THE SON FROM THE WEST

THE SON
FROM THE
WEST

EVELYN CROMER

Matador
9 De Montfort Mews
Leicester LE1 7FW, UK
Tel: (+44) 116 255 9311 / 9312
Email: books@troubador.co.uk
Web: www.troubador.co.uk/matador

ISBN: 978-1905886-746

Typeset in 11pt Bembo by Troubador Publishing Ltd, Leicester, UK
Printed in the UK by The Cromwell Press Ltd, Trowbridge, Wilts, UK

Matador is an imprint of Troubador Publishing Ltd

This book is dedicated to the memory of
H.S.H. Princess Vibhavadi Rangsit
and to
Shelley, Alexander and Venetia

"If you've heard the East a'calling
you won't ever heed aught else"

Rudyard Kipling

Also quoted by the 1st Earl of Cromer,
statesman, who lived most of his life
in India and Egypt, in his unpublished
'Autobiographical Notes, 1905'.

Contents

PART ONE
THAILAND, LAOS AND VIETNAM

PART TWO
SINGAPORE, PHILIPPINES AND HONG KONG

PART THREE
CHINA

Acknowledgements

I would like in particular to thank the following people who assisted me in the writing of this book: Dickie Arblaster who corrrected my English grammar and jogged my memory, Dick Chan for providing his story, Charles Letts for his encouragement, Helen Booth for her creative suggestions and editing, Sumet Jumsai for advice on Thai protocol, Chris Buttery for his many inputs and many others who provided encouragement, especially my wife, Shelley, who had to live with this book over the five years it took me to write it.

Preface

I have endeavoured through the pages of this book to answer an enigma posed by many who have known me over the years: why did a young man from what would be called today a privileged background, a scion of two of the most influential families in the land, with a title and financial prospects, give up a comfortable and assured future in England to become an adventurer in the Far East?

With my father, 'Rowley' the 3rd Earl of Cromer, as Governor of the Bank of England and possessing the Baring family name, an entry into a comfortable City career was assured. A leisurely retirement on the red leather benches of the House of Lords was there for the taking.

Or my maternal grandfather, Esmond, the 2nd Viscount Rothermere, proprietor of the last great newspaper dynasty in England, might also have welcomed the eldest of his three surviving grandsons into his far-flung media empire.

Neither the Barings nor the Harmsworths however, had achieved their wealth and success without risk-takers and adventurers amongst their ranks. The first Earl of Cromer, Evelyn Baring of Egyptian renown, would have understood as would the first Viscount Rothermere or his brother Lord Northcliffe. But these days we do not live in adventurous times.

The question posed here is – was it all worth it? I fought fiercely for my independence, at one point becoming a banker but never using the Baring influence, at another point becoming a journalist but never writing for a family newspaper.

After my early years in Thailand, you may think that it was time to return home and take up family responsibilities. But a fresh incarnation materialised in Singapore which led on to a new life in the Philippines. Hong Kong beckoned and then the maw of China swallowed me for the next seventeen years. I lived in the Far East for twenty-nine years and not a day was wasted. This is the story of those three decades – a period when Asia was changing fast around me: the American war in Vietnam, the emergence of China on to the world stage, a period of rapid economic and social changes. I was witness to it all.

Evelyn Cromer
Somerset, 2007

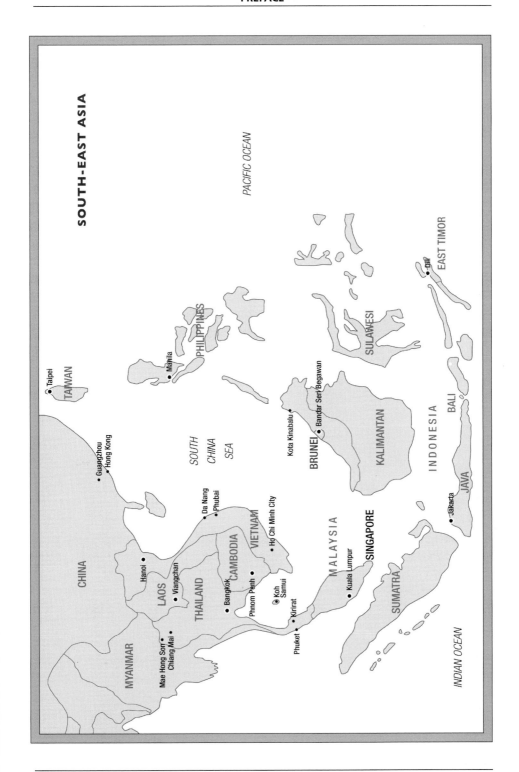

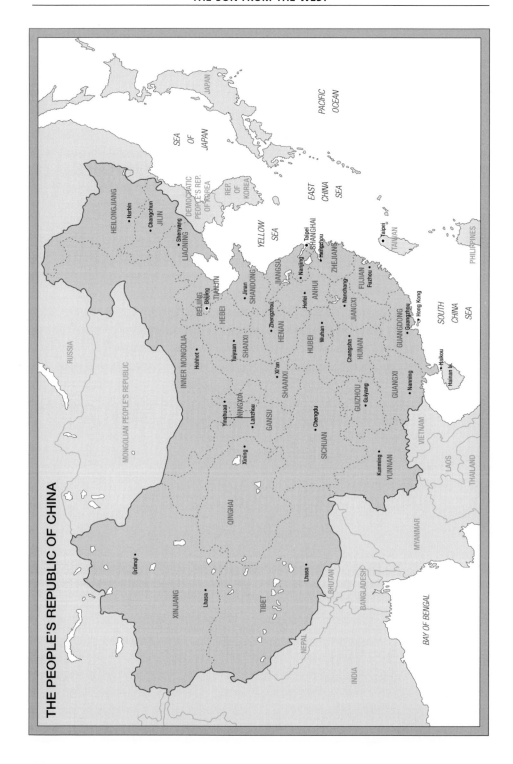

THE PEOPLE'S REPUBLIC OF CHINA

PART ONE

Thailand, Laos and Vietnam

1967–1971

1

Jungle Sickness

I had been lying here for what seemed like a very, very long time. It must have been days, maybe weeks. The humidity had seeped into my watch and it had stopped at nine-thirty one morning, or maybe evening, back in the mists of time. I lapsed in and out of consciousness, distantly aware of my delirious ramblings as if they were disembodied voices. Sometimes I thought I was not alone. Voices spoke to me and I would prize open a gummy eye but nothing moved and the voices stopped. There was nobody there. Today, I felt slightly better but I was pitifully aware of the rank smell exuding from my own putrid body.

I was lying on a bamboo *charpoy*, a sturdy bedframe made from thick bamboo trunks. A flat layer of beaten split bamboo gave a smooth but hard surface. My emaciated body was covered by a sweat-stained and sodden *pakoma*, a length of checkered cotton Thai men wear around their waists which serves a multitude of different tasks from towel to blanket. Hanging from a wooden rafter was a torn mosquito net, yellow with age, that kept the larger insects at bay and was probably helping to keep me alive.

My body oozed sweat. It ran in ever-changing courses across my chest and down my sides. Like raindrops on a window, it started as beads on my forehead, united and ran into my eyebrows, cascaded into my eyes, around my nose, down my face and into my mouth. The beaten earth under the *charpoy* turned a darker brown where puddles of sweat formed.

The *charpoy* was the only piece of furniture under the lean-to structure. The roof and sides were of palm fronds and on one side there was a gap which led into a small room supported by bamboo uprights. There were no windows, running water, furniture, electricity or any other hint of the 20th Century.

Prostrate on the *charpoy*, during fleeting moments of lucidity I could see the canopy of the tropical jungle over my head through half opened eyes. Immeasurable meranti, teak and other tropical trees soared into the thick green mat above, blocking out natural light save for the occasional patch of dappled sunlight that played off the ferns and orchids hanging tenuously from trunks and branches. Screeching monkeys crashed overhead swinging noisily from tree to tree or sliding down the jungle creepers, like a small army of miniature Tarzans.

I languidly watched the leeches squirming their way across the mud floor. Inch-long tubes arching and waving their backs in the air trying to sense whether there was any flesh within range. Sometimes I caught them worming their way up the *charpoy*'s bamboo legs, intent on reaching my body. Usually I was too late to stop them. I would feel something heavy on my thigh or arm and would tear off the *pakoma* to find a long slug attached to my body, gorging on my blood.

I called "Narong, Narong!" and again more urgently, "Narong, *ma ni reo!*" "Come here quickly!"

Narong entered quietly and sprinkled salt on the leach until it fell off leaving a small hole bleeding profusely for hours until the anticoagulant was flushed out of the wound.

I knew that at the age of twenty-two I was perilously close to death. The end in a remote tropical jungle in Thailand was profoundly depressing. I would be cremated on a pyre of brushwood in the jungle as the Thais do not bury their dead. My far away family would never know what had really happened.

Perhaps two more days had gone by, maybe three. It must be five days now since the party of doctors and soldiers carried me off the shallow draught boat with its long-tailed engine and left me in the care of the *Wat*. It should take the team another two days down the river to reach the road-head at Phra Saeng and a further day to the hospital at Nakorn Sri Thammaraj. The return journey, assuming that suitable medication was available, might take a day longer. It would be at least a week before a doctor could get back to the Buddhist temple, or *wat* in Thai. I was not sure I was going to make it.

The privy was in an *attap*-thatched hut some hundred feet from my shelter. There a deep hole was crossed by two thin slimy wooden planks a foot apart. I needed to perch with one foot on either plank while wracked by the agonising cramps that come with amoebic dysentery, sometimes vomiting at the same time. The trick was not to slide off the planks into the hole below. The privy provided sustenance and shelter to a menagerie of insects and little reptiles but I was past caring whether they had malicious intentions or not.

Sometimes I never made it but would collapse on the path outside my hut where I would be found by Narong whose gentle hand would cool my sweating, fevered, brow and although waif-like himself, he would pick me up and carry my thin body back to the *charpoy*. There he gently washed the sweat and vomit off my face and the slime from my legs. The slight smile never left his face, never for a second revealing the revulsion he must be feeling at the gore and stench oozing out of me.

I looked down at my emaciated limbs, bones and sinews. Surely there was not much in the way of physical reserves remaining.

My chain of thought was broken by Narong. He was a novice Buddhist monk, no more than fifteen years old and slight of build. He had been instructed to care for this strange *farang* who had been washed up on the shores of this little jungle community. His smoothly shaved head and eyebrows revealed a finely shaped skull and moon-like face with two dark eyes, a flat nose and a mischievous mouth set off by ears that sprung sideways out of his head. I communicated with difficulty – I had been in Thailand a little more than eighteen months, had mixed exclusively with Thai people and could speak the language fairly, but here was spoken a southern dialect quite different to the refined Thai found in Bangkok, the capital city, five hundred kilometres to the north.

Narong bustled around the *charpoy* with a broom made from rushes, sweeping the detritus of the night into a small heap: ants, dust, beetles, leaves and a red centipede the size of a cigar. He removed my dripping *pakoma*, rinsed my body with a half-coconut bowl of water drawn from a large earthenware jar at the foot of the *charpoy* and covered me with a fresh *pakoma*. This was no normal nursing task: my face was caked with dried vomit from the night before, my buttocks and legs with faeces, slime and blood. Throughout my ablutions the smile never left his face. He then gently lifted my head from the solid block of kapok that formed a hard pillow and spooned a pungent broth into my mouth.

Then as silently as he entered, he faded back into the jungle.

My eyes closed as the black curtain of unconsciousness wafted over me and my wavering distant thoughts turned to how I had found myself in this dire situation.

I had been marooned in a unique place, far from the traditional concept of a Thai *wat* with its green and orange tiled roof and golden *naga*s on the eaves, an architectural design that had not changed for centuries. This *wat* had been founded by a monk who believed that Buddhism in Thailand had varied too far from the original philosophy. Theravada Buddhism, in its pure form, aims to achieve enlightenment through meditation but Buddhism as it had come to be practised in Thailand, especially in the countryside, was much closer to idolatry. Worshippers went to temples with offerings which they laid in front of the Buddha image and prayed to Buddha to save them from their sufferings, grant their wishes, help them to buy a new car or win the lottery, conceive a child, or achieve any other human ambition in much the same way as Catholics pray to the image of the Virgin Mary and Protestants to the crucifix. This may be a human need but it is not Buddhism.

This particular monk had left his monastery in Bangkok and had carved a small retreat out of the jungle near Nakorn Si Thammarat. In his retreat he did not permit the presence of an image of the Buddha and concentrated solely on meditation. He was to be joined by other monks of like mind and gradually a unique new monastery appeared. Each monk went into the jungle and created his own cell, in fact a small shelter made out of what could be found in the jungle. There were many such cells each connected to each other by walkways through the trees. A central building housed the administration and dining area. There was a large circular clearing in the jungle where the monks met to pray and chant.

Such was the remoteness of the temple that the monks could not rely upon daily donations of food from worshippers, so it was not possible for the monks to sally forth every morning with their bowls to gather food in the manner one sees on the streets of Bangkok. This monastery relied on cash donations from people who supported their particular mission and they would then buy food in the nearest market and transport it back to the temple.

Once I had set out on the road to recovery from the dysentery, I fell into the daily routine of the monastery. I was not the only *farang* there: once I stumbled across an American but he had taken a vow of silence and although he looked at me curiously when we met each other on a jungle path he quickly retreated to his cell and was not seen again throughout the time that I spent there.

It was a simple life – rising at four o'clock, assembling in the clearing, listening to lectures or sermons, eating, meditating, sweeping up the leaves (a constant occupation), more praying, more meditating and early to bed. Chanting in Thai monasteries is in Pali, a language descended from Sanskrit and unknown to me. I was hardly familiar with the Buddhist sutras from the Tripitaka and could not understand the intellectual Thai used by the monks during their lectures. The monks were extraordinarily kind and considerate to the stranger in their midst. I was allocated a spare cell and a novice to care for me. As soon as I was well enough, I ate and lived with them and followed their daily life as best I could.

I spent much time observing the tropical rain forest and learning its ways. Dark, forbidding and not a little frightening to most people, it became a source of fascination to me. The massive bulk and height of the trees was a wonder. The multitude of life never ceased to astound me. Armies of ants marched through the jungle devouring everything in their way. Poisonous centipedes a foot long lurked under giant teak leaves on the ground. Many other insects and reptiles were so well disguised that one did not notice them until after remaining motionless for a considerable period of time, something on a tree trunk, branch or leaf would suddenly move. The jungle is a busy metropolis where different species of insect and animal life live in harmony but for the occasional predator, dangerous to the uninitiated without doubt but not without its fascination. My jungle education was to come in useful when I found myself in Vietnam not so many months later on long-range reconnaissance patrols with the American military.

One elderly monk, who spoke more than passable English, took me under his wing and spent several hours every day debating Buddhist philosophy and teaching me the art of meditation. I would then be left on my own from noon to dusk to practise what I had learned. It was a unique, valuable and spiritually rewarding experience but as my strength recovered I began to tire of the monastic life and I started to think of returning to the outside world.

So it was that after I know not how long in the jungle, the day came when I joined a group of monks on their way to Nakorn Si Thammarat on a provisioning expedition. Once in the town people stopped in their tracks to turn and stare at the little group of orange-robed shaven-headed monks chatting intimately to a lone *farang* in their midst. That evening I bade farewell to my new friends and caught the night train back to Bangkok.

2

S.S. Ben Nevis

It was a cold, foggy, Dickensian October afternoon in the Pool of London. Moored alongside a quay derelict of workers or any type of activity was a rust-streaked freighter that, even to a non-mariner such as myself, looked as if it should have met its destiny in the wrecking yard many years before. It had, as I learned later, been constructed in the 1930s as an American flat-top aircraft carrier but had never quite worked out in that role and was converted to a general tramp steamer, acquired by the Ben Line, and put on the Far East service. Soon surpassed in speed and technology by more modern vessels it was put out to pasture like an old cart-horse. For many years it quietly rusted in the Pool of London making the occasional cocoa run to Africa. The Ben Line kept the old lady in reserve, to be used as and when an unexpected demand arose.

This was not at all what I had expected. In June 1967 at the age of twenty-one, I had visited the offices of Killick Martin, the Ben Line agents in London and was shown magnificent brochures and glossy pictures of the fine ships in their fleet that whisked one to the Far East in air-conditioned comfort in six weeks. The Suez Canal was closed at the time due to hostilities so the journey was protracted by having to sail around Africa and the Cape of Good Hope. The thought of taking an airplane was something that I had not even considered – too easy, too quick and no sense of distance.

I had the rather vague intention of taking a ship to Bangkok, staying there for a few weeks while the ship continued its local calls around Asian ports and then re-embarking on the same ship back to London where I would give my future career some further thought. How very differently life was going to turn out.

My poor mother and father, distraught at seeing their son flee the family nest to such distant lands – and this was long before students started to back-pack around the Far East in their 'gap' years as they do today in such an organised manner – looked even more forlornly than I at this scarcely-floating rust bucket.

Things had started to go wrong a week before my scheduled departure. The Ben Line telephoned to say that a dockers' strike had been called for the following day and it looked as if it might continue for months. The vessel I had selected could not be readied in time, but I was assured that luck was on my side as the S.S. *Ben Nevis* was there for this very purpose and could sail on the afternoon tide two days hence with an 'urgent and secret cargo.' Could I make it?

Clambering up the perilous companionway on to the main deck, my parents and I were greeted by Captain Robert McPhee, a jovial weathered Scotsman with twinkles in both eyes. I was shown my cabin, in fact a small grey box with a steel bunk and a porthole looking out onto a rusty side deck. As the rain poured down outside, I saw my mother dabbing her eyes and my father, looking very much out of place in his city suit, having a quiet word in Captain McPhee's wizened ear. The word, I later heard, was that the captain was to put me off at the next port and make sure I caught a flight back to London.

That was, however, not to be.

Somehow we missed that afternoon tide but sailed anyway and within two hours found ourselves stuck hard on a mud bank in the Thames estuary. The captain thought this was a cause for hilarity, one of life's little tricks and an opportunity to crack open a bottle of Johnnie Walker and get to know the passengers. Somehow this did not augur well for a journey to the other side of the world.

It did however give me time to acquaint myself with my motley fellow passengers. There was the feisty Betty Parker, wife of a British officer serving in Seremban, Malaysia on her way to join her husband. Hearty and jovial, as time went by she became ever closer to Captain MacPhee and by the time we had entered the warm, smooth waters of the Indian Ocean the two would disappear into the captain's quarters behind the wheel-house for hours at a time. "Showing her my charts," he used to say with a wink.

There was Alonzo, a missionary on his way to Indonesia, who paced the foredeck Bible in hand. Quite what he thought of Betty Parker was never revealed but over meals you could see he was earmarking her for redemption. A honeymoon couple on their way to join the British embassy in Manila completed the passenger list. Although only a couple of years older than me the groom already possessed that slightly superior air and condescending attitude that characterises junior members of the British Foreign Service. His wife resembled a thin, white bantam.

So there we were, five passengers and the captain gathered in the officers' mess contemplating half-full tumblers of whisky. We were joined by 'Curly' Bell, the chief engineer, a round burly Scotsman and Robert Clarke, the conscientious, dour first officer. Central Casting could not have picked a more interesting or varied selection of characters. We were warned of an additional member of the crew: Captain Nicholls had commanded the *Ben Nevis* on her previous voyage but died off the Malabar coast. In time honoured fashion, the ship's carpenter knocked together a makeshift coffin and, according to Curly Bell, it was only as the coffin was sliding into the ocean that the burial crew realised that the coffin was upside down. It was said that on stormy nights the phantom of Captain Nicholls was to be seen stalking the deck.

Floating off the Thames mud with the rising tide, we set off down the English Channel. I was somewhat alarmed when entering my cabin the first evening to find the walls, floor, ceiling and even the bunk itself alive with small black beetles. I called the captain who gave the cabin a cheery glance and announced, "Aye, cocoa beetles, they'll not be harming you but remember to put cotton wool in your ears when you're sleeping." The Ben Nevis was not long back from a passage to the Ivory Coast and where there is cocoa, there are cocoa beetles. So I started an extermination campaign in my cabin keeping a careful score of the numbers squashed. I think it was something over fifty beetles for each of the first few days and then the numbers gradually diminished so by the time we crossed the Equator my cabin was beetle free but the final tally was in the high hundreds. They kept appearing all over the ship at the most inopportune moments: in the soup, amongst clean laundry, at the bottom of whisky bottles or in the Corn Flakes box at breakfast time.

Life on board seemed an endless alcoholic party with Captain McPhee, quite one of the most humorous and cheerful characters with whom one could wish to be confined on a ship, being the host, cheerleader and entertainer rolled into one. He would frequently end the evening by playing the bagpipes on the bridge. The late night tuneless wailing of the pipes caused our Chinese crew to quickly vanish into their quarters fearing the instant arrival of Captain Nicholls. Curly Bell spent most of the day spread-eagled in an armchair nursing a bottle of Johnnie Walker. Only First Officer Clarke seemed to have some idea where the ship was going. Once across the Bay of Biscay, the Atlantic calmed and we gently steamed into slightly warmer waters although I still recall wearing a thick sweater crossing the Equator. We stopped for a week in Dakar, Senegal where the open drains and squalor, did not invite further investigation.

The Ben Line had thoughtfully issued each of its passenger-carrying vessels with an ancient 35mm cine projector and a meagre but appropriate collection of films only three of which I can recall: 'Mutiny on the Bounty', 'Robinson Crusoe' and an early black-and-white version of 'Titanic'. The crew set up our cinema on the narrow side deck, using a sheet for a screen. The old ship slid through the tropical deeps, the path ahead lit by the stars and behind our wake created a milky way of fluorescence as we watched the flickering sheet, nursing the inevitable tumblers of whisky.

Events took a turn for the worse when we approached the Cape of Good Hope. The seas turned mountainous and were breaking over the bow. Then we lost way, there was a mechanical problem, the propeller stopped turning and we were no longer able to keep the ship's bow into the seas. The old ship creaked and groaned while something heavy crashed around in the bowels of the ship. There was a danger that we could swing abeam of the waves which might have proved dangerous to our little ship. The captain called us to life-boat stations. This was somewhat confusing as we had never had a life-boat drill, but we knew where the boats were so we went on deck and hung for dear life onto whatever looked reasonably stable. In the far distance we could see Table Mountain and Cape Town nestling below but that was another world away. Captain McPhee was in his element tunelessly belting out Scottish hymns into the wind and the spray, as the bow buried itself in the breaking waves which rolled seething along the deck crashing into the wheelhouse.

The honeymoon couple held on to each other with tears in their eyes. Betty Parker stood by the railing, hair plastered to her face gazing enraptured at the captain. The missionary took on the elements personally raising his small head, like a diminutive Moses and challenged the seas to quieten by threatening menacingly from the Scriptures.

Eventually power was restored and we chugged on into the calmer waters to the East of the Cape. The next day the Captain thought it a fine idea to hold a life-boat drill so we stood by the life-boats and watched with humour and horror as not a single life-boat could be made to leave its chocks. All were rusted as one with the ship. For most of the next ten days we smoothly slid across the Indian Ocean in the direction of Colombo, as the crew worked away with blow-torches and jack-hammers strenuously trying to free the life-boats from their positions.

We had been at sea for over a month by now and the routine was becoming tedious. Reading on the deck in the morning, an alcoholic lunch, a game of poker with the officers in the afternoon, a boozy dinner and then a black-and-white film on the side deck. The black ocean rushed past us, the odd flying fish landing on the deck, the Indian Ocean moon hanging oval and low on the horizon and the Captain and Betty Parker raucously whispering loud secrets to each other meant only for the sea captain and the colonel's wife but heard by all.

Noticing I was at a loose end, 'Curly' Bell decided I could be put to use painting the side of the ship. He rigged up a gantry which he hung over the side with a bucket of paint and a roller and this kept me as happy as a sand boy for many a long day as I sat suspended on a plank with the Indian Ocean seething far below.

It was only when we arrived in Colombo and were made to lie away from the main roads some way from the harbour, that I discovered the nature of our mysterious cargo. We were in fact carrying munitions bound for the American forces in Vietnam and destined to be offloaded in Bangkok. I doubt whether I would have aborted sailing on the *Ben Nevis* if I had known about our lethal cargo but it was a somehow sobering thought. It was my first brush with the war that was raging with intensity on the other side of the world in Vietnam. It was to become a cloud that sometimes hung over the horizon but at other times dominated life in the Far East in the late '60s and early '70s. Unbeknownst to me, only four months previously the North Vietnamese Politburo had determined that the time was ripe for the final stages of their revolutionary war: the 'General Uprising' which was to lead to the Tet Offensive in South Vietnam only three months later. Television was to bring the Vietnam War suddenly and dramatically into homes around the world.

Colombo was my first introduction to the Orient and it captivated me. We were caught up in another dockers' strike so did not know how long we would be there. Robert McPhee, in a rare serious moment, warned me to keep my porthole closed as although it was little larger than my head, I was assured that a supple Sinhalese could squeeze his whole body through this small aperture and make off with my few possessions. Tamils and Sinhalese swarmed all over the ship anyway. Producing dirty cotton handkerchiefs from their dhotis, they laid them on the deck to reveal star sapphires the size of gulls' eggs and ruby and gold bracelets of dubious purity. Like so many young men before me down the centuries, I was relieved of my slender savings, the hawkers happy to accept my sterling cheque at a time when foreign exchange controls in the U.K. would have made it impossible to cash. Who was cheating whom?

In fact these purchases did prove to be much more valuable than I had ever imagined and some years later and hard-up, I sold a star sapphire I bought at that time in exchange for a diamond engagement ring for my first wife.

Colombo was a steamy paradise of dark sari-clad women, lush vegetation new to my eyes, elephants padding silently along the pot-holed roads, pedicab jams and afternoon thunderstorms. Its heady, pungent, over-heated atmosphere sunk into my brain, still befuddled by claustrophobic, cold and stifling England. The colour and vibrancy of Colombo was infectious. It awakened the adventurer within me; I paced the deck eager for the ship to weigh anchor and steam further into the Indian Ocean.

Dinner on the *Ben Nevis* was always a light-hearted meal, when the small group of passengers and officers sat around the long table with its finely starched white tablecloth, served by some of the uniformed Chinese crew. Even on the *Ben Nevis*, discipline was maintained, though one could only guess at what the crew made of the liberal drinking amongst the passengers and officers. One evening Captain McPhee asked me with an uncharacteristic note of gravity in his voice whether I had seen any of the flying jellyfish often found in the Indian

Ocean in the winter months. This was news indeed; the thought of being hit on the back of the head by a flying jellyfish opened my eyes wide. I earnestly promised to keep my eyes skinned. The next day I searched the ocean far and wide, flying fish there were everywhere but not a flying jellyfish to be seen.

With the heat building, the crew assembled a swimming pool on one of the hatch covers out of wooden railway sleepers and canvas which was pumped full of seawater. Primitive, but effective. Hardly what one would expect on an ocean-going freighter but everything on the *Ben Nevis* seemed to have a unique charm of its own.

Then came the night when after a particularly rowdy evening, I staggered back to my cabin to find lying on my bunk what could only be described as an enormous jelly-fish, at least two and a half feet long and a foot wide. It lay there wobbling gently and rocking with the ship's motion. This creature could only have flown in through my porthole! A fairly tight squeeze, I thought. I went in search of the captain who was found on the bridge in singlet and shorts with nightcap in hand and his eyes surveying the night sky. Betty Parker lolled on a deckchair beside the binnacle gazing at the captain dreamily.

"Aye," he said, "the difficult part is to get the wee bugger off your bunk." Recruiting Curly Bell and First Officer Clarke on the way, by the time we got to my cabin most of the ship had heard of my plight and there was quite a crowd around the door staring at this strange creature. I took all this very seriously, assuming that I had an interesting zoological specimen on my hands, until Robert McPhee could contain himself no longer and erupted into an endless gale of laughter. Curly Bell carefully rolled the 'jellyfish' into a towel and let it drop into my basin where it exploded revealing that it was no more than a condom filled to bursting point with water.

The ship sailed on through the placid waters of the Andaman Sea rolling gently with the breathing of the ocean. Day followed day of bright, fierce sunshine and nights of warm velvet as the ship sliced through the deep ocean. Then we turned Southeast into the muddy waters of the Straits of Malacca with Peninsula Malaysia hidden in the mist on one side and the Indonesian island of Sumatra on the other. Finally, eight weeks after leaving London and two weeks behind schedule, we reached Singapore.

Captain McPhee called the four young British ratings and myself into the wardroom and gave us a little lecture the night before we docked in Singapore:

"I know you've been at sea for two months and there'll only be one thing on your mind. But," he warned, "Singapore can be a dangerous place for a young man who doesn't know the ways of the East and I don't want any sick men on my ship."

With no further ado we were each issued with a single condom. Then with a bellow of laughter and a swig of the bottle he was away leaving me in a state of confusion and anticipation.

So when we docked the next evening, I put on my trendiest London gear, (remember this was the swinging '60s): yellow and green striped canvas trousers and a thick long-sleeved velvet jacket with a Nehru collar and gold braid down the front. Looking like heaven knows what, but melting inside in the tropical heat, I set off out of the gates of the Port of Singapore Authority.

Within seconds a large crowd of trishaw drivers surrounded me trying to win my attention by pulling at my sleeves and grabbing my elbows. I selected a diminutive Chinese with legs the size of a professional football player and settled myself in the back of his trishaw. He jumped onto the saddle and pedalled away, legs pumping like pistons. We flew through the narrow streets of Singapore, scattering dogs, children and chickens, the lights, shops and people just a blur as we sped past.

"What you wannee? Velly pletty sister? Nice black Tamil girl? Honest Malay virgin? I know, pale skin girl just arrived from Arabia?" shouted the driver over his shoulder.

I was twenty-one years old and even if my sexual experience had been somewhat limited, this all seemed dangerously tantalising. After all, I was a man of the world now and had to act like one. Scarcely knowing the difference between a Tamil and a Malay and thinking that the 'pale-skinned Arabian girl' might be a little less exotic, I told the driver to show me the goods.

Night had fallen and I was now bouncing faster and faster through narrower and narrower streets, the roofs of the houses seeming almost to meet overhead. We skidded to a sudden halt outside a very shabby concrete building stained with years of grime and mouldy slime. Still in my immaculate green velvet jacket, I was ushered into a small room with a few pieces of broken plastic furniture where the driver was greeted as an old friend by a hunched and wizened crone. Money changed hands – from me to the driver and from the crone to the driver – and he disappeared leaving me in a remote corner of Singapore to a fate I was beginning to think might not be in my best interests.

I was hurried into a small room with a steel bed frame on which lay a hard and stained kapok mattress. A naked 20-watt light bulb glowed faintly in one corner. The ceiling was cracked and a grey hairy fungus hung undisturbed in one corner. I waited a longish while and eventually lay on the bed and closed my eyes dreaming, perchance, of the Arabian beauty at this moment dashing to meet her destiny.

I was half awakened by a hidden hand turning off the light switch and a weight sitting on the hard bed. So this was she. My heart opened to her, poor innocent child. What had the trishaw driver told me? Just seventeen and only arrived in Singapore a few days before? Probably a virgin from Araby sold by a slave trader into a life of prostitution. She gently undid the buttons of my velvet jacket, now soaked with tropical sweat, and eased off my trousers. Her bare and silky arms slid up my body but instead of an exotic perfume of musk and myrrh, my nostrils were assailed by the worst case of halitosis I could ever remember encountering. As I gagged, her other hand grabbed my over enthusiastic member in a vice-like grip. Things were not going quite as planned. I jumped off the bed and with my trousers around my ankles, hopped to the light-cord, and gave it a firm pull. The light revealed the true identity of my paramour: the toothless crone who had paid off the trishaw driver.

I was away in a flash and running, zip and buttons undone, through the anonymous streets of Singapore until I found a trishaw and made my way back to the ship. Captain McPhee was slouched in an armchair in his quarters, whisky in hand, Mrs. Parker on his knee, and in a philosophical mood. Noting my dishevelled appearance and flushed face, he murmured "Aye, young Evelyn, the ways of the East are not to be learned in a single night."

Now my father was not one for volunteering a helping hand to his children. Maybe he thought we would somehow let him down, or, more likely, he was not a man to place himself under obligation to anyone. At that time, amongst the many peaks of his career, he was the senior partner of Baring Brothers & Co. Limited, merchant bankers to governments and royalty and riding high at the time. It was not for nothing that the Duc de Richelieu had observed in 1818 that 'There are six great powers in Europe: England, France, Prussia, Austria, Russia and Baring Brothers.'

Of the unlimited contacts that he had at his disposal in the Far East, he provided me with a single introduction: a letter from Tony Keswick. The Keswick family controlled the vast Far Eastern conglomerate Jardine Matheson whose tentacles extended into every Asian country and many Asian businesses. The relationship between Baring Brothers and the Keswicks was cool as Baring Brothers had some years before bought the Jardine family's shares in the business and had thus become substantial shareholders in Jardine Matheson. Not wanting to involve themselves in the politics of the business, Barings left the management firmly in the hands of the Keswicks. My father was fond of Tony Keswick who had been a member of the Court of the Bank of England when my father was Governor. Whether this feeling was reciprocated is not known but certainly Tony Keswick was not going to put himself out for 'Cromer's boy.'

Tony wrote a routine note to his man in South-East Asia by way of introduction. The note was along the lines of 'Rowley Cromer's boy Evelyn is passing through your area, lend a hand if he needs anything.....' and was probably the same as he issued for many visiting sons of acquaintances and meant 'don't bestir yourself needlessly'. Charles Letts was their man in Singapore and his area of responsibility within the Jardine's empire included most of South-East Asia. I arranged for the letter to be delivered and was duly rewarded with an invitation to meet this great dignitary at his house for a drink. In the meanwhile I checked into an hotel for a couple of days as a welcome change from my cell on the *Ben Nevis* before it left for Bangkok. The ship had been moved out of the harbour and into the hazardous goods anchorage due to its explosive cargo and that meant at least a forty-five minute run in a bumboat to reach Clifford Pier on Collyer Quay, then, as now, one of the main marine entrances to Singapore.

Charles Letts lived in a vast colonial-style house in Tanglin Hill. Tall rain trees in the large garden housed a colony of fruit bats which darkened the sky as they flew in every night from the Riau Archipelago to the south of Singapore. Charles proved to be a giant of a man in every way and was to play a significant role in my life, although it seemed unlikely at that time. Over six feet four inches tall and immensely strong, he was one of those few men who need but a few hours sleep every night, in bed by three a.m. and in the office by six a.m., day after day. Captured by the Japanese during the war, he was put to work on the infamous Death Railway linking Thailand with Burma where stories of his derring-do became legion amongst the few survivors.

He was in his mid-forties at the time, more than double my age, but we got on well and he invited me for dinner that night. We ate Chinese, a new experience for me as I quickly realised that what passed for Chinese food in England bore almost no resemblance to the real thing. Then we moved on to the Great World Amusement Park which housed a well-known night club, named after a notorious pre-war establishment in Shanghai.

In this large darkened dance hall a tall, willowy girl was softly crooning a Mandarin love song into a microphone while a few couples stood almost motionless on the dance floor swaying slightly to the music. We were shown to one of many small tables where a red-shaded lamp cast a small circle of light. Charles ordered Dom Perignon champagne and called for the *mamasan*. This was a routine which over the following years was to be repeated in a hundred different nightclubs across the Far East but for me it was something very new and exciting.

After a while two girls joined us, both, I guessed, little more than eighteen years old. I leapt to my feet like any well-brought up Englishman. Charles remained seated. The girl sitting next to Charles, clearly no stranger, snuggled up to him and laid her hand on his thigh. With one hand around her shoulder caressing her hair, Charles' other hand parted her cheongsam and a finger ran slowly up her leg almost to her midriff. My girl, name long since forgotten if ever known, sensed my unease and embarrassment and asked me to dance. She was tall, nearly my height, and had long luxuriant black hair falling to her waist. It smelt slightly of fresh shampoo, coconut and some exotic perfume I could not place. She glued her slender body to mine and lightly brushed my sweating face with her cool, pale skin. One of her arms circled my waist, the other hand rested gently on my shoulder, one finger slowly stroking my ear lobe.

By the end of the second bottle of Dom Perignon I was beginning to forget the *Ben Nevis* and Bangkok. Perhaps, I surmised, I should spend the next two months in the Great World Amusement Park.

Charles thought it time to leave and asked if I wanted to take my new friend with me. I was taken aback by this suggestion and I stammered that of course she had to stay at the club to work. Charles looked amused at my lack of experience in these matters and with one arm he hooked his girl out of his lap and we made off to his car with me rather foolishly following. Charles drove his large American car with an aggression that I later got to know was very much his style in life, one hand on the wheel, the other enveloping the girl's slight body, gently tweaking her left nipple and causing shy squeaks and the playful slapping of his hand. I sat alone in the back of the car beginning to think that the Far East was going to prove much more interesting than I had imagined.

Singapore in the late '60s was a small city with colonial characteristics; the British administration had departed only a short time previously and the Ministry of Defence still owned more than a third of the island. Lee Kuan Yew was the Prime Minister but had yet to start the transformation which was to turn this small island into the amazing city-state it became in later decades. This is not a travel book so I will not give a detailed description of the Singapore I found and to which I was to return to live not too many years hence. But between then and now there were to be many visits to Singapore and much more of Charles' life was to be revealed to me.

The *Ben Nevis* sailed at dawn the next day and headed northeast into the frequently ill-natured South China Sea. Three days later we dropped anchor off the Thai island of Koh Sichan in the Gulf of Siam where we were to wait until it was our turn to cross the bar at the entrance to the Chao Phraya River which winds its way through mangrove swamps to the river port of Bangkok. I was the only remaining passenger by then and I remember the ten days that we lay off Koh Sichan as being stiflingly hot. Curly Bell made a hammock for me which was suspended in what was known as the monkey's nest, a small deck behind the wheelhouse at the highest point on the ship where there was the best chance of catching any breeze.

I was warned that, as in Colombo, Thais would swim out to the boat, shin up the side of the vessel and squeeze through portholes. But these would not be thieves but lissom Thai girls keen to provide a service. Hopeful, I left my porthole open all day and all night but of visitors came there none. The swarm of sinister-looking sharks that circled the stern of the vessel hungrily snapping at the rubbish that the crew threw overboard might have been a deterrent.

During the night the crew amused themselves by hanging arc lights over the side of the ship to see what would rise to the surface. All sorts of creatures from poisonous sea snakes to meaty crabs were attracted by the bright lights.

At dinner on the tenth day Captain McPhee announced that permission had been granted to enter Bangkok and we would be crossing the bar with the tide at first light. My ten-week odyssey on the *Ben Nevis* was drawing to a close. I slept not a wink that night and climbed up to the monkey's nest at 5 a.m. as the ship slipped silently and unnoticed into the muddy and surprisingly narrow Chao Phraya. I understood, for the first time, what Kipling had in mind when he wrote 'An' the dawn comes up like thunder outer China 'crost the Bay!' The sun rose out of the grey haze in the East gathering a speed, heat and intensity never seen in northern climes. Somehow I was beginning to realise that everything in the tropical East was more vibrant in every way, be it brightness, colour, flavour or sheer spectacle, than in damp, dim, distant England.

With a deep sense of nerves and anticipation I watched the shadowy banks of the river slide by. Beyond stretched a sea of coconut palms fading into the dawn mists. Chains of half-moon shaped straw-covered wooden rice barges slipped downstream pulled by a single brightly coloured tug separated by a tow rope so long it looked as if tug and barges had no connection. I saw my first 'long-tail' boat – thirty-feet long, three-feet wide with rows of passengers squatting on the floor, two to a row, sheltered by a brightly striped canvas cover. On the stern of the boat balanced a large V8 car-engine from which extended a fifteen-foot propeller shaft. Herds of water buffaloes swam across the river, only their eyes, nostrils and horns showing above the water. Everywhere there were boats, fast and slow, roaring noisily along the river between ocean-going ships moored in midstream.

So this was the country I had travelled so many thousand miles to visit. I wondered anxiously whether my only letter of introduction, to Her Serene Highness Princess Vibhavadi Rangsit, had gone astray? Perhaps she was overseas? Perhaps she did not welcome visitors? She had not responded to my letter announcing my arrival – I had never even met her. The Rangsits were a very imposing family. The Princess's father, Prince Rajani, had been a famed writer and philosopher. Prince Rangsit's father, a son of the great King Chulalongkorn, was raised by Queen Sawang Vadhana, one of King Chulalongkorn's three official wives. As a senior and the most able prince he was appointed the Regent to the young King Ananda and the future King Bhumibol when they were being educated in Switzerland in the late 1940s. He had been almost a father to the two future kings whose own father had died when they were very young. Prince and

Princess Rangsit's marriage, I learned, was the only marriage officially blessed by the late King Ananda during his short reign.

This was the complex and forbidding world of the high Thai aristocracy. There was so much that could go wrong, I thought. Perhaps it was all a mistake.

At 7 a.m., there was a loud clattering as we dropped anchor in the middle of the river. I returned to my cabin one last time and rested my head on my pillow, wondering what would happen next. Soon I fell asleep.

I was awakened by the strange sight of an old man's head protruding tortoise-like from a long and scraggy neck, peering through my porthole.

"*Sawaddi krap,*" the disembodied head said to my amazement, "Good morning. My name is *Khun* Shit."

This then was my introduction to Bangkok where I was to spend the next four years of my life.

3

Vippy

It was 1965: I was nineteen years old and had just started working at Baring Brothers as a 'trainee' merchant banker. The first of those years was the last of my father's five year term as Governor of the Bank of England, a position he had achieved at the age of 43 – the youngest Governor the Bank of England had ever known.

'Rowley', the 3rd Earl of Cromer, was not close to his three children. His business life and onerous duties were his main priorities and he found it difficult to show more than a passing interest in his offspring or their needs. As children we saw him infrequently. Throughout my early days at Frenchstreet Farm in Kent, my father commuted to London, leaving early in the morning and returning just before dinner, when I was already asleep. In later years he was more interested in mixing a shaker of dry martinis and discussing the day with my mother than he was in playing with his children.

Weekends were no different: he worked Saturday mornings in London, returned for a brief lunch and then slept in his deep red armchair all afternoon. He slept all Sunday morning, would resurface for a slightly grumpy lunch and then back to the armchair. When he was awake he would busy himself making amateur films in the special circular room he had converted for this purpose in an oasthouse. By the age of sixteen I had become an awkward teenager, probably in need of careful parental guidance but my father always put his extremely eminent and successful career ahead of the psychological requirements of his growing children.

His overwhelming power in the City of London and the respect heaped upon him, not only by the pink-liveried Bank of England footmen who seemed to constantly float around him with an envelope here and a pouch there, but also by the press and any adult I met, seemed to place him on a remote pedestal to be approached only in silence and genuflection. Leaving Eton at eighteen, I found myself at something of a loose end, and tied down by a girlfriend who was determined to carry me off to the altar; an ambition appealing to me less and less as day succeeded day.

Parental advice was rarely available and when it was, my stubborn nature paid little attention. Both my mother and father were understandably on an altogether higher mission and difficult teenagers were inconvenient. My sister Lana, twenty-one at the time, was married and breeding and my brother Vivian, fourteen, was still at boarding school.

Apart from the Bank of England's familiar edifice in the City, the main administration centre was in a vast building complex known as 'New Change' at the other end of Cheapside next to St. Paul's Cathedral. From a discreet wooden door, marked 'No. 35 Cheapside', a private lift whisked one to the seventh and top floor of New Change where lay the Governor's formal reception rooms and, at the end of a long corridor, a polished wooden door opened into the Governor's private flat. It had an institutional, anonymous feel about it, scarcely a home but more a perch in the rarefied atmosphere in which my parents lived.

Living in the City of London was a strange experience. Occupied by millions during the daytime, by evening it was deserted, but not silent. Throughout the night articulated lorries thundered down Cheapside on their way to the Port of London, the roar from their diesel engines amplified by the canyons of dark, unoccupied office buildings.

It was convenient insofar as I had the luxury of a five minute stroll from 35 Cheapside to Baring Brothers' offices at No. 8 Bishopsgate every morning, but inconvenient as my friends lived in the West End of London. I can still recall the look on strangers' faces when I would give my address as 'above the Bank of England.'

It was a custom that any member of the Baring family, vast as it was, was given a single chance to work for the merchant bank that bore their name. If it turned out that their capabilities would not in time take them into the hushed sanctum of the Partners' Room, then a secure and appropriately senior position in a stockbrokers' office or insurance company would be found elsewhere in the City where a Baring was always welcomed. Family members (male only) would not generally be accepted by the bank until their late twenties or early thirties, by which time all wild oats should have been sown and the young executive-in-waiting would be married and ready to settle down to assume serious responsibilities. Of course I fitted not one of these prerequisites.

Barings seemed a convenient solution to keep me out of harm's way and my father easily allowed himself to be persuaded that I should start work there at the age of nineteen. A single telephone call probably fixed the job and I duly started the daily grind on a salary of £23 per month. By working overtime up to 10 p.m. I could raise this scarcely generous sum to £30 but even by the standard of the day I was barely adequately rewarded.

Unlike the slick investment banks of today with their gleaming marble and chrome offices, No. 8 Bishopsgate had not changed much since Baring Brothers bought the Georgian building in the City in 1806. One still entered the building through a covered alley where earlier partners had arrived on horseback. An antique rope and basket haulage system transported the mail from the ground to the first floor. Most of the managers and staff worked out of the warren of nooks and crannies in the ancient building. The pervasive dust from the decaying mountains of defaulted Imperial Russian, Argentinian and Chinese bonds filled the halls, glinting in the occasional ray of sunshine that penetrated through the grime of centuries encrusting the building's few windows. Many of the bewhiskered older staff could have been employed since the first Duke of Wellington cashed his cheques there. The investment department, the hub of a modern merchant bank, was concealed in a corner so remote that I never found it. The foreign exchange department, an airport size room in Merrill Lynch today, was to be found up a small flight of stairs where three men stared lethargically at their wooden telephone consoles whose buzzers would occasionally disturb the peace.

I was put to work in one department after another, in each case being the dogsbody, which is no bad thing for a young man. One week my job was to sift waste paper baskets rescuing paperclips for reuse. Several weeks were spent writing out bank statements by hand for fastidious clients, though why anybody would have wanted my ink-splodged, scribbled and messy efforts escaped me. Nothing had changed in decades: Wyndham Baring, my great grandfather's second son joined the bank in 1903 and found himself 'engaged in transcribing entries from a ledger onto a sheet of paper' which he thought was 'devilish tricky work'. More than sixty years later I was performing the same mundane task and could understand his sentiments perfectly. All the bank's cheques, many for millions of pounds, were written out by three clerks, myself one of them, perched on high stools using dip-pens and black ink and inspected by a schoolmaster-type who would more often than not find some minute fault, tear up the cheque and send the slip back to the clerk for rewriting.

Assorted bowler or top-hatted men in tail coats strode around the office. Foreign potentates, Indian maharajas, Texan millionaires and every month the entire harem of an Arab ruler cashed cheques for many times my annual salary, the large white five pound notes disappearing into open Gladstone bags. The travellers' cheque had scarcely come into its own and it was more usual in those days for well-connected world travellers to journey with a personal Letter of Credit drawn on Messrs. Baring Brothers which was instantly recognised in every corner in the globe.

I laboured in this salt mine for something over eighteen months. During my second year my father completed his term at The Bank of England and returned to Baring Brothers as senior partner. This was not, as I understood later, to the total pleasure of some of the other partners, who were torn between the prestige of the Governor being a member of the family with the attendant reflected glory on Barings itself, and the awareness that he was likely to remain senior partner for a long time to come. He was only forty-eight at the time, thus blocking the ambitions of some of the other partners.

Accustomed to being treated in a very grand manner in the Bank of England, his first move at Barings was to announce that he would not be taking his desk in the Partners' Room together with the other partners but would work out of his own suite of offices on another floor. Red and green traffic lights were installed outside his new office to indicate whether or not he could be disturbed. Even at my lowly station in the bank this raised a few eyebrows so I could only imagine the reaction of his fellow partners.

We moved from Cheapside back to our London home at 167 Pavilion Road in Belgravia in the summer of 1966. This meant a modest commute on the London Underground to 8 Bishopsgate but brought me back to living in the West End of London. It did strike me as slightly ironic that father and son would leave the same house at more or less the same time every day for the same office in the City: one by public transport and the other in the back seat of a chauffeur-driven Rolls-Royce.

It was however, proving difficult to be the new boss's son in the bank. While my father was at the Bank of England I was free to associate with my fellow clerks and join in their evening merriment in Leadenhall Market and the surrounding pubs and wine bars. But with the Earl behind the reins I was suddenly my father's son and relationships changed in many subtle ways. What little fun there had been ebbed away.

It was time to flee the nest and spread my wings. The first objective was to move out of 167 Pavilion Road, but how? My salary was derisory, but in addition I had been receiving a monthly allowance from my father of twenty pounds, bringing my monthly total nett income to around forty pounds; far from sufficient to rent a room and feed myself. At that time it was just possible to take an undemanding girl out for a modest evening for one pound: ten shillings would buy a hot but simple meal for two at the Chelsea Kitchen in the King's Road and a further ten shillings would buy two tickets at the Chelsea cinema.

In the event I opted for an affordable and original solution: the *M.V. Patriarch*. The *Patriarch* was an infantry landing craft of wartime vintage converted into a houseboat and moored off Cheyne Walk, not far from the World's End in London's Chelsea. I managed to scrimp, save and borrow enough to buy the little boat. It was reached by crossing a bridge onto a pontoon from the Embankment and then walking over a precarious gangplank. The *Patriarch* had electricity but for plumbing and sewage there were a series of chemical buckets emptied occasionally by a service company to which one paid moorage. The *Patriarch* rose and fell with the tide spending some six hours each day sitting on the mud and the rest of the time floating merrily on the River Thames.

The *Patriarch* was pleasant enough on a warm summer's day but claustrophobic, humid and depressing in the cold when moist mists would drift along the Thames. The adjoining houseboat sank one night when an old children's pram, gently finding its way along the river bed with the flow of the river came to a halt right underneath when the tide was ebbing and punctured the probably unsound plywood hull. When the tide rose and the other houseboats floated off the mud, my neighbour stayed put and was only awoken by cold water lapping against his bunk. He leapt out into electrically charged water with deeply shocking results.

I had an old wooden clinker-built dinghy which came with the *Patriarch* and was moored to the stern. I bought a small Seagull outboard motor and with oars as backup used to motor up and down the river visiting the pubs on the South Bank. This proved a very pleasant spring evening occupation until one day, with a fiercely flowing ebb tide, the motor died in mid-river. Undaunted, I inserted the oars into the rowlocks but at first stroke one of the oars snapped in half leaving me with no form of propulsion and drifting at speed towards three barges moored abreast in midstream. I could see my small dinghy was about to be capsized under the blunt bow of one of the barges and sucked under-water by the fast-flowing current.

I shouted and yelled and waved my oar stump in the air but there was no sign of life from either shore. I sat on the thwart to consider my approaching fate, which looked no more than sixty seconds away. But not for the first, and certainly not for the last time, my luck held out. One of my neighbours had been sitting on another of the Cheyne Walk houseboats watching me through his binoculars and had seen the entire incident. He, fortunately, also had a dinghy (most houseboats did not) and he took to the water with a more powerful outboard motor and snatched me to safety scarcely twenty yards from the jaws of the barges. Two days later the dinghy broke free in the middle of the night leaving two feet of wet and frayed rope hanging from the stern of the *Patriarch*.

For some reason the friends that I had made at Eton College were generally a year older than me, so that by the time my turn came to be released into the world, they had all dispersed for a year overseas, into the army, their country estates or wherever. I then formed a new circle of friends, none of whom had ever been anywhere near Eton. One of the supposed advantages of being educated at Eton was that you were introduced to people from similar backgrounds from which one would draw one's lifelong friends. For me, at least during my years in Asia and afterwards, I very rarely met anyone I had known at

Eton. When I did I found them generally arrogant, insular and unworldly. Eton, if anything, proved a handicap to me: an expensive education that I constantly needed to disguise.

So my new friends, Geordie Gordon, Martin Jansen (who had been to Eton but left prematurely after a contretemps with a loaded revolver in the dining room ended up with a bullet through the Corn Flakes box), Donald Cameron, Philip Monbiot and my cousin Robert Mercer Nairne, had all come from different schools and different backgrounds and were the more interesting for that. We threw ourselves into the spirit of the '60's with varying degrees of enthusiasm. These were the days of 'flower power', outrageous clothes, the Beach Boys, longer and longer hair and barefeet in the King's Road. But no drugs: spliffs were not smelt too frequently in London at that time.

We got up to all sorts of rudeness and excesses that delight young people and the more so if one succeeded in shocking the elders. We used to eat on the *Patriarch* at night and then, if the tide was low, would jump into the three feet of mud that lined the bottom of the river and indulge in mud-flinging battles until exhausted, cold and covered with evil-smelling sludge from ears to toes, would slip back onto the *Patriarch* for a cleanup.

Geordie at the time was taking some extra tuition at a school in Brighton and had acquired a beautiful and exotic Thai girlfriend who was also studying in Brighton. Her name was Vippy Rangsit and she was to change my life. I first met her when I visited Brighton for the weekend: there was Geordie and beside him was this pale-skinned girl with dark almond eyes. Her glossy black hair was cut short so as to frame her face. Much better dressed than us would-be hippies, she wore a figure-hugging grey striped top with a thick gold chain and a gold heart dangling in her cleavage.

One evening I was complaining to Geordie and Vippy about Baring Brothers and life in London when Vippy said, "Why don't you go to Bangkok? My mother and father are lonely now that their two daughters are studying overseas and I am sure they would love your company." Although I only had the vaguest idea of where Bangkok was in the world, I thought this sounded like an excellent idea and agreed there and then, probably over the third bottle of cheap wine, that I would take her up on her offer. True to her word, Vippy did write to her parents and that was how it all started.

One remaining string needed to be cut. I accordingly found myself sitting outside my father's office at Baring Brothers waiting for the traffic light to change. At length the light turned green and I entered his office and, still standing, told him that I had decided to leave Barings. He raised his eyes from his desk and looked at me for a long time over his half-moon reading glasses.

"I told you that you joined too young. Well, they won't have you back you

THE SON FROM THE WEST

know." He lowered his eyes and the interview was over.

know." He lowered his eyes and the interview was over.

I looked back as I walked out of his office. The traffic light had turned red once again.

Back on the Ben Nevis, I dressed in my only suit, ordered specially for the voyage from my eclectic tailor in London: a 1960s Sergeant Pepper wonder of thick beige cotton, pseudo-military style with epaulettes, patch pockets and brass buttons. Apart from having my hair 'cut' by Curly Bell while sitting on a bucket one fine day in mid-Indian Ocean, it had received little attention. I must have looked a very curious sight. Mr. Shit waited outside my cabin. When I had dressed he summoned some coolies who lifted my few possessions onto their muscular sweating backs, with a band around their foreheads taking the strain, and carried them off the ship. I bade farewell to Captain Robert McPhee, Curly Bell and Robert Clarke and to the *Ben Nevis* itself. It had been my intention to rejoin the ship after it had been to the Philippines, Indonesia and points East. It was returning to Bangkok in about a month's time.

So it was '*au revoir*' rather then '*adieu*' but could I read in Captain McPhee's eyes a certain sadness? A finality? Did he know something I didn't?

"Look after yourself, son, you'll grow up quickly here," he murmured.

I looked at him quizzically but he had turned away. It was some time before I understood quite what he meant. In the event I was never to see Captain McPhee or the *Ben Nevis* again.

My belongings and I were loaded into an ancient Volkswagen Microbus and we lurched into the city of Bangkok. This was a world away from the rather more organised life in Colombo and Singapore, both beneficiaries of many decades of British administration. This was a wild shambolic city where one was meant to drive on the left but only if there was nothing coming on the right. Roads and canals intermingled, everyone was in a hurry. The heat had already turned my shirt into a sodden mess and I could feel the sweat trickling down my back.

Mr. Shit (could this really be his name?) told me in broken English that the Princess was expecting me but the Prince was 'upcountry', wherever that was. I had no idea what to expect and my anxiety increased the more I thought of the uncertainties ahead. I had a few pounds in my pocket, was eight thousand miles from home and my only other contact was another note from Tony Keswick, this one to his man in Bangkok, a certain Alec McCallum. Judging by Charles Letts' bemused reaction to Tony Keswick's note, I was unlikely to receive a particularly hospitable welcome from the Jardine's Bangkok representative.

Charles Letts was his boss and he had dismissed Alec McCallum with a wave of his hand when I mentioned his name. "He will do nothing for you," Charles had said.

   As we bounced along in the VW, dodging potholes, dogs, children, bicycles and a multitude of other forms of life and machinery, my mind drifted back to the fateful evening in Brighton when the seeds had been sown that brought me to this distant land.

4

The Son from the West

Mr. Shit swerved suddenly across two lanes of traffic and drove into a narrow road bordered by palm trees bringing my reverie to an abrupt end. After a couple of hundred yards the drive opened into a tree lined circular carriageway with a garage block on one side. Facing the drive was a strange-looking house – I can only describe it as Teutonic–Tudor with an oriental air. It was a large three-story building, painted in faded yellow, open shutters beside each tall window. The Volkswagen bus lurched around the carriageway and grunted to a halt under a shelter in front of open double front doors at the top of a small flight of marble steps.

"*Wang Vidhyu*," announced Mr. Shit mysteriously. "Welcome to Vidhyu Palace."

A diminutive maid was waiting on the top step, clad in a long black sarong with a white short-sleeved cotton top, her long thick hair tied behind her head in a pony tail. She bowed her head and placed her hands together in what I was to learn was the traditional Thai form of greeting, the *wai*, and gestured that I should enter.

I walked into the outer of two adjoining formal drawing rooms. The room was sparsely furnished with plain upright wooden arm chairs and a few occasional tables. I anxiously sat on the edge of one of the chairs, sweat dripping down my back, the thick heat gently stirred by an overhead fan. After a while another maid entered the room carrying a small tray with a glass of steaming brown water. She walked hesitantly to within ten feet of me then dropped to her knees and shuffled towards me. This must have needed a lot of practice without her sarong falling to her knees. She put the glass on a table beside me and then reversed, backing away from me still on her knees and then rising and swiftly walking out of the room.

The hot Chinese tea, for that is what it was, seemed refreshing. Strange, one would think that a cold drink would be more suitable, but the hot tea seemed pleasantly cooling.

I waited another twenty minutes and then with a slight rustle, a striking lady of medium height and a kind-hearted face full of character entered the room smiling broadly. Her Serene Highness Princess Vibhavadi Rangsit wore a formal two-piece silk suit and was barefoot. She walked straight towards me then hesitated and, unless I was mistaken, a look of sheer incredulity crossed her face; she looked as if I had just arrived from outer space instead of England. I leapt to my feet and extended a hand in greeting. Without exactly ignoring my outstretched arm, she walked slowly around and behind me and then perched on a chair opposite mine, her dark and sympathetic eyes fixed on mine.

I sat down again; beads of sweat were gathering on my brow. I knew they would soon start to course down my face in rivulets, dripping in a spreading and embarrassing patch on my shirt. I was being observed, carefully, from top to toe. She looked at my shoes and frowned imperceptibly. I awkwardly crossed my leg allowing the sole of my shoe to point towards the Princess and I thought I saw another look of disapproval. I quickly put my foot back on the floor. I was not creating a good impression.

I was becoming unnerved by this scrutiny and tried to remember whether Vippy had told me if her mother spoke English. At that point she said in a clear, unaccented voice but with a slight quaver,

"Did you have a pleasant voyage?" as if I had just crossed the road. I assured her the passage had been long and eventful.

After another painful pause, she asked

"Do you know anybody in Bangkok? Some friends perhaps? Maybe the ambassador?"

I told her I knew not a soul in her country. I knew little of her family except what Vippy had said in Brighton so many months previously. Likewise, she knew nothing of me other than what Vippy had told her. Or perhaps had not told her. I was beginning to think that I had made a terrible mistake in coming all this way.

"Well," the Princess said, "we are going to have to get you organised then aren't we?"

She stood abruptly and walked out of the room. As she did so, a dark brown Great Dane dog appeared by her side, its shoulder nearly as high as her waist. We walked back towards the front door and waited while a driver brought around a yellow, two seater, Volkswagen Kharmann Ghia sports car.

The driver got out of the car and the Princess took the wheel. As she turned the ignition she turned abruptly to me and said, "Try to remember never to wear your shoes into a Thai house again and never, ever, point your foot at someone's head. My husband had a foreigner ejected from the house for doing that."

I learned many lessons in a few seconds, the most important being that the Prince was not to be trifled with, and the second and more intriguing was that the Princess was sufficiently interested to proffer some advice. I found this reassuring.

Deftly, the Princess threaded her two-seater back into the main traffic stream in Wireless Road, passed the American embassy, a few hundred yards from *Wang Vidhyu*, around a teeming and lawless round-about and off at an angle down South Sathorn Road. There is a North and a South Sathorn Road, and the two Sathorn roads appeared, from the road signs at least, to be parts of a one-way system. But nobody seemed to be paying any attention to the road signs. Cars, motor-cycles and three-wheeled *tuk-tuks* drove in every direction, some on the road, some on the muddy shoulder, heading towards each other on a collision course and then veering to left or right in a lawless game of chicken.

Some way down South Sathorn Road, the Princess swung to the left between a Shell petrol station and some tennis courts and came to a halt in front of an apartment block. There were actually two blocks, one behind the other separated by an open space and a garage block. Each block looked as if it had been there for many years, albeit clean and tidy and freshly painted. On the ground floor of the first block, there was a ladies' salon by the name of Kesya.

"This," informed the Princess, "is my little hobby. They are going to turn you into a new person."

We entered through the glass door into the heaven-sent cool of an air-conditioned room. The place was abuzz with female titters which were silenced by our entry. The Princess summoned the manageress and introduced her to me. I then stood in painful embarrassment as a long conversation in Thai took place while I was subject to close examination by a number of young girls in tight white uniforms. After a while the Princess told me that I would be 'looked after' and she would return later to see the finished result.

I was then ushered into a cubical and had my hair washed and cut short, shorter than it had been for many years. I was shaved, manicured and generally civilised after so many weeks aboard the *Ben Nevis*. Throughout my pampering the door constantly opened and closed as different women of all ages, I assumed all employed by the Princess, found some reason to enter my private room to take a quick look at the young Englishman the Princess had delivered into their care. I later discovered this had been a signal honour; the only other men allowed inside Kesya were the Prince and his younger brother who, like most Asian men, came to have their black hair dye renewed every month.

When she returned the Princess seemed pleased with my freshly groomed appearance and said she would now introduce me to my new home. We walked to the second of the two apartment blocks, climbed the stairs to the second floor and entered one of the three apartments on that floor. It was a large airy flat with a balcony running the entire length on the far side overlooking an unkempt garden, a row of casuarina trees, a *klong* choked with weed and some dense tropical vegetation beyond. The flat had been designed before the advent of air-conditioning and thus each internal wall ended some two feet short of the ceiling to allow the air to circulate. There was a large sitting/dining area, two bedrooms, a kitchen and a bathroom with no bath or shower but a tall brown earthenware jar filled with water in the corner. There were a few pieces of cane furniture and a cane bed with a hard kapok mattress.

I noticed to my surprise that my few belongings had already been delivered from the ship: a school trunk tied with baling twine, a record player and a steel filing cabinet which for some inexplicable reason I had decided to bring with me from England.

"What do you think? I know it is not home, but will you be comfortable here?" enquired the Princess anxiously. "If you like it, you may stay here as my guest."

This was much, much more than I had expected. I had hoped that I might be invited to stay in the *Wang* for a few days and would then need to find some accommodation for myself, but now I was to be lent an entire apartment.

"I must apologise about the furniture but I was not to know your taste." She continued, "If you like the flat we can choose some new furniture, upholstery, curtains and whatever else you may need. I have to refurnish this flat anyway," she added as if she felt she was being overgenerous.

I was overwhelmed. I mumbled my thanks.

"Right, that's settled then, this will be your new home."

The very same day we chose a complete new set of cane furniture, colourful Thai cotton curtains, sheets, blankets and everything else to make the flat comfortable. I offered to contribute but this was brushed aside. Within hours workers had arrived to install air conditioners, the partitions were brought up to ceiling level to contain the cool air and by the evening I did indeed have a new home. I remained puzzled, however, at the lack of washing facilities and wondered what I was meant to do with the jar of water. It was round and tall, almost up to my chest, with a narrow opening at the top. Was I meant to get inside? How would I get out?

Next, the Princess decided that I needed some transport and a Volkswagen Beetle was produced which I was to borrow until my own car arrived from London. I was becoming a little impressed by the vast quantities of VWs the Rangsits appeared to have at their disposal.

I had noticed quite a few more VW Beetles at the *Wang*. It was only later that I discovered that the two Princely brothers owned the company which imported and distributed VWs in Thailand. I had planned to bring my own car on the ship with me but such was the Ben Line's haste in dispatching the *Ben Nevis* from London that distant October day, that my car together with most of the other freight had been left on the quay. In the event the dockers' strike in the

U.K. continued for many months and it was a long time before I was to see my car again.

That evening I was invited back to the *Wang* for an informal dinner in the garden. The Prince was still 'upcountry'. There were about thirty guests and I was the only non-Thai amongst them. This was the first time I had met Thai people on their own ground: they were polite, highly civilised, cultured and very international. All could speak perfect English and all showed more than a passing interest in my long sea voyage. It had been rare for many years for people to travel such distances by ship. I bit on my first Thai chili bringing tears to my eyes and causing fresh rivers of sweat to course down my face. I was alone in being pursued by a swarm of giant mosquitoes that took a particular interest in my ankles, my black socks proving irresistible. Thai food was served from a table in the garden, while we ate sitting on the marble steps at the back of the *Wang* overlooking a small *klong* which separated the respective houses of the two Rangsit brothers.

This separation took greater significance over the years as the relationship between the brothers gradually broke down and degenerated into outright warfare. That night at least the gate between the two houses at the end of the *klong* was open and there was a free flow of guests and servants between the two houses. Within a few short years that gate was to close, never to be reopened. That evening, magical in my memory, was my introduction to Thailand, to the Rangsits, their close friends and followers, and was a taste of the years to come during which I was to be embraced totally by this rich and powerful clan.

Over dinner the Princess introduced me to a young girl, about my age, who had been brought up with the Rangsit daughters but was a dependant. She lived in the *Wang*, was almost treated as a member of the family but was still an attendant. Her name was Nying. She had a round, jolly face, was quick to laugh, a happy extrovert. A cut above any of the masses of servants that thronged the *Wang*, she travelled with the Princess and had visited Europe many times. Nying was to become a close friend, adviser and supporter to me, a constant source of measured advice on Thai culture and habits. Looking back it is clear to me now that the Princess had singled her out to be my mentor: somebody of my own age who could teach me the ways and customs of the Thai aristocracy. I was going to be transformed from an English youth into, if not a Thai, at least someone who would understand the Thais and their ways, and who would behave appropriately.

Nying was Mr. Shit's daughter. Mr. Shit, whose name fortunately turned out to be Mr. Chit, was the senior driver at the *Wang*. Frequently drunk, he was not well suited to this role: one evening I remember him returning to the *Wang* with a very battered VW Beetle swearing that a tree had unexpectedly crossed the road and collided with his car. Mr. Chit's father had been a captain in the Royal Bodyguard in the early 1900s when Queen Sunanta's boat capsized as she was crossing a narrow stretch of the Chao Phraya near the Royal Palace at Bangpa-In. The Royal Bodyguard stood by helplessly, no one daring to lay hands on her royal body as she thrashed wildly in the waters before drowning. King Chulalongkorn, the grandfather of King Bhumipol, was mortified at the loss of one of his three Queens (all of whom were his half-sisters). Princess Rangsit took pity on Mr. Chit's family who were languishing at Chitrlada Palace, the King's one square kilometre moated palace in Bangkok, and provided them with employment at the *Wang*.

Before returning to my new home that night, the Princess took me to one side.

"Now we have found you a home, tomorrow we will discuss what you are going to do in Bangkok. Do you have a profession?"

I admitted I had none. The Princess looked thoughtful. She was hatching a plan.

Her confidence growing, she then said, "Nying will prepare your lunch every day which you will take with the staff at Kesya. You will eat with me every evening at the *Wang*. If I am out for dinner Vippy's old nanny will try to prepare some Western food for you. Will that be alright?"

My amazement knew no bounds. In just a single day someone had entered my life who had shown more kindness and consideration to a complete stranger than could possibly be justified by a normal display of hospitality. I was being welcomed into the Princess's family – what was happening to me? What exactly had Vippy told her mother before I arrived?

The answer did not reach me for many years; it was in fact my mother who solved this riddle. The Princess was Queen Sirikit of Thailand's principal Lady-in-Waiting and would accompany the Queen on her overseas trips. On a visit to London a year or so later with Queen Sirikit, the Princess joined my mother for tea. Over sandwiches and biscuits, the Princess told my mother that it had been her custom for many years to consult a *more doo* or, for lack of a better translation, a fortune-teller. Such people are very widely respected in most Asian countries and many an Asian prime minister would never make a major decision without consulting his personal astrologer, *bomoh, feng zhui* geomancer or fortune-teller.

In the summer of 1967 the Princess's *more doo* had told her that her life-long wish to bear a son was to be granted and that she would be 'favoured with a son from the West'. This was an enigma for her: her marital relations with the Prince were not going to produce another child and anyway she was scarcely interested in having more children and what did it mean 'from the West'? The *more doo* was not forthcoming and so she relegated this mysterious prediction to the back of her mind. She had two beautiful daughters but it was a disappointment that she had never been able to give the Prince the son that he wanted.

Then she received a letter from Vippy telling her that 'my friend Evelyn Errington' was going to visit Bangkok. Evelyn being accepted as a girl's name in most countries, she naturally assumed that I was one of Vippy's girl friends and so was expecting to meet a young lady that morning in her drawing room. But it was not to be; she was introduced to a young man and not only that, but also someone who knew nobody in Bangkok and who had been delivered to her personally and exclusively. I could only be the 'son from the West'. It was the only time in my life that I was genuinely grateful for my parents for giving me an androgynous name.

That night I returned to my new home and climbed into the vast jar of cold water in my bathroom. I gave myself a thorough soaping and clambered out. That left the large and heavy jar full of dirty soapy water. With great difficulty I pushed it over onto its side which caused a flood in the bathroom until the water had drained away through a hole in the wall. I righted the jar and filled it from a hosepipe attached to a tap. It was a very laborious process; surely there must be some other way of bathing? I made a mental note to ask Nying in the morning.

5

Khirirat

It was the King's Bounty that had brought me to the temple in the jungle. Perhaps the greatest unifying factor in Thailand is the people's respect for the monarchy. H.M. King Bhumipol earned this respect through a life totally committed to his people. A modest and sincere man, he realised in the 1960s that the whole fabric of his country was threatened by the communist terrorists who were achieving some success in selling their policies to the illiterate jungle-dwellers. He sponsored many programmes to improve the lot of the peasants but it was the King's Bounty that I came across first.

Princess Rangsit, as a courtier and confidant of the King, had been chosen as the King's emissary charged with distributing the Bounty amongst the remote villages deep in the far south of Thailand near the Malaysian border. It was an area where the communist insurgents had met with a great deal of success and where troubles continue even to this day albeit of a different type.

The Bounty consisted of a programme funded by the King to distribute a small package containing a blanket, a mosquito net, a bar of soap and a few other daily necessities to each inhabitant of every village that the Princess and her party passed through. The party itself consisted of the Princess, some of her own personal staff including Nying, several doctors and nurses, the local area administrator and some of his staff and a handful of soldiers to provide security. I beseeched the Princess to take me with her on one of these expeditions. She was reluctant at first, not knowing how the villagers would respond to a *farang* in their midst and what message this would carry but, in June 1968, she eventually relented.

We assembled at the seething Hua Lamphong railway station in Bangkok. Boarding long-distance trains anywhere in the Far East is a special excitement: much shouting, laughing and weeping, wicker baskets of mangos pushed through windows, trussed chickens and ducks rammed under seats, much jostling and shoving, vendors shouting their wares, teenage girls thrusting *oleang*, a tamarind-based iced 'coffee' in plastic bags with a straw poking out of the top, through carriage windows or *gai-yarng*, a bright red barbecued chicken splayed flat on a bamboo frame. A special carriage had been reserved for our large party and its hundreds of boxes of the Bounty which were hastily loaded onto the train through the doors and windows. A few sweaty policemen vainly tried to keep the crowds apart, some liveried Palace attendants stood by, a 'Bangkok Post' photographer struggled to keep his camera level, the excitement growing to a fever pitch as whistles blew and flags waved. The crowd on the platform suddenly bent as a wave and *waied* low with hands together as they saw the Princess at the window in her sunhat and mauve silk shirt. Then with a sudden lurch the train set off on its eighteen hour journey along the west coast of the Gulf of Siam and into the Kra Isthmus.

Ban Doem was just a stop on the railway line to Malaysia. The town had no hotel so we spent two nights sleeping in the town's hospital gathering supplies and assembling the rest of the team. The Princess had her own room in the hospital but as all the other beds were taken by patients, the rest of us slept in rows on the wooden floor of an empty ward. Nying slept on the floor across the door to the Princess's room as a deterrent to any night intruder.

When our preparations were complete we left Ban Doem at dawn in a small convoy of pick-up trucks for Phra Saeng, a village and road-head on the Mae Nan Ta Pi River. Phra Saeng, no more than a few wooden houses and sparsely stocked shops, was, although we knew it not at the time, to earn its fatal reputation in history many years later as the place where the Princess was murdered. But when we arrived it was thronged with people who had come from miles around to see the Princess, the emissary of the King.

On the river there were half a dozen shallow draught wooden boats, twenty foot long with wooden thwarts and rusty corrugated iron roofs to shelter us from the tropical sun. The boats were laden almost to sinking point with the Bounty: stacks of blankets and boxes of soap and medicine and other paraphernalia. Our party, now fifty strong, clambered onto the boats and we set off upstream in high spirits. The Princess was in the first boat together with the senior local officials, her staff from the Palace and me. We were distinguished by having two framed photographs of the King and Queen mounted on the roof of our boat.

It was not long before bottles of *Mekong*, the cheap and pungent Thai rice whisky, were broken out and circulated around the fleet. A Thai drum appeared and one man stood on the front of his boat with a flute-like instrument and the whole party started singing Thai folk songs which filled the air, echoing off the rocks and boulders as we made our way upstream. This was pure Thai theatre: a happy and cheerful people for most of the time, they would seize any opportunity for a party.

We meandered our way up the river. Gradually the landscape changed from flat rice paddies to hilly jungle and then to dramatic sheer limestone rock faces rising several hundred feet on either side of the river. Patches of sun-dappled triple canopy jungle forced their way between the rocks, jungle creepers hanging into the water from the tops of mahogany trees high overhead. Monkeys followed our procession along the riverbank, whooping as they swung from tree to tree. The river sometimes narrowed forming deep, clear pools into which we dived, swimming alongside the boats as they chugged their gentle way upstream. The trees on either bank met overhead creating cool green tunnels through which our wooden fleet processed in Indian file.

At other times the valley broadened, the river spread out and there was only a foot of water under the boats. Then everyone jumped off the boats and pushed them upstream amidst much shouting and hilarity. A long rope was attached to the front of each boat and, one by one, they were pulled and pushed over the shallows. On one occasion the rope broke and all twenty people pulling found themselves prostrate in the water.

Occasionally we rounded a bend in the river to come across wild elephants or buffaloes drinking or bathing in the water. The few houses we passed were built on high stilts fifteen feet from the ground with a ladder that was brought in at night to protect the inhabitants from the tigers that lived in this part of Thailand. We met several villagers on our journey who had been maimed or deeply scarred from tiger attacks.

We saw no villages for the first two days and spent each night lying in rows on patches of sand beside the river under a tarpaulin that was stretched over thick bamboo poles cut from the jungle. Each evening was a continuation of the party with the men cutting firewood and the women cooking searing curries in the pots that were tied onto the roofs of the boats during the day. *Mekong* flowed freely and there was singing and dancing late into the night.

I noticed that each morning a man would disappear into the jungle and return with a few branches of spindly leaves that he left on the boat's corrugated iron roof to dry during the daytime. In the evening the leaves, now brown, were crumpled and dropped into the curry. Some of the leaves were rolled and wrapped in newspaper to form a thick cigar which the men smoked and passed around the circle in front of the fire. Some wild tobacco or herb perhaps? No, this was *ganja* or cannabis growing wild in the jungle and which the Thais have used in their cooking for centuries. Virtually all the men, including the soldiers and doctors, happily puffed away and it all added to the hilarity of the evening festivities. This is not a drug feared or abused as in the West, but a wild herb that provides fun and entertainment and has always been part of life in Thailand and the surrounding countries.

By the third day we had passed through the deeply-fissured limestone karst hills and the jungle evened out. It was not long before we came across signs of human life. We negotiated a sharp bend in the river to be met by an amazing sight: all the inhabitants of a village, and jungle dwellers for miles around, several hundred people, had gathered on the river bank and were squatting in neat rows. Like statues, they squatted in complete silence with their hands raised in a *wai*, the traditional Thai gesture of greeting. When they saw the lead boat with its pictures of the King and Queen and the unmistakeable figure of the Princess in front, a hushed murmur passed through the ranks and, as one, they bent their bodies forward and raised their hands above their heads in respectful greeting.

We clambered ashore, the parcels of blankets and soap were stacked in a pile and the King and Queen's portraits were placed on an easel. The villagers lined up and one by one they approached the doctors and the Princess. Most of the women carried children, many showing signs of malnutrition: swollen bellies, weeping sores or distorted limbs. The doctors inoculated each villager against smallpox. They would cry and try to wriggle free at the sight of a needle disappearing into their arm but the Princess was quick to comfort them and hand over their little parcel of Bounty in front of the portraits to which they would *wai* in respect and appreciation.

Later the doctors and the few nurses accompanying them held an impromptu surgery and the sick and maimed came from miles around, sometimes travelling for days, to seek the scant medical attention that our doctors could offer. Pills were handed out for malaria, wounds treated and other acute problems attended to, but it was obvious that most of the problems were either chronic tropical illnesses or originated from malnutrition. There was little the doctors could do for these cases but provide sympathy.

When the inoculations and surgery were finished we retired to a wooden shelter where the local headman gave a speech and exotic food was passed around accompanied by a local brew which varied from village to village, sometimes made from rice, sometimes coconut and occasionally pineapple. Then somewhat the worse for wear, we clambered back on the boats and continued upstream.

This ceremony was repeated several times each day. Sometimes the crowds were large and sometimes sparse, but wherever we went we were met with the traditional warmth and hospitality for which the Thai people are renowned.

I was a particular attraction. None of these remote villagers had ever seen a *farang*, or white skin before. I was a source of complete fascination to them. Whatever I was doing, they gathered around and observed me. My blue eyes filled them with fear – if I was to fix one with a look they darted away in sheer terror. The men kept their distance. The women were braver, some came quite close just to stare at me. As their curiosity and temerity grew, they ventured even closer to gently tug the hair on my arms or legs. Thais, like most oriental races, have little body hair.

In the evening it was our custom to find a quiet place on the river to bathe but this was quite an ordeal for me. I was followed by a large throng of women and children in the hope that my *pakoma* might slip and my naked body would be revealed. Thai men and women bathe covering their body with a *pakoma* neatly tied so that it does not slip. This was quite an art and one which took time to acquire. Frequently I found that my knot became untied while washing and the current ripped off my *pakoma* leading to a surge in the watching crowd in the hope that they might see whether I was built to the same penile specifications as their own men folk.

Urinating or defecating was another thing altogether. A walk into the jungle generally accomplished this and Thai modesty allowed people to complete these tasks in privacy. But not for me. Once again curiosity overcame modesty and whenever I walked into the jungle a whisper would go around and there would soon be a small group of children following my every footstep. I would generally have to wade far out into the river so that I could urinate in deep water unobserved.

Now that we were amongst villages we slept at night in a couple of houses, built high off the ground on stilts which the inhabitants vacated in our honour. We slept on the floor, packed like sardines. The Thais were used to the heat and it never bothered them, but I found it unbearable. Sleeping on wooden floors with no mattresses was also a torment. The Thais actually prefer to sleep on the floor as they say it is cooler and anyway is their general custom outside Bangkok, but I found that my hips, shoulders and all sorts of protruding bones that I never knew existed, complained at this treatment.

Occasionally we had to visit villages that were distant from the river. Then elephants were provided and we clambered onto their backs, half a dozen on each elephant, and swayed down the jungle paths. The Princess on the lead elephant alone with the village headman and a soldier, the portraits of the King and Queen mounted on the front of the *howdah* like talismans. One day I noticed that there was a young elephant tagging along with the group, less than half the size of an adult. This handy-size model looked easier to mount and dismount and I decided to ride it.

The Princess peered down from her perch on the tallest elephant to see me struggling with the chain around the ankle of this docile-looking youngster.

"I wouldn't try that one, Evelyn," she warned. "They say it hasn't been completely broken in yet."

"We'll see about that," I shouted back, "anyway there is only a few feet to fall."

As I clambered onto its back, I caught some of the elephant-handlers eyeing each other; the Princess talked avidly to her *mahout* and then laughed. My elephant lurched placidly along the jungle track in the way elephants do, grabbing the odd banana tree with its trunk as it walked, until at one point our path traversed a riverbank, some twenty feet above the river. The elephant stopped. It had caught sight of a particularly delectable green shoot just below the path on the bank. It's trunk went out and very slowly the elephant lost its footing and started to slide down the bank - trunk, feet and me waving in the air, until we landed in the river with an enormous splash. I would not recommend falling into a river with the possibility of many tons of elephant landing on top. Elephant and I clambered back up the bank, wet and muddy, much to the amusement of our party who had gathered to watch these antics from the top of the bank.

Almost from the moment we left Phra Saeng I noticed that one of the nurses was a winsome lass. Her hair was shoulder-length at the back but in the front it was cut in such a way that it frequently fell across her eyes which she would then flick away in a particularly feminine gesture revealing large and, I thought, flirtatiously deep brown eyes. She was used to working in the jungle and her skin was burnished a copper reddish brown. I often caught her watching me in an inquisitive way, observing my every move.

My Thai was improving by the day, no other language was spoken, and by this time I could manage a fairly decent but rudimentary conversation. It was certainly sufficient to make her laugh and laughter is the way to any Thai girl's heart. She would bring me little delicacies, perhaps a fresh pineapple or a mango from the jungle. The Princess noticed what was going on and wagged her finger at me in a slightly disapproving way.

The tropical evenings are the best part of the day. This was a time for us to bathe in the river or explore the surrounding countryside. I took to walking with the nurse around the villages practising my Thai. One evening we walked out of the village and climbed some nearby high ground to the base of a limestone outcrop rising several hundred feet out of the jungle. For once the villagers and children left us alone. From our vantage point we looked out over the top of the jungle which stretched before us like a green sea with waves formed by the higher stands of trees. In the distance and surrounding us on every side the Khirirat mountains rose like islands and headlands in the ocean.

We lay together on a patch of grass and watched the sun sink into this expanse. There is something magical about the tropical sun. So intense during the day, at dusk it grows larger and its anger dissipates as it is swallowed by distant clouds on the horizon.

I felt her fingers lightly brush mine and linger a little. Her shoulder touched mine; I could feel the heat of her body through her cotton shirt. This nurse, prettier and braver than the others, was letting her curiosity get the better of her.

I gently lifted myself on one elbow and looked down at her. She was waiting. I lowered my lips towards hers when suddenly her courage failed her and she leapt to her feet, sending me sprawling on the grass. Gathering her sarong around her thighs, she ran like a frightened deer down the path into the jungle and back to the village. She kept her distance after that and there were no more little culinary delicacies.

This was a world untouched by the twentieth century. There was no electricity, no telephone, no television, no exhaust fumes. The only sign that the long arm of the Thai government had reached these villages was education. The larger villages had a small shelter under which there were some wooden benches and tables and a blackboard. A few teachers, dispatched reluctantly from the city, spent some months in the jungle providing one or two mornings of education every week. The children often had to walk miles, leaving their homes in the early morning as soon as it was considered safe from tigers and other wild animals.

I have not been back to Khirirat for over thirty years but now I hear there is a road through the valley and the loggers have moved in. The jungle is gone, the river is a tourist attraction and a whole way of life has been destroyed. European backpackers routinely hitch-hike past the limestone rocks and hills and internet cafes line the road. They could not guess that not so long ago it took days to reach this fabled place, a place where few *farang* had ever ventured.

We continued in this way for over two weeks, distributing the King's Bounty, treating the villagers and, hopefully, winning the hearts and minds of these people from the communist terrorists. We never encountered any of the 'enemy' but we knew they were there. The village headmen told us that strangers came into the villages at night and asked for food. They were armed and gathered all the villagers together to tell them how the government was neglecting them. If the villagers would only support these strangers then a new and better life would be theirs. At this stage the terrorists behaved well and did not harm or threaten the people.

Later, when the government started to react, different and more traditional tactics were introduced. The teachers were murdered first: they were often the only literate people in the area, could read out public notices and were much respected. Then any village headman who did not cooperate was shot in front of the assembled villagers. Later still, any villager who would not provide food or shelter was executed in front of his family. Sometimes children were murdered in front of their parents. The usual tactics of terrorism. But this was still in the future for these people.

The villagers were not ignorant. Many of the men, though none of the women, had made the five-day trip to the road-head at Phra Saeng and many had ventured into a bigger town with its bars, bright lights, fat-cat businessmen and government officials in their air-conditioned Mercedes-Benz cars. They may have known nothing of communism or the war that was being fought ferociously in nearby Vietnam, but they did know that they were not getting their fair share of attention from the central government.

This was my first expedition into the Thai jungle with the Princess but it was not going to be the last. Many more followed, some back to Khirirat, some to other areas in the far south of the country, to the distant islands in the Gulf of Siam and, as we will see, one particularly fateful expedition to the far north in the remote jungle on the Burmese frontier. I became the unofficial expedition photographer and my photographs and the stories I wrote were published in the English-language press upon our return to Bangkok. The Princess had been making these expeditions for many years before I came to Thailand and continued to do so for many years after I left the country, until it was to come to a sudden end with her untimely and savage death.

Back in Khirirat, we had exhausted our medical supplies, distributed all the Bounty and it was time to turn our boats around and head back downstream to Phra Saeng. As an alternative means of transport, some of the local villagers had built rafts out of bamboo cut from the jungle. Each raft consisted of thirty long lengths of thick bamboo bound together with creepers with a palm-frond shelter in the middle. These rafts could be punted down the river by two men with long poles balanced at each end of the raft and with two people sitting under the shelter. Fully loaded the rafts were flush with the river, the water lapping over the top of the raft.

Near the mountains the water was clear and inviting, further downstream it became muddier with the runoff from the jungle. But nowhere in the tropics is it safe to drink untreated water. Years later I was tempted to drink crystal-clear water at an altitude of fifteen thousand feet in the high Himalayas, a long way above any human habitation, but was reminded by a sherpa that however high I was, there was always the risk of a dead animal polluting the water just a little further upstream.

The river was running fairly fast and it needed some skill to steer the rafts down the river, round the bends and through the rapids across which, only a few days earlier, we had laboured to push and pull our laden boats upstream. The rafts slipped silently through the jungle, surprising birds and wild animals as we went. I took the front pole on the leading raft and energetically steered the raft for many hours as it sped down the river. This was hot and thirsty work. Arriving at one village around lunchtime, I was offered a bottle of water by one of the villagers. Without looking or asking what I was drinking, I quickly gulped the contents of the bottle.

The Princess stared at me aghast. "Evelyn, what on earth are you doing? Are you crazy?" she shouted at me.

It was too late. I had drunk a whole bottle of river water.

By that evening I was running a fever and by the next day I was showing symptoms of amoebic dysentery. The doctors could only sympathise and shake their heads; all their medicines had long since been distributed to the villagers. The next day I lay on the raft as the fever rose and my condition deteriorated. By the end of the second day I became delirious and the doctors recommended that I should be put ashore.

The next day we arrived at the *wat* in the jungle and it was decided that I should be left with the monks while the party continued downstream. One of the doctors would return with whatever drugs could be found. I was carried ashore and left in the care of the monks, though by this time I was scarcely conscious and knew little of what was happening around me.

One evening several days later, as the bats emerged and flapped noisily in the trees above, I was awakened from my delirious groaning by the muted sound of hundreds of bare feet padding around the outside of my shelter. Then there was a scuffling as the feet settled followed by absolute silence abruptly punctuated by the deep boom of a buffalo-skin drum: the signal for a hundred male voices to start chanting in a single low key. Volume gathered and reverberated off the very trees of the jungle. Immensely soothing, I could understand not a word but I knew the monks were chanting their Buddhist sutras in the ancient dead language of Pali; praying for my recovery.

On and on they chanted, deep into the night, vibrating the tropical air in my fragile shelter and filling my confused brain, for the first time since I had been abandoned deep in the jungle, with a sense of peace.

Then as suddenly as they had started, they ceased. I never heard the padding of bare feet away into the jungle but I knew that the monks into whose hands my life had been entrusted had called upon Buddha to give me strength.

With my health fading, Narong had moved into my *attap* hut. He slept on a rush mat on the earthen floor and attended to me during my brief moments of consciousness. He forced my narrowed and sore throat to swallow coconut milk and strange tasting broths made from the roots of plants and herbs growing in the jungle.

Early one morning Narong gently shook me awake and I saw through a half-open eye that he was pointing at a praying mantis that was slowly, very slowly, making its stately way along a palm frond beside my *charpoy*. This grotesque yet beautiful insect, like an alien from outer space with its helmet-like head, spindly arms and bright green body – at least six inches in height – became a friend. I would talk to it and whether it heard me or not it would turn its head and peer at me. Each day it would walk sedately along the palm in slow motion to a point level with my eye, turn and walk back: an eight hour journey to cover eighteen inches. Narong told me that it signified my troubles would soon be over.

Some days later I was aware of firm hands picking up my body, the sound of new Thai voices and an instant sharp pain as a syringe the size of a knitting needle was inserted into my thin buttock. A doctor had returned; salvation was at hand. My life had been saved but it was going to be weeks before I was strong enough to leave this mysterious temple in the middle of the jungle.

6

Blood on my Shirt

Princess Rangsit had given a lot of thought as to what I should call her. She was respectfully known by her servants as Tan Ying, *Tan* loosely meaning honourable. Her friends called her Ying but in formal Thai society it would never do for someone of my age to refer to an elder without an honorific. She wrote me frequent little notes which would be delivered to my flat and which she signed 'Vippy's mother' which then became 'V.M.' This clearly was not satisfactory so, in the spirit of the Son from the West, she announced that I should call her 'Tan Mair' or 'Honourable Mother' and so that became her name from then on. This was a great honour and amused the Thais enormously, but it solved many problems at a single blow and it clearly defined her relationship with a much younger man that otherwise might have been misinterpreted.

The next problem was how I should be addressed. It was hopeless to expect the army of Thai servants at the *Wang* to call me Lord Errington; they would never be able to wrap their tongue around such a long name and Evelyn would be far too informal. The Thais are meticulously formal people; the language changes in many subtle ways according to whether you are speaking to a social inferior, equal or superior. Members of the greater royal family, of whom there are a considerable number, must be addressed in what is almost a different language. So Tan Mair christened me 'Tan Lord' and that remains my name in Thailand to this day. As Buddhists, the Thais do not of course have Christian names as such: they have a first name and then the family name. A *Khun* Narong Adisorn, with Adisorn being the family name, is known as *Khun* Narong and is filed as such in the telephone directory leading to endless head scratching amongst foreigners visiting the country who would understandably look for him under "A" for Adisorn.

All Thais have nicknames from birth and it is to these odd-sounding names that they normally respond amongst friends. Thus it was not surprising to meet a beautiful and elegant Thai lady who would answer to the name of 'egg' or 'rat'.

The Thai ambassador in Austria was known to his friends as 'elephant' (and his brother, an important banker, as 'crocodile'). Tan Lord was more a nickname than an honorific: it was a pun, the Thai word *lord* means a straw so to many I was just an 'honourable straw' no more or less humorous than many other Thai nicknames and quite in keeping with the Thai sense of humour.

On my second day in Bangkok Tan Mair came to my flat to discuss my future plans. I told her that I was thinking of taking the *Ben Nevis* back to England in a month's time, a notion she dismissed with a wave of her hand.

"No," she said, "we must arrange some employment for you that gives you sufficient spare time to see my country." She decided that I would become an English teacher. Within a few days she had lined up a selection of pupils: none of the staff at Kesya could speak English so the manager and two senior stylists were co-opted as was one of her friends who owned a Thai silk exporting business. Then the VW agency was told that they also would be learning English and a meeting room in their substantial offices was converted into a classroom.

So every morning the Kesya manager would come to my flat for her hour of tuition and the two tittering stylists would follow her; one was very pretty and would gracefully flirt with her teacher. I would then drive across town to Rajprasong and give another hour of tuition to the owner of the Thai silk business. In the late afternoon I would appear at the VW agency and would teach a classroom full of mechanics and car salesmen.

One day I was introduced to a Thai working for Philips Electronics. He had a problem: Philips had sold a communications system to the Thai Police and a number of policemen were to be sent to Germany to attend a training course. Could I teach them English? So three times a week I set off to the Police Headquarters to teach a room full of policemen some rudimentary English. Now the Thais at that time generally thought there were only three languages in their world: there was *pasa Thai*, spoken by everybody, *pasa jin*, spoken by the large ethnic Chinese population, and *pasa farang* spoken by all white people. *Pasa farang* was of course English. It was not long before I discovered that the Thai police were to attend a German-language course in Hamburg so they were learning the wrong language. Should I tell them and thereby lose my job, or should I teach them English anyway and let them in for an unpleasant surprise when they arrived in Germany? I decided discretion would be the best course of action.

I soon discovered that I knew very little about my own language. Rules must exist for English grammar and spelling but I had no idea what they were. And then there were the idioms; the language seemed full of them. I bought some books and found that I was learning as much about English as my pupils. In fact I was not sure who was learning from whom.

I had lunch with Nying and the Kesya girls every day, which was a source of endless amusement. To them I was a novelty and my fumblings in Thai would be greeted by gales of laughter. Nying solved my bathing problem: I was not meant to get into the jar of water but use a ladle made from half a coconut shell to splash water from the jar over my body. Tan Mair instructed Nying to give me a lesson in washing in the tropics. In English boarding schools one bathes twice a week. At home in England I used to bathe once a day. The Thais on the other hand shower at least three times a day. Unless one washes very frequently in the tropics one can soon become fairly 'high' and it was not long before I saw Nying wrinkling her nose at me and declaring that I '*men kee tow*' or smelled like tortoise shit.

So I adopted the Thai regimen and the problem was solved. I soon found that insufficient bathing was not the only *farang* behaviour that upset the Thais; there were many offensive western characteristics from the volume of one's speech to body contact – the Thais never touched anybody, never shook hands, never kissed a cheek – and at all times I had to remember where to put my feet. There was a lot to learn.

Every evening I drove the short distance to the *Wang* for a swim and dinner. Most days Tan Mair would attend a funeral in the evening. Funerals, as I was later to discover to my cost, are social occasions and are held every evening for as long as ninety days from the day of the death until the day of cremation. Each evening the relations and friends would gather at the *wat* where refreshments would be served, a Thai band would play and orange-robed monks would chant from time to time. The unfortunate departed, depending on their position in society, would preside in a sitting position from inside a square coffin or large urn. Funerals are happy events and there would be much conversation and discreet laughter with children running around the temple. Death is not to be mourned but welcomed as a release from this life and an entry to a better life through reincarnation.

After the daily funeral, or sometimes several funerals, Tan Mair would return to the *Wang* and we would dine alone. After dinner we would sit in her formal drawing room, barefoot on a rare turquoise Persian rug given to her by the Empress of Iran. She would tell me about her life as a writer and courtier, her trips overseas with the King and Queen and the ways and traditions of the Thai people. Tan Mair's father, Prince Rajani Chaemcharas was educated at Cambridge University and became a poet and a scholar. He had owned a newspaper but its offices, archives and his extensive library were all burnt during the Second World War. During his later years Prince Rajani's eye-sight deteriorated and Tan Mair became his right hand and amanuensis.

Tan Mair inherited her father's literary genes and became a renowned and prolific writer of Thai romances, many made into films or television dramas, as well as historical novels based on Thai and European history. I was an avid and enthusiastic listener and relished our evenings as we sat at either end of the Persian rug. Several evenings a week she would attend dinner parties at Chitrlada Palace or be on duty welcoming foreign royalty and I would eat with Nying at the *Wang* or alone watching the *jinjoks* crawling across the kitchen ceiling in their pursuit of mosquitoes. They would occasionally lose their grip and fall with a plop onto the floor, or, as luck would have it, on to the table where I was eating.

I had been in Thailand for over a week before I met Prince Piya Rangsit whom I was to address as Tan Chai. A handsome man in his fifties, he had a superior and somewhat overbearing manner and tended to greet every comment with a "tsk, tsk" followed by a high-pitched laugh. Everybody in the *Wang* was clearly terrified of him. His word was law and he did not brook any view except his own. He had a distinctive aura of power emphasised by his royal birth, his position as chairman and proprietor of a large and successful business and as an extremely wealthy man.

Tan Chai's father, Prince Rangsitprayurasak, later given the grand title The Prince of Chainat, was another of King Chulalongkorn's descendants. His mother died when he was a child and he was raised as a son by the present King's grandmother, Queen Savang Vadhana. While King Bhumibol was in Switzerland finishing his education, the Prince of Chainat was appointed Regent for the last five years of his life. He died in 1951, the year King Bhumibol returned to Siam to be crowned the ninth King of the Chakri Dynasty.

Most weekends we would drive to the Rangsit seaside home in Sriracha. It was a wooden house overlooking the Gulf of Siam. Not far offshore was the island of Koh Sichan, the same island where the *Ben Nevis* had anchored waiting to cross the bar into the Chao Phraya River and where the sharks had swum hungrily around the ship. That seemed a long time ago. These days one can drive to Sriracha on a four-lane superhighway but then a small road led from Bangkok to Paknam at the mouth of the river and down the east side of the Gulf across salt pans and marshes. From Sriracha we would drive further south to Pattaya Bay with its small fishing village. There was a single hotel, the Nipa Lodge, and a small restaurant, Barbos, from where I could water-ski, swim in the crystal waters or hire boats to visit the nearby islands. Today Pattaya is a nightmare of dingy hotels, bars and nightclubs populated by hookers, transvestites and armies of sex tourists from Europe. To swim in its dirty, sewage-filled water would be to court disease, to walk in its filthy alleys to invite mugging.

The Rangsits generally travelled in one or two VW microbuses. There would always be Tan Mair and Nying, a couple of maids, Nying's brother Tuk, and a few other Thais who lived at the *Wang* or family friends. Tan Chai would join us when he was not 'upcountry'. We made expeditions to Khao Yai, a national park north of Bangkok where we searched for mouse deer and other wild animals or braved the rapids and falls on tyre inner tubes. We frequently drove the few hours to Hua Hin on the west coast of the Gulf opposite Sriracha where Tan Chai's brother Tan Sanidh owned a house. The King spent a month every year at his palace in Hua Hin and Tan Mair was allocated a house in the royal compound where she would stay with her retinue. I would stay at Tan Sanidh's house where the Swiss artist Theo Maier was living.

He filled the house with colourful tropical paintings of Bali where he had lived for most of his life and was besotted with the resident maid who, much to Tan Sanidh's amusement, had moved from the servants' quarters into Theo's bedroom.

Several times a month, Tan Chai gave formal dinner parties at the *Wang* and I was a frequent guest. There I met many other members of the Thai aristocracy: Prince Subhadradis Diskul, the chairman of the National Museum, the diminutive Princess Chumbhot of Naga Svarga, Seni Pramoj, a previous prime minister, and his brother Kukrit Pramoj a future prime minister. Occasionally the King and Queen came to dine. As interesting as those who were invited, were those who were not: no political leaders, who were deemed corrupt and socially undesirable, and very few business people, who were almost exclusively ethnic Chinese, ever saw the inside of *Wang Vidhyu*.

The Chinese had been fleeing the poorer parts of China for a new life in Southeast Asia since the the middle of the nineteenth century. Those who settled in Thailand came mainly from the *chaozhou*-speaking part of Guangdong Province in the south of China. Known as *teo-chiu* in the local vernacular, they were a rough peasant people who naturally took to trade. Before long they dominated the easy-going Thai farmers who rapidly fell into debt to the immigrant Chinese. Despite this, Thailand became the most successful country in Southeast Asia in assimilating the Chinese, many of whom took Thai names (albeit loosely based on their original Chinese names), embraced Buddhism and married Thai women (though not the other way around: Chinese girls rarely married Thai men).

Upper class Thais tended to be condescending towards the ethnic Chinese in their midst, referring to them as *jek* with a knowing nod and a wink. They laughed at the Chinese tendency to over-excitement and would whisper "*jek deun fai*" or "Chinese walking on fire" whenever they saw an ethnic Chinese starting to raise his voice. The Thais knew that the Chinese were by no means as integrated as they appeared: they tried hard to pass on their own Chinese dialect down the generations, maintained Chinese schools for their children, published Chinese newspapers and preferred to mix with their own ethnic group looking down in turn on their Thai hosts. Nevertheless other countries in the region were nowhere near as successful at integrating the flood of Chinese immigrants: racial conflicts broke out from time to time between the Chinese and the local population in Malaysia, Indonesia and the Philippines then as they do today. The true tension between the ethnic Chinese and the Thais was not to be brought into focus until I was to meet my future wife two years later.

At my first dinner party at the *Wang* I met one couple who were to become life-long friends: Peter and Sanda Simms. At that time Peter was working for the Time-Life news bureau in Bangkok. His wife Sanda was a Cambridge University-educated Shan aristocrat of an ancient lineage, whose father had been elected the first President of the Union of Burma in 1947. In later years Peter was to live in Singapore at the same time as I and even later he was to move to Hong Kong where I was also living. Our paths were to cross frequently over many decades.

As the months slipped by, I absorbed the Thai culture and way of life. I met many Thais but few *farang*. It was not easy in those days for foreigners to live in Bangkok. Visitors had to obtain visas that were only valid for ten days and could be extended for a maximum of a month. Tan Chai solved this problem by arranging to have a work permit issued to me on the grounds that teaching English was a national priority. The days of the backpacker and budget tourist had not yet arrived. *Farang* living in Bangkok were mainly diplomats and long-term residents, many of whom worked for large foreign companies in Thailand, and of course the rapidly expanding number of American soldiers.

One day I decided that I should deliver Tony Keswick's letter to Alec McCallum, the Jardines' man in Bangkok. A florid man, he greeted me warily and immediately summoned one of his underlings and waved me out of his office. His underling was one of the army of young 'Jardine Johnnies' that the company sent to the Far East, and who were moved from department to department, country to country, spending a couple of years in each, until it was thought they had learned enough about the ways of business in the East. They were then sent to the head office in Hong Kong to take on more serious responsibilities.

My contact was Robert Friend and he invited me for lunch. I learned that there were many young Englishmen working in Bangkok for companies such as Jardine Matheson, the Borneo Company and the Anglo-Thai Corporation (both units of the world-wide Inchcape trading empire), BOAC, Shell or the many other British companies with interests in Thailand. These young expatriates had, as the English had done throughout the world down the centuries, recreated a little England for themselves: there was the British Club, a couple of English pubs, games of football and in fact everything to help an Englishman forget that he was in a foreign country. Most important of all there was the Royal Bangkok

Sports Club where it was possible to meet attractive and well-bred young Thai girls fresh from English boarding-schools or American colleges.

This sounded like an interesting prospect worth investigating but I was not a member of the Club and, given my particular disinterest in organised sports, coughing up the entrance and monthly fee in the hope of meeting some nice girls would put too much of a strain on my slender income. Tan Mair was a member but she rarely went; like me she was not one for organised sports.

As I became more familiar with the Bangkok social scene I learned how the young expatriate male, and particularly the Jardine Johnnies, operated. There was always a small clique of English-speaking western-educated Thai girls who were keen to demonstrate their newfound westernised ways by mixing with the young foreigners. A romance would develop which would shock the girl's parents: after all the girl had been expensively educated overseas in order to attract a rich and eligible Thai husband, not so that she would be wasted on a hairy young white man from an alien culture who would move on after a few years.

The romance would continue for as long as the expatriate remained in Thailand, generally two to three years. The girl, deeply in love and devoted to her boyfriend, hoped that marriage was going to be the next step but generally the young man was transferred to his next Asian posting leaving the distraught girl behind. By that time no Thai man was interested in the girl. All oriental men have a sneaking feeling that they are physically inferior to the western male, and this was going to lead to an unfortunate comparison in bed. This was in fact no idle speculation: years later when I was working for Inchcape one of my responsibilities was managing the Durex condom agency in Vietnam. The London Rubber Company, then manufacturers of Durex condoms, had experienced sales difficulties in Thailand and market research found that their condoms were not popular as they tended to slip off. A tighter-fitting model had to be introduced.

So the Thai girl, rejected by her own race, could only return to the Royal Bangkok Sports Club, don her sexiest bikini and wait for the next *farang* to come by. The public school educated Jardines executives in particular, many from the English/Scottish border counties, formed an exclusive circle and socialised together allowing in only a few like-minded (which generally meant originating from similar backgrounds) young men from other companies. The girls ended up being passed down from an outgoing to an incoming expatriate in an endless chain until age had withered her attraction and was coveted by neither European nor Thai.

This is not to say that *farang* males did not form lasting relationships with Thai girls, far from it. Many *farang* married Thai girls and mixed marriages became more frequent as they became more acceptable. Things had come a long way from the 1950s when an expatriate in the East had to resign his club memberships, an important part of the expatriate's life, before he got married. He would then have to reapply for membership: if his wife was a *farang* then re-election was automatic but if oriental then his resignation might become permanent. The expatriate's boss also had to be consulted and permission to marry might or might not be forthcoming. By the 1960s mixed marriages were reasonably common but by the 1990s they were so frequent that the majority of children at the International School in Bangkok were of mixed parentage.

Mixed marriages did however lead to problems, though not so much with the Thais who generally accepted the mingling of the races, as long as it did not involve their own daughters. The males would generally keep to their own race for the reason given above. Opposition always came from the community of *farang* wives. Western women are at a distinct disadvantage in the Far East. Large and clumsy compared to the lissom and graceful figures of the oriental woman, they feel themselves out of place with their dyed wiry hair compared to the long and sleek black manes of the Thai, Chinese or Vietnamese; their skin white, blotchy and perforated by insect bites alongside the darker, smoother and hairless skin of a young oriental female.

It was not only physical differences that set the *farang* female apart from her oriental sisters. The *farang* women tended to dismiss the oriental woman as compliant, submissive and obedient. Nothing could be further from the truth: oriental women generally possess an active intelligence, intuition and insight that far exceeds the male. Women are to be found in positions of power in business, politics or government in Thailand far more frequently than in any Western country. Oriental female presidents, prime ministers and chairwomen of boards are also often found. But combined with their undoubted mental acumen is their capacity to flatter their man's ego in a subtle way which pleases the man at little cost to the woman.

Tansannee was my first Thai lover. She was a sensitive seventeen-year-old student, quiet and gentle in appearance but with a sharp mind and a perceptive eye. The first time we slept together I was lying on my bed waiting for her to finish brushing her hair which fell to her waist like black molasses. She silently wafted into the darkened room, a sarong around her waist, her breasts hidden behind her waterfall of hair, approached the bed, dropped onto her knees and *waied*, bending so her head nearly touched the bed. It was profoundly touching and feminine gesture. She murmured into my ear that this was a Thai custom, all women must *wai* their man before climbing into their bed at night – a small sign of appreciation for being there, of love, of gratitude. Today's modern woman might recoil in horror, but does feminism deserve to supersede centuries-old traditions of gentleness and affection?

Most unattached young men would take up with a Thai girl and many a husband found themselves irresistibly drawn to their secretary, a girl at the office party, an airline stewardess or, heaven forbid, some lady of the night. The western wives could only circle the wagons and try to insulate their husbands from temptation. But they were often fighting a losing battle and, as I saw so many times over the years, an oriental girl would often displace the western wife.

All this tended to make the western female in Asia an embittered species. They could only look down haughtily from what they perceived to be their high moral ground and avoid any contact with young oriental females. They stuck to their own expatriate communities and moaned about the heat, the food, their servants and reminisced about life 'back home' while their men worked and played.

The Thai girls did not know it but they were risking their futures by marrying a young *farang*. Generally these young men came from middle class homes in the west. They were tempted to work in the Far East for a few years by a generous salary, a large house, servants, a chauffeur-driven car and many other benefits. Such a lavish living style was of course irresistible to many oriental girls who assumed that when they moved to the West their young husband would enjoy the same standard of living. It would come as a shock to find they were expected to live in semi-detached or terraced houses in suburbia and had to bring up the children, cook, and clean the home themselves. All but the poorest of Thais had their own maids in Bangkok and so marrying a *farang* in many cases brought a temporary uplift in their way of life in Bangkok, but a long-term decline once in the West.

Robert Friend was sounding me out. The Bangkok Post, an English-language daily, had already reported that a young English lord was living in their midst and Robert was wondering whether I would fit into their tight circle. I can only surmise that he found me too strange a bird: I was not employed by an established company and was living exclusively amongst the Thai community under the umbrella of one of the most powerful families in the land. This was beyond his ken: young expatriates had few opportunities to meet and mix with upper class Thais at that time. They would certainly have liked to do so, but they were really skating on the surface of a very alien culture, whilst I was gradually immersing myself into Thai life under the careful guidance of Tan Mair and Nying.

The British Club was not for me; in fact I never crossed its doorstep once throughout my many years in Bangkok. Robert realised this and sensed also the loner within me. Although in time I was to meet most of the Jardine executives and trainees in Thailand. I would sometimes go to their parties but remained an outsider. Some of them became friends; Robert in particular kept in touch with me throughout my years in Asia.

I spent my first Christmas in Thailand with Sanidh at his Thai-style wooden house on the banks of the Ping River in Chiang Mai in the far north of Thailand. Chiang Mai is a walled city and in the 1960s there were very few buildings outside the city wall. Today it is a vast sprawling metropolis and the old walls have almost vanished but in those days it had an atmosphere of its own. There were few cars, local transport being by pedicab. The weather was cool during the day, almost cold at night. I was allocated a small wooden guesthouse with a veranda jutting over the river. I looked across the muddy swiftly-flowing river to an island given over to a leper colony. In the distance rose Doi Sutep, the first foothill of the ranges that roll into Laos and Burma and eventually thousands of miles to the west rise into the high Himalayas.

Sanidh was the exact opposite of his brother. Where Tan Chai was austere, Sanidh was a jovial extrovert and bon viveur. He lived with Christine, his third wife, vivacious and very French. It was never clear to me, or I suspect anybody else, whether he had divorced his other two wives. Marriage is something of a vague concept to most Thais. It involves signing a book in the *umphur*, or local administrative office; alongside this book there is another in which a simple signature then undoes the marriage. It was legal to be married as many times as one liked simultaneously as long as it was in a different province. Divorce, at least for males, was something of a minor technicality.

Sanidh and Christine lived grandly and extravagantly and were very much part of the international jet set. They were amused by Tan Mair's 'Son from the West' and often invited me to their parties in Bangkok which they threw for passing visitors like John Paul Getty, the notorious film director Roman Polanski, the dark Italian Prince Dado Ruspoli or the occasional film star – Alain Delon being a frequent favourite. The only problem for me was that the language generally used was French in which I hardly excelled. Sanidh often amused himself by taking his guests to the Mosquito Bar, a particularly sordid joint by the harbour with sawdust on the floor, frequented by sailors and their molls. Punch-ups between drunken Russian and Norwegian sailors were a nightly event.

That first night in Chiang Mai we ventured into the town and ate by a *klong*, a canal that ran through the centre of the town. We drank a great deal of Mekong rice whisky mixed with soda water and fresh limes. The food was exotic in the extreme: whole baby frogs skewered on a stick and grilled over an open fire, deep fried frog skin which we ate like chips before the meal, small mounds of ants eggs like white caviar served on a leaf. The soup was a warm sticky concoction with a spring onion floating on the top. By the time we made it back to Sanidh's house we were very much the worse for wear.

The next morning I found to my horror that the shirt I had worn the previous night was covered with bloodstains. I asked my host whether we had become involved in an accident or maybe even a fight the previous evening. He assured me that we had not but I had spilled my soup. One of the delights of Chiang Mai cuisine is to serve fresh pig's blood straight from the pig into a bowl. From then on I vowed to examine my food much more closely before eating, regardless of how much Mekong I had drunk.

7

The Islands

Southeast Asia is blessed with some of the most beautiful islands in the world. Sometimes mountainous, occasionally flat, they were created by nature in myriad ways: many are volcanic rising as sea-mounts from the ocean floor, others are vast coral reefs covering huge areas just a few feet above the surrounding seas, some are limestone outcrops jutting starkly out of an emerald sea while others are sand banks that disappear with the rising tide. Even those with no evidence of fresh water boast lush tropical vegetation, blood-temperature water so clear that depth becomes an illusion and a normally hospitable indigenous populace.

Two of the largest Asian countries by area, the Philippines and Indonesia, are massive island archipelagos. Thailand, Malaysia, Cambodia, Myanmar and Vietnam are all surrounded by constellations of temptingly seductive tropical islands. Exploring these islands became a way of life: most have some sort of accommodation varying from five-star resorts that may cost thousands of dollars a night in today's money, to an *attap* hut on the beach for less than a dollar.

That first year in Thailand slipped past quickly. I laboured away at teaching English and learning Thai and spending most of my free time with the Rangsit family. Tan Mair continued to treat me as her Son from the West. We made frequent trips around Thailand to many places *farang* did not or could not visit. The seasons scarcely changed, the monsoon rains came and went, the heat remained. I remember these as happy times as I began my long education into the ways of the East. I was becoming seduced by the tropical sun, the vivid colours that infused one's every day, the courtesy and unselfconscious friendliness of the Thais, the elegance of the women and a way of life so different from what I had known in England.

During the school holidays Tan Mair's two daughters, Vippy and her younger sister Priya, a headstrong teenager, returned to Bangkok. If they were surprised to find how Tan Mair had absorbed me into their family life, they never showed it. The daughters were expected to join their mother on her trips into

the tropical rain forests which they did with reluctance. The jungle expeditions were a source of endless fascination to me, but held no excitement for them; they preferred to stay in Bangkok with their friends where the lights were bright and the night-clubs stayed open until the early hours.

It was not only the jungle; we made many other trips outside Bangkok. On one occasion the family set off to visit an island owned by one of Tan Mair's friends near the Cambodian frontier. It was called Koh Kradat, or Paper Island, so flat that one could scarcely see it from the sea. The island was unoccupied save for an ancient mariner with skin burned to the texture of parchment who oversaw a handful of itinerant fisherman and looked after the absentee owner's small wooden house. We were to live off the land, and that meant fishing for food, which I thought was a little optimistic given that there were at least a dozen in the Rangsit party.

There was no sign of any fishing activity throughout the first day and it was looking as if our dinner was going to be limited to coconuts. Then as dusk approached one of the fishermen suggested to me that it was time to fish for dinner. We walked down to the jetty. I was a little puzzled, as I could see neither fishing boat nor fishing equipment. He strolled down to the end of the jetty, reached into his *pakoma* and pulled out a stick of dynamite, ignited a short fuse and threw it into the water where it exploded with a massive whoosh.

Almost immediately the surface of the sea was covered with dead, dying or writhing fish. I assumed that he was going to scoop up his catch and take them ashore but he said we could not eat these fish as their internal organs had probably burst and the meat would be inedible. Instead we both dived into the water where we found a large number of fish just beneath the surface which had been merely stunned by the explosion. I could swim up to them and they would lazily swim away a foot or so and then hover, dazed. With a little practice I learned to approach them from behind, grab them firmly and whisk them sharply into a net. This way we caught more than we could possible eat and all within thirty minutes. Far from ecologically or environmentally correct but we were living in a different era in the 1960s.

There were also large numbers of giant clams living on the coral reef that surrounded the island. I was shown by the fishermen how to sever them from their anchorage and swim back to the shore where I forced them open with a knife, cut out the flesh which was tossed back into the sea and scraped off the small white muscles which were delicious raw, dipped into a mixture of lime juice and chillies. Many years later, and as the holder of a scuba diving qualification, I was to learn that these clams are an 'endangered species' and within a few years it became illegal to kill them in most Asian waters.

The old man of the island used to follow me closely observing my every

move. By now I was quite used to the curiosity that Thais showed towards *farang* but his attention became intrusive and I would noisily complain about him to Vippy and Tan Mair in the safe knowledge that he could not speak a single word of English. On our last day on the island we packed up our few belongings and prepared to climb onto the boat, which had come from the mainland to collect us. At the last moment the old man came up to me, smiled as Thais do and said in perfect but rusty English with a slight American intonation.

"I do hope that you enjoyed your stay on the island. You are the very first *farang* I have seen for over twenty years."

I could have fallen off the jetty in amazement, the more so when he went on to tell me that he had graduated from Harvard in 1912.

Our trips to the south of Thailand took us fairly frequently to the island of Phuket. We normally stayed in a Chinese hotel in the centre of the town and would explore Phuket's faded splendour from the days when it was a rich tin mining centre. The Thais, eager to keep their skin as pale as possible, never visited Phuket's fabled beaches which remained remote and road-less on the west side of the island. On my second or third trip Sanidh joined us and he suggested that we might like to visit some land he had purchased many years before. We set off down a dirt track, our jeep bumping for miles over the hills until the track rose over the last and steepest climb to reveal an emerald bay of astonishing beauty spreading in front of us with headlands on either side and a small island in the middle. It could have been a film set, scarcely credible in its perfection. The road dropped sharply to the beach where there was a small wooden house that Sanidh had built a few yards from the sea.

I was overwhelmed by its natural beauty, with the clear sea lapping against an untouched sandy beach and evidently praised it so much that Sanidh, in his characteristically generous and expansive manner, said that the land was of little use to him and offered to sell me a five-acre piece by the beach. How much would it cost? He pondered for a while and said that five thousand dollars would be a fair price. Five thousand dollars! Not much today perhaps, but at the time it was a king's ransom to me. It had to remain a dream.

Today that bay, Kata Yai, is the home of a huge Club Mediterranee complex and there are other hotels as well as bars and nightclubs spread along the beach. This half-mile strip of sand, empty except for sea eagles and dolphins in the 60's is now, 45 years later, a phallanx of North European flesh frying under rank after rank of gaudy mauve parasols. Sanidh sold his land long ago and it is now some of the most expensive real estate in Thailand.

Phuket was an island to which I returned again and again over the following decades. Parts of it gradually metamorphosed from a somnolent paradise to a modern hell of motor-cycles, tawdry transvestite bars, 'resort' hotels with their pallid pot-bellied *farang* tourists, vendors hawking knock-off watches and 'brand-name' clothes; all to the constant background noise of ghetto-blasters hanging from palm trees or blaring along the beaches. The oriental entrepreneur is no slouch when it comes to smelling out a quick buck and if a single tourist is to be seen strolling down a deserted beach then it is only a very short time before there is a row of hawker stalls peddling every known fast food and tourist tat.

Many years later I was again tempted by the Phuket property market. This time it was not Sanidh but one of his many children, now grown up and a would-be property developer, who 'owned' a delightful coconut plantation on a ridge overlooking two pristine bays. Purchasing land in Phuket required taking a great deal on faith: the Thai land title laws are complex in the extreme and operate on many different levels. Ultimately uncleared jungle belonged to the first person to hack away the undergrowth and attempt some form of cultivation regardless of whether any right to the land had been registered with the authorities. It was therefore quite likely that one could acquire a piece of land, build a house and develop the property only to have a farmer appear one day to claim that it was his grandfather who had originally planted a mango tree on the site many years previously. In such cases the 'authorities' would always support an indigenous islander against some rich developer from Bangkok, another world away, or, even worse, a *farang*!

I look at Phuket today and see many new developments and beach-side houses apparently owned by Germans and Americans and imagine those crafty islanders biding their time before reclaiming their birthright.

This was not the only opportunity I missed: one of Tan Mair's expeditions to distribute the King's Bounty took us to the islands in the Gulf of Siam. The largest island is Koh Samui, in those days a very remote place. There was one small town on the island and a handful of villages. A single *farang* lived there, a Dane who managed a small coconut-processing factory owned by the East Asiatic Company. There were no hotels on the island and, as usual, we took over the town hospital and slept on its wooden floors. The *nai umphur* or head man of the island was enormously amused by my faltering Thai, my pathetic efforts to sing Thai folk songs and, evidently, the respect and affection that by now all the Rangsit party showed to the 'Son from the West'.

One evening he took me out to a headland sprinkled with large boulders

and otherwise covered with thick elephant grass, where the land dropped spectacularly into the Gulf spreading in front of me like a carpet of shimmering gold in the setting sun. I imagined building a house there and disappearing from the world. The *nai amphur* approached Tan Mair and solemnly told her that this land was no good to him or the villagers as it was not possible to grow rice there and the soil was poor. He would like to grant the whole headland to me. Tan Mair said she was sure she could find a way around the law prohibiting *farang* from owning land in Thailand and I became very excited at the prospect. Sadly, back in Bangkok, Koh Samui faded from my mind with its remoteness, which necessitated an overnight trip by train from Bangkok, a longish drive to the port, and a slow crossing in an antiquated ferry.

I never did anything about it and the opportunity slipped through my fingers. Today Koh Samui is one of Thailand's main tourist attractions with its own airport and daily direct flights from Bangkok. The island is littered with hotels, inns, nightclubs and restaurants. Although I did return to Koh Samui several times in the years to come, I never ventured back to my headland.

Some days later we were walking along a jungle path to visit a remote village some hours away. The path meandered some twenty feet above a fast-flowing river. Apart from our usual complement of doctors and nurses, many of the local villagers had turned out to accompany us. Some way in front of me was a young girl, maybe ten years old. Suddenly she slipped and slid down the riverbank into the river. There was an outcry as she was swept out into deeper water and downstream towards me. The mother screamed, others shouted and ran back along the path towards me but nobody jumped into the water. The girl could not swim. I dived into the water, swam out to the girl who had panicked and was gulping water, got my arm around her and pulled her back to the shore.

That night when we were sitting around the open fire discussing our day's activities the *nai amphur* came up to us followed by the mother, the daughter dutifully following behind. Was I mistaken or was the girl crying? Slowly she came out from behind her mother's sarong, walked reluctantly towards me, *waied* and sat quietly cross-legged at my feet. All talk around the fireside ceased, only the fire crackled, all eyes were upon me. The *nai amphur* stood before me, *waied* deeply and announced that the mother would like to formally thank me for saving her daughter's life. I told her that anybody would have done the same and to think no more about it. But the mother seemed to be weeping as well, or so it appeared in the flickering light of the fire and the torches burning around our campsite.

The *nai amphur* softly but firmly explained to me that it was their custom that as I had saved the girl's life, her life now belonged to me. I glanced at Tan Mair who nodded her head slightly and gestured to me to stay silent. The *nai*

amphur continued with his speech of thanks and told me that although the mother loved this daughter as her favourite child, she had six children and sufficient sons to look after her. What was I to do? Accepting this daughter as a gift was an interesting thought but I could see it also meant a life-long commitment. I told the *nai amphur* that I was touched by the offer but in my country a life belonged to the individual and could not be given away. He listened, amused, but paid little attention. The mother turned tearfully away and faded into the darkness. The girl looked at me and I saw for the first time that she was very beautiful.

For days afterwards the girl followed me everywhere: folding my *pakoma*, fetching my food, her constant attention becoming an embarrassment. She said nothing but looked at me imploringly through huge dark brown eyes partially veiled behind strands of long silky black hair, desperate to anticipate my every need. She was pathetically eager to please, as if my rejection would cause her family to lose face amongst the villagers. Tan Mair was enormously entertained by the incident and teased me constantly about my latest conquest.

As time went by I spoke to the *nai amphur* on many occasions explaining to him that it was difficult for me to take the girl back to Bangkok, that she would be home-sick, that I might not even stay in Thailand for very long. Tan Mair eventually relented and released me from my dilemma by ruling that the girl should stay on Koh Samui but should never forget the *farang* who saved her life and should pray to Buddha to protect me each day.

Face was saved, the mother looked delighted and the girl smiled for the first time in days. Their customs had been respected and honour was saved.

There was another incident on one of those remote islands that has remained in my memory. This involved Priya, Tan Mair's younger daughter. The islands to the north and west of Koh Samui are of the same geological limestone formations that extend from Guilin in south China, recurring in many locations in Southeast Asia from Halong Bay in Vietnam, across southern Thailand into Malaysia and again on the other side of the South China Sea in the islands to the north of Palawan in the Philippines. In each case limestone rocks, the ancient cores of much larger rock masses, rise sheer out of the sea or paddy fields to a height of several hundred feet. As islands they are often uninhabited, as they offer no foothold to get ashore. The islands near Koh Samui are home to swallows which make their nests high on the rock face. The Thais used these islands as penal camps. A convict could choose to serve out his sentence in the austerity of a conventional prison or be sent to one of these islands where his sentence was halved in recognition of the additional hardship. His dangerous task was to climb the sheer rock faces and harvest the swallow's nests destined to be served in Chinese restaurants in Hong Kong or Singapore as bird's nest soup.

This may sound like a strange way to complete a prison sentence but stranger things happened in Thailand. It was possible at that time for a rich man found guilty of some offence, to send a substitute to prison while the culprit remained at large. On one occasion the editor of the Bangkok Post, a well-known *farang* in Bangkok, was found guilty of *lèsè majesté* and was given a prison sentence. His chauffeur served the sentence in his stead.

On one occasion our modest fleet of boats anchored offshore a steep rocky island. There was a small village nestling under a sheer cliff and I suggested to Priya that we go ashore and explore the island. So the two of us accompanied by three soldiers from our guard took a small boat ashore. We walked through the village noticing, but not registering in our minds, that men appeared from between the houses, took a quick look at us and then swiftly darted into the background. When we reached the far side of the village, the cliff rising high above us, we found an animist shrine filled with phalli of different shapes and sizes cut from driftwood, coral or stone. This was not the only strange feature of the island: it gradually dawned on us that the village was only occupied by men: there was not a female to be seen.

As we were admiring this fascinating collection of phalli one of the soldiers ran towards us shouting. He yelled that we had to get off the island, and fast. As we ran back through the houses we saw that the male occupants were talking amongst themselves and making threatening signs at us. By the time we reached the beach and had thrown ourselves into the boat, some of the men were running down the beach towards us shouting, gesticulating and throwing stones. I felt like Captain Cook about to meet his end with a spear thrust through me on some remote tropical shore.

Back on our mother boat we were told that the authorities did not allow women on these islands and as a result the resident sex-starved criminals had not seen a woman for, in most cases, many years. An animist religion had sprung up on the islands featuring a male-hungry Goddess who protected the convicts as they climbed the precipitous cliffs in pursuit of the nests. The phalli were offerings to appease the Goddess of the island. Priya's arrival had caused consternation at first and then a fear that her presence would anger the jealous Goddess. Priya was to be sacrificed.

ॐ ॐ ॐ

I was commissioned by Thai Airways International to write a guide-book on Bali to commemorate the first jet flight to this Indonesian island. The night before I left Bangkok I joined Tan Mair for dinner at the *Wang*. While swimming before dinner her pet pug dog nipped my ankle in play drawing a bead of blood. The dog died during the night. A hasty post mortem revealed that the dog had died of rabies although it had shown none of the usual symptoms. I was rushed to a doctor who prescribed the only antidote available in those days: a series of ten daily injections through the stomach wall.

I was handed a box containing ten glass phials which I kept in the airplane's refrigerator during the flight to Indonesia. Arriving at the 'Tanjung Sari', one of only a handful of hotels on the island at that time, I arranged for a doctor to make a daily visit to administer the injection. That evening, a large moustached woman appeared clad in a sarong, a grimy shirt and a bandanna. She had a belligerent and truculent look to her. She snarled at me to lie on the bed and bare my stomach while she produced from her battered bag a syringe more often seen on a farm with a needle the size of a kitchen skewer. Wearing a decidedly satisfied grin, she growled that I would experience a pain I would remember all my life and holding the syringe high in the air she plunged it straight into my stomach. The pain of being stabbed in the stomach was only exceeded by the sheer agony of the serum contacting the stomach wall. She left me bathed in sweat and gasping for air. With a smug smile on her face she said she would be back the next day. She gave quite a new meaning to the term 'bedside manner'.

I spent the next twenty-four hours dreading the doctor's return and nursing a bruise the size of a pigeon's egg on my stomach. That evening the torture was repeated and so it continued for the next eight days. Each day produced a fresh bruise and by the fifth day she broke the bad news, with an even larger grin on her face, that she was going to have to plunge the skewer through one of the earlier bruises. Strangely I began to feel a little like a mad dog myself; while not exactly nipping at the shins of the other guests, I found myself becoming inexplicably irritable and snapped at anybody who crossed my path. I could have cheerfully bitten the doctor in the leg.

I have been to Bali on countless occasions since but the face of the doctor still haunts me. I see her walking down country roads with a child bouncing on her hip, in temples balancing a tower of fruit on her head, in coffee shops, playing in the *gamelan*. I see her everywhere with the skewer just hidden behind her back ready to raise it above her head and plunge it into my stomach.

8

The Invaders

I completed my year of teaching Thai policemen the rudimentaries of English in December 1968. I am not sure that they had learned very much from me; they really only showed interest in chat-up lines and how to swear fluently. Prasert, the Philips Electronics manager, telephoned to invite me for dinner to celebrate the end of the contract.

After a fiery Thai meal he suggested, with a gleam in his eye, that we should go to a Thai massage parlour. These were fairly common in Bangkok although not as widespread as they are today. I had never visited one as I had scant interest in having my back rubbed and my limbs twisted, but went along anyway. I was somewhat surprised to find myself looking into the 'goldfish bowl' at several hundred scantily clad young girls with plastic number disks pinned to their postage-stamp bras. This was not at all what I had expected: the last time I had had a massage it was by a muscular sweating Serb in Belgrade. I followed Prasert's example and selected one busty long-haired number, making the mistake of choosing youth and beauty over experience.

She undressed me while I stood self-consciously in the middle of the small room not knowing quite what to do with my hands. She smelled of cheap soap and cigarette smoke. Indicating that I should clamber into an oversize plastic bathtub but remaining almost fully clothed herself, she leaned over to quickly rub soap over my body, studiously avoiding any sensitive areas, and then hosed me down. She averted her eyes while I climbed out of the bath and quickly patted me dry with a towel like sandpaper. I lay on the huge circular bed while she spent thirty minutes feebly pressing her hands into my back. She seemed nervous, perhaps terrified, and said not a word to me in Thai or English. Perhaps I was her first *farang* customer. Somewhat dissatisfied, I met Prasert in the reception area. He had a broad smile on his face, looked like a cat that had overdosed on double cream and made all sorts of salacious signs at me. Clearly I had missed the plot somewhere. I did not go to another massage parlour in Bangkok for many months but when I next ventured inside, I picked an older girl who knew the ropes: a different experience altogether.

A reinvigorated Prasert then suggested that we should visit a traditional Thai nightclub. We drove to Rajadamnoen Avenue, not far from the Grand Palace, and walked into a pitch-black room. A saxophone was playing lazily somewhere in the darkness and a girl was crooning softly in Thai. The only light came from the penlight torches carried by the waitresses which flashed narrow beams of light. We stumbled into a booth, sat on what felt like two small benches on either side of a table and stared into the blackness. My eyes gradually grew accustomed to the darkness but even then I only vaguely made out Prasert's silhouette hunched opposite me. I was unable to guess the size of the room and, except for the occasional fleeting shadow, could not see any other people. I heared them though, the occasional murmur, the clink of ice in a glass, the odd laugh, some strange grunting and the distant ethereal Thai music.

Then I became aware that I was not alone. Somebody had sat beside me. Not a word was spoken but a nose gently stroked my cheek. Or I assumed it was a nose as I was engulfed in a cloud of garlic fumes, so I knew a face must be very close to mine. I felt a hand running gently up my thigh, then to my zip which it confidently undid and reached inside. There was no dancing in Thai nightclubs.

In the late 1960s Bangkok certainly did not have the sordid reputation that it suffers from today but the ready availability of young women and their uninhibited attitude to sex was irresistible to most visitors. Frequently this would prove a chore to the foreign resident in town as one was expected to traipse around the fleshpots, frequently translating for the visitor and negotiating a short term contract in Thai. With friends this could be amusing but sometimes visitors I did not know so well used to irritate me with their demands.

Henry was a well-bred young Englishman, a friend of a friend, on a jaunt around the Far East. He invited me for dinner. We met, dined, and, as usual with the English, Henry did not offer to pay or share the bill mumbling vaguely that he hoped I would look him up in London on my next visit. The English were by far the worst spongers: I often received letters from people whom I had never met claiming some remote acquaintanceship with someone I had not seen for years: their son was coming through Bangkok and could I keep an eye on little Willie in case of trouble? Willie would then call, expect to be entertained and would very rarely write a note of thanks. Should I make the mistake of calling the parents when in London, there was always a moment of hesitation and a shallow excuse proffered.

That evening Henry was particularly insistent and so I took him to the Safari, a nightclub well-known to the residents of Bangkok but far from the tourist circuit. As usual it was full of lovely girls. Henry got drunk, noisy, upset a chair, spilled a glass of beer and insulted the *mamasan*. I told him I was going home but he begged me, before I left, to negotiate the price of a girl for the night. He had selected a particular beauty, taller then the rest, larger breasts, long smooth legs, hair to her waist, wearing a green silk dress that was glued to her impressive body. On this occasion I obliged. I spoke to the girl and agreed a price. Henry was delighted, could he buy me another drink? I simply must not forget to call when next in London.

I saw the happy lovers off in a taxi and went home feeling fairly smug: a job well done. The girl was a 'lady-boy' well-known on the street and I chuckled to myself as to what Henry might do when he found out.

The next morning I met Henry in his hotel. He thanked me cordially for the previous evening's entertainment and said that the night had lived up to his every expectation. I looked at him searchingly but he seemed genuinely appreciative. I never found out what passed between them: I had been told that it is possible to spend a night with a transvestite in Bangkok and never know that 'he' was not a 'she'. Perhaps Henry did not know he had slept with a boy. Or perhaps he did.

By early 1969 I was tiring of teaching English and started to look around for some other gainful employment. I had to keep food on the table and pay the rent on my flat in the Rangsit's apartment block in Soi Suanplu. My break came over dinner one evening with Peter and Sanda Simms. As well as working for the *Time-Life* news bureau in Bangkok, Peter was also a stringer for the *Financial Times*. It emerged that the *Financial Times* was planning to publish a survey on Thailand. Peter was handling the editorial for the survey and he suggested that I took on the advertising side. For the next six months I struggled to sell advertising space for the survey, and to prove that nothing succeeds like success I managed to sell so much space that the *Financial Times'* survey of Thailand became one of their largest surveys ever conducted in Asia.

Working with Peter put me in touch with other journalists based in Thailand and I soon became a member of the Foreign Correspondents Club, which had no fixed premises but met fortnightly in a room in the Oriental Hotel. Soon I was filling in for other journalists when they were on leave, and within a short period of time I was writing articles for a number of newspapers both in Thailand and in the United States. It was not long before I was writing regularly for *Business in Thailand*, the country's predominant business magazine and by the end of that year I was appointed its assistant editor.

Thailand at that time was governed by the military. Both Prime Minister Thanom Kittikachorn and the minister of the interior, Prapass Charusatien, were fields marshal; in fact generals filled almost every senior post in the government. Even the director of the Tourist Organisation was a general. Perhaps this was not surprising in a country where there were more generals in the army than there were tanks. Democracy was not to come to Thailand for many years; student uprisings, elections, vote-buying and corrupt politicians were all in the future for Thailand. In the late 1960s the country was under the firm grip of the armed forces and their cronies. Wary of the spread of communism and China's ambitions in the region, Thailand had become the foremost U.S. ally in that part of the world.

Thanom had been prime minister since 1963 and he had brought the country even closer to the U.S. The military politicians became the delighted recipients of billions of dollars in economic and military aid. Such policies attracted the enmity of not only the Chinese and North Vietnamese but also many third world countries opposed to the American war in Vietnam.

In many ways Thailand was at war. There was an ongoing communist insurgency actively sponsored by China with some two thousand well-organised armed terrorists in the jungle to the northeast of the country on the Lao border and an equal number in the far south near Malaysia. I remember a briefing by General Sayyud Kherdpol, the officer in charge of CSOC, the Communist Suppression Operations Command, who showed me a map of Thailand illustrating the rapidly spreading areas of the country under the control of the communist terrorists.

On another occasion an American officer at JUSMAG, the Joint United States Military Advisory Group, pointed to a map of the Far East on his wall and likened the looming bulk of China to an orange sitting on a pin, the pin being all the small countries of south-east Asia. He intimated that whatever China wanted, the other countries were too insignificant to resist. In 1965 China had established the Thai Patriotic Front which broadcasted Radio Free Thai, a radio station in China's Yunnan Province beaming communist propaganda in Thai dedicated to overthrowing the Bangkok government. Thailand was fertile ground for communist propaganda: the farmers were poor and squeezed by Chinese money-lenders; much of the land was owned by absentee landlords. Government officials were poorly paid and always on the lookout for ways to increase their income at the expense of the rice farmers.

The Americans used Thailand as a rear base for their war in Vietnam. There were some 50,000 American troops in Thailand, mainly airmen and their support staff. There were seven air bases in the country on Thai sovereign land, but used exclusively by the U.S. air force. B-52 bombers flew sorties around the clock bombing South Vietnam and later North Vietnam, Cambodia and Laos. The Americans generally kept to their bases and one would not know that the country was at war except for the occasional army convoy thundering along country roads bringing ordnance from the naval base at Sattahip to one airbase or another.

The same could not be said of the American soldiers based in Vietnam. Soldiers were granted ten days 'rest and recreation' (generally known as 'sex and intoxication' to the Thais) in every twelve month tour of duty. Uncle Sam flew them to a number of destinations ranging from Hawaii to Australia, Tokyo to Taiwan but the most popular destination of all was Bangkok. It was close, it was cheap, and most important of all it was full of young girls eager to satisfy the sex-starved GIs in exchange for US dollars.

The Patpong area of Bangkok, later to become notorious for its gaudy nightclubs and bars, was at that time the business centre of Bangkok. It was highly respectable and hosted the Thai head offices of Shell, Air France and many other multinational companies. The area the GIs frequented was a strip known as the New Petchburi Road Extension where a hundred night clubs and bars with names such as Thai Heaven and Big Boy provided every service that a GI could desire.

The GIs rarely ventured far from the bars, motels and massage parlours along this strip but when they did they went by taxi. Bangkok taxis were miniature rust buckets, known as Datsun Bluebirds and were recognisable by two coloured lights on the shelf behind the rear seats. I would frequently drive along the streets of Bangkok behind a taxi occupied by a huge GI, his crew-cut lit up by the yellow lights of the taxi and beside him I could just make out the top of a diminutive Thai girl's head, his 'hired wife' during his 'R and R'.

The Thais tended to take a relaxed view of this plunder of their women-folk. They were poor girls from the provinces and the GIs were no threat to their wives or daughters. Many foreign visitors wondered why prostitution was so common in Thailand; it was of course fairly common in Indonesia, the Philippines and other Far Eastern countries as well, but no race embraced it so enthusiastically as the Thais. The answer seemed to lie in Thai men's traditional view of women. They were chattels and were treated as such. Men could divorce their wives at the stroke of a pen but women could not divorce their husbands. Women's rights did not exist in Thailand.

As soon as they could afford it Thai men acquired a 'minor wife' or *mea noi*, as opposed to a *mea yai* or 'main wife'. The number of mistresses added lustre to a man's position in society. The *mea noi*, often a beauty queen and a third of the man's age, would be paraded in public and photographs would appear of her in the society columns in the local newspapers. The *mea yai* had to accept an unfaithful husband as her lot but there were certain rules. The husband had to provide for the *mea yai* in such a way that her 'face' was preserved: on no account could the *mea noi* have a larger house, a newer car or more ostentatious jewellery. 'Face' must be preserved at all costs.

The husband had to spend most of his time with the *mea yai* and was expected to be a decent and loving father to their children and accompany her to formal Thai gatherings and the evening funerals. Then at weekends or other times he would disappear from the family home to go 'upcountry' an aphorism universally understood as meaning the man was chez *mea noi*. The Thais had preserved this way of life for centuries and it continues today, the only difference being an increase in the stakes: one has to be a wealthy man to afford a *mea noi* and run two households. The modern, possibly western educated Thai girl is also less likely to tolerate an erring husband and stories of husbands wearing their underpants backwards when they go to bed to avoid a well-aimed snip of the scissors are legion.

In March 1968 President Johnson announced that he would seek a negotiated settlement with the North Vietnamese. The Thais began to wonder whether their ally was about to let them down and, once again demonstrating the same diplomatic skill that had kept Thailand a free country during the period of colonialism, the Thai generals began to distance themselves from the U.S. and move closer to China.

One evening in April 1968 I was invited to a dinner party at the *Wang* where I was introduced to the foreign editor of the *Financial Times*. One of their stringers in Vietnam had been wounded and he was in Bangkok to find a replacement. He asked me whether I knew of any suitable candidates. The next morning I visited him in the Oriental Hotel and proffered my services. Within a month I had received accreditation and was on an Air Vietnam flight for Saigon.

9

Phubai

The twin rotors of the Chinook shook the aircraft so much that I could feel my teeth vibrating against each other. I could see neither the sky nor the ground below just a grey sheet of water that whipped around the outside of the helicopter and through the open glass-less windows. I sat alone on the webbing, my fatigues sodden, water everywhere, streaming down my face and gushing in rivers along the Chinook's floor, first one way and then the other as the craft bucked like a wild horse, buffeted by the wind and the rain.

I had caught a lift that morning on a Huey, the helicopter workhorse of the Americans in Vietnam. I had been at the U.S. Special Forces camp at Lang Vei for three days – a desolate and exposed muddy base from where the cloud-covered hills overlooked the embattled U.S. Marines' base at Khe Sanh. In the far distance lay the steep mountains of Co Roc from where the North Vietnamese Army's 130mm and 152mm artillery pounded Khe Sanh and the surrounding hilltops around the clock. The NVA mounted their artillery on railway tracks which led deep into caves in the mountains out of reach of American B-52 bomb strikes.

Lang Vei had achieved notoriety two months previously, in February 1968, when it was attacked and taken by nine NVA Russian-made PT-76 tanks supported by a battalion of the NVA's 66th Regiment, 304th Division. The twenty-two Americans and four hundred South Vietnamese were overrun and the survivors sealed themselves into their command bunker and directed artillery fire from Khe Sanh onto their own positions. By March Lang Vei had been retaken and was back in operation as a base for small groups of Special Forces to mount long range reconnaissance patrols into Laos to report on activities on the Ho Chi Minh Trail – the network of tracks through the dense jungle used by the North Vietnamese to transport men and materiel to support the war in the south. It was a desolate place, the rebuilt command centre dug deep out of the hillside's mud. Water coursed constantly down the reinforced sand-bag walls and through the mud and timber roof, now built to withstand anything short of a direct artillery hit.

Khe Sanh was destined to remain under concentrated NVA attack until the end of March when a combined U.S. Army and Marines operation relieved the base. The North Vietnamese had hoped that Khe Sanh would prove to be the American's Dien Bien Phu, the final battle in 1954 that spelled the end of the French occupation of Indo-China. It had looked for a while as if this might be the case, but the North Vietnamese had not taken into consideration the weight of American air power and the devastating accuracy of the B-52's 'arc-light' bombing missions which turned jungle into moonscapes two miles long and half a mile wide.

The Huey dipped and dived not twenty feet above the ground, the edgy side gunners occasionally firing aimlessly at dogs running on the ground below. We flew over the Rockpile with its 175mm artillery, touched down briefly at Camp Carrol and then landed at Dong Ha. It was raining there, the landing strip a sea of red mud and the wind fierce from a typhoon, stationary in the Gulf of Tonkin. The weather forecast said that the typhoon would move southwest in the direction of Danang, cross the coast and dissipate over the land before it hit the Annamese Cordillera, the range of mountains that followed the Vietnamese coast, sometimes dropping into the sea, sometimes retreating inland.

I did not relish the thought of spending the night at Dong Ha, the most northern town in South Vietnam, not far from the De-Militarised Zone from where the North Vietnamese lobbed rockets into the town and the Marines base. But an overnight or maybe even a two or three day stay was looking inevitable. Such weather conditions brought the war to a halt. American F-5 Phantom fighter-bombers were grounded, soldiers on both sides hunkering down from the torrential rain which turned the landscape into a mudscape.

I had filed my travel plan that morning with the U.S. Marines Public Affairs Office, the unit with general responsibility for keeping a weather eye on the whereabouts of journalists in their area saying that I was on my way to Phubai, the huge Marines base near Hue. It was looking less and less likely that I was going to make it. No sweat, I would find a bed somewhere in Dong Ha and let them know sometime over the next day or so where I was. They were not going to concern themselves with a missing British correspondent for a few days, it happened all the time.

On the point of giving up, I saw a Chinook starting up its engines on the far side of the airstrip. Chinooks were not my favourite means of transport. Noisy and cumbersome, they slowly lurched through the air, easy pickings for an enemy gunner on the ground. With windows removed so that they would not splinter if hit by gunfire, the theory went that in a crash landing one could easily jump through an open window. But this just increased one's exposure to the noise and the wind howled through the body of the aircraft like a typhoon of its own making.

Beggars can't be choosers, so I grabbed my kitbag, ran across the tarmac and shouted at the pilot to ask where he was going. "Jump aboard," he yelled back, "we'll be the last chopper to Phubai today." So I scrambled into the belly of the helicopter and it lurched through the rain and into the clouds, pitching along just a few hundred feet from the ground.

The weather conditions deteriorated from severe to atrocious as we flew south and closer to the core of the typhoon. We dropped below the clouds and I could just make out the tops of coconut palms through the rain and spray below. We dropped further, the trees got closer and suddenly parted to reveal an airstrip. We hit the ground with a bruising thump. The engines stuttered into silence and the helicopter sat there, still shuddering in the wind, like a bedraggled bird. I jumped into a deep muddy puddle, cursed and made my way round to the front of the aircraft where the two-man crew were crouching under the nose of the helicopter vainly trying to keep dry. "It's no good," the pilot shouted through the wind, "I couldn't see a damn thing. We'll put down here for the night, see what it's like tomorrow."

At that moment a jeep drove up, the two airmen jumped into the back, and it sped off splashing through the red muddy puddles leaving me alone on this deserted airstrip in the middle of God knows where. I looked around: there was nothing to see. Just a small laterite airstrip, no aircraft except for the Chinook, no buildings, no people, no sign of habitation. Shit, I thought, just my luck!

I splashed my way across the airstrip, soaked and cold. The light was fading and it would be dark within half an hour. I set off along a potholed track that led from the airstrip down a small hill hoping that sooner or later I would find some shelter in a Vietnamese farm house. Things did not look good: I had no idea where I was and who was to know whether the locals were friendly or not?

After a couple of hundred yards some U.S. Marine 'hootches' loomed out of the gloom. A 'hootch' was a prefabricated plywood hut: home for up to a dozen GIs. I splashed up to the first hootch and banged loudly on the door. No answer. I tried the second and after a few minutes the door opened a crack and a pair of bloodshot eyes peered down at me from a coal-black face. Seeing the miserable specimen on his doorstep the GI opened the door wide and I stumbled inside.

A strange sight befell me: a small mountain of beer cans, empty I assumed, rose from the floor. There could have been three hundred of them, perilously supporting each other so the top one was nearly five feet from the ground. Around this aluminium mound slouched a dozen marines in various states of undress and very, very drunk. This was no surprise to me: I was inured to the lack of discipline amongst the U.S. forces who spent much of their time drinking beer or smoking joints.

I asked if I could spend the night there and the tall GI who had let me in gestured at some floor space in the corner of the hootch. Dead tired and hungry by now, I rolled out my army blanket, lay down in my sodden fatigues and almost immediately fell asleep despite the racket of the drunken marines noisily arguing with each other over heaven knows what. I was past caring.

Some time later, it could have been minutes or it could have been hours, I was awoken by something pointed being thrust into my neck. I looked up, instantly alert, into the eyes of another black GI who had stuck his M16 assault rifle into my neck, just below my chin.

"We'se a been talking about yer," he grunted, alcoholic spit spraying onto my face, "and we'se decided yer no American. Y'er a Russian. A spy. We'se been warned about the likes o' you."

This was palpable nonsense, you found all sorts in Vietnam but the one person you were not going to meet was a white-skinned Russian spy! But the Americans were very sensitive about the Russians who were supplying war *materiel* to the North Vietnamese and had their own ambitions for the American naval base at Cam Ranh Bay. Still, I was dumb-founded by this accusation!

"Yer don't talk like an American," he went on.

I rotated my eyes and looked around: there were half a dozen faces, all nodding approval. Another half dozen bodies lay around in various stages of inebriation. Things looked grim.

"We'se a goin' to shoot yer. Y'er russkie bastard."

So it had come to this. I had spent months in Vietnam: with the marines here in 'eye-corps', the most northern of South Vietnam's five military regions, the USAF, the U.S. Army, the Special Forces, the U.S. Navy out in the Gulf of Tonkin, even the Koreans, the Thais and the Australian military contingents. I had dodged incoming Viet Cong rockets, been shot at by all and sundry and now my end was going to be delivered by a drunken GI in this hell hole. It would be all too easy, a bullet in the head and my body would be unceremoniously dumped in the flooded ditch outside, just another war death. Nobody knew where I was, my disappearance would not be noticed for days and my body would not be discovered for weeks, if ever.

Very carefully and slowly, I opened my mouth and muttered that I was a British journalist and had walked from the airstrip.

"Fuckin' crap, the airstrip's been closed for two days now," and his finger tightened on the trigger.

I suggested that he check my ID. One or two of the others nodded and he let me slowly feel one pocket after the other until my shaking fingers located my Military Assistance Command Vietnam press pass and my non-combatant card which identified me as a British correspondent with the assimilated rank of a major in the US Army. These were passed around from one to each other.

"Shit," said one, "ah bet the russkies turn these out ev'ry day." They were not impressed.

Playing my last card, I suggested they call up the Marines Public Affairs Office who would verify my status. I was counting on sowing some doubt in their minds. I doubted that the local PAO would have heard of me as I had last reported in with the PAO in Camp Carrol and had told them I was on my way to Phubai. There was no reason why anybody should know that I had hitch-hiked a lift on a Chinook in Dong Ha which had made an unscheduled landing at this God-forsaken spot.

The drunken marines muttered interminably amongst themselves as to what they should do as I lay on my back on the ground, the M16 never wavering from my neck. One fat white GI, cigarette dangling from the corner of his mouth, wearing a sweat-stained singlet which I could smell from two yards away said,

"Hell, I say let's shoot him anyway."

The others shouted in agreement, "Yeah, let's kill the bastard."

Well, that was that. I had done my best. There was no escape, the slightest movement would have caused that finger to squeeze the trigger. I closed my eyes, held my breath and waited.

At length one of them, perhaps less drunk than the others, said, "Well, let's give 'em a call anyway."

He stumbled over to the corner, narrowly missing upsetting the mountain of beer cans which seemed to have grown another foot while I was sleeping and picked up the RT. With surprising speed he was patched through to the local PAO and he told them they had arrested a Russian spy who was right now on the floor of their hootch. It was late at night and judging by the voice crackling over the RT, this news must have been a major surprise to the young officer at the other end of the line.

The disembodied voice asked for my name and ID.

"Hey man," said the voice, "so you've found the Brit. We had been wondering where he'd got to in this storm." So for once the machinery had worked. Somebody at Camp Carrol had remembered to file a travel plan for me and, even more amazing, somebody in Phubai noticed that I hadn't turned up!

The M16 was removed from my neck and the marines instantly lost interest and cracked open a few more cans of beer.

I spent the rest of the night wide awake on the ground. As soon as the first hint of dawn cast some light through the cracks in the hootch's wall, I was out of there.

The rain had stopped, the wind had died down, there were some hints of blue sky through the clouds. The humid air had been cleansed by the passing typhoon. It was going to be a beautiful day.

10

Motor Sport and Other Games

I learned two new sports while I was in Thailand. One day Tan Mair called me to say that she was going water-skiing the next day and invited me along. We drove down to the Chao Phraya river and took a long-tailed boat a couple of miles upstream, dodging the chains of rice barges and clumps of mauve water-hyacinths floating downstream.

We disembarked onto a small wooden jetty where some slippery steps led down into the grey-brown river. Thais living along the riverbank use such steps to wash themselves and their clothes, brush their teeth and many other daily activities best left to the imagination. We were met by an antique plywood speedboat with a vintage outboard motor. With a wave and a flourish Tan Mair leapt onto a single mono-ski and slalomed down the river amongst the barges, tugs and long-tailed boats holding the rope with one hand, the other touching the water as she gracefully leapt over the boat's wake. It was a performance that left me breathless with surprise. When she returned she timed her arrival so perfectly that she stepped off the ski right onto the steps without getting a foot wet.

Now it was my turn. Never having water-skied in my life, I viewed the fast-flowing river with some trepidation. Soon a pair of water skis had been attached to my feet and with shouts of exhortation from Tan Mair and Nying, I launched myself down the river. The thought of falling onto any of the dead pigs and bloated dogs floating down the river, or having my leg severed by a *he-ya*, a type of iguana that grows up to five feet long and lives in the river, was enough to keep me on my feet. I was perhaps one of very few people who learned to water-ski without ever falling into the water.

This was soon to become a weekly activity and it was not long before I was also to be seen slaloming down the river in front of the Oriental Hotel oblivious to the dead dogs, sewage and clumps of malodorous weeds, much to the surprise of the guests sitting primly on the hotel's famous veranda.

ॐ ॐ ॐ

The car I had left sitting on the dock in London, a white MGB GT sports car, my pride and joy, and my father's gift on my 21st birthday, eventually arrived in Bangkok. It proved to be ill equipped for the tropical heat, could not sustain an air-conditioner, and was hot, uncomfortable and subject to frequent mechanical failures. But it gave me greater freedom and I was able to return the VW beetle borrowed from the Rangsits for so many months.

By early 1969 The United Nations had completed the section of the Asian Highway between Vientiane in Laos, through the entire length of Thailand and Malaysia, to Singapore, a distance of some 1,500 miles. The U.N. decided to hold a motor rally to publicise their achievement. The target of the Asian Highway project was to link existing trunk roads together to a uniform standard so that it would theoretically be possible to drive from London to Singapore on a sealed road. Politics were to ensure that this project still remains on the drawing board today, more than thirty-five years later.

I jumped at the chance of entering this rally and chose Vivat Snitwongse, one of Tan Chai's young executives, as my co-driver and navigator. Vivat was a tall, handsome Thai with a reputation for being something of a playboy but also considered a gifted mechanic. We drove northeast to Vientiane, the capital city of Laos, crossing the River Mekong by ferry at Nongkhai and spent two days there priming the car by day and exploring Lao nightlife by night.

The notorious White Rose nightclub was in its heyday. Perhaps tame compared to the lascivious excitements available in Thailand today, where at that time dancers had to be fully clothed, Playboy magazine was illegal, prostitution was banned and heavy emphasis was placed on the preservation of 'Thai cultural values'. Of course everyone knew this was a facade but at least there was a skin-deep veneer of probity. Not so in happy-go-lucky Laos where there were few laws and uninhibited Thai girls from the nearby U.S. airbases were happy to strip, harbingers of things to come in later years. The more conservative Lao girls generally steered clear of such places.

Also appraising the scenery at the White Rose was Dickie Arblaster, a fabled man in the world of Far Eastern motor sport, who was covering the rally with a team from Radio Television Singapore. Our paths were to cross frequently in the years to come.

The rally took us the whole length of Thailand with a brief overnight stop in Bangkok. Tan Mair visited me during the stop and a Bangkok Post photographer snapped a shot that appeared in the next day's newspaper under the heading 'Elvis Presley at the Rally'. I was used to teasing from the Thai press with one Bangkok Post article describing me as 'Lord Errington, son of Duke

[Ellington] the well-known bandleader'. 'Elvis' however, was a nickname that was to stick with me for a while. Although I could never see the likeness to the crooner myself, I only had to enter a bar and there would be shouts of 'Elvis! Elvis has come!'

This was the first international motor rally that Thailand had ever seen and it attracted enormous publicity. Through day and night crowds several thick lined the sides of the highway. Whole towns came to a halt as the people thronged around the cars allowing just a narrow avenue for us to race through. It became an Asian Mille Miglia.

Many well-known Thais joined the rally: the famous grand prix driver Prince Bira drove one car and entered his three wives in another. He joked with me that he had chosen his wives carefully: one to cook, one to educate his children and the third, well, she was a beauty queen. I would not like to say how the wives fared together under the strain of the rally but their car fell into a ditch sometime during the first night and they were spied by the next car standing at the side of the road berating each other.

My rally ended somewhere in the jungle between Ipoh and Kuala Lumpur in Malaysia when a wheel bearing seized and we ground to a halt in a cloud of smoke. Vivat had forgotten to check the bearings before we started and also had no idea how to make the repairs. By the time we had found a garage, secured the spare part, had it fitted and set off again, we were twelve hours behind the pack. Driving like the wind we finally arrived in Singapore but with so many penalty points that we reckoned we were completely out of the race. But as luck would have it all the other cars in our class save one had crashed or broken down somewhere along the road so we ended up second in our class and received a small prize.

I had arranged to stay with Charles Letts in Singapore and arrived in the middle of one of his formal dinner parties. The black-tie clad guests must have assumed we were the cabaret when we drove up dirty and unshaven wearing our racing overalls emblazoned with sponsors' tags.

The next day was the official prize-giving day to be held on the Padang in Singapore, a sort of central parade ground or *maidan*. But all was not well. All the top prizes had been won by *farang*. Not a single Asian driver had won an award (scarcely a surprise to me given the appalling driving standards in all Asian countries). But this was a matter of 'face': it was after all an *Asian* Highway motor rally. The U.N. officials scrambled for a compromise and soon announced that there would be a special prize for the first Asian driver. 'Face' was saved. Hardly sporting, but worse was to come.

The United Nations seemed pleased with our effort: I was invited the next year to become the judge for the second, and last, Asian Highway motor rally.

This was a much more adventurous affair starting in Iran and passing through Afghanistan, Pakistan, India, Nepal and ending in Bangladesh. I flew from one city to another waiting for the rally cars to arrive. I spent nearly a week in Kabul and took the opportunity to visit the Buddhist monuments that some thirty years later were to be dynamited by Islamic extremists. At that time Afghanistan was at peace but it was soon to be enveloped into a seemingly interminable civil war.

I was later to join several long-distance motor rallies in Thailand with mixed success. On one rally I teamed up with Prince Panya Souvanna Phouma, the younger son of the prime minister of Laos and a good friend, and the French director of the Lao waterworks. Our windscreen shattered within the first hundred miles and we ended up that night driving along a muddy flooded logging track in the middle of the jungle near the Cambodian frontier. The water and mud was so deep that we took it in turns to walk in front of the car testing the depth of the water. Finally the car fell into one pothole so deep that the engine flooded and died. We spent the rest of the night in the car, soaked by the tropical rain, huddled together in the back seat. Nothing fazed Panya: Gauloise cigarettes were produced, a bottle of cognac appeared and the night faded into oblivion.

Another time I led the VW rally team in the first Round Thailand Rally with Vivat again acting as my navigator. He was so hesitant and indecisive at plotting our locations and speed objectives that we missed checkpoint after checkpoint. In the end we stopped the car and had a lengthy stand-up shouting match. Vivat refused to drive another inch with me and was all for giving up and returning to Bangkok. I convinced him that we should at least finish the rally for the sake of our sponsors and so we drove on, Vivat silent with his arms crossed flatly refusing to navigate or even look at the rally instructions. We finished the rally and went separately to the prize giving the next day.

To our utter astonishment, it was announced that we had won the rally! There was a universal outcry as other drivers said that they had passed us going in the wrong direction, others saw us standing by our car arguing, others thought that there was monkey-business afoot and I had bribed the judges, but the truth was that by some miraculous accident of fate, we happened to achieve the right number of points. Vivat and I glared at each other across the crowded room, neither of us wanting to collect the silver cup. Finally we walked up to the dais together and shared the cup between us. When I left Thailand some years later, I gave it to him.

By that time the lessons of the first Asian Highway motor rally had been learned. Although *farang* filled the first six places, by far the largest and most ostentatious trophy was handed to the team in seventh place: the highest placed Thais!

ॐ   ॐ   ॐ

The proprietor of *Business in Thailand* was Bill Heinecke, an entrepreneurial young American, not yet twenty-one and born and educated in Bangkok. Bill was to become a good friend and remains one today. He is a natural businessman and had started a janitorial business when he was a teenager, cleaning offices himself and featuring in *Business Week* and *Fortune*, mop in hand, with an army of Thai cleaners. He is one of that rare breed of people who are born to succeed in business and so he did; eventually founding a business empire that is one of the largest foreign-owned enterprises in Thailand today.

Bill was a keen motor-sports enthusiast and we decided to buy a second-hand racing car to race on the Grand Prix circuits in Asia. We scouted around for a suitable car and eventually learned that an American in Hong Kong had an Elva-BMW prototype for sale. We flew to Hong Kong to see the car.

Walter Haskamp was nothing if not a salesman.

"So, Walter, why do you want to sell the car after only one race?" enquired Bill.

"It's too fast for me, I just couldn't handle it," said Walter.

"If it is that fast then why didn't you win a race?"

"It was me, not the car. The car was always the fastest on the track. It was just too powerful to handle," insisted Walter.

Bill and I looked at each other failing to understand the logic. We bought the car. It might have been very fast; we never really found out. On its few outings it would crackle like a Catherine wheel for a few laps and then expire in a cloud of steam.

At that time there were formula races in Macau, Malaysia, Singapore and a few other Far Eastern countries. The only proper circuit at that time was at Batu Tiga in Malaysia; the other races were on open roads or through the city streets as in Macau. We obtained sponsorship from Shell, Malaysia-Singapore Airlines (MSA), various hotels and other companies keen to have their names on the side of our car. We called ourselves 'Team Thailand' the Thai national motor sports team and raced under Thai colours, the first time the Thais had had a motor racing team since the days that Prince Chula backed Prince Bira in the 1930s and 1950s on the European Formula One circuit.

The Elva-BMW provided Bill and I with some frustrated enjoyment on the Grand Prix circuit and a great deal of publicity. It was not long before I was greeted by strangers in the street in Bangkok with a thumbs-up and *cup rod gaeng* or 'crack racing driver' a great accolade from the Thais, who viewed every car as a racing car and every road as a Grand Prix racetrack.

11

Bear Cat

I was not exactly asleep, but more in a semi-trance, staring sightlessly at the shadows cast by the moon through the rubber trees. Evenly spaced out, the trees exactly thirty feet from each other in neat ranks marching into the darkness. Whichever way I looked the trees formed perfect lines of glossy trunks glinting in the moonlight. The man hunched next to me nudged me gently in the ribs; I could feel his hot quick breath and smell his rank body fumes steaming through his unwashed fatigues. His breath stank of last night's joints and unbrushed teeth.

He was staring into the gloaming. He had seen something. His body had tensed and he softly worked his M-16 assault rifle onto the top of the thin dusty earth wall made when we scraped the soil away to excavate our shallow two-man foxhole the previous evening. We did not dig deep, we were too tired. I was all for collapsing on the ground and sleeping where I fell but he said that would be unwise. He said we should always take precautions. Tonight might be the night.

I stared into the gloom but could see nothing unusual. The night was still, not a leaf stirred. Tropical night noises echoed around me as they always had: the cicadas whirred, frogs croaked loudly, a distant bird was screeching, it all seemed the same as it had for the previous ten nights. But he did not think so, he was awake, alert: I could feel the tension mounting. I wiped the sweat from my forehead, a drip stinging my eye and peered deeper into the plantation. Still nothing.

Chip Stevens was wiry, red-haired and from Arkansas. He was a Special Forces advisor attached to the Royal Thai Army. He was the only American in the contingent, speaking no Thai and the Thai soldiers spoke no English. But he got what he wanted with just a look or a gesture. The Thais were frightened of him. Perhaps it was the deep bullet scar that creased the stock of his M-16 assault rifle; perhaps it was that he had volunteered to renew his tour of duty again and again. Perhaps it was his knowledge of the jungle and his intuitive understanding of the Viet Cong mindset. He had been in Vietnam for four years; most soldiers wanted to leave as soon as they could and few ever signed on for another tour.

Another twelve months of hell, of not knowing when the VC bullet would strike: in a bar, walking down the street, in the security of a base camp, it could be anywhere – that was the trouble with Vietnam, you never saw your enemy: it could be the old lady hobbling down a dusty village path who would suddenly whip out a gun from her *ao-dai* and fire a single shot: one dead American. It could be the children who swarmed around the American army trucks laughing and joking, "Hey, GI, you gimme beaucoup chocolate?" The same children would wrap a rubber band around a hand-grenade, pull the pin and drop it into a truck's fuel tank. One moment the children were jumping all over the truck, the next moment they had disappeared and then WHUMP, a truck had exploded and there was another dead American slumped over the wheel of his truck, flames melting his flesh like candle wax.

Or perhaps a VC rocket fired from a bamboo launcher deep in the jungle. Unaimed and unpredictable it could land anywhere, killing Americans and Vietnamese alike. The GIs had got quite good at guessing from where these missiles were launched but the VC only launched one at a time and by the time the Americans had got a chopper to the right location and had started blasting with their rockets, the VC had slipped away and was back sleeping in his village.

The platoon had camped at one edge of the plantation in the proscribed L-shaped ambush. Along the edge of the plantation was a jeep track and beyond that there was an open area of elephant grass. The Thais had set up their only machine gun under a rubber tree beside the path; the remaining twenty-eight soldiers had dug two-man foxholes some twenty feet apart from each other in a line stretching a hundred yards into the plantation. In front of our positions they had placed a line of Claymore directional anti-personnel mines which would be detonated by trip-wires laid along the ground between the rubber trees. I could just make out the camouflaged helmets of the Thai soldiers in the foxhole nearest to mine. They had not been wearing their helmets the last time I looked. They had also seen something.

If the VC came, they would not be walking down the track. They would walk inside the plantation, parallel to the track amongst the rubber trees. The point man would trip a Claymore, the Thais deeper in the plantation and furthest from the track would then open fire driving the VC out of the plantation, across the track and into the elephant grass where they would find no cover and would be raked by the machine gun. That was the plan of action explained by Chip the previous evening. He had drawn a diagram in the dust with his bayonet; the Thais had listened attentively and followed his instructions without a word.

VC had been active in this area for some time. Perhaps they thought the Thais were a soft touch. The small Thai military group in Vietnam was long on machismo but short on action. Thai casualties were few; in fact when the Thai 'Black Panthers' returned to Bangkok at the end of the war the general in charge was asked by a reporter to explain their very low level of casualties compared to the other international combatants in the war. "Our tactics were superb," said the general. "Whenever we made contact with the enemy, we withdrew." Their base camp at Bear Cat was a sprawling affair but protected on a mammoth scale by ramparts and a perimeter of cleared land that stretched almost to the horizon in every direction. The Crusaders would have admired the thick earthworks, ramparts and tank-proof moats that the Thais had constructed to protect themselves. I had been dropped off there by an American army jeep. We had to wait for an hour to pick up an armed guard in the form of another jeep with a heavy machine gun mounted behind the driver for the last ten miles.

One week before, an American jeep with four soldiers on board had been ambushed while driving down this road. The driver and the soldier in front had been killed instantly but the two sitting in the back had been thrown out of the jeep. They had run through the rubber trees down to a stream where they had been cornered by their attackers. They were held down while their fatigue trousers were ripped off and their genitals sliced away and stuffed down their throats before being garrotted. This was fairly common: it angered the VC that they should be hiding womanless in the jungle while the Americans screwed around openly with young Vietnamese girls, maybe their sisters or daughters.

Peering through the dark, now completely awake, had I seen something moving? Was that a shadow that had darted from one tree to another or had I imagined it? It might have been a mouse deer, or an owl, or was it a man? A VC? I reached for my helmet but could not find the damn thing; I remembered putting it in the foxhole the previous evening but now it had gone.

I would have felt better if I had had a gun in my hand. It was a moot point whether journalists should carry weapons or not. Most did, but the common wisdom said you should not: if captured by the enemy one was meant to hand over one's 'non-combatant' ID card which the VC was meant to read, shake you by the hand and wish you 'good day'. If you had a gun then your status as a non-combatant was compromised and they could use the gun on you. It all seemed hypothetical to me: if you fell into VC hands you would be dead with or without a gun. Better have one and you then stood a slight chance that you could shoot yourself out of a situation. So I usually kept a 32mm Beretta automatic in my kitbag or in a shoulder holster under my fatigues but that was not going to be much use here in the rubber plantation.

Nor had it been much use anywhere else. When I first acquired my automatic I tried it out at the police shooting range in Bangkok. Not a single bullet ever reached the target, which was fairly large and not very far away. So much for cowboys picking off Indians with a revolver at a hundred yards on horse-back as they cantered over the prairies. A week later I had stumbled across a king cobra in my house in Bangkok and tried to dispatch it with my 32mm. I shot holes in the wooden floor, walls and some furniture but the snake just glared angrily at me. A passing jeep stopped outside the house and a Thai man got out holding a much meaner weapon. He crept into the house and shot the snake through the head with a single bullet at twenty paces. In those days most people were armed, nearly all Thais keeping a gun in their car and another at home. When I flew from Bangkok to Saigon or Vientiane, I generally took my automatic with me: there were no body checks and metal detectors had yet to be introduced to airports.

The Thai sector was adjacent to the South Korean sector where I had spent two days the previous week. The Koreans kept a clean sector; no VC had been caught in their sector for months. These muscle-bound, bullet-headed Koreans had little to do except play basketball all day. I asked them why the VC never gave them any trouble. When they set up their camp they caught four VC red-handed, three men and a young girl, placing satchel charges inside the perimeter. They tied the men to posts for a couple of days while they played with the girl. They then meticulously skinned alive two of the men and the girl, and hung up the skins by the camp gates *'pour decourager les autres'*, sending the sole survivor home to relate the tale.

Suddenly there was a white flash and an explosion. Then another. The Claymore directional mines were detonating. M16's were firing all around me, men were shouting, somebody was screaming in pain. Chip was kneeling, body above the mud wall, firing in long measured bursts. I scrambled for cover, hands futilely trying to protect my uncovered head. Flashes revealed people running all over the place. One shadow was running straight towards me when whoosh, a rocket-propelled grenade was fired from behind me and the shadow dived into the ground. The machine gun opened up down by the track firing long steady bursts. A huge explosion shook my rubber tree and showered me with stones and dirt, something hot thumping into the ground beside my shoulder. Had I been hit?

As quickly as it had started, the noise stopped. Guns fell silent. Nobody moved. The only sound was Chip's panting, somebody groaning, another screaming in high-pitched Vietnamese and behind me a Thai voice speaking into his radio. He kept repeating our position. The screaming stopped. My whole body was shaking, almost in spasms. A massive explosion shook the ground and a wave of hot air went over me, the rubber trees bending backwards pushed by an unworldly force. "Incoming!" shouted Chip over the explosions. A 105mm artillery fire-base some five miles away was lobbing shells into the plantation a hundred yards or so ahead of us to discourage the VC from regrouping.

The pummelling of the plantation continued for another hour and then abruptly ceased leaving me choking in the dust, smoke and cordite. Dawn came up slowly and revealed a scene of devastation. A giant hand had upset the ordered ranks of rubber trees: some fell where they stood, others had been decapitated, some deeply scarred, some bent and tottering. One by one the Thai soldiers ventured out of their foxholes and tentatively probed around the undergrowth. Solitary shots rang out as the Thais put a bullet into the head of any wounded VC. Few prisoners were taken in this war. Both sides killed the wounded. Sometimes the VC would capture an American and use him for intelligence purposes but few were ever sent back up the Ho Chi Minh Trail to the north. Many times I had seen VC caught by the Americans; they sat cross-legged on the ground tied tightly with rusty wire cutting into their wrists and ankles. The Americans handed them over to the South Vietnamese Army, the ARVN, to do as they wished. This would mean torture, interrogation and not infrequently being thrown out of a helicopter at two hundred feet.

I walked over to where I had seen the shadow charging me a few hours earlier. The top third of his head had been completely blown away. The remaining eye hung out of its socket. Something had ripped open his stomach and his intestines had spilled over the grass. One arm was flung wide, the other was hanging from a bush twelve feet away.

In the distance I could hear the familiar whump, whump, whump of an approaching helicopter. It came in fast over the trees and lowered itself over the elephant grass beside the plantation, whipping up a storm of dirt and stones and flattening the grass. A couple of wounded Thais were helped on to the Huey and it took off vertically without touching the ground.

We spent the morning pulling the thirty-nine dead VC out of the plantation and lining them up on the track. They were a sorry looking lot; few had shoes, some a sandal or two, their trousers and shirts torn and bloody. There were two small and emaciated women. I inspected their kit: most had a bag of cooked cold rice and a little dried fish. They all had an aluminium box attached to their plastic belts containing some field dressings and a small IV drip. We gathered up their weapons, threw them into one of the fresh 105mm shell craters and exploded them with a charge.

That morning I sat beside the line of mutilated corpses, opened a can of C-rations and ate my tasteless lunch. I ruminated on how just a short time ago a dead human body was something that would have repelled me and yet here I was surrounded by carnage and quietly spooning canned peaches into my mouth.

Intelligence reports were coming in suggesting that the VC were regrouping not far from our location and would probably attack in force again that night. Early in the afternoon the distant firebase resumed its pounding of the far side of the plantation. This was fairly nerve-wracking, as at any moment one of the 105mm shells could have fallen short.

I needed to file my story back in Saigon and put in a request for a helicopter. I did not have to wait long. Within an hour a helicopter was to be heard thumping at tree level towards us. The service that the U.S. military provided to correspondents throughout this strange war was incredibly impressive and was also their undoing. There were so many accredited reporters in Vietnam. Some experienced responsible war correspondents knew that civilian women and children do unfortunately get killed in a war. Others leapt at opportunities to show people 'back home' the murders that their boys in Vietnam were perpetrating in the names of freedom and democracy.

I readied myself for the chopper which dropped like a stone within a few feet of the ground laying the elephant grass flat and throwing dust and gravel into my eyes, ruffling the clothes on the line of corpses and causing one lifeless arm to lift in a wave as I jumped into the back of the chopper which ascended like an express lift and swooped away just feet above the rubber trees. The sweat-stained side-gunner grinned at me, "Another hot LZ, huh?" I agreed the landing zone had not been a friendly place to be and closed my eyes.

Within minutes I was back in Saigon searching for a lift from Tan Son Nhut airport to the UPI news bureau in Saigon. A military police jeep obliged and before long I was handing in my films and my hastily written report to a bored Vietnamese girl in the UPI office. My story was wired out to the world's newspapers and was honoured the next day with two-page spreads in all the Thai newspapers as evidence of the bravery of their boys helping their American allies in Vietnam.

I checked into the antiquated Caravelle Hotel and revelled in the luxury of a hot bath. I was not to know that in a few short years time the victorious North Vietnamese and their VC allies would occupy this hotel. The young soldiers never having seen a flushing toilet in their lives, used them to hold live fish before cooking them. When one of the soldiers accidentally flushed the toilet and the fish disappeared, they machine-gunned the toilet deciding it was some evil booby trap left behind by the Americans.

That evening I dined alone on the top floor of the hotel from where there was a panoramic view over the city. In the distance flares were illuminating faraway military bases, artillery flashes lit up the sky and periodically the hotel would shake with the prolonged roar of a B52 arc-light strike somewhere outside the city.

The contrast was too great: for days I had been living in the jungle and yet here were polite waiters, starched tablecloths and fresh French bread. That night as I lay between clean sheets I thought briefly of Chip Stevens facing another night in the tense, steamy plantation before I fell asleep under the softly turning overhead fan gently stirring the thick Saigon heat.

12

The TV Star

Early in my third year in Bangkok I had a fleeting encounter which had a subtle effect on my relationship with Tan Mair.

One evening Tan Mair returned to the *Wang* from a funeral commenting on one of the daughters of Prince Chakrabandh who had been invited to a party at Chitrlada Palace. She had sung while the King played the saxophone. Tan Mair remarked that she sang like a bird and looked like a 'pocket Venus', small but perfectly formed. She had an elder sister, born from a French mother, whom Tan Mair described as a 'man eater'. She recommended that I keep my distance, but of course my interest had been awakened.

I eventually contrived to meet this *femme fatale* and her first impression did not disappoint. Tall for a Thai, and with defined European features, she spoke fluent English with a seductively French accent. Pretty, alert and intelligent, she intrigued me. If she really was a man-eater, then I was happy to sacrifice myself. Her name was Supinda.

That she had short hair, while all my girl friends had very long locks, and that she painted her face geisha-style with thick foundation cream leaving her neck a different colour to her face all meant nothing to me. Elegant and thin, most women would not find her attractive, but she oozed sex appeal.

She worked as a presenter at a television station owned by the Thai army and soon I found myself meeting her there and taking her for intimate meals. She showed me a different side to Bangkok, and explained her city to me through a lover's eyes in a way that Tan Mair could not. I saw new beauty in the temples, a fresh taste in the food, a happier laughter amongst the Thais.

I took to spending my evenings with her, not returning home until dawn. We were playing a dangerous game: she was to be married within a few weeks to a rich and powerful Malaysian Indian. He would fly up from Kuala Lumpur every weekend and she would then spend the weekdays and nights with me. He had no idea I existed, or so I assumed: in moments of passion she had the off-putting habit of calling out his name, maybe she called out my name when she was with him.

Tan Mair disapproved. I was not sure whether she was missing my company in the evenings, was not pleased with this new influence in my life or generally disliked Supinda's promiscuous lifestyle.

Ultimately I decided to move on; Supinda's fiancé had powerful friends and it was cheap and easy to have a rival eliminated in Thailand. I allowed our relationship to drift apart. Supinda saw the wisdom of this.

So I became aware that living in the Rangsit apartment compound in Soi Suanplu had mixed blessings: my every movement was detected by a gardener, a driver, one of the Kesya girls or a night watchman and reported back to Tan Mair who would look at me reproachfully as if her 'Son from the West' was somehow letting her down. Nying also would find out one way or another and would tease me about my previous evening's activities.

It was not long before I moved away and rented an apartment on the other side of Sathorn Road. This was not a good idea: Tan Mair was offended, and the apartment shook ominously every time a heavy truck went by.

13

Bangkok – A Day in the Life 22nd October, 1969

The Bangkok dawn was a magical experience, so unlike the gradual watery dawns in England where the sun weakly rises over a pinkish grey horizon. The Thai dawn brooked no hesitation. Within minutes the seething, burning disk was high over the glistening fronds of the coconut palms declaring another broiling day. My bedroom in Soi Suanplu faced east and even with the Thai cotton curtains tightly drawn, the penetrating sunlight forced the air-conditioner to take on a more purposeful note and soon I was wide awake.

Outside the *salika* birds began their relentless chatter. A gibbon was starting its early morning swing through the casuarinas and teak trees that fringed the *klong* at the back of my flat, whooping as it leapt from one tree to the next, shaking rustling plate-size teak leaves to the ground. The sinister *tuckear* lizards had begun their dawn croaking. Soon I was to hear my maid Sawannee boiling water in the kitchen. She was not a Thai but a round-faced, placid *Mon* hailing from the Thai frontier states with Burma. One of the multitude of peoples who make up the Union of Burma, the *Mon* living in Thailand had long been assimilated with the Thai race.

By 7 a.m. I was washed and shaved, wearing a cotton sarong and a Thai farmer's shirt fastened by tie-strings, eating my breakfast of *papaya* and lime juice. I sipped a cup of ginger tea as I cast my eye over my collection of Khmer brass rubbings recently bought in Phnom Penh. Tan Mair had recommended papaya for breakfast. I thought it foul-tasting and slimy, but perhaps useful to my constitution, so forced it down dutifully. Only much later did I discover that most Asian armies feed the fruit to their soldiers to reduce their libido.

At 8 a.m. my two remaining students came for their English lessons. I had long given up teaching English but I still had a few students to whom I felt particularly attached and whose enthusiasm I could not disappoint. My first student was a thin, emaciated Chinese girl desperate to become a doctor. She was attending Chulalongkorn University, one of the finest in Thailand, and had ambitions to become a doctor. She struggled with her English but had no talent for languages. I admired her perseverance and single-minded intent and helped her as much as I could.

At 9 a.m. Khun Somchit slid into the room. She was a tall, handsome Thai-Chinese with high cheek bones and severely cropped hair. She was a *mamasan* in a nightclub and spoke the sort of English common to many Thais: no verbs, sporadic instructions only. She was in her late thirties but looked forty-five. Although much older than I, she would also *wai* me in a most respectful way showing deep reverence for the status of the teacher, woefully inadequate though I was. We had an excellent arrangement: I charged her no fee and she looked after me in her nightclub.

By 10 a.m. I dived into the heat and started up my MGB GT. Throwing myself into the maelstrom of the daily Bangkok traffic I weaved my way to the head offices of ECAFE[1] where I was due to interview the director-general for a newspaper article. The traffic was intense as usual. Bangkok traffic lights change every seven minutes giving me a chance to read that morning's Bangkok Post as I waited in my low-slung sports car, only feet off the ground, amidst a cloud of exhaust fumes and the deafening cacophony of motor-cycles, *tuk-tuks* and Datsun Blue Bird taxis whose exhaust mufflers had long been consigned to the Bangkok gutters. The heat was unbelievable. Within minutes my shirt was glued to my back. I felt the first spring of sweat on my brow and then a drip would slowly make its way down my cheek and onto my shirt. Within seconds my whole body had burst into sweat, coursing down my face and onto my freshly-ironed shirt. My trousers turned a damp dark grey around the waist.

At each traffic light stood an energetic policeman, whistle clenched between teeth. All Thai policemen seemed too large for their uniforms, stretched tight across their melon-like stomachs. It has been said that an earlier police general ordered all policemen on traffic duty to blow their whistles constantly to prevent them from swearing at the drivers. By and large I found them friendly, recognising the cars they saw on a daily basis but then Bangkok was a small city in those days.

I was twenty minutes late for the interview. I staggered into the director-general's cool air-conditioned office and gasped with relief as the cold air wafted inside my shirt and began to dry the perspiration. The D-G was not impressed by what he saw; I was just another sweaty journalist to him. He was an earnest Swede, a type which the United Nations favours, and pontificated at length over the reasons why the planned dams were not being built on the Mekong River

---

[1] ECAFE: The Economic Commission for Asia and the Far East. A United Nations Agency responsible for promoting major infrastructural developments in the region.

and why his projects, while consuming vast amounts of money and employing many hundred expatriates (mainly Scandinavian or from the Indian subcontinent), never left the drawing board. As I took my leave the D-G asked whether he could see the draft of my article. I thought it unlikely he would agree with the tenor of my script so I declined.

There was just time to drive down Silom Road and into the Oriental Hotel for a quick drink at the Foreign Correspondents' Club before heading off for lunch at the *Wang*. At that time the FCC occupied a small suite at one end of the old wing in the venerable hotel famed for housing Grahame Greene, Somerset Maugham and countless other authors down the years. The only people in the FCC that day were Dennis Bloodworth, up from Singapore and researching a new book, and the Daily Mail's Noel Barber, at that time a prolific author and an old friend from yore. I reluctantly headed back into the traffic slightly the worse for wear to arrive at the *Wang* fifteen minutes late and once again bathed in a flood of sweat.

Tan Mair's Great Dane nuzzled my hand and I sank into the tropical oasis of timeless peace that the *Wang* provided in the centre of Bangkok. A maid silently brought me a fresh lime juice on her knees after *wai*-ing me deeply. Tan Mair was sitting under a *nipa* palm in the garden working on a novel. We lunched on the marble terrace overlooking the *klong*. In the middle of our lunch of searing pork and noodles a Burmese farmer in a loin cloth was brought in by one of the maids. He squatted on the marble floor and opened a sack revealing some rare Burmese bronze Buddhas. The Princess examined them closely, made an offer, haggled briefly and the man bowed deeply and left on his knees, shuffling backwards. Tan Mair handed me one of the Buddhas, magnificent with a jade green patina. "For you," she said, "respect it always." As I write, I am looking at this Buddha, sitting in his correct position on a shelf higher than my head so I must always look upwards to see his impassive yet beneficent expression.

The afternoon was taken up with writing my article and once again forcing my way through the 'dodgem' traffic to the dilapidated central post office in New Road to file my story by telex.

That evening I joined Axel Aylwen for dinner. Axel, the Anglo-Greek step-son of an erstwhile Lord Mayor of London, had allowed himself to be addressed as 'Lord Aylwen' and the Thais had been happy to welcome him as a member of the English aristocracy. My arrival had caused Axel to downgrade himself slightly but his other talents more than made up for any social pretension. Later Axel was to horrify the staff at the venerable Tanglin Club in Singapore by pulling out the starched white table cloth from underneath a loaded table to prove that all could be left standing, only to see glasses, plates and candelabra crash to the floor.

Axel was entertaining some European celebrities, with whom he had a particular following. We met at his house before moving on to dinner. The house, off Soi Ruamrudee, not far from where I lived, was a typical Thai wooden house elevated off the ground on two levels set in a dense tropical garden. It was not long before we moved on to the Galaxy Restaurant. There we sat on the floor in a private room around a large table with a pit underneath our feet. We were five men. Between each man sat a young girl, naked but for a thong. The rule of the house was that the men's hands were not allowed to touch the table or the food. So the girls fed us tasty morsels with their chopsticks, sometimes the girl on my left and sometimes the girl on my right. Another naked girl had slipped into the pit and was making mischief where eyes could not see. There was much hilarity, the Thai sense of *sanuk* always rising to the surface.

After dinner we moved on to the 33 Bar in Silom Road. In 1969 there were only a limited number of night-clubs in Bangkok that were not catering for either the American military or traditional Thai taste. Club 33, small and dark with a minute dance floor and a sultry saxophone player was an occasional haunt of mine. I had been eyeing a particular girl there for some months. She was tall and usually wore a cat-suit which emphasised her thin waist and long legs – far too long for a Thai girl.

After a while Axel and his friends moved on to another night-club. I stayed behind at a small table observing the electricity between the clients, mainly *farang* Bangkok residents, and the girls eyeing their next mark. The cat-suit was dancing with a bald-headed man half a head shorter than her. After a while she came and sat with me. I offered her a drink which she declined much to my surprise as commissions on drinks would have been her second main source of income.

"You look sad and lonely," she said in Thai. "Shall we dance?"

We shuffled a little around the miniscule dance floor. She was nearly as tall as me, her shiny hair felt like strands of silk against my face, tickling softly. We did not talk. The saxophone played lazily in the corner, a girl wearing a few purple feathers crooned smoothly into a microphone. She whispered in my ear, "Let's go, I think you need some company tonight. I'll meet you behind the night-club in ten minutes." I offered to pay her 'bar fine' to reimburse the night-club for their loss of income if one of the girls left before closing time. "Not for you," she said with a toss of her long hair.

I drove her the short distance back to my flat. She undressed, showered and slipped into my bed. When I awoke in the morning she had left. Although I had made sure that she had not gone empty-handed, at no time had she ever mentioned the subject of money. This was normal for Thai 'working' girls: however poor they were, money was a secondary consideration and you were trusted to do the right thing. Time and time again I found this to be the case. If you were liked and trusted, money was not an important issue unlike so many other places in the world.

14

The Plain of Jars

The elderly DC3 lurched down the runway at Vientiane, bounced once and tentatively took to the air, struggling to gain altitude, skimming over the trees at the airport's perimeter. I was the only passenger on the airplane; a single canvas seat had been attached to the floor for my benefit. It was near the door towards the back of the plane beside some crates of chickens noisily protesting at the nearest they would ever get to flying in their short lives. A goat was tethered to the fire extinguisher, its hooves scrabbling to keep its balance on the slippery aluminium floor.

I heaved a sigh and stretched my legs out on one of the cartons of cigarettes that filled the rest of the aircraft, stacked in neat piles the length of the plane. Certainly the cartons were clearly marked 'State Express 555' but it was curious that each carton had taken two men to carry onto the plane. More likely munitions, I thought. Laos was meant to be a neutral country, a buffer between Vietnam and Thailand but the place was crawling with American military-types in ill-fitting civilian clothes. Strange things were going on.

Welcome to Lao Air Charter, one of two airlines that flew services from Vientiane, the Lao administrative capital, to Luang Prabang, the royal capital. The road between the two capitals had been closed for years by now and with the recent sinking of one of the few shallow draught cargo boats that used to motor up the Mekong to supply Luang Prabang with the town's necessities, the DC3s provided the only remaining passenger and cargo link. It was an uncertain flight at the best of times: soon after leaving the flat plain around Vientiane the ground rose into the foothills of the Annamite Cordillera, the mountains that separated Vietnam from western Laos and Thailand. Only two passes crossed the mountains but they had been closed ever since the French evacuated Vietnam in the 1950s.

One of the two American pilots weaved his way through the cigarette cartons back to where I was sitting. The chickens clucked furiously causing a maelstrom of feathers and dust. He was a lean, rangy Texan who had been flying in Southeast Asia for several years.

"I've been flying this route for months and still don't know which clouds have hard centres," he ruminated peering out of the cracked window at the mountains rising into the clouds.

Crashes on this route were almost a weekly event. The DC3 flew at three thousand feet, on either side the peaks of the mountains rose out of the clouds far above the aircraft. The objective was to fly above the twisty Mekong River Valley, make a tight circle around Luang Prabang to lose altitude and drop onto the laterite landing strip.

"It'll be a hot LZ today," grumbled the pilot. "The Pathet Lao have been mortaring the airstrip for the past three days. We'll come in steep. Jump as soon as we stop and sprint to the terminal," he advised.

As soon as the plane lurched to a halt I followed his advice and ran across the dusty apron but seemed to be the only person in a hurry. An elderly Liberator truck coughed into life and disappeared in a fog of blue exhaust, lumbering out to the DC3 to collect the 'cigarettes', chickens and the goat. Smoke coiled lazily into the sky on the far side of the airstrip from that morning's mortar shelling. The terminal was a deserted shed beside the airstrip. I waited for an hour, watching the surrounding hills change colour and depth as the sun played through the whispy clouds, until a passing *cyclo*, the ubiquitous pedal-powered trishaw, picked me up and pedalled me sedately into town.

Luang Prabang was an enchanting town located on a promontory in the Mekong River with water on three sides. There were almost more temples than houses. Golden spires and *naga*-heads, orange tiled roofs and pointed wooden gables glinted in the sunshine as they had for centuries. Little moved. A few orange-robed monks swept up brittle leaves in the temple courtyards, a teenage soldier shorter than his rifle slumbered in the sentry box outside the palace gates, a solitary *cyclo* pedalled in slow motion along a dusty street, a dog scratched itself under the shade of a pipal tree. Here there was no sense of time, a haven of peace surrounded by the oily brown waters of the Mekong, mountains and jungle beyond. I wandered aimlessly into one of the deserted temples and lay on the oiled teak floor. Beams of slanting sunlight cast patterns through the drifting dust. A sense of inner peace filled me.

That afternoon, as I strolled around the town I found a magnificent French-style chateau complete with a carriage drive and wrought-iron gates, one of which hung askew on a single hinge. The words 'Hotel de ......' were legible in cracked stucco above the portico, the last word having crumbled away. Anticipating a better hotel then mine, I walked up the driveway and entered the imposing building. The reception area had once been as grand as the outside of the building had suggested. There were signs of gold leaf that had at one time adorned the cornices and threadbare velvet drapes hung beside windows and doors. But there was no sign of a receptionist and the bar seemed to be closed.

I soon found a lounge with some comfortable chairs and an overhead fan gently stirring the afternoon heat, so I made myself at home and presently fell asleep. Upon waking some time later, I felt an urgent call to inspect the plumbing facilities. Failing to find a loo on the ground floor, I climbed the chipped marble staircase and eventually found relief in an upstairs bathroom where I realised, to my chagrin, that there was no paper and the loo refused to flush. Somewhat out of sorts, I decided to retreat to my hotel.

As I descended the stairs and crossed the huge hall, I noticed that the hotel commissionaire had arrived. He was standing beside the front doors splendidly clad in a blue uniform with gold epaulets and rows of medals upon his chest.

I addressed him in French: "Although your hotel is certainly the most attractive in Luang Prabang, there are some serious deficiencies." I went on to berate the man on the deplorable service: the receptionist had disappeared with all the other staff, the bar seemed to be permanently closed and there was no paper in the loos which anyway would not flush. What was he going to do about it?

He listened patiently and respectfully to my ill-tempered tirade and when I spluttered to a halt, he bowed politely and replied in perfect English, "I'm indeed very sorry to hear of your dissatisfaction and I will endeavour to put these serious matters to rights as soon as possible. But I fear you may be under some misconception: this is not an hotel, it is the town hall, the *Hotel de Ville*."

At that moment a cavalcade swept up the driveway complete with motor cycle outriders. My 'commissionaire' was helped into a large Mercedes Benz and with a cursory wave the Governor of Luang Prabang and chief Aide-de-camp to the King of Laos sped away leaving me standing in a cloud of dust.

The next morning I left in a jeep for the Plain of Jars to see how the American-backed Royal Lao Army was faring in the secret war with the North Vietnamese-backed and well-armed Pathet Lao troops. The international press was full at that time of the fierce duels between the opposing sides and I wanted to see for myself what was going on. The eastern part of the country along the Vietnamese border was firmly under the control of the Pathet Lao under the leadership of Prince Souphannouvong while the western part was under the control of Prince Souvanna Phouma's neutral but western-leaning government. The two princes were half-brothers but had not met since 1960 when the 'Red Prince' had escaped from prison in Vientiane and had made his way to Phong Saly in the north-east to lead the Pathet Lao troops.

After two gruelling hours of bouncing over dusty tracks the jeep ground to a halt and a further three hours walk brought me to the front line. There a platoon of royalist soldiers was sitting around some dusty foxholes playing cards. We chewed the fat for a while and then at midday a whistle blew and a fire was lit. A chicken was produced, a pot boiled and lunch was prepared.

Suddenly a column of men appeared through the scrub in front of our positions carrying AK47's and Russian-made rocket-propelled grenades. The Pathet Lao had arrived. Were we to be taken prisoner? Was it going to end here in this dusty scrub? The communists did not look particularly menacing, in fact they paid me little attention.

One strolled over to me, AK47 waving in my direction, and stopped to stare at me. Opening his mouth to reveal a few black teeth, he spat a stream of crimson betel juice between my feet. I edged away and anxiously looked around but the royalist soldiers scarcely stirred, just looked up and muttered a few words of welcome. I offered a cigarette which the soldier seized gratefully and then squatted beside me to share the smoke. The rest of the communist soldiers piled their weapons around a tree and producing a bag of rice also squatted down and started chatting to their supposed enemy. Soon a bottle of rice whisky appeared and was passed around from soldier to soldier. I was told that many on both sides in this conflict were related and, as fate had decreed, some were on one side of the conflict and some on the other. It was not their war; they had just been dragged into the conflict.

The sun beat down from a cloudless sky. The heat rose in waves off the parched brown plain. The soldiers lay around well-fed and slightly drunk, murmuring to each other of absent friends and girls back in their villages. After a while the whistle blew again and the Pathet Lao soldiers desultorily picked up their weapons and sloped off back to their lines. The royalists wandered back to their foxholes. Some time later I heard gunfire but I doubted that the two sides were shooting at each other, more likely someone had seen a wild pig in the brush.

Such was the war in Laos in the early 1970s. It was not to remain so friendly for long. Soon the Americans were to pulverise these mountains with B52 bombers and Laos was to become the most heavily bombed territory in the world. Later still the communist North Vietnamese were to sweep through the country annihilating, imprisoning and 're-educating' as they went along. The secret war was to end in death and tragedy for many; Laos was to enter a dark tunnel from which it was to emerge decades later but a shadow of what it had been before.

Some days later I had progressed as far across the Plain of Jars as it was possible to go. I had walked for several days by now with my guide, a *Hmong* named Ngu. He was a cheerful soul with long Rasta locks, a soiled and torn shirt, loin cloth and no footwear. He carried my cameras and water bottles. I carried a light backpack with some dried pork, candles, a mosquito net and a fat bundle of Lao currency, the Kip, of little use in such a remote area. We slept under the stars or in villages deserted by the local people, fleeing the impending war.

On the third day we came across a small gathering of wooden houses where some unaccountable celebrations were being held with muzzle-loaded rifles fired noisily and carelessly into the air and giant home-made rockets launched amidst much hilarity. Several hundred tribespeople were milling around, the women in their best costumes of gaudy red and black blouses heavily embroidered with sequins and silver coins. They were laden with silver bangles stretching their necks and through extended holes in their ear-lobes. The elder women squatted topless, their dry and wrinkled breasts touching their knees. We arrived in the early evening and it looked as if we had missed the best of the party; many of the younger men had already collapsed underneath a huge banyan tree. Others were sitting in circles smoking pipes of opium or *ganja*.

I was welcomed with exaggerated enthusiasm and invited to sit beside the one-toothed village headman who plied me with a heavy rice liquor in a battered aluminium saucepan that was passed from hand-to-hand around the circle.

As the evening developed, some of the men linked arms, stood waveringly and attempted to sing popular folk songs to wild applause. The worse they sang or the drunker they became, the louder was the appreciation. Then a group of comely maidens appeared and danced in front of the men gathered cross-legged around the fire. One of the dancers was especially alluring with bright flashing eyes and plump tight breasts jiggling jauntily. The village headman caught my look of appreciation and made an unmistakeable gesture followed by an eyebrow raised in query. I think I nodded my head but it might have been the liquor.

When the celebrations had exhausted themselves and the fire began to burn low, I rolled out my bedroll under the banyan tree, covered myself with my *pakoma* and gazed drunkenly at the myriad stars swimming over the Plain of Jars.

I was not, however, to rest for long being nudged awake by a shadow who beckoned to me. I struggled to my feet and followed him through the dark houses until at the end of the village he gestured for me to enter one of the shadowy houses. Not knowing quite what to expect I walked through the open door into a pitch black room. I stood for a second blinking while my eyes got used to the inner gloom, illuminated slightly by the stars outside. A soft female hand took mine and led me over to the far side of the room. I heard a dog growl but a finger was gently pressed over my mouth to reassure me.

My knee bumped into what felt like a bamboo bed and I allowed myself to be turned and pushed gently back and down so I was resting on my elbows with my feet on the floor. There I stayed while my ears detected the unmistakeable rustle of clothes being removed. A hand reached for mine, lifted it and placed it on a soft and firm breast. With her other hand she swiftly untied my sarong, pushed me flat on to the bed, and slid on top of me. By now my eyes could make out a little of the room, the lighter patch of a window and the door through which I had stumbled. I traced my fingers over her face and down the length of her body. She must have been the dancer I had been admiring around the fire. We kissed, her lips soft as a fresh mango. Her body, warm and silky on top of me, began to move. I closed my eyes thanking the god of travellers for the mercies sometimes thrown my way and began to move with her rhythm.

Suddenly on the far side of the room a match scratched and sprung to life. I looked up and to my complete horror saw face after face around the room. It was full of people, all sitting quietly cross-legged on the ground looking at the performance on the bed. The whole village seemed squeezed into the room. They must have been sitting there for a long time with their eyes completely adapted to the starlight coming through the window.

The girl giggled slightly but continued her rhythmic moving. I should have completed the show, maybe even added some sound-effects or improved my performance but sad to relate I leapt to my feet and ran naked through the village leaving my sarong on the floor. Laughter was still ringing in my ears as I made my way back to my banyan tree.

15

The Opium Fields

My journalistic work in Thailand presented me with many opportunities. One of the most memorable was standing in for Peter Simms to cover U.S. Secretary of State Henry Kissinger's visit to Thailand when he disappeared for three days, to the mystification of the press corps. It was later revealed that he had made a clandestine trip to China to pave the way for the restoration of American ties with the People's Republic, severed since 1949. Little was I to know that Kissinger's visit to China was going to place a heavy, albeit distant, influence on most of my working career.

One brilliant sunny day late in 1970 Tan Mair told me that she was planning her first trip to distribute the King's Bounty to the hill tribes that live far to the north of Chiang Mai on the border with Burma. This was a new area for me and promised an expedition into the heart of what was later known as the 'Golden Triangle'. It was an area notorious for producing much of the world's supply of opium and its derivatives. It may seem strange today when the north of Thailand is home territory to back-packers, and tour groups of blue-rinse ladies can safely take a coach almost anywhere around that formerly remote area to gape at the quaintly-clad Meo tribes-people, paraded like living tableaux in a museum but in the 1960s the road came to an end, to all intents and purposes, in Mae Sariang, some 150 kilometres south-west of Chiang Mai. Dense jungle then rolled north and west into the hills rising higher as they crossed into Burma only thirty kilometres to the west, Laos far to the east and China to the north.

Warlords of different allegiances, but none to the Thai government, controlled the jungle and knew no borders. It was a dangerous place to visit: the communist terrorists were active, the warlords unpredictable, and asking too many questions about the opium trade was not advisable.

Long before the term 'Golden Triangle' had been coined, drugs had been a significant business in Thailand for many years but the Vietnam War lifted the industry to a new dimension. The 500,000 American soldiers in Vietnam were a ready market for any type of drug. Here was a mainly conscripted army fighting a war they did not understand for a people who did not want them. The tour of duty for most GIs was just one year. If they could stay alive for that time then they were home and dry. Drugs made the time pass quicker, the hell easier to bear.

When I first visited Vietnam, packets of twenty machine-rolled, filter tip marijuana joints in sealed Marlboro cigarette packets complete with unbroken government revenue stamps, were being sold on every street corner together with real cigarettes. Many GIs smoked joints as if they were smoking cigarettes, and this had a depressingly negative impact on their fighting spirit. Indeed to the GI a marijuana smoke-filled hootch was a much more enticing prospect then venturing into a jungle filled with booby-traps, Vietcong, the North Vietnamese Army and wild animals lurking behind every tree.

The drug trade in the 1960s was creating vast fortunes across the Far East from the refiners in the jungle, to the wholesale dealers in Bangkok and the financiers, otherwise respectable businessmen and bankers, in Hong Kong. The Thai generals-cum-politicians seemed to do best. They were either directly involved themselves in the business or were paid to turn a blind eye, and paid very generously. Thai generals did not get to live in extensive compounds with fleets of Mercedes-Benz cars on a soldier's salary.

Rumours had been circulating around the Foreign Correspondents Club for some weeks to the effect that a cabal of American logistics officers had organised a means of getting drugs directly to their soldiers in Vietnam without going through the normal supply channels so cutting out the generals in Bangkok. The rumour suggested that Air America, the CIA-owned 'civilian' airline operating throughout the area, was running secret drug flights from Chiang Mai directly to Saigon and other U.S. bases in Vietnam. I had even heard that U.S. air force C-130 Hercules transport planes had been diverted to carry tons of marijuana and heroin directly to Vietnam. In some perverse way the Americans were apparently reviving their habits honed twenty-five years earlier in another war, when the U.S. Army Air Corps dropped opium into Burma to pay their Kachin guerrillas, but this time it was their own boys who were the recipients.

It was a moot point as to whether some in the American embassy in Bangkok knew what was going on but most journalists assumed they did. The whispering in the Foreign Correspondents Club intimated that Thai intelligence had learned that a U.S. embassy truck driving between Chiang Mai and Bangkok had been routinely ferrying drugs. This was a step too far for the Thai generals. The truck was protected by diplomatic immunity and could not be legally intercepted. The generals arranged for the embassy truck to be 'accidently' rammed and it ended up on its side having spilt its cargo across the highway for all to see. A diplomatic incident followed which both the Thais and the Americans went to extraordinary lengths to deny.

Now journalists took their careers, and their lives, in hand if they were to write about the illicit drug trade and most considered it a subject worth avoiding when there was much else to investigate. The story was common knowledge around the bar in the Foreign Correspondents Club but as every journalist learns, there is a time for speaking out and there is a time to keep the Olivetti typewriter quiet in its little blue case.

By this time I had become the 'stringer' for a number of newspapers and it was my custom to advise them when I was about to make an expedition with Tan Mair into the remoter areas of Thailand. So when I informed an American newspaper for which I wrote, that I was about to travel deep into the northern jungles, the editor responded promptly, asking me to keep an eye out for any signs of opium cultivation or any other controversial activity.

In November 1970, I travelled to Chiang Mai with Tan Mair and her usual assembly of doctors, nurses, local administrators and an unusually large contingent of Thai soldiers. From there we set off in a small convoy of army trucks and spent the night at the road-head in Mae Sariang. There was a dingy wooden hotel memorable for the small holes drilled into the plywood partitions between each room by inquisitive voyeurs eager to see whatever might be happening in the next room. Each room had a 'squat' in the corner, encrusted with ancient dried faeces, around which a multitude of insects and cockroaches gathered whenever the single naked light-bulb hanging from the cobwebbed wooden ceiling was extinguished.

The next day our convoy stopped at Mae La Noi, due north of Mae Sariang where the road petered out into a jungle track. A hundred or so Meo tribespeople had gathered to meet us. Distinguishable by their colourful clothes, these mountain people spoke their own language and even the Thais needed an interpreter to communicate. The Meo were hill-dwellers and their villages were always located at the very top of a hill, useful for defence but inconvenient for water. The women folk formed an endless chain carrying earthenware water jars on their heads filled from the rivers in the dark bottoms of the valleys to the top of the hills, two thousand feet into the clouds.

There were no boats to carry the Bounty here. Each box of blankets, soap and medicine had to be tied into wicker panniers, thirty kilogrammes each. The men hauled these up and down the steep hills on their backs with a band around their forehead taking the strain, walking bare-foot, their splayed toes struggling to catch hold on the narrow muddy path.

We walked for hour upon hour, mile after mile. The path crossed flat river valleys with young rice growing in shallow terraces on either side and then led directly into thick undergrowth on the sides of the valleys and up near-perpendicular hills, three thousand feet or more, to hilltop villages only to descend sharply to another river valley. Uphill was a sweaty grind, downhill became positively dangerous as bare feet would slip on the mud, and man after man would cannon down a slope sometimes losing his pannier of medicines colliding with the next man knocking him off his balance until the hillside was covered with loose panniers, and men hanging onto tree roots and jungle vines, struggling to keep their balance.

After a while I noticed that we seemed to be crossing the same river as it wound its way around the hills. It puzzled me as to why we did not follow the river along the flat floor of the twisting valley rather than the constant pattern of ascent and descent. I noticed that the Meo were much happier, and moved faster, when they were climbing than when they were walking along the flat. Their legs and feet seemed to be designed for walking up and down; when they were not climbing they appeared cumbersome, as if their feet had been adjusted for hill-dwelling.

We spent each night in a hilltop village, a small huddle of draughty wooden huts built on beaten mud at ground level unlike the high stilted houses of Khirirat. Tan Mair was allocated the headman's house, which gave her a degree of privacy. There was however nowhere else for the rest of the party to stay. It was too cold to sleep outside as we had done on our southern expeditions. However each village had a 'house of the dead' reserved for the laying out of corpses. When not being used for its main purpose it was otherwise occupied by a menagerie of chickens and pigs which were kept in at night, safe from wild animals. This house was brushed clean of animal refuse and made available for us. As there was nowhere else for the animals to spend the night, we had to share the house with its usual occupants, which led to some strange incidents. We would lie on the floor together with the pigs and chickens; the pigs in particular seemed to enjoy their new guests and more than once I found a bristly friend snuggling up to me while I slept.

As we progressed deeper into the hills the paddy fields in the valleys became less frequent and the jungle closed in. We saw much evidence of tiger, panther and wild elephant activity. Then we began to come across slash–and–burn farming and in the clearings there were fields of mauve and white poppies. Meo women worked in the fields, slicing the poppy heads with diagonal cuts to allow the resin to ooze out of the flower head and harden. The sticky black resin was then scraped off and formed into balls or bars of raw opium.

We met many mule trains threading their way along jungle paths laden with sacks of opium. These mule caravans were heavily guarded and our out-numbered lightly armed Thai soldiers were occasionally questioned in case they were on official business. The drug merchants seemed amused to find a party of doctors and nurses in such a remote area and our encounters always ended up with drinking some fiery homemade liquor.

The villages where we stopped for the night also hosted the drivers and guards of the mule caravans and so I was able to learn much about the workings of the opium trade and the upstream refining industry from the point of view of the farmers. After a couple of weeks we emerged from the jungle at Mae Hong Son, a prosperous little town not far from the Burmese frontier. This was surprising, as it was not connected with the rest of Thailand by road except for a 120 kilometre muddy track through dense jungle that was impassable for six months of the year. It did however have a small landing strip occasionally used by planes flying the northwest Thailand routes. The town seemed well supplied, the houses were concrete and there was electricity for a couple of hours every evening supplied by a diesel generator. There were restaurants, food of all sorts and Hennessey VSOP brandy in cases stacked outside shops selling every conceivable type of Thai or American cigarettes or Burmese curly cheroots.

Tan Mair disapproved of this place and wanted to return to Mae Sariang down the jungle track after just one night. The doctors and soldiers were all for a few days' rest. We dined that night with the local 'mayor', a rotund Sino-Thai who wore a diamond-encrusted gold Rolex. Even more surprising, as there were no roads outside the town and even the roads inside the town limits were just muddy tracks, we were driven around the small town in his Mercedes-Benz limousine.

The Princess looked ill at ease sitting beside, and breaking bread with, one of the world's most notorious drug merchants, a veritable king himself with his own army probably better equipped than the Thai army itself. He smiled through his golden teeth, swilling brandy and munching whole ricebirds in single mouthfuls, boasting of the profits to be made dealing with the Burmese over the border.

If the 'mayor' was surprised to see a *farang* amongst this strange group of doctors, soldiers and Meo porters that had suddenly appeared out of the jungle, he certainly did not show it; he was far too confident to be alarmed. Why should he? We were two weeks walk from the nearest Thai town and our armed guard of Thai soldiers had no interest in making trouble. Within minutes of strolling into town they had parked their guns and broached the brandy. The Thai generals posed no threat, they were his allies. Over the second bottle of VSOP, he presented me with a jadeite ring and allowed a photograph to be taken with his fat arm reaching up around my shoulders, his head at chest-height, a greasy and evil grin fixed upon his fleshy face.

All through the night mule trains trekked into Mae Hong Son, the muleteers exhorting their stubborn animals, cracking whips over their heads. Mountains of jute sacks appeared, were reallocated and moved out of town on fresh mules. Now it is a typical Thai town, connected by an all-weather road with the rest of the country, but at that time it was the nerve-centre of the opium industry, a major junction point where the Shan, Karen, Wa and other tribes living on the Burmese side of the border handed over their crops to the Thais to take further along the maze of jungle paths that covered the hills in the Golden Triangle. This was where the business was done. It was a forbidding place.

My description of Mae Hong Son in 1971 must be difficult for the modern traveller to believe thirty-five years later. A modern guide book indicates that there are four aircraft a day from Chiang Mai to Mae Hong Son and that one is likely to encounter 'hordes of travellers'.

After a couple of days in this strange town we set off back to Mae Sariang. This was no mean feat. A Rangsit VW microbus had been sent to collect us and it had taken the driver and two men three days to travel the 130 kilometres. We were to understand why: some two months after the monsoon had passed, the track was still waterlogged. For much of the distance we had to walk, pushing or pulling the VW through the mud. Rivers and streams were crossed by balancing the vehicle on two logs, slippery with mud. We were a sorry sight when we eventually reached Mae Sariang, oozing mud and covered with mosquito and leech bites.

As usual, throughout the expedition I took photographs with my two Nikon cameras. I had rolls of photographs of poppy cultivation, of the jungle refining centres we passed through, the mule trains and the muleteers themselves and also of what I had seen in Mae Hong Son. Bearing in mind the warnings of my colleagues in the Foreign Correspondents Club, I did not intend to write a story on Thailand's flourishing drug industry but thought I might find a buyer for the pictures in one of the photographic news agencies.

That was how my problems started.

Upon my return to Bangkok I delivered the thirty or so rolls of film to a processing laboratory that was used by many journalists in Thailand at the time. Their normal practice was to prepare contact prints that I would collect after a couple of days. I knew the laboratory well and never asked for a receipt for my films.

When I returned two days later to ask for the contacts however, I was met with a blank stare: they were sorry but I had not visited the laboratory for a couple of months and I had not given them any films to process! As I was talking to the very same man who had accepted my films scarcely forty-eight hours earlier, I could only stare at him in amazement. Was it my imagination or was there a muscle flickering on one side of his face, and why did he not look me in the eye? He seemed particularly keen for me to leave and was relieved when the door opened to admit another customer.

About a week later I noticed a black Toyota Corona parked outside the house I was renting in the north of Bangkok. Through the tinted glass I could make out two men with dark glasses, quietly smoking. The car was there all the following week. I thought little of it then, but it was to come back and haunt me in time, eventually expediting my departure from Thailand.

16

The Silk Queen

Tan Mair had an inner circle of about a dozen close female friends and they met for lunch at the *Wang* monthly. I met all of them over time. There was the Queen's private secretary, the deputy governor of the Bank of Thailand and various other ladies at the pinnacle of Thai society. Amongst them was Khun Payung Isarangkul na Ayudhya.

Khun Payung had a short severe hair style, a pockmarked face, deep voice and a rather masculine bearing. She managed a Thai silk business in Patpong Road, the centre of the commercial district in Bangkok at the time. Unusually for a Thai, Khun Payung was a Christian; ninety-eight percent of Thais are Buddhists and Christian missionaries experienced little success in attracting converts down the centuries. But then she was not like the Thais in many ways. She seemed to lack the soft charm, easy humour and subtle mind so often found in the Thais. I was not therefore surprised to learn that she had French and Vietnamese blood.

Khun Payung invited me to lunch.

Over a fiery curry she talked of her family and in particular of her only blood daughter who was married to a wealthy British-educated Thai of Chinese extraction, and was living at the time in England with her infant son. A photograph was produced which I studied carefully. It showed a serious young Chinese-looking man standing beside a taller Thai girl. He was squinting at the camera and was pitched forward slightly as if he had custom-made heels on his shoes to make him appear taller.

She was quite beautiful with a round face, a wide but rather sad smile and lustrous black hair falling to her waist, but there was a hint of unhappiness in her eyes. Standing between his parents was a small boy, a miniature image of his father. The mother had an arm around her son's shoulders but the father stood on one side; the body language did not portray a close, loving family.

It was a familiar story: that of a pretty Thai girl marrying into a rich Chinese merchant family. Over the previous one hundred years there was massive immigration of Chinese from China's poor southern provinces into Thailand, a land of comparative milk and honey compared to the grinding poverty and frequent famines that swept China with regularity. These new immigrants worked hard and gradually took over much of the mercantile, banking and industrial sectors in Thailand creating vast fortunes in the process.

"What do you think of my daughter?" enquired Khun Payung. I assured her that she looked beautiful and that she must be a proud mother and grandmother. Looking me straight in the eye, she then said, "Would you like her?"

"Uh, in what way?" I stammered,

"I mean, would you like to have her?"

"But, but she is already married. Very married," I said pointing at the husband and child.

"That can all be arranged," she said quietly. "She is returning to Bangkok next week and you will meet her."

Sure enough, a week later Khun Payung telephoned to invite me for lunch again but this time we were to meet at the Hilton Hotel where a fashion show was to be held and her daughter was one of the models. Would I like to take a closer look? Intrigued at this turn of events, I naturally accepted. There were a number of beautiful Thai girls strutting their stuff on the catwalk between the tables but one stood out above the rest. After the show she joined our table and Khun Payung introduced me to her daughter, Plern. She was infinitely more attractive than her photograph, and as we looked at each other I felt that kick in the stomach that only happens a few times in your life, when something is telling you that a milestone has been reached and that nothing will be quite the same again.

Thus started a love affair which was to continue for many years, made all the more piquant by being illicit. We would meet in dark corners, quiet bars, grab a few fleeting minutes with each other before Plern would have to dash back to her husband. The marriage had been arranged by Plern's mother and eminently suitable it was: Plern's family was 'comfortable' but a better future was to be assured by marrying into a vast fortune built on rice mills and property. Plern's father was a doctor and soon to become the chairman of Bangkok's largest hospital; there was not much money in the family and there were two other sons to consider. There were many social changes afoot in Asia in the 1960s and 70s: arranged marriages were no longer the norm. Oriental women were taking hesitant steps in the direction of their western sisters who by then had passed through the bra-burning stage and were well on their way to achieving the sorry state of decayed feminism that surrounds us in this day and age.

Plern was not happy with Sakda, her husband. He was a solitary and taciturn structural engineer given, she said, to bouts of violence, and kept a gun under his pillow. The strictures of a close Chinese family tied down this headstrong and fun-loving girl and she viewed her future with gloom. Plern had been educated at a convent in Bangkok and at the University of California at Berkeley where she was just beginning to learn that there was a life apart from nuns and her severely Catholic mother, when she had suddenly been pulled out of college to return to Bangkok and marry a Chinese boy she had scarcely met. She felt her life had been cut down as it was only just starting.

I could only assume that Khun Payung realised that she had committed her daughter to a life of unhappiness and thought there may be an edge in introducing her to Tan Mair's 'Son from the West'. Here was a young single Englishman who had learned the ways of the East and had been 'adopted' by one of Thailand's foremost ladies. He had a title of his own and where there are titles there is frequently assumed to be money. What mischief could there be in introducing these two young people and seeing how matters fared from there on?

We gradually fell in love as two people do when both are seeking new adventures. I was tiring of life in the *Wang* and ready for the next chapter in the great adventure; Plern was looking for a way out of her marriage with Sakda. But there were many obstacles: the main one being the oriental male's lack of confidence when confronted with competition from the western male. If he had found out that his wife was becoming involved with a *farang* then 'face' would have made the situation impossible to resolve. Indeed, things could have turned dangerous: Thai men were always quick on the draw and a hired killer could be found for a handful of Baht. One of the contributing editors to *Business in Thailand* had been shot recently outside his house after being warned several times not to go out with a certain Thai general's daughter.

Tan Mair was not happy at our deepening relationship. On many occasions she took me aside to warn me against becoming too involved, especially since Plern was married with a child. She rallied her friends to the cause: I was sent to see her closest friend, Khunying Suparb Yossuntara, the deputy governor of the Bank of Thailand, who gave me a stern lecture not to take things too seriously. Others weighed in with similar advice. But Plern was the forbidden fruit at the top of this exotic tree.

Khun Payung, on the other hand, was doing all she could to get Plern's marriage annulled. As wives could not divorce their husbands this involved petitioning the Prime Minister's office requesting that the marriage should be negated on the grounds of mental and physical cruelty. Quite what the unfortunate Sakda made of all this is difficult to say: he was resolute in denying Plern a divorce and seemed, understandably, incapable of realising why she was so single-minded in pursuit of her independence.

Ultimately she was successful but at some cost: she received no alimony from Sakda, only an abiding hatred. Sakda severed relations also with Ariya, his only son and heir, and contributed nothing towards his son's education until he went to university, when I was no longer willing to continue to bear the financial burden on my own. Only when Ariya grew up and became a successful businessman in his own right did relations with his father start to improve.

Meanwhile, back in Bangkok, Plern and I were finding it difficult to find trysting places which were both safe and discreet. Then suddenly, like a knight in shining armour, the Prince from Laos rode onto the scene on his black steed shedding light and laughter in every direction. This was the time when Prince Panya Souvanna Phouma entered our lives.

I had been in Bangkok for three years by now and although I did not yet know it, clouds were beginning to gather on the horizon.

My parents, perplexed at what was detaining their eldest son in far off lands, made a fleeting visit. We toured the fabled ruins of Angkor Wat which had been closed to the outside world for the previous decade, and within twelve months were to close again as the Khmer Rouge began to tighten their grip on Cambodia. Angkor was not to reopen for a further quarter-century and at that time I was to be one of the first foreigners to venture back into the ruins. By then many of the statues and friezes that had decorated the ruins in the 1960s had been stripped only to magically migrate into private salons in Paris and Fifth Avenue.

My mother found Thailand uncomfortable: the mosquitoes targeted her white flesh, she was suspicious of Thai food, often eating only plain boiled white rice and, like all western women before and after her, felt cumbersome compared to the much smaller and neater oriental females. A beautiful woman herself, she was five foot ten inches tall, half a head higher than most Thais. Every Thai girl she met was carefully scrutinised in case she might be the reason why their son had fallen under the spell of the East.

They returned to England not quite knowing what to make of my life in the Far East, but by that time my father's eyes were on a new challenge: he had been asked to accept the post of British ambassador to the United States, the highest pinnacle of the diplomatic corps and a rare honour for a non-diplomat.

I had moved into a small house quite close to Plern's family compound. It was hot, dark and characterless with a faintly sinister atmosphere. Preoccupied with Plern, I saw less of Tan Mair. My work as a journalist and as an associate editor of *Business in Thailand* continued. These were happy days: my Thai language continued to improve, although I took no lessons. Bangkok was a fun and enjoyable city in which to live, I was young, independent and I spared no thoughts for the future.

17

Thai Justice

On the 15th May 1969 a towering thunder squall loomed black on the horizon, its anvil head building to tens of thousands of feet in minutes, to burst in a torrential storm flooding some outlying areas of Bangkok. Lightning cut the power across most of the capital. Unsuspecting people in the street caught by the unseasonable tempest scampered for cover from the warm sheets of rain. It was the harbinger of greater storms to come as the monsoon winds started to turn in Thailand's direction.

I was driving down Ploenchit Road in my MG, passed the extensive British embassy grounds where Queen Victoria, surrounded by Indian Civil Service designed buildings, stared sightlessly through a cast iron gate into the smoggy exhaust-filled maelstrom outside. The President Hotel was on my right, where Plern managed a boutique for an obese Thai princess with a handicapped husband. The princess was reputed to kick the unfortunate husband out of bed onto the floor if he displeased her, where he would languish for hours until he repented, when she would deign to help him back onto the bed! I continued passed the Police Hospital and the headquarters of the Criminal Investigation Department with its permanently closed shutters on my left and a hundred metres further there were some traffic lights at the junction with Henri Durrant Road.

The lights were red and as I braked I felt a slight bump as a car behind touched my rear right bumper. It came to a halt alongside me in the offside lane. The car was a beaten-up red Toyota, with rusting chrome, a cracked windscreen and a badly dented passenger door. A thin-faced man with a droopy, wispy moustache and a mole on his cheek from which sprouted several long hairs was driving the car. His passenger looked similarly evil and they both spelled trouble. As soon as their car stopped, the passenger jumped out and stuck his head through my window shouting in very fast Thai. His eyes were red and the liquor on his breath was stale from the night before.

His right hand shot through the window and in one smooth movement he grabbed my car's ignition key, killed the engine and jerked his head out of the window still holding the key. He then danced around the outside of the car waving my key chain in the air. "Damn it," I thought. "Another Thai jealous of a *farang* in a sports car."

The driver meanwhile came around from his side and started to make threatening gestures with his fist, shouting loudly that the *farang* had crashed into his car. We were all stuck in the jam at the lights and traffic lights in Bangkok change slowly. I got out of the car and asked, in Thai, for my keys back. The driver grabbed me and pinned me across the side of the car while his companion prepared to practise his Thai kickboxing in my direction.

I hastily looked around but the other drivers were studiously staring in front of themselves not wishing to get involved. We stayed this way for at least three traffic light rotations. Fists were threatened but no violence materialised although I knew that at any moment a knife might be drawn and I would be left bleeding on the roadside. Miraculously a police motorcycle drew up, the policeman took charge and told all three of us to follow him to the nearby Lumphini Police Station.

Once there, the two attackers gave a long garbled explanation to the policeman. I calmly explained my side of the story in a few sentences and expected to be asked whether I would bring charges against the two hooligans.

"One hundred Baht each," the policeman said to the assailants. They handed over the money and slunk away complaining.

"Thank you," I said to the policeman, "at least you saved me at the right moment."

"You. Seven hundred Baht," the policeman replied.

"Oh, what for?" I enquired politely.

"Fine for making trouble."

"But I was the innocent party here," I persisted.

"You *farang*. *Farang* always trouble. *Farang* always rich. *Farang* pay seven hundred. Thai pay one hundred."

I handed him the money which he stuffed into his pocket. I went on my way pondering over his logic and wondering about the Royal Thai Police Force.

That evening I recounted the story to Tan Mair. She looked thoughtful and I saw she was uncomfortable. "Keep away from the police in Bangkok," she warned. "They are little more than criminals themselves."

Some five months later I was passing through Bangkok for one night on my way between Laos and Singapore. The monsoon rains were in full force and the flight from Vientiane had been particularly rough, the light plane thrown around like a paper kite with lightning seeming to strike the wings in a constant image from hell. The airplane eventually emerged from the tormented clouds just feet above the runway in Bangkok and hit the ground heavily.

As we taxied to the terminal it flashed through my mind that my motorcar insurance had expired the previous week. Insurance is not mandatory in Thailand and there was, after all, a negligible risk in driving downtown that evening. I would renew the insurance as soon as I returned from Singapore.

I took a cab back to my house, showered and climbed into my car, drove out of the dripping carport and threaded slowly between the puddles down the mile long lane to Klong Tan, a larger road which would take me onto Sukhumvit Road, the main highway into the centre of Bangkok. The lane was narrow with high grass on either side; there was no pedestrian footpath. The rain came down in torrents and I drove slowly with the windscreen wipers working at maximum speed. I was wary of the potholes: all filled with water, one merging into the next, some just a few inches deep, others could swallow a car. Many were manholes with their covers missing waiting to consume an unwitting pedestrian. I knew from long experience which puddles to avoid but nevertheless I drove with caution.

It was very dark; the Bangkok municipality did not believe in streetlights. One navigated by the car's headlights or in the more populated areas by lights from the shops or neon advertisements. Roads were rarely repaired and certainly never in the monsoon season.

Pavements and sidewalks were obstacle courses most pedestrians avoided at risk to their lives. Suddenly out of the corner of my eye, I saw something dark move swiftly out of the long grass and straight into the left wing of my car. I did not have time to react. By the time my right foot had jammed onto the brake pedal, the object had hit the car and slammed into the windscreen smashing it more or less in the centre and was then thrown back into the long grass.

It is in situations like this that one's instincts take over and rational thinking stops. When learning the skills of driving in Thailand, and it is a very different set of skills compared to those needed for the well-regulated and immaculately manicured roads of Europe, one is always told that in the event of an accident keep driving as long as the vehicle can move. To stop can easily lead to experiencing the other side of the famous Thai smile. Many drivers carry handguns in their cars and emotions tend to detonate in accident situations. I recall seeing a minor shunt in a traffic jam in Bangkok. The two parties got out to remonstrate with each other, within seconds tempers flared, one party walked purposefully back to his car, returned with a handgun, calmly shot the other in the chest and drove off.

My instincts though had been conditioned by my upbringing in England, my training as a driver there, and the need to do what my intuition and education told me was right. I therefore made the 'mistake' of stopping my car to see what I had hit. Lying in the sodden grass, a few feet from the side of the road, was a man. He was twitching but otherwise not moving, blood coursed down his face mixing with the torrential rain. I looked around: there was not a soul to be seen. Everyone was at home sheltering from the rain. I was alone with the wounded man.

In the minute or two that I stood there, shocked, with a thousand jumbled thoughts rushing through my brain, I saw some headlights approaching. I stood in the middle of the lane and the vehicle stopped. It was a covered pickup truck with half a dozen men inside. They saw my damaged car and leapt out to assist. They carried the wounded man to the back of the pickup truck and laid him on the flatbed. I climbed in afterwards and we drove off towards the police hospital some thirty minutes away. I knelt on the floor of the truck and cradled the man's bleeding head in my lap. His legs were jerking spasmodically, blood dribbling out of his mouth and nose. Half way to the hospital he shuddered and went still. I was holding a dead man's head.

I accompanied the stretcher into the empty A&E room in the hospital. A sleepy doctor appeared, washed his hands in slow motion, walked over to the body and felt for the vital signs. He looked at me through cracked glasses as if seeing me for the first time and quietly told me the man was dead. "From head injuries," he added, looking at my bloody hands as if I might be holding a blunt instrument. I must have stood there in shock, gaping at the doctor not altogether believing what I had heard and yet knowing that it was true. In a moment of compassion, he put his arm around my shoulder and advised softly that I should go to the police station and report the accident, the pickup truck would take me there. An accident, yes, I thought, that is what it was, an accident. How could I be blamed for such a tragedy?

The Bangrak Police Station was a scene out of purgatory. A madhouse of drunks and hookers, drug addicts and criminals all shouting, screaming, punching, shoving, hair pulling and eye gouging. The Thai police wore over-tight, sweat-stained greyish fatigues, looking little different from the other inhabitants. There were seething masses of people ebbing and flowing like waves eddying from one fist fight to the next. The stench was overpowering – vomit, stale cigarette smoke, sweat and sweltering fetid air. Crowded beyond belief, everybody was pushing and kicking each other, the floor a slimy mess of spit, phlegm, vomit and broken glass. Tempers flared. Steel gates banged open and slammed shut. I made my way to the duty sergeant and shouted at him that there had been an accident, someone had died. He paid no attention, shouting down a woman with a torn and bloody blouse who was screaming at him, while another man tried to stove in her head with a broken broom handle.

The Kirirat Expedition

Villagers awaiting the arrival of Princess Rangsit

Princess Rangsit distributing the King's Bounty

S.S. Ben Nevis

Wang Vidhyu, Bangkok

Vippy Rangsit and me

Water skiing on the Chao Phraya in Bangkok

Princess Vibhavadi Rangsit

As a war correspondent in Vietnam

After the ambush in the rubber plantation

ELVIS PRESLEY AT THE RALLY
— Yes, he looks so much like the Roc
'n Roll singer, but he is none other tha
Lord Errington, who was a competito
in the rally.

From the Bangkok Post [Elvis Presley at the Rally]

Macau Grand Prix, being welcomed by the Governor of Macau

My father (aged 43) entering the Bank of England on his first day
as the Governor.

My mother, Esme, Dowager Countess of Cromer, Sir Richard Southwood,
Vice Chancellor, and my uncle Vere, 3rd Viscount Rothermere, on their
investiture as members of the Court of Benefactors, Oxford University

Plern

My grandfather Esmond, 2nd Viscount Rothermere, chairman of the Daily Mail & General Trust

My father, Cabinet Secretary Sir Burke (later Lord) Trend, President Nixon,
Secretary of State Henry Kissinger

Kenneth, 3rd Earl of Inchcape, the chairman of the Shanghai No 1 shipyard
and Dick Chan

Eventually an officer noticed that there was a single *farang* in the midst of this maelstrom, and forced his way over to me shouting and enquiring in English as to what I was doing there. He pointed towards a crowded bench of nearly naked prostitutes fighting each other with bloody fingernails and gestured for me to sit. The hookers paused and looked at me for a moment and went back to their bickering. I took stock of myself: I could pass for any of the crowd, my shirt was soaked with rain and blood, my face streaked with sweat, my trousers blood-stained, my shoes covered in mud.

Time dragged by. I was in shock. Within a few hours I had been torn from my civilised life, hot croissants that morning at the Patisserie in the Lan Xang Hotel in Vientiane, to be treated like a common murderer. Hours went by, maybe six, maybe more, before I saw three young men, adolescents really, fighting through the throng towards me. The eldest reached out and grabbed me by the throat, the younger hit me hard in the face. A couple of policemen seized my assailants by their shirts and forced them away from me where they stood snarling. A policeman told me that they were the sons of the dead man, called to the police station so that they could personally see the *farang* who had killed their father. The police were pleased that they had been able to solve this death in record time.

Two other policemen seized my arms, forced them behind my back, handcuffed me and roughly shoved me into another room. I was thrust onto a wooden bench in front of a desk and the interrogation began. Over the next couple of hours a succession of policemen asked my story which I repeated again and again. Finally one officer took a statement from me that he laboriously wrote down in halting English and asked me to sign. It seemed like a reasonable rendition of what had transpired and I signed it. He said that normal Thai procedures were to hold me in detention until bail could be produced.

I was allowed to make a single telephone call. Mercifully, for once, the Thai telephone system actually worked. I called Plern and explained my predicament to her. Within minutes she was standing in front of me deeply shocked at my appearance. She took it all in within seconds, ordered the slightly shame-faced policemen to remove my handcuffs, and dropping names and threats in all directions, managed to introduce a little civility into the proceedings. A whisper went around the room, police eye met police eye, *"Tanlord? Tanlord!"* They had caught a fish in their trap far larger than the rest of the flotsam in the station. This could be a man with connections, maybe with money as well, a victim they could play with and squeeze dry in the time-honoured way of the Third World. Not for the first time and certainly not for the last, I cursed having a handle to my name. Another telephone call and Khun Payung appeared clutching the title deeds to some property. Bail secure, I was allowed to return home for the night with instructions to return the next morning.

After a sleepless night I returned to the Police Station where the statement was rewritten twice more and translated into Thai. I was told that I had certain responsibilities to discharge and that would be the end of the matter as long as the widow was satisfied.

The requirements were to settle a sum of money on the widow to provide for a comfortable old age; to pay for the funeral to the satisfaction of the family, and to pay for the education of all three children to graduation from college.

The dead man was a senior technician at the Thai Tobacco Monopoly and the family had expectations. Khun Payung advised that it was important for me to show 'sincerity' and contrition or the family could turn difficult. She offered to carry out the negotiations with the family on my behalf.

The police officer said that their preliminary investigations into the accident bore out my statement. They added that the man had been urinating under a tree, had been drinking and was probably drunk, had turned without looking and walked straight into my moving car. The police fully accepted my story; I had nothing to worry about. They would however keep my passport until the family had been satisfied in case I thought of doing a bunk.

The first ordeal proved to be the funeral. Funerals, as we have seen before, tend to be quite an occasion in Thailand: evening services can be held nightly for thirty days and then a weekly service for the remaining weeks until the cremation on the 100th day (giving, according to ancient custom, sufficient time for the body to become dry enough to burn easily). Although these elaborate services can be curtailed in the interests of economy, with a *farang* footing the bill the family naturally opted for the long version. They wanted the full thirty day version, with a complete complement of monks, a band, appropriate flowers, and fully catered refreshments for every evening of the funeral. I was advised to agree to all their requests and did so willingly.

I was also told that I should openly demonstrate my contrition by attending the funeral every evening. This proved to be a very harrowing and humiliating experience: I sat in the temple grounds alone on a chair while I was pointed at, stared at and occasionally spat at. I sat there from six to nine o'clock every night unable to help myself to any of the refreshments I was paying for, looking downcast and saddened – it did not require any acting skills. The widow on the other hand looked quite radiant as the hostess with her large family in attendance and, it seemed, the entire staff of the Tobacco Monopoly, an enormous business in Thailand, enjoying the music and eating their fill.

Night after night I sat on my solitary chair watching people milling around the temple grounds. Most nights one well-dressed portly lady with a large ruby brooch would waddle up to me, wait until she saw others watching and then spit straight into my face. I never blinked an eye. Other times a man in a well-pressed dark suit with a gold button in his lapel would slowly pour a glass of some sticky orange drink into my lap. It dripped down my trouser leg and within minutes started to attract ants which nibbled their way painfully up my legs.

During those thirty days Khun Payung was in contact with the widow and used an array of other intermediaries to convince her of my unabated remorse. Finally a very large sum was mooted as the family's requirements. It amounted to most of my life's savings, a considerable sum for me. I tried to negotiate but in vain.

By chance one day I met an English friend, John Houseman, a struggling stockbroker. A man had fallen to his death under the wheels of John's car the month before. John had contributed a relatively modest sum to the family and that was the end of the matter. The police had scarcely bothered to open a file. We discussed my situation and his advice was that I was mistaken in agreeing to such a lavish funeral. If I could afford such a protracted party then there was more to be mined from that lode. "Anyway," he said in parting, "fortunately I am just a plain mister."

Finally I agreed to hand over the sum requested and there was a modest ceremony at the police station at which the widow signed a document confirming that she would have no further claim against me. The case was closed; it was the end of the tragedy, so could I have my passport back please? The police officer told me to return the next day.

The following day I returned to be met by three solemn policemen who said there was bad news. A handful of witnesses had unexpectedly and voluntarily come forward to say that I had been driving at great speed and I was to be charged with dangerous driving, maybe even manslaughter. I looked at them askance and surprised; there was some shuffling of the feet and averting of the eyes. A young police lieutenant was to shadow me in case I flew the nest. For the next few weeks I went everywhere with the police officer, an earnest and polite man of my own age – to restaurants, nightclubs, bars, everywhere. He tried hard to befriend me but I was constantly aware that a more sinister motive lay underneath his polished charm.

After a month it was hinted that the matter could be resolved by a contribution to the police station which would be shared amongst the policemen who had worked so diligently on my 'case' and that would close the affair. Welcome to the Third World! Best to go along, I thought, and handed over my few remaining Baht. I was promised my passport would be returned within a week, just a few official signatures were needed.

Not so fast. A week after the brown envelope changed hands I was told that a skid mark had been found on the road that corroborated the witnesses' accounts. I protested that some months had gone by and in any case the road was slick with rain at the time, to no avail. A larger contribution was now required.

At this juncture I made a fatal mistake: seeing no end to this extortion, I appealed to Her Britannic Majesty's ambassador to the Kingdom of Thailand for advice. The ambassador, a balding anonymous bureaucrat enjoying his first and last ambassadorship, listened patiently to my tale and assured me that my problems were over. For years the British embassy had cultivated the friendship of a senior police general with generous invitations to dine at the ambassador's table, doubtless backed up by allocations of duty-free Scotch whisky and now a favour would be called in and his influence would end the matter.

By that time my father had taken up his new position as British ambassador to the U.S.A., so one can assume that 'our man in Bangkok' was indeed doing his level best to assist. I can easily imagine the discussion that must have taken place between the ambassador and the police general. Something along the lines of, "Look old chap, the son of one of our VIP's has got into a spot of bother, be a good chap and help us out here will you?"

The predictable result was that the police general reported to his colleagues that they had hit pay dirt and to mine it for all it was worth. The next time I went to the Bangrak police station the expectations of the Policemen's Benevolent Fund had multiplied. I had been forced to cable my father for funds, a step I took with great reluctance as it compromised my entire justification for splitting away from the family and seeking my own way in life.

More money changed hands. The ambassador washed his hands of the affair pleading that he had done his best. Still my passport was not returned. It occurred to me to flee the country but Khun Payung would lose the title deeds to her property and Plern's support throughout this ordeal had been unwavering. I could not take the coward's way out.

Then one day, some nine months after the accident, Charles Letts came through Bangkok. We dined and I told him the whole sorry story. He was silent for a few minutes and then told me to leave it to him. He would have my passport back within seven days. Three days later he called me from Singapore:

"You will go to the Siam Cinema and buy a ticket for the 3:30 p.m. performance tomorrow," he quietly but firmly instructed me, "You will sit in seat 34 in row Y, near the back. After exactly forty-five minutes a man will sit beside you. He will be wearing jeans and a red batik shirt. He will not look at you or speak to you. You will have 250,000 Baht in a brown supermarket paper bag under your seat. He will reach for the bag, check its contents with a torch and then hand you your passport."

I was incredulous. It all sounded too clandestine. Had Charles been seeing too many James Bond movies? Many questions bubbled to the surface.

"But, but Charles, supposing the seat is already taken? Suppose it's the wrong man? Suppose he doesn't give me the passport? Suppose the police persist with their corruption? Suppose………"

He cut me off: "Evelyn, trust me, will you? You really have no choice," he purred down the international telephone line.

Appealing to my father to release more funds, I duly drew the cash from the bank and apprehensively made my way to the cinema at the appointed time. I sat on the edge of my seat anxiously scanning everyone entering the cinema. I am not sure that I ever knew what movie was showing. Sure enough, exactly forty-five minutes after the movie started, a shadowy figure in a red shirt sat beside me, reached underneath my seat and picked up the brown paper bag. He peered inside with a small torch, ruffling through the wads of banknotes. Without saying a word, he reached inside his shirt, withdrew an envelope and pressed that familiar little cardboard book into my hand and silently slid away.

I never heard another word from the Royal Thai Police. It was as if nothing had ever happened. My shadow disappeared and life returned completely to normal.

Charles Letts' standing soared in my mind. Well-known as a man with friends in all corners of the Far East, a 'Mr. Fixit' par excellence, he had ridden to my rescue without hesitation and had known precisely which button to press although he was living over a thousand miles away in Singapore. But Charles was a man of mystery: he spoke Malay, the Chinese Hokien dialect and Thai fluently. When a prisoner of the Japanese during the war working on the Death Railway in Thailand, he had been the only Thai speaker in the camp and it was his lot to break out of the camp at night to forage for food for the other prisoners. He was caught by the Japanese guards on countless occasions and suffered for it. Finally the camp commander summoned him:

"Why, Private Letts, do you think we built a fence around the camp?"

"Well," said Charles, "I assumed it was to keep the Thais out!"

18

The Last Monsoon

The monsoon was late in 1971. Clouds gathered on the horizon, rose in pregnant columns and threatened rain, only to fade during the tropical nights and reveal clear blue sky the next morning. By night dry storms rumbled and flashed but the rains would not come. The *soi* outside my house was parched. The frogs squatted quietly on the cracked mud, wild dogs wandered aimlessly along the lane snapping at flies or scratching their bald stomachs; the clacking of the Indian peanut seller's coconut shell had fallen silent. Miniature dust storms eddied down the *soi* spiralling soiled toilet paper and old lottery tickets into the air to flutter, spent by the heat, a few yards further down the road. The world was waiting.

The dark clouds brooding over Southeast Asia's political theatre were also threatening America's war-show in Vietnam. It was not going the way the directors had intended. The generals were claiming victory, only a little more time needed, only a few more American boys to be sacrificed. But the evidence was not convincing: the Viet Cong's Tet offensive of 1968 had seen to that. The American people had had enough, there was no more spirit in the fight. The South Vietnamese were resigned to defeat, only needing the Americans for their greenbacks. Politicians in Washington might have been wondering why they had never learned their lessons from the years of propping up Chiang Kai Shek and his corrupt cronies in 1949 against a people's movement in China. But do politicians ever study history or learn from it?

Elsewhere things looked similarly gloomy: the terrorist movement in Thailand was spreading unchecked with the Thai generals only interested in how deep they could dip their snouts into the American trough of plenty.

Neutral Laos was being bombed into a moonscape. Cambodia was suffering the same fate but ultimately would experience the self-annihilation of two-thirds of its population. Maoist terrorists in the Philippines were enjoying a new lease of life. The Domino Theory was on everyone's lips; if one country falls to the communist threat, they all fall.

The Americans I met at briefings were no longer so smug. Their foreheads were pale and greasy. Their mouths still uttered the same meaningless words of victory but there was no back-slapping. Their eyes were watery and lifeless. They knew they were beaten, humiliated by the unseen men in black pyjamas, but could not understand why.

Then in July 1971 a bombshell dropped: President Nixon announced that he would visit China. Such a momentous event was the prelude to a dramatic change in U.S. foreign policy. America's longest war was soon to be over. The Thai government, which had not been consulted, was horrified: its U.S.-backed anti-communist policy was in shreds and, as China moved quickly to join the United Nations in October that year, the Thais scurried to befriend China along with the rest of the world.

I had been in Thailand nearly four years now. It seemed a long time since Captain McPhee had said, "Look after yourself son, you'll grow up quickly here," as I stepped off the *Ben Nevis* into a new world, blinking in the tropical sun. But it also seemed as if my luck was turning against me. Was it that the East had finished with me? Just another young Englishman like so many who had gone before, who sowed his wild oats in the orient only to return to the motherland and conform. Was it time to return to London, cap in hand, and seek another perch at Baring Brothers?

My old friends were going their own ways. Vippy was to marry a promising young Thai diplomat and was soon to move to New York. The Souvanna Phoumas seemed settled in Laos. Peter and Sanda Simms were moving to Singapore. Plern had retreated to Chiang Mai fed up with her stubborn husband and her troublesome lover. But the play was not quite over; a few stings remained in the tail.

Once again I began to see the black Toyota Corona parked down the road from my house seeking some shade under a flame tree. Inside the two men smoked incessantly. Cigarette smoke curled through the car's open windows and hung in the hot still air. They were not there all the time and not every day, but frequently enough for me to realise that I was being watched.

Then one day I was invited to visit the Press Office at the Ministry of Information. I was welcomed by an urbane press officer who said that a special briefing had been arranged for me and would I care to accompany him? I was ushered into a large meeting room where I was regaled for over an hour with a detailed briefing on the Thai Government's war against narcotics. Statistics were produced showing how poppy cultivation had declined, photographs showing happy tribesmen growing coffee instead of poppies, maps illustrating how whole swathes of jungle had been cleared of narcotics. All very impressive, I said, but why had I been chosen to see this particular presentation, frequently trotted out to gullible correspondents from abroad?

An envelope slid across the glass surface of the table. Out of it spilt the contact prints of the pictures that I had taken in the north of Thailand when on safari with Tan Mair so many months previously. The same photographs that had so strangely disappeared from the photofinishing laboratory. There were colour photographs of poppy fields stretching endlessly over the northern hills, processing factories, mule trains laden with opium, smugglers and warlords, the whole infrastructure of Thailand's flourishing illicit drug industry. "It always pays to stick to the facts," the press officer murmured silkily and ambiguously as he scooped up the prints and put them safely back into his file.

This gentle warning was not sufficient however, for the Thais. I had inadvertently trampled on holy ground and must be deterred. I can surmise that the Thai generals may have exchanged a quiet word with their contacts in the American embassy in Bangkok, who in turn may have arranged to pass a discreet message to their equals in the British embassy in Washington for suddenly, quite unexpectedly, there was an urgent flurry of confidential cables and letters between my father in Washington and the new British ambassador in Bangkok. Apart from his single trip to the Far East and a solitary telephone call during the saga of the car accident, I had scarcely heard from my father for three years. Now he was taking time to write to the British ambassador in Bangkok desperately seeking ways to have me removed from Thailand with all haste.

Somebody had told my father that I had become involved in the drugs trade and the ambassador in Bangkok took it upon himself to do some research. He reported back that he could find no evidence and indeed, "whenever I have seen him he has appeared quite normal." But the ambassador saw me rarely because, in his words, "I was aware of his attitude towards officialdom." More telegrams flashed between Washington and Bangkok and evidently my father urged the ambassador to find a way to talk to me, but this he found difficult. The ambassador complained "when he comes to the Embassy on business, as he has to do from time to time, he makes a point of treating the visit as a strictly business one and leaves as soon as his business is done, avoiding any opportunity to linger and chat." In telegram number three (there were at least seven, maybe more) my father suggested that some form of "constraint" might be put upon me to leave Thailand. The ambassador was not keen, especially as he had earlier reported that he had heard no ill of me, "I am sure that before we think of any attempt at constraint every effort should be made to make him leave voluntarily."

Two weeks later the ambassador had a change of mind. He began to echo my father's concerns and wrote that new "facts" had come to his attention: "I have had more general reports which I am afraid are disturbing and which lead me to conclude that there must be substance in the gossip widespread in Bangkok that he has some connection with the drug traffic." He hastened to add that "I have no direct evidence of this" but could not resist adding more speculation: "An American woman resident here who was formerly a journalist....... has told a member of my staff that a group of journalists here believe that your son is actively engaged in trafficking drugs and are trying to unearth evidence which they can substantiate." But he did not want to wait until evidence was produced and cabled "I am bound to suggest to you," he reported to his colleague in Washington, "that we should now take steps to get him out of Thailand." He was hatching a plan: "I think it might be possible to cause enough quiet pressure to be put on him ...... to convince him that it was best to get out. We have the right high-level contacts with the police and immigration authorities and I think they might be prepared to cooperate."

What was going on here? The hunter had become the hunted. But who was doing the hunting? Were the Thais acting on their own initiative or was the misguided ambassador in Bangkok raising the stakes with the Thai authorities? An expedition into the heart of the Golden Triangle and a couple of dozen rolls of film seemed to have opened a floodgate of official mischief. An attempt had been made to brand me as a trafficker of drugs: a career choice which had never entered my mind. Someone had turned the tables: what better than to discredit the inquisitive journalist by painting him with the same brush as those he was investigating?

Not for nothing had my colleagues in the Foreign Correspondents' Club warned me off writing a story on the drugs business in Thailand. It was too close to the power, the money, the generals. Just too dangerous, many people had died for less in Thailand. Others might have been shot walking down a *soi* one dark night, or killed in a traffic jam by a hired gunman, or a grenade thrown into a bedroom by an unseen assassin. For me the officials had turned to other methods: no investigative article had appeared, no generals had been interviewed so no harm had been perpetrated as yet, but there were those troublesome photographs. Few people in those days had penetrated the opium fields as I had done with Tan Mair. Some of the people I had photographed had not liked having their pictures taken. The photographic laboratory had a lot to answer for!

The name of H.M. ambassador's mysterious American woman informant was never revealed. I knew many Americans in Bangkok, as the city was flooded with them, but it was very unlikely that an 'ex-journalist' would be offering her services to the British embassy to unearth evidence that I was involved in the drugs business. It all seemed too preposterous to be plausible, but the two ambassadors, one in Washington and one in Bangkok, were becoming increasingly frenzied in their mutual hysteria.

It was more probable that the conniving Thais had leaked a little information to the Americans or the British that a certain journalist had been

THE SON FROM THE WEST

poking his nose too closely into their business and the photographs provided all the evidence that they needed. The ambassadors thought they were taking the initiative but, with the benefit of hindsight, it seems they may have just been pawns in a much larger game.

By this time news had filtered back to me that the British embassy were creating some trouble and I thought that a call on the ambassador might be useful. The ambassador reported to Washington: "Evelyn looked perfectly fit and, although I claim no expertise in these matters, he showed no sign of the dissipation which one would expect from drug-taking." He sounded a little disappointed but he was not going to give up easily. He contacted the very same police general who had proved so unhelpful the previous year over the car accident. He was still very much in favour at the embassy in Ploenchit Road. The ambassador reported to my father that "quite by chance (!) I ran into a police Major-General who has been most friendly with this embassy for as long as anyone here can remember...... I asked him whether he had any reports on Evelyn's behaviour and he said that he himself had investigated the matter and was happy to assure me that he had nothing on Evelyn on that score."

So that should have spelled the end of the matter, but the two ambassadors were not so easily appeased. The ambassador in Bangkok in particular seemed keen to have me off his patch. He thought that he might raise the matter with the Thai Foreign Minister but would only do this with the permission of the British Permanent Undersecretary of State and would my father like to have a word? He was not deterred in the slightest by the fact that "the Thais have nothing against Evelyn of a criminal nature (eg drugs) [so] they will not take the initiative to get him out of the country or prevent his return" so perhaps it would be better if the British took the law into their own hands! The ambassador in Bangkok began to think that he had bitten off more than he could chew. The Thais, he wrote, "would have grave reservations about taking such an action against Lord Cromer's son. I do not think I exaggerate in saying that there is probably no present Minister who would do this without the personal sanction of the King." So, and here we have the essence, "if an initiative is taken it must therefore come from us."

But then it seemed the ambassadors lost interest in their mayhem. The last correspondence on file was a letter from my father who wrote "if he [Evelyn] questions me on my sources of information ...... I will merely tell him that I have a number of sources of information in that part of the World [sic], some American. This is in the bounds of the truth as indeed I have."

Thus ended a particularly scurrilous episode which could have been resolved easily by a little plain talking, but is typical of the mindset of the British Foreign Office. With very few exceptions, I found British embassies or high commissions in the various countries in which I lived to be hives of misinformation and inaccurate gossip. It was to be some years before I learned to turn their natural tendency towards a casual interpretation of the facts to my advantage. Their main difficulty appeared to be an over-reliance on obsolete contacts, a deeply embedded arrogance and an instinct to deal only with local anglophiles who tended to feed the diplomats with whatever would please their ears. Other countries must face the same problems but have learned to be objective; the British seemed too steeped in tradition to open their eyes a little wider.

I was never popular with British expatriates: I did not join their clubs, avoided their social gatherings, and showed no interest in their sporting activities. I had not travelled around the world to seek out a little England. I was more interested in becoming involved in the countries where I lived, in meeting the indigenous people and learning their ways. The result was that the British tended to gossip, often invent some incredulous stories about me, and generally behave in a peevish manner. Thailand was my first experience of this attitude but it was to be repeated in other places over the coming years.

In the meantime Tan Mair had chosen to fade into the background. She had grown remote from her 'Son from the West' since the car accident the previous year. During that trauma, fearing embarrassment, she had elected to distance herself. My preoccupation with Plern was a disappointment to her: she did not approve of the liaison and frequently remonstrated with me but I was stubborn and to spare further disputes I saw her less and less. My frequent trips to Vietnam caused her further worry as she lost sight of me. She had formed a discreet liaison with my parents and had kept them informed of my activities, but now she felt that she had somehow let them down.

Tan Chai, perhaps never altogether approving of my close relationship with Tan Mair, sensed the change and bided his time.

19

T'at Dam Pagoda

At about the same time as Plern and Sakda returned to Bangkok from England, so also did Vippy return from perfecting her German in Munich, and a new celebrity arrived in town in the form of a lissom Salika Siddhisariputra from Paris. Sali was a Thai beauty in every way: tall, elegant and much in demand as a model on the catwalk circuit. She was fun, gregarious and intelligent. Although she might have fallen prey to the 'Jardine Johnnies' at the Royal Bangkok Sports Club, she was far too bright to be taken in by the transient expatriate male and preferred to select her own companions.

It was not long before she attracted the eye of Prince Panya. They were a good match: Panya was dashing, good-looking, cosmopolitan and with a superior bearing that comes naturally to those of royal birth in the Far East. Generous to a fault, he took great pleasure in entertaining his friends to the last Lao *kip* in his wallet. His father entrusted him with many responsibilities, from managing the Lao national water works and irrigation schemes on the Mekong River to running the national airline, Royal Air Laos. Perhaps something of a dilettante to the more serious minds in the American embassy, to his friends in their twenties he provided boundless hospitality and entertainment.

Plern and I took to making monthly trips to Vientiane, the capital of Laos, by train from Bangkok. The 'express' left in the evening from Hualomphong Station with Vippy, Sali and Plern on board seen off by their respective parents and husband while I discreetly met the train at Don Muang, a station twenty miles up the track. We would arrive at Nongkhai on the banks of the Mekong early the next morning and cross the river by ferry to be met by Panya.

Panya lived in a villa beside the *T'at Dam* Pagoda, a stone *stupa* on a grassy circle in a quiet area in the middle of Vientiane. He slept on a mattress on the floor, an assault rifle on one side, Sali on the other. These were lazy, hazy days of sunshine and wine, authentic French food for lunch, Chinese delicacies for dinner (including whole baby pigeons stuffed with birds' nest: a dish renowned throughout Asia). We water-skiied on the muddy Mekong and swam with the French colonials in the swimming pool of the splendid but crumbling Lan Xang [million elephants] Hotel.

Frequently we dined with Panya's father at *La Residence*, the prime minister's official house beside the Mekong. Government ministers, visiting foreign politicians and dignitaries and ambassadors were all regular guests. Laos had become a critical pawn in the political game that had engulfed South-East Asia. The prime minister used to deliberate aloud as to how ironic it was that his country, formerly a French colonial backwater, was now being courted by the great powers. The Americans were anxious to shore up the regime to prevent a domino from falling, the Russians ponderously supported their North Vietnamese allies a few hundred miles away, while the French had seen it all before and prophesied doom. But nobody seemed to quite know what the British were doing in their large embassy except that the ambassador was writing a book on the Mekong's unusual freshwater fish (the largest in the world, he claimed). Memories were rife of the French defeat at Dien Bien Phu in 1954 and the French colonials, sipping their Ricards in Vientiane's road-side cafes, smugly predicted that the American military excursion in Vietnam would end the same way.

The Souvanna Phoumas spoke French *en famille* and had acquired the very best French habits. Panya was adept at preparing *pate de fois gras* and his speciality was a leg of lamb so lightly roasted that the flesh still quivered. His father ceremoniously mixed Roquefort cheese with cognac to be enjoyed after dinner. While the best French wines were served the conversation inevitably centred on politics.

After dinner we generally visited Monsieur Fab, a diminutive shrivelled Vietnamese who owned an opium den in a wooden house in the centre of Vientiane. There we would sit on the plank floor with M. Fab cross-legged on a straw mat in the centre of the room surrounded by his paraphernalia. He would hold a marble-sized amber-coloured ball of raw opium over a candle until it softened and turned viscous when he would spin off a small amount on a long needle which he would rotate over the candle until it began to smoke. Then one or other of us would stretch out on the mat, rest our head on the hard opium-smoker's pillow and hold the ivory pipe to our lips. As M. Fab inserted the needle into the pipe's bowl delivering a small pellet of smoking opium, one would begin a slow, long intake of breath. That single breath had to be sufficient to inhale all the smoke from the burning pellet. The result was an inhalation so deep that one's lungs completely filled with smoke.

Most of us could only manage three or four pipes an evening, but the Lao could smoke many more. Panya often smoked twenty or more pipes in the course of the night. The opium was a stimulant and activated the brain. The war was won many times over every evening. Everybody participated: government ministers, diplomats, businessmen: it seemed that it was *chez M. Fab* where most of the Lao society congregated several times every week. There was nothing illicit or underhand about smoking opium in Laos. It was a deeply ingrained custom and an essential part of their culture, as it was in most of the neighbouring countries.

Then came the day when Panya and Sali were to marry. The Lao prince and the Thai beauty created a great stir amongst the socialites of both countries. Television crews from around the world came to broadcast the long, formal and colourful ceremony. For reasons that escape me I was invited to be the best man though many others were more qualified. I borrowed Tan Chai's *jonggrabane*, a complicated tunic worn in Thai court circles for centuries consisting of a length of silk wound around the lower body, passed through the legs and tucked into itself behind. It looked and felt very insecure, threatening to unravel in mid-ceremony.

The newly married couple settled into the villa at *T'at Dam* Pagoda. Sali started a boutique, children arrived and all was peaceful in that oasis in the heart of Vientiane while storm clouds gathered outside as the war in Vietnam escalated and began to spread into Laos. There was a sense of *fin de siecle*. It was all too peaceful to last.

My last trip to visit the Souvanna Phoumas was in 1972. I flew from Bangkok in Royal Air Laos' only Caravelle jet, unique in that a parachute was deployed when the plane landed to provide additional braking as the aircraft had no reverse thrust.

Panya met me at the airport and drove into town. A new friend accompanied him: a Lao girl in her teens wearing black trousers, a black shirt and with long black locks cascading to her waist. She was of such astonishing beauty that she left me gasping for air. Panya did not introduce us, perhaps intentionally. They spoke French softly to each other while driving into town. Panya stopped the car near the centre of Vientiane and let her out. She turned, waved and caught my eye for a second. It was a look that froze in my memory. I could not have guessed that we were to meet again years later under very different circumstances.

Some months later I was back in Luang Prabang. I stumbled across some Americans in a bar who had become maudlin over their Tiger beers imported from Singapore. They had been manning a secret communications base in the

Lao jungle guiding squadrons of B-52 bombers on their way to North Vietnam. The northeast provinces of neutral Laos had suffered badly during the war. For years American bombers jettisoned their bombs over Laos on their way back to their Thai bases if they had failed to find a target in Vietnam or if they were frustrated by the weather.

Some of the most pristine tropical rain forests in the world were rendered a barren mountainous desert where only elephant grass now grew.

"It's all over, yer know. Just like that," one of the crew-cut Americans grunted, clicking his fingers. "One moment we're bombing the hell out of the gooks, the next we're told to leave. No packing. No explanation. Just get the hell out."

"Shit! And did we have them on the run!" said the other.

"Fucking politicos," said the first. "What a way to run a war."

As the war began to wind down in Vietnam, the first hints of American retreat were detected in Laos as the Americans abandoned the clandestine bases whose very existence had been denied for so long. The Americans were declaring a victory but to those on the ground it looked very different. Soon it was to turn into a rout as the South Vietnamese army crumbled without American support and the North Vietnamese swept in.

When I got back to Vientiane, the city was rife with rumours: the Pathet Lao had come out of the jungle and were dancing in the streets (the city looked particularly quiet to me), the North Vietnamese army was massing on the North Vietnam/Lao border (true), the Americans were evacuating their vast sprawling airconditioned base outside Vientiane (true) and the King was dead (not proven for some time). Nobody had yet grasped the prospect of the real horror of the reprisals and forced 're-education' camps that were to become a feature of life in Laos for the next decade.

That night we dined as usual at *La Residence* with the old Prince, the prime minister. It was an historic evening. He had an unusual guest: his half-brother Prince Souphannavong, the leader of the communist Pathet Lao, who had finally come out of the jungle after living for years in caves dodging American bombs and murder squads. The two half-brothers, who had plotted and schemed against each other for so long, shared cigars and reminisced as if they had never been separated.

After dinner the Roquefort cheese and cognac were mixed as usual by the prime minister. The two princes put their feet up and gazed out over the Mekong as distant gun-fire rattled in the city.

"Oh well," said Panya, "Let's see if Monsieur Fab is still in business."

He was.

20

The Curtain Drops

It was September 1971 and the telephone rang on my desk in Bangkok. Tan Mair was on the line, she sounded hesitant, almost shy. I had not spoken to her for several months. She said Tan Chai had gone 'upcountry'. Could I drop by the *Wang* that evening?

I drove slowly down Silom Road, the three-wheeled *tuk-tuks* overtaking me, their thin, wiry drivers glancing sideways to see why the *farang* was not participating in Bangkok's twenty-four hour grand prix. The car filled with exhaust from the buses racing passed, passengers clinging to the open doors and window frames. I drove down Rama IV Road and turned left into Vidyu Road. I looked across the garbage-encrusted lake in Lumphini Park to see the sun sinking into the thick soup of humidity and smog that covered Bangkok on most days. It was a familiar sight and one that I had grown to love. It was my home now, this mad, seething, broiling city. I had got to know its many characteristics, the way it worked, its eccentricities and its beauty.

The *Wang* seemed strangely neglected. Gone was the army of servants and retainers. Only Tao, Tan Mair's personal maid, and Eart, the maid who had received me that far off day so many years before, remained. Desiccated teak leaves rustled restlessly in the monsoon drains. Weeds were growing through the gaps in the paving stones. One of the shutters was hanging askew. The large house felt unloved, deserted, its spirit gone. A *towkair*, a giant lizard, croaked loudly from behind a pillar.

That night at the *Wang*, Tan Mair had made a special effort. Nying, who by now was the proud proprietor of a Rangsit-sponsored Cordon Bleu cooking school, had prepared a western meal for us, a rare treat. As usual, I walked through the back entrance into the cavernous kitchen with its netted food-safes standing in little saucers of water to keep the ants at bay. Seemohk, Tan Mair's Great Dane, lollopped over and started to lick my hand, delighted to see a familiar face.

"*Sawaddi ka*, Tan Lord," said Nying in her invariably mocking way, smiling broadly. "What have you done today to please your Tan Mair so much?" She leaned against the black wooden door frame, a red sarong reached to her bare feet. Her thick hair was tied behind her head in a luxuriant pony tail. Nying was my first friend in Thailand and I had grown to love her ways over the years. She had been a constant shadow to Tan Mair, accompanying her on every trip into the jungle, on every shopping expedition to Paris. Nying had guided me through my chaotic life in Thailand; we held no secrets. We had shared so much for so long but I knew Nying had also become disappointed with me as my path had led away from the *Wang*. She thought I had let her down, she could not understand that people and events had moved on. She wanted, as we all do, for time to stop.

It was a particularly hot evening and Tan Mair and I ate at a round table on the marble terrace at the back of the *Wang*. Tao and Eart shuffled soundlessly across the floor on their knees serving Nying's exquisite cooking. We overlooked the *klong* with its rare Victoriana water lilies so proudly sunk by Tan Mair months previously. I forget now what we talked about. It was a quiet evening, the constant whirring of the cicadas punctured by the calls from the vendors walking down Soi Ruamrudee on the other side of the *klong*. Although we were in the centre of Bangkok, the *Wang*'s vast gardens made it seem as if we were deep in the jungle once again.

After dinner we walked slowly into her drawing room, the same room where we had met four years before. We sat barefoot on the Persian rug given to her by the Empress Farah Diba of Iran and admired the rug's brilliant turquoise border. We talked haltingly about our adventures in the jungle distributing the King's Bounty and all the people we had met, water-skiing on the river and the many journeys and excitements that we had shared over the previous four years. A single candle flickered, casting moving shadows onto the walls. She was nervous, fidgeting with the large emerald cut diamond she had bought to console herself when Tan Chai started to spend more and more time 'upcountry'. The diamond cast shards of coloured candle light into her dark eyes.

"Evelyn," she murmured, "you know that the time has come."

Her eyes filled with tears which she tried unsuccessfully to blink away. She bowed her head to avoid my eyes. Her tears dripped onto her mauve silk shirt making little dark circles.

"We did have fun, didn't we?" She looked at me imploringly. "You were a good student, you know," she hesitated and then added with a slight smile, "and a good teacher too."

In a few words Tan Mair had accomplished what the two ambassadors had been striving for months to achieve. I knew in my heart that it was time to move on.

I walked slowly down the *Wang*'s marble steps for the last time, lost in thought and memories.

PART TWO

Singapore, The Philippines and Hong Kong

1972–1979

1

Consolidated Commercial

Before we left Bangkok Plern and I decided to get married. I asked Tan Mair whether Tan Chai could formally approach Plern's father to ask for permission as this was the custom in Thailand. He reluctantly agreed. Tan Mair wrote to my mother, "Evelyn wants my husband to represent his father because it is customary here that the father of the man goes and asks the girl's parents for her hand. My husband grumbles a bit, saying if he jilts her the good doctor and his wife [Plern's parents] will kill him. I am a little worried knowing Evelyn as I do." Tan Mair was resolutely against the marriage. She was to write again to my mother, "they are badly starred together, no good will come of it.....Evelyn has his moods and he needs a strong and intelligent girl to deal with them. A sweet, well-brought up, pretty creature with long hair is not enough." A comment, I thought, that scarcely did justice to Plern's lively intelligence.

Plern and I were eventually married at the Tunbridge Wells Registry Office on October 25th, 1971. We were both twenty-five. There were few guests. Geordie Gordon and Vippy's sister Priya were the witnesses. My sister gave a small party after the civil ceremony. None of our parents attended. My grandfather, the newspaper tycoon, was not amused. He wrote to my mother, "The whole episode has made me feel sick and I want to forget about it. Evelyn might have tried to make it look respectable by asking some members of the family to be present but bad taste ruled to the last[1]. I am getting too old to understand the young. I have not yet met your daughter-in-law and don't intend to be in a hurry to do so."

We found ourselves in London with no home, no employment and no money. But good fortune strikes at unexpected times. The night before we left Bangkok a few weeks before our wedding, we had dined with Panya and Sali. Salika's father, Khun Prasit, turned pensive when he heard that we had nowhere to stay in London. He was a much-propertied man with houses and flats in

---

[1] A most hypocritical comment: he had caused considerable distress in the family by marrying Mary Ohrstrom, his third wife, in complete secrecy only a few years earlier, he aged 79 and she 17.

Switzerland, London and elsewhere. Neither Plern nor I knew Khun Prasit well but evidently our plight must have appealed to memories of his own youth as he took me on one side and invited me to stay in his empty flat in London. He brushed off any mention of rent, "No, stay there as my guests. Shall we say six months? All I ask is you give me a bed when I pass through London occasionally."

Khun Prasit's flat overlooked the River Thames in Barnes, a fifteen minute drive from the centre of London. It was modern, had two bedrooms, a spectacular view and was our home for the next six months.

Once married I needed to find a more regular source of income than working as a freelance journalist. There was always the possibility that I could seek my father's cooperation and return to the high desks and dusty managers in the dungeons of Baring Brothers in Bishopsgate but this had to be the last resort. But once again Geordie Gordon stepped into my life; I had not seen him since I left England four years previously but friendships can survive long absences. His brother, Andrew, was starting a new business and asked whether I would like to join his fledgling team. He was a little vague as to what sort of business it was and anyway I had little experience as a businessman. He said it might be a wild ride, but quite how wild I was to find out as the years unfolded.

Andy was a stocky man with prematurely balding dark hair, a booming and infectious laugh and immense charm. He was in his early thirties, had been married briefly to a Sri Lankan belly-dancer and seemed to have an infinite supply of long-legged blondes pursuing him down every street in London. Andy was a man who firmly believed in form over substance.

He had just acquired the leasehold of 21 Charles Street, just off Berkeley Square in the centre of Mayfair. It was a large four-story Georgian mansion undergoing a make-over by Muriel, an Amazon-like interior decorator, a giant in reputation and size, who sailed through the house daily like a Spanish galleon scattering the ranks of artisans, carpenters, painters and plumbers as flotsam in her wake. She scoured the nearby auction-rooms acquiring rare and eclectic works of art as if they were groceries.

A Bentley Continental with liveried driver hovered outside in Charles Street, while Dewhurst, Andy's batman-cum-butler awaited his master's call in the pink marble kitchen, itself some twice the size of Khun Prasit's flat.

The early 1970s were boom-times for a new type of businessman: the asset stripper. Now an established practice, in those days these latter-day buccaneers were ruffling the cosy clubs of industrial boardrooms across the country. 'King' stripper was Jim Slater, a Henry Kravis prototype, while legendary property dealer Black Jack Dellal was the prince of strippers. There were hundreds of wannabe Jims and Jacks filling the pink pages of the Financial Times daily, buying up 'shell' public companies, desperately seeking assets to strip, their highly valued paper cascading over the City of London like confetti.

This was the sort of oxygen on which Andy thrived. He had already achieved something of a reputation as an entrepreneur and had been through a few ups and downs, but each up had been higher than the one before. Now it was his turn to take control of a public company and the unlikely victim was a particularly bland company by the name of Consolidated Commercial. CCC, as we came to call it, owned only two assets and neither was strippable: forty-nine percent of a biscuit factory in Nigeria, and all of a grain silo in Liverpool. Synergy was not a concept that applied to either CCC or Andy's view of corporate philosophy.

The biscuits were popular in Nigeria and the factory paid large dividends, but the profits could not be remitted outside Nigeria, so much to Andy's considerable frustration there the funds remained. CCC appeared to the shareholders to be flush with cash: there was no hint that the funds were stuck in a bank in Lagos. The grain silo on the other hand produced steady and consistent profits that were mainly channelled into Muriel's capacious hands and transformed into Regency mirrors, Louis XIV furniture and a dazzling array of baubles, trinkets and beads.

There was a blurred line between Andy's personal belongings and the company's assets, a line which became increasingly hazy until the day came when the house of cards collapsed and the Department of Trade & Industry inspectors called, but that was to be sometime in the future. It was a line, I discovered later in my commercial career, that was not only crossed by the buccaneers of the 1970s: in fact within many companies, even amongst the most revered, the higher echelons in the corporation have little respect for their shareholders when opportunities come to feather their own nests. Lip-service was always paid to the noble tenets of increasing shareholder value and returning profits to shareholders but I rarely saw evidence of this hype turning into reality.

Meanwhile the trusty grain merchants of Liverpool worked away primarily to finance the decoration of a palace in Charles Street. And a palace it was: the first three floors offered reception rooms amongst the finest in London, whilst the top floor was the nerve centre of CCC. There Andy had his lair in a large sunny room whose massive floor boards had been hewn from a rare and protected species of tree only found on southwest-facing Andean slopes of Peru. In a single room at the back were the rest of the team: an ex-Heinz executive gambling with his career, a wide-boy stock trader, and myself.

We pored over balance sheets and profit-and-loss accounts into the small hours searching for the holy grail: a public company with undervalued assets, a board of slumbering directors and acquiescent shareholders willing to sell their shares in exchange for overvalued CCC paper and Andy's smile. And Andy was good at the talk: the CCC share price had gone from 19p when I joined the company to 36p within six weeks. Newspapers were commenting favourably and he was occasionally invited to the high table to chat with King Jim's boys but, in spite of the talk, deals failed to materialise. Not for lack of trying.

There was a constant stream of visitors to Charles Street who gazed in awe at the affluence and taste on display, were treated to Andy's widest smile and loudest laugh, and listened to Andy's breathless vision of CCC's global ambitions. The punch line was always the same: "Sell me your business. It is better to have a small piece of a big cake than all of a small cake."

In the meanwhile with my new found job-security, Plern and I had moved out of Prasit's flat, taken on a mortgage and bought a small house in South Kensington. We were beginning to settle down. Plern liked London and I missed the Orient less as time went by. But London was still a gloomy place for me. I would frequently stare out of the rain-streaked windows at five o'clock in the darkening afternoon, watching passers-by wrestle with their umbrellas in the wind and the hail, and imagine myself swimming in the tepid, crystal waters of the Gulf of Siam.

One day Andy called me into his office. He was sitting in a leather armchair smoking a ten-inch Cohiba cigar, wearing Yves St. Laurent jeans and a Dunhill golfing shirt, Gucci loafers resting on the table. He slid the Financial Times across the two thousand year old table's marble surface, recently rescued by Muriel from the ruins of a Roman administrator's villa in Ephesus. It seemed that the Jims and Jacks had discovered the Far East. Some Slater acolytes had taken control of Haw Par, the revered manufacturer of Tiger Balm in Singapore and had discovered a whole new cornucopia of under-valued assets ripe for stripping.

"What about it? You're the expert on the Far East."

"Well, yes, but I was just the assistant editor of a business magazine in Bangkok."

"So you must know all about doing deals out there."

Andy had recently suffered a few setbacks in his plans for CCC but that morning he was reinvigorated. A new plan was in the making and Andy paced up and down the room with excitement. He had a new vision: CCC's first global step outside Liverpool and Nigeria was to be a foothold in the Far East.

"We'll steal a march on the others. Pack your bags. We'll leave on Monday. The FT says this Haw Par is in Singapore. We'll go to Bangkok first and then to Singapore. Get weaving!" He had already reached for the telephone to call his blonde long-legged travel agent.

Thus are great commercial initiatives launched.

Three days later Andy and I found ourselves peering into the 'goldfish bowl' at the Mona Lisa Massage and Sauna in Bangkok. Andy was staring open-mouthed, not unlike a goldfish himself, at the several hundred girls sitting in the amphitheatre on the other side of the oceanarium-size window where young girls in bikinis, one-piece swimming costumes or negligees, were painting their nails, gossiping, playing cards, smoking or posing for the invisible customers on the other side of the one-way mirror. Andy had never seen anything like it. He was bewildered by the multitude of assets to strip.

I nudged him, "Come on Andy, make your choice." As soon as he pointed at one, a quicker client had already called her number and she was on her way out of the door, but then an even more beautiful girl would enter from the other side: he was spoilt for choice. Finally he selected number 138, a solemn but pretty girl with short hair framing her face and pale skin. They walked together up the staircase towards the private rooms hand in hand. He was bulky and western, she was slight and oriental, her head not quite reaching his shoulders.

One is allocated an hour for a bath and massage before a bell rings and the fun is over. When my hour was finished I sat in front of the 'goldfish bowl', one amongst several other clients waiting for their friends. There was no sign of Andy and I assumed that he had extended his bath by another hour. I watched the girls coming and going. They were a happy group smiling and laughing, teasing and playfully pushing each other. If they had been sold into slavery and forced to work in a bathhouse in Bangkok, as newspapers in England would have us believe, then they were certainly making the best of it. The truth is that for most of them it was just another job, a well-paid job too, and in clean air-conditioned surroundings. Most of them sent money back to their families in the countryside, built houses, bought fruit orchards, a BMW and some jewellery. Then aged thirty or so, when it was all over, they returned to their villages and lived on the orchard, opened a coffee shop or hair salon and became respectable.

By now Andy was into his third hour. I was about to call him to say I was going back to the hotel when he appeared, smile unwavering, number 138 clinging to his arm.

"Evelyn, help me out can you? She can't speak a word of English, but I want to bring her back to the hotel tonight." In Bangkok most things can be arranged but amongst the few impossibilities would be to smuggle a massage girl into the staid formality of the Oriental Hotel.

"Now, Andy, that is just not going to be possible......" I started but was interrupted by a wave of the hand.

"Nonsense. Please tell Wannee to get changed. She's coming with me." I explained to the girl what Andy had said and she looked doubtful, or rather Andy thought she looked doubtful. I knew her brain was working like a calculator. This was not a girl who was going to take things on trust and Andy was clearly not a Bangkok resident.

"Five thousand Baht," she said, quoting a figure at least eight times the going rate.

I started to negotiate in the time-honoured way but Andy looked shocked, almost offended, and took ten thousand Baht out of his wallet and thrust the wad of notes into her hand.

Sneaking her into the Oriental Hotel was easier than I had thought. All it required was a thick roll of 500 Baht notes distributed fairly evenly between doormen, security guards, front office staff, receptionists, the manager on duty, more security guards, the lift boy and even more security guards.

The next morning Andy brought number 138 to the Oriental Hotel's formal dining room for breakfast. Daylight did not flatter her, and with her mauve mini-skirt, orange skimpy top and tottering heels she hardly looked like a typical Oriental Hotel guest.

"Evelyn, I love this soft jewel," whispered Andy in the hushed silence of the dining room. He was holding her hand under the table. "She has had such a difficult life and I would really, really like to help her."

"But Andy, I know she is lovely, and all the girls in the Mona Lisa have had hard lives or they wouldn't be working there."

"No, this little peach needs to be rescued and I am lucky that I am in a position to do something to help," said Andy as visions of Nigerian biscuits and Liverpudlian workers labouring away at the grain silo flashed in front of my mind. "Tell her that I would like to give her as much money as she needs to leave the Mona Lisa. I will send her a monthly allowance from now on."

Now this was something one just did not do in Bangkok. I tried to remonstrate but he would only stare into her eyes and tell me to get on with the translation.2

We spent three days in Bangkok, during which I scarcely saw Andy. We then headed south to Singapore. There we were met by some of Jim's or Jack's boys and invited out for dinner with some B-list Singaporean movie stars. Andy, only just recovering from his exhausting schedule in Bangkok, was once again at his most charming. He was intending to pick the brains of the entrepreneurs at dinner, keen to identify opportunities for CCC, but his attention was distracted during dinner by an Eurasian model who took him by the hand in the middle of the main course and led him out of the restaurant.

---

2 Andy honoured his word and contined to send number 138 an allowance for some years but she never left her work at the Mona Lisa.

I did not see Andy for another forty-eight hours. Just before we were due to leave the hotel for the airport and the long flight back to London, he called my room.

"Right, Evelyn," he yawned down the telephone,. "I have finished my research and I've decided that what CCC needs most is a deal in the Far East. Bangkok or Singapore will do fine. I will get the merchant banks working on it." Then after a moment's hesitation he added "Now I know what kept you in the Far East all those years. You lucky dog!"

The next chapter in my life had started; I was on my way back to the East.

2
Outsider to Winner

Investment bankers were a rarity in the Far East in those days, but were soon to become as common as spots on an adolescent's face. The family-owned businesses that dominated corporate life in the area saw no point in them – they could deal amongst themselves in their own languages without hiring some highly-paid *farang* to tell them how to do it. In 1969 my father stationed a Barings executive with the Hong Kong & Shanghai Bank to advise on business potential for merchant banks in the Far East. Although Barings had an unrivalled portfolio of clients with Far Eastern interests and was well-placed to ride the crest of the wave of economic growth that was gathering momentum in East Asia, the executive returned to London with the advice that it would be many years before the region would be ready for London investment bankers.

The next year Flemings, a rival British investment bank, formed a joint-venture in Hong Kong with Jardine Matheson, in which it will be recalled Barings had a substantial financial interest, and the race was on. Within a very few years all the major London investment banks had formed strategic alliances with Asian institutions and were touting their wares. Barings was left to catch up.

Thus are great commercial opportunities lost.

Our small team in Charles Street began the process of scouring Singapore for an undervalued public company. Andy had a sneaking preference for Bangkok but the absence of a working stock market created few opportunities for the asset stripper. The Singapore government was beginning to understand what asset stripping meant: it certainly was not honest foreign investment as first thought. It was almost colonial in its reach and that was something that the Singaporeans were not going to brook. To them it looked like a gang of British opportunists riding into town with borrowed money, buying up solid Chinese companies, inflating prices, selling off assets patiently acquired over generations by hard-working Chinese immigrants and then flying back to London with suitcases bulging, never to be seen again. And that was precisely what Jim's and Jack's boys had in mind, with Andy pawing at the ground anxious to join the party.

I suggested to Andy that the Singaporeans could be harsh on those who did not play by their rules and the strict regime on the island could make life difficult if one was to fall foul of their views on foreign investment.

"Nonsense," was Andy's response, showing me another Financial Times article lauding further successes by one of Jim's boys who had just acquired another Singaporean public company, "if they can do it, I can do it."

Many trips to Singapore followed and a new manager joined our team: David Evans, a solid corporate salary-man who had never been east of Margate, was seduced from his reliable middle-management career and persuaded by Andy that he was the man to lead our challenge into the Far East. *end GB 4*

We fell into somewhat dubious company from the start. Tan Sri Khoo Teck Phuat was on his way to becoming the second richest man in Singapore. Reputed to be the thirteenth son of a Chinese rice trader, he evidently thought large families had their advantages as he is reported to have spawned a total of fourteen children of his own. Khoo, a Malaysian, had a chequered career as a banker and had recently been forced to cede control over Malaysia's largest bank after a run on deposits caused by uncertainties over extensive loans to Khoo's family businesses. Such *legerdemain* was to be repeated in 1986 when the Brunei government took over another Khoo-controlled bank when it was discovered that ninety percent of its total lending had been granted once again to Khoo's family businesses without collateral or documentation. Khoo's only recognised son served a two year prison sentence in Brunei for conspiring to defraud the bank. Khoo was not a man to be trifled with.

Khoo was an unprepossessing man of small stature, pebble glasses and little charm. In fact he was the antithesis of Andy, master of the firm handshake, the intimate pat on the back, the big smile. But Andy's charm failed to make an impression on Khoo's impassive features. Khoo saw Andy as prey, ready to be stripped of his money. It was the wealthy Asian asset creator versus the English asset stripper. Neither understood each other: Khoo thought Andy had more money than sense, whereas Andy had much sense but little money. Andy thought he could tempt Khoo into CCC's grand design with the bigger cake theory, but Khoo had all the cake he needed.

After the debacle in Malaysia, Khoo channelled much of his substantial fortune into the hotel industry in Singapore. Amongst a plethora of other businesses, he controlled three public companies whose sole assets were hotels. These companies always traded at a premium to their underlying asset value. This may have been due to the allure surrounding the Khoo name, or possibly due to speculation that one day the hotels would be replaced by more profitable shopping centres or luxury apartment blocks.

The hotels relied on the sandy foundations of the tourist trade. Few tourists visited Singapore as a destination; there was little to see or do on the small island at the tip of Malaysia in the Straits of Malacca. It was a resting place for the tired traveller en route between Europe and Australia. All the BOAC, Qantas and Malaysia-Singapore Airlines flights stopped in Singapore for crew changes, and often travel agents would include a couple of free nights in Singapore into the cost of the ticket to Australia. The hotel business in Singapore was a down-market, tight margin industry susceptible to the variable winds of the economies of Europe and Australia.

Khoo surrounded himself with a small army of sycophants of dubious quality, amongst whom were teams of 'creative' accountants. Andy and his imported lawyers and investment bankers spent interminable hours negotiating with Khoo's men over imaginatively constructed profit and cash-flow projections but try as he did, Andy still could not find any undervalued assets. Far from it, every asset that Khoo owned seemed to have a price tag far in excess of any reasonable valuation.

Andy was not to be deterred however: if Jim's and Jack's boys had succeeded in Singapore, then so would he. One of Khoo's toadies was a Hokkien Chinese with a glass eye who purported to be a management consultant. One evening he cornered Andy in his hotel suite and muttered that he could introduce Andy to a prominent family in Singapore who controlled a small flush of public companies. One of them, a building materials manufacturer, might be for sale. I warned Andy that 'One-eye Chan' had done time in Changi Prison for criminal breach of trust, but Andy fixed me with a tired look and admonished me for having old-world values.

So we were introduced to the three remaining Yong brothers; there had been a fourth but he was killed racing a rare 'D-type' Jaguar in the Johore Grand Prix in 1967. The Yongs had built a substantial business out of construction and property development, a route to riches familiar to many emigrants from China. The Yong cast of characters was headed by Yong Nam Seng, sombrely respectable with his dark suits, polished shoes, slippery manners and lugubrious hangdog expression. Nam Seng was the brother brought out to deal with the politicians, negotiate the government's public/private 'Urban Renewal' development projects and smooth over troubled waters while projecting a thin veneer of sophistication. Younger brother Yong Tet Miaow, commonly known as 'T.M.', was the rough and tough brother responsible for the family-owned construction business. Oleaginous, he waddled around the construction sites keeping the workers in order; one would not pick a fight with T.M. In a co-starring role was Micky, a half-brother who did not get on well with either Nam Seng or T.M. and had not shared in the family wealth. Micky was a loudmouthed salesman, given to making expansive statements and sweeping gestures, a wagging toothpick permanently lodged between his teeth.

The Yongs owned a majority interest in Malaysia Tile Manufacturing Company Limited, a publicly-quoted ceramic tile factory in Singapore. MTM had been set up to provide bathroom tiles to Singapore's booming construction industry and that meant primarily the Housing and Development Board, a government department charged with building low-cost high-rise housing for Singaporeans. At that time the government was committed to moving the inhabitants of the Malay village *kampongs* and the so-called Chinatown (a misnomer in a city mainly inhabited by Chinese) into modern high-rise apartment blocks all of which needed ceramic tiled bathrooms. As the Yongs already controlled their own property development companies, which also needed tiles, as well as one of Singapore's largest construction contractors, there had seemed to be synergy in a move into building materials.

A new factory was constructed on a large site off Bukit Timah Road in the centre of the island and the very latest technology in Italian tile-manufacturing machinery was installed. But operating costs were high: all raw materials had to be imported, the cost of electricity to fire the furnaces was rising, labour was becoming expensive compared to neighbouring countries, and royalties on sales had to be paid to the Italian equipment suppliers.

The unpalatable truth was that it was cheaper to import tiles from larger manufacturers overseas which benefited from economy of scale, than it was to produce tiles in Singapore. The company also suffered from having only one main client, the Singapore government, whose objective it was to produce reasonable quality accommodation units at the lowest possible cost. The Yongs played the nationalist card and were able to use their influence with the government to persuade the authorities that Singapore needed to have a tile plant of its own. The government acquiesced and introduced duties on imported tiles so making MTM's products cheaper than imported tiles. But the Housing & Development Board, under its fearsome chairman Teh Cheang Wan, continued to squeeze the tile prices to such an extent that MTM had never made a profit.

I warned Andy that this might not be the right business for him: whereas the government had protected the Yongs by import tariffs, they might not take such a benign view if the company was owned by foreigners. And did CCC know anything about manufacturing? After all, tiles in Singapore had little to do with biscuits in Nigeria. If the Yongs could not make any money out of the business with government support, then what secret did Andy have up his sleeve that would change matters?

Such reservations were brushed aside. I was not being imaginative. And in any case Andy had spotted the holy grail: MTM's factory was occupying a large amount of land valued at cost in the books and which might be worth several times more.

The Yongs assured Andy that all MTM needed was a cash injection and then its problems would be over. Andy did not hesitate. He talked his bankers into the project, borrowed more money, and CCC's Far Eastern arm was born amidst a surge of expectations as Andy pontificated that he would now be building an empire in the East based on acquiring other assets using MTM shares. The MTM share price climbed from S$1.20 to S$2.60 on the announcement of the deal. Andy was cockahoop. He had bought into the company at ninety Singapore cents a share.

David Evans and I were immediately mobilised and dispatched to live in Singapore. Before long, with Charles Letts' assistance, I had procured a lease over number 24 Bukit Chermin, a black and white colonial house with large verandas perched on the top of a hill with lawns sweeping down to the narrow straits between Singapore and the neighbouring island of Pulau Blakang Mati (now transformed into a tourist haven and renamed Sentosa). Ocean-going freighters needed to navigate these straits, no more than a quarter of a mile wide, on their way to Keppel Shipyard and it would seem from the house as if these huge ships were passing just at the end of the lawn.

A long pebble drive wound around the hill on its way to 'the Bukit', as we called the house, and frequently I would round a corner to meet an iguana crossing the road. Some six feet from darting tongue to tip of its tail, it demanded right of way and was not to be deterred by the sight of an approaching car. It lived in a culvert under the house and devoured rats, chickens from the nearby *kampong*, and the neighbours' pets.

My responsibility in those early days in Singapore was as 'project director' for MTM which meant searching for other deals for Andy. David Evans was to concentrate on running the tile manufacturing business. He did this proficiently and expanded the business by buying other building material factories in Singapore and Malaysia. I travelled around South-East Asia following up all sorts of leads passed to me by Andy.

Having spent quite some time in the Far East by now I began to find that my reputation preceded me: on one flight to Hong Kong I sat next to a voluble Chartered Bank executive determined to impress me, a complete stranger, with his extensive range of contacts in the region. Amongst the other luminaries in his select constellation was a certain Evelyn Errington, "a very close friend and invaluable source of knowledge on the Far East." Had I met him?

In those days I still talked to people on airplanes. Over the years, like most people, I gradually dropped this courtesy. This was a shame as I came across all sorts of strange people flying the Asian skies. One of the most surprising was on a flight from Bangkok to Kuala Lumpur when I found myself sipping champagne with a pleasant middle-aged man who introduced himself as the regional director of Oxfam, a large British charity. I enquired whether the charity sent all their executives first class? After all, was not the charity supported by countless generous people in England and other countries who donated a few hard-earned pennies to alleviate starvation in the Third World? Were these pennies really being spent on first class travel?

My neighbour was bemused. "Well," he said. "I used to be a corporate executive for a multi-national like you on a handsome salary with a package that included first class travel, and then I was head-hunted by Oxfam. They wanted a professional businessman instead of the brown bread and sandals types who used to run the charity. They took me on, paying me the same salary and offering the same perks as my old job."

"But, but……….are you sure you are projecting the right image?" I asked.

He winked at me and called the stewardess to replenish our glasses.

At one moment MTM was going to build an ice-skating rink in Singapore, at another it was to be a cold store in Bangkok or an undervalued rubber plantation in Sumatra. But none of these deals came through and meantime the tile business continued to lose money.

Then Andy made an error of judgement which was to spell the end of his Eastern ambitions almost before they had started. He had stumbled across another undervalued asset: the Paris Hotel in New York. MTM, he announced, was to acquire this 'prime' real estate by issuing MTM shares to various companies controlled by Andy. David Evans was horrified and sent me to New York to investigate. The Paris Hotel turned out to be in a down-at-heel neighbourhood on the upper West Side and was in a very poor state of repair. I reported to Andy that it was unlikely that the Singapore government was going to support this adventure. "What the hell has it got to do with them?" he retorted.

By that time the Singapore government was wise to the antics of the British asset strippers and was making their lives more difficult. Different government agencies had to approve any sort of corporate activity and they turned their critical eyes upon MTM the moment they heard that the struggling tile manufacturer had decided to buy a run-down hotel in New York. Shareholders had also wearied of the lack of progress in either turning the manufacturing business around or any new deals and the share price slid from S$3.00 per share to less than S$2.00.

There was no chance that this deal was going to be endorsed by the Singaporeans but Andy had made commitments without realising that he needed permission from the authorities in Singapore for such a transaction. David Evans took the high moral ground and resisted the deal. Andy gave ample vent to his anger and frustration by repeatedly calling David in the middle of the night (early evening in London) and accusing him of lacking Andy's concept of entrepreneurial flair. Andy decided that he had best take hands-on control over his Far Eastern empire. David was fired.

Andy's spotlight next fell on the technical director, Peter Wegmann, a skilled Austrian ceramic engineer, who was struggling to get the tile factory operating once again at full capacity. His problem had been one of finance. The factory needed a constant supply of refractory rollers from Italy. But the Italians were reluctant to supply them as they had not been paid for several years. Peter pleaded for money to settle the Italian debt but there was none available. Eventually one of the two kilns had to be closed down reducing the factory's output by fifty percent. Andy was horrified. It had to be Peter's fault. He was also dismissed.

So of the original three-man team that Andy had sent to Singapore some twelve months earlier, I was the sole survivor. I was twenty-seven and with little business experience. "Not to worry," said Andy. "You run the ship. It just requires a little common sense," and, he should have added, to follow orders from Charles Street with no questions asked. I was therefore appointed the managing director but, I surmised correctly, with little promise of long term tenancy. Nevertheless, I relished the challenge and moved into the corner office, took over the managing director's chauffeur-driven Jaguar, and started to deal with MTM's impatient bankers, the increasingly restless and subversive Yong family and Teh Cheang Wan at the Housing and Development Board.

The Paris Hotel affair had alerted the Singapore government to the activities of what they had now correctly identified as another British asset-stripper. The ripples resulting from the Paris Hotel deal began to spread far and wide: the tariff protection that MTM had enjoyed was suddenly withdrawn. Imported tiles flooded the market, MTM's reduced capacity increased manufacturing costs and the Housing & Development Board stopped buying the more expensive locally-manufactured tiles. The writing was on the wall: the government was going to force Andy out. It did not take long for the local shareholders to speculate that all was not right between MTM and the authorities and the share price dropped to eighty Singapore cents, below Andy's purchase price.

I laboured on for another twelve months until I could see no future and eventually told Andy that I could not continue unless more finance was forthcoming. He rightly decided that any further investment would be throwing good money after bad and balked. I resigned. I had been in Singapore for two and a half years.

The Singapore government eventually achieved its ambition. It forced MTM into insolvency; the share price fell to less than ten cents. Teh's Housing and Development Board made a bid for MTM and acquired the business for a song. CCC and the minority shareholders received almost nothing from their original investment. The government cared little for the minority shareholders anyway, the main objective having been accomplished: the foreign pirates had been vanquished. The Housing & Development Board then applied to the Ministry of Finance for reimposition of tariffs which was speedily granted allowing the company to increase its sales price and to become profitable once more.

For me the MTM experience was an essential lesson in business. For most of the time I was managing a company on a shoestring, not knowing how the next week's salary was going to be paid to MTM's eight hundred employees. Some months salaries were paid late, and this immediately led not only to sabotage of expensive machinery but also to threats against my life. Years later when I was working for Inchcape, an organisation with vast reserves generating hundreds of millions in profits every year, it was inconceivable to imagine a shortage of cash but my time of scrimping at MTM proved a powerful influence throughout my business career.

Then there were the oriental wrinkles to the problems. At my first board meeting as managing director, there was considerable discussion as to why MTM continued to lose money. We all knew the reasons but T.M. Yong, normally a most pragmatic and down-to-earth man, suggested that we should call in the feng-shui doctor. The feng-shui expert reported back that the MTM factory at the base of a hill was disturbing the dragon sleeping on the hill-side and the only way to avoid this particularly bad feng-shui was to move the aspects of all the doors and gates in the factory some thirty degrees to the west so the dragon could not look directly into the factory or its offices. I wearily asked a contractor to estimate the cost of all this work and the sum came to several hundred thousand dollars.

At the next board meeting I reported the feng-shui doctor's recommendations and commented that it would be impossible to implement his suggestions due to the cost at a time when every cent was needed to pay salaries and essential overheads.

This was received in silence by my fellow directors. I thought they were tacitly agreeing with my analysis of the situation but far from it. T.M. looked at me as if I was an ignorant westerner, and said that of course we had to spend the money to move all the doors even if salaries were going to be paid late that month. I looked around the table hoping for some dissent, but all eight Singaporean heads, an Indian, a Malaysian and six Chinese, were nodding in agreement in a rare demonstration of unanimity. Only Micky, the half brother, removed his toothpick to say that he had never heard such utter rubbish in all his life. So the next week the contractors moved in and every door was moved thirty degrees to the west making it quite difficult to enter certain offices except by sliding in sideways. Even the vast rolling steel gate to the factory had to be realigned which involved recasting the concrete entrance. Our fortunes however showed no sign of improvement: evidently the dragon was not impressed.

Singapore was an enjoyable place in which to live in the 1970s. It was small enough to be intimate without being claustrophobic. There were no traffic jams, high-rise buildings were just beginning to appear, and the government had yet to adopt the hectoring, authoritarian tone it was to assume later. The Jurong industrial zone, soon to become one of Asia's electronics manufacturing centres, was being reclaimed from mangrove swamps. It was a lush and verdant city. The multi-hued Singaporeans had none of the racial complexes so often found in ex-colonies.

My life settled into something of a routine: my chauffeur drove me to the factory in the morning and returned me to the Bukit in the evening. Or that was what he was meant to do. Once I employed a Chinese driver who was so reckless that I continuously criticised him from the back seat for running lights, overtaking on blind curves, pursuing a vindictive vendetta against bicyclists, and similar bad habits. Evidently he was as furious with my back-seat driving as I was by his irresponsibility. The day came when I criticised him particularly harshly after he had swerved in front of a school bus forcing it to take to the pavement scattering pedestrians in every direction. With no notice the driver jammed on the brakes and the car skidded to a halt in the middle of the outside lane. The driver got out and shouting over his shoulder, "Drive yourself!" walked away leaving me looking somewhat foolish in the back seat of the Jaguar with a rapidly growing traffic jam behind me.

Weekends were spent on a small speed-boat I imported from England and which gave almost unceasing problems as boats are wont to do. On one occasion Plern and I were rounding one of the outer Singaporean islands when the engine died. There was a strong wind blowing with squalls in the vicinity and we were being blown towards the centre of the Straits of Malacca. On the other side of the Straits, and in clear visibility, lurked the Karimun Islands in Indonesia, the lair of the piratical Bugis. Distress flares failed to gain altitude in the wind and it began to look as if we were destined to become castaways with no food, water or shelter. Suddenly out of the dusk approached a Thai fishing boat, a long way from home. Thai fishermen have a well-earned reputation in such situations for murder, rape, and pillage, and Plern tried to cover herself with a tarpaulin while I hailed them in Thai. Fortunately they were delighted to rescue a Thai-speaking *farang* so far from Thai waters and towed us back to Singapore, refusing to accept any money, before continuing on their way.

At 5:30 am every Sunday morning as the sky began to lighten in the east, Charles Letts picked me up from the Bukit and we set off for a ten mile hike through Singapore's only remaining patch of jungle around Bukit Timah, the highest point on the island. Whilst I struggled to keep up, Charles slipped through the jungle panther-like, his years evading the Japanese making him at home amongst the thick undergrowth, the insects and the heat. Rising at such an unearthly hour on a Sunday morning was not always easy, and there were many mornings that I hid underneath the bedclothes hoping that Charles would oversleep. But he was always punctual and threw stones at my bedroom window until I reluctantly dragged myself out of bed.

Charles also introduced me to the life of the Chinese *towkay*, or 'big boss', generally a businessman who had made his fortune out of rubber, tin or property development. A group of such people would rent an apartment as a joint 'mess'. They met there several evenings a week for a night of drunken carousing. A nearby Chinese restaurant provided food and serving staff who placed bottles of Hennessy VSOP cognac on the table. The brandy was poured into tumblers and mixed with ice and water and knocked back with each toast. It was not uncommon for each guest to drink a whole bottle of brandy in an evening. Needless to say, half way through the meal most of the Chinese, who are not natural drinkers, became incapacitated and by the end of the dinner many needed assistance to find their cars which they drove unsteadily home and, I assumed, to their irate wives.

At some stage in the evening a bevy of 'hostesses' would arrive, generally aspiring models or B-list movie stars. They joined in the drinking, often matching the men drink for drink, and could be lured into one of the bedrooms for further mayhem. Whilst most of the men chose to drink, others tempered their drinking, preferring the girls.

Few *farang* were invited to the messes as little English was spoken and the heavy drinking was not to everyone's taste. But it did enable me to understand much more of the local life in Singapore and Malaysia, where the same custom was maintained with a slight difference: some Malays would join the party and the more Islamic-minded amongst them preferred to be seen drinking vodka with a dash of orange juice.

Business life in South-East Asia almost always involved the provision of girls. One dined with the Chinese, not always consuming cognac on a wholesale basis, and at some stage girls would appear. If I called on a businessman in Ipoh or any other Malaysian town, a girl would be sent to my hotel room. Sometimes just checking into an hotel would precipitate a call from the concierge within ten minutes enquiring, not whether I wanted a girl, but the type of girl I would be needing. On one occasion I checked into an hotel in Songkhla, in southern Thailand, very tired after a long journey and received the usual call from the concierge.

"Thank you but no," I said, "I am very tired and would like to sleep."

"Alone?" enquired the concierge in an amazed and slightly shocked voice.

"Yes, alone."

"But the girls here are renown!"

"That may be the case but I am very tired."

"This can be solved easily. There is a new girl here, from Chiang Mai. Very pale skin."

"I am sorry, the answer is no."

A light flashed on in his brain, "Ah, I understand. You prefer a boy? Can do also." The idea that anybody would prefer to spend the night alone was an alien concept to him!

On one occasion in Kuala Lumpur a businessman sent a young bronze-skinned Bugis girl from the Indonesian islands to the south of Singapore and prized for their beauty, to my hotel room. For one reason or another I sent the girl away with a tip and asked her not to tell the businessman that I had dispensed with her services. The telephone rang early the next morning and the businessman was on the line, sounding deeply offended. Why did I not like the little present that he had sent me? My explanations sounded feeble and he put me down as a prig, and not the sort of person that he wanted to do business with.

Such Asian customs put enormous strains on a marriage. Most western wives, if they knew what was going on, took an understandably dim view. *Farang* with oriental wives may have been more fortunate, but not necessarily so. Plern, whose father was an inveterate womaniser, knew the customs of the East and never questioned me when I would return home very late at night and slide into bed pretending not to know the time.

There was an active social life in Singapore and Plern and I met many new friends and some old. *Time-Life* had moved Peter Simms to their bureau in Singapore and he and Sanda lived in a delightful old apartment off Holland Road.

Dickie Arblaster, last seen in Laos, was managing an automotive business in Orchard Road. Not far away was an ancient bar, with equally antiquated customers and staff, called the Ai Hou Kee to which we would repair after work. A few other characters came into my life who were to reappear in other guises as years went by: Ong Beng Seng, working for another British asset-stripper more successful than Andy, popped up everywhere on his way to becoming one of Asia's most successful tycoons, although one might not have guessed it at the time.

Philip Monbiot pottered around town on a motor-cycle, living in a small flat in Orange Grove Road. Philip had started an essential oils business in Indonesia, the first step towards the creation of a cocoa-based fortune. He lived with Chan See-Foon, an Indian-Chinese girl who captured the imagination of all the men in Singapore by starring in a television advertisement, during which she emerged suggestively from the sea wearing the smallest of bikinis, whispering soft words about the soothing benefits of a skin cream she was promoting. Philip, evidently influenced by his girl-friend (and probably in need of a dollar or two) attempted modelling himself and one time I found him hiding behind a column outside the Kuala Lumpur Hilton anxious that nobody should see him, while posing for a photo-shoot for the Malaysian Tourist Board.

Remo Riva, destined to become the senior partner of Asia's largest architectural practice and to design most of the modern buildings one sees today in Central Hong Kong and other Asian cities, was a struggling young architect. Everybody had their difficulties with the no-nonsense authoritarian government and Remo seemed to have more than his fair share.

Singapore benefited from a lack of pomposity, a relaxed atmosphere, and a lack of urgency. For most *farang* it did not have such an alien environment as Bangkok; the British had seen to that, but it was still very much an Asian city.

When I resigned from MTM, I was allowed to stay at the Bukit, which was rented by the company, for a further three months. I had assumed this would give me sufficient leeway to find a new job. I had however not taken into consideration the vindictiveness of certain Singaporeans. David Evans had not been the best judge of characters and one of his poorer decisions had been to hire Wee Teow Swang as his office administrator. In his late-50s, Wee had a round, grey face and the few remaining strands of hair on his head were scraped over his bald scalp. A retired civil servant, Wee was greasy and obsequious towards David, but mean and petty to his colleagues. When I became the managing director Wee tried to ingratiate himself with me. I should have let him go, recognising him as the snake he undoubtedly was, but I was still inexperienced and allowed him to continue in his sinecure.

When I resigned, Wee took it upon himself to remove me from the Bukit and even Singapore itself. At that time wives of expatriates on work permits were not allowed to take on employment. Plern had started a small business importing Thai silk for the household furnishing industry, and as she did not receive a salary we did not consider that this amounted to employment. Wee thought otherwise and using his contacts in the civil service, he lodged an official complaint with the Immigration Department along the lines that my wife was working illegally and should be disciplined. I was duly summoned to the Immigration Department, advised of Wee's act of treachery, and told that it would be best if we were both to leave Singapore within a week or two.

This was not the only act of slyness I encountered in Singapore. One day not long after I had arrived in Singapore, T.M. called me to say that he could help with my house-hunting. The Yongs had just finished the construction of a luxury apartment block and he offered to sell me one of the flats at well below the market price. I did not want to live in a high-rise block and so declined the offer, but he persisted and said he would hold the option open should I change my mind. A few months later he visited my office to tell me that he had sold that particular apartment for tens of thousands of dollars more than the original asking price. As he had granted me an option at the original price, he was happy to let me have the difference. He then passed over a very substantial cheque made out to me personally. Smelling a rat, I handed the cheque to David Evans and suggested that he paid it into MTM's bank account.

About a year after I left Singapore, I received a letter from the Singaporean taxation authorities to the effect that they had received information that I had accepted a cheque from T.M. and had not declared it on my income tax return. I explained that I had not received the money personally, and that was the end of the matter. The Yongs had lost considerable 'face' over the whole Andy Gordon experience and long after CCC had withdrawn they still persisted in making trouble. Evidently T.M. had remembered the trap that he had laid for me three years previously, and hoped that he could spring the trap even after I had left Singapore.

As for Teh, the fearsome tyrant at the Housing and Development Board – many years later he was charged with corruption and hanged himself.

I now threw myself onto the job market. I quickly became aware that I was at a disadvantage compared to my peers. That I had not been to university had never worried me until now. When the subject of university had come up with my parents when I was at school, my father brushed the subject aside. He went to Cambridge University for a year, disliked university life, and left to join Baring Brothers. His advice to me was that it was a waste of time – but then in his day a man found his way through life according to his contacts, rather than his academic qualifications. I had obtained the basic academic qualifications at Eton but now found that in competing for jobs, there were many others more suitable than I. I was now twenty-eight years old, with a wife to support, little money in the bank, and scant experience other than a few years working as a journalist in Thailand and a short career in industry.

Expatriates needed work permits in nearly all countries in the Far East and in those days most countries were trying to phase out expatriates in favour of promoting the local inhabitants. I was quite determined to stay in the Far East but it was beginning to look as if I was not going to succeed.

I was soon to lose the Bukit and the roof over my head. Then, once again, Charles Letts came to the rescue.

3

Bancom

There were not many people who counted in Southeast Asia who had not heard of Charles Letts. An inveterate and professional networker, he kept in touch with everybody who was influential or might become so in the future. One particular contact was Washington Sycip, the founder of the accounting firm Sycip Gorres Velayo or SGV, headquartered in Manila and with offices throughout the Far East. SGV was the only large accounting firm in the Far East that was Asian in ownership and management and yet purportedly international in its accounting practices. 'Wash', as his friends knew him, was a cosmopolitan Filipino-Chinese, at home on the international conference circuit and friend to corporate chairmen from New York to Sydney. Charles had a word with 'Wash' on the lines that you should never turn a good man down. 'Wash' in turn had a quiet word with Sixto 'Ting' Roxas, the chairman of Bancom Development Corporation. Suddenly I found that an unexpected new chapter in my life was beginning.

Bancom had become an overnight success story in the world of Asian finance. The brainchild of 'Ting' Roxas, the ethereal and academically-minded scion of a well-known Filipino family, Bancom prided itself on becoming the first truly Asian investment bank. It had cornered the arcane market in short-term commercial paper in the Philippines at a time when Filipino companies could not raise long term finance. Backed by American Express Bank, which held a minority stake in the company, it had rapidly expanded into other businesses from insurance to commodities. 'Ting', whom I had met previously in Singapore, invited me to Manila for an interview.

'Ting' was a deep ponderer, a visionary; he gave the appearance of stumbling into the world of business by mistake. He greeted me warmly, discussed the security in Manila which was under a night-time curfew at that time, and then asked if I would like to join Bancom. The company had a subsidiary in Hong Kong and after a year in Manila I would be posted to Hong Kong as the deputy general manager under Noel Escaler, a blue-blooded

Filipino. This sounded an interesting new challenge, albeit quite different from anything I had done previously. I was then interviewed by the two executive vice presidents: Rolly Gapud, a serious no-nonsense banker, and Luis Villafuerte, a motor-mouth politician who gabbled without drawing breath for an hour, as I nodded in enthusiastic agreement understanding little of what he was talking about. He then thanked me for my intelligent contributions, and I was hired.

Plern and I moved to Manila in January, 1974. Neither of us knew very much about the Philippines. The last time I was in Manila was the previous year for Philip Monbiot's wedding: a grand affair of which the highlight for me had been the opportunity to walk down the aisle of the cathedral with the bride's sister, the fabled Margie Moran, one of only two Asians to have won the Miss Universe beauty contest. At the appointed time, we had both left our respective pews opposite each other, but instead of linking arms with me, she swept down the centre of the aisle by herself at great speed leaving me trotting in her wake.

On our second day in Manila we hired a guide to take us around Intramuros, the old Spanish citadel in Manila. The guide thought that an introduction to the Filipino race was appropriate and he started off by saying:

"We Filipinos are members of the brown race."

This was a description new to me. What was this brown race?

"Well, you know," he explained. "Our skins are brown like the Thighs and the Malays."

"The who?"

"The Thighs," he repeated, impatiently slapping his leg. "From Thighland."

His ignorance spoke volumes. As members of the Association of South-East Asian Nations and well within the geographical boundaries of South-East Asia, the Philippines are somehow set apart from the rest of the region. Although some of the Portuguese settlements in East Asia were much older, the Philippines had been colonised by the Spanish long before the British had moved into the area. Then after the Spanish-American war, the United States took over the administration of the Philippines in 1898 and ran the country until 1946 when the Republic of the Philippine Islands was established. Filipinos therefore tended to look either west to Spain, or more likely across the Pacific to the U.S.A. where their mainly agricultural economy exported most of its produce. If a Filipino travels overseas he will go to Los Angeles or Madrid, not Singapore or Bangkok.

The Philippines had little contact with the great trading blocks of the British Empire with its Far Eastern possessions of India, Malaya, Ceylon and Burma and its trading posts in China, or the French with their Indo-Chinese colonies and

Chinese concessions or indeed the Dutch with the Dutch East Indies. There was another important difference: very few overseas Chinese settled in the Philippines. There is a small Fujienese community but nothing on the scale of the Chiu Zhou invasion of Thailand or the Hokien, Hakka and Hainanese Chinese populations in Malaysia and Singapore. Much of Indochina was under Chinese administration for over a thousand years and the Chinese have been integrated with the native population there for centuries. The British valued the hard-working, commercially able Chinese and encouraged them to settle in their Far Eastern colonies, but the Spanish did not share this view and so few ventured across the South China Sea and settled in the Philippines.

The culture of the Philippine Islands is also very different from other countries in South-East Asia which draw their cultural inspiration mainly from the ancient Hindu religion, later modified by the introduction of Buddhism and even later by Islam in some countries. The Philippines however had little indigenous culture or religion before the arrival of the Spanish in 1521 who quickly eradicated any animism that might have been around and yoked their subjects to a particularly severe form of Roman Catholicism.

It came as a surprise to find that all Filipinos have Spanish names. Why should this be? Indians, Pakistanis, Malaysians and Singaporeans did not adopt Western names so why did the Spanish force the Filipinos to adopt Spanish names? Most Filipinos did not seem to know the answer although I did hear some quaint theories. The most likely was that the Spanish experienced some difficulty in keeping track of the Filipinos as they sped from island to island creating mayhem for their colonial masters. An early Spanish governor had the idea of calling everybody from a given area by a particular Spanish name. So everybody in Iloilo in the far south of the archipelago, for example, was to be called Trinidad, while everybody from Vigan at the other end of the islands was a Perez. They were then able to keep track of the troublemakers as they moved around the country. True or not, this is as plausible as many of the other theories that seem to abound.

Then there is the question of inter-marriage with western races. In most countries in the Far East, except for China and Japan, mixed marriages had taken place for as long as the respective races first encountered each other. As we have seen before, the British discouraged this practice. The Asians tended to tolerate it but Eurasians were until recently, a sub-species not quite one and not quite the other and often sidelined as a result. But not in the Philippines: to have some western blood is a social cachet, the more the better. The 'mestizo' families, as they are called, are the aristocrats of the Philippines. As *mestizos* married *mestizas* down the generations, their skin grew paler and their Filipino physical characteristics diminished to the extent that some appear completely caucasian.

The Philippines in 1974 was going through one of its difficult periods. President Marcos had declared martial law in 1972 and there was a curfew between 10 p.m. and 6 a.m. Curfew violators were treated in the same lenient way as convicts in Thailand. Although it was not possible to nominate your driver to serve your sentence on your behalf, the penalties for being caught outside during curfew hours were not too onerous: one was sentenced to wear a yellow T-shirt proclaiming 'curfew violator' and made to cut the grass on the central divider on highways in Manila for half a day. That is, of course, assuming that you did not have any 'special contacts' in which case even this minor inconvenience was waived. I would frequently arrive in the office to find several managers missing only to be told that they had been seen watering the plants that morning on Epifanio de Los Santos Avenue, the eponymous highway that connects Quezon City and Makati City in the heart of Metro Manila.

My new job with Bancom involved a major reduction in my standard of living. Gone were the high salary, the chauffeur-driven Jaguar and the large house with its sweeping lawns. They were replaced by a salary of US$800 per month, a battered old Japanese car and a small bungalow in a nondescript 'village' in Makati, Metro Manila's business district. The 'villages' were another American import: gated communities with their own armies of security guards, they were fenced in to keep others out – not that this concept succeeds anywhere in Asia as it depends entirely on the reliability of the security guards.

Many years later I was living in Harbour City in Hong Kong, a complex of several apartment blocks with a single vast underground car park. Harbour City boasted its own two hundred strong army of security guards, electronic barriers, CCTV and a range of other security systems. Notwithstanding this security barrage, thieves managed to steal three consecutive brand new cars from my allotted underground car park space within two months from right under the noses of the guards. Each time the event was recorded on CCTV and each time the security guards expressed total astonishment as to how the thieves were able to carry out their business without being detected.

The house rented for us in San Miguel village was not without its interesting features. It had a central corridor with rooms leading off on either side. One of the doors opened onto a spiral staircase which led to a box-room, a dark and depressing unused cellar. The house was air-conditioned so the windows were always closed. Both Plern and I remarked that doors, which had been firmly shut, seemed to open and stay ajar. We put this down to poor workmanship, perhaps the doors had not been hung properly or the catches were not correctly aligned. Then one Sunday when the maid was off-duty and all the outside doors were locked, I came out of the kitchen at the end of the corridor just in time to see a man walk through the door into the box-room. I assumed he was a workman called by the landlord and thought no more about it.

Later than morning I mentioned it to Plern and she looked at me in surprise. Who had let him in? She had not and the doors were all locked on the inside. I walked down the stairs into the box room but there was nobody there. We searched the house: it was empty save for the two of us and the doors were still locked. I had not seen the man's face but I had definitely seen somebody. That evening the maid returned and I told her what I had seen.

"Hah!" she said. "I knew it was only a matter of time. I didn't want to tell you. Most other people have left this house in a hurry!"

When the house was under construction the son of the owner visited the house before the steel spiral staircase had been installed. He opened the door off the corridor. It was dark inside, the electricity had not been connected, and he walked through and fell fifteen feet to his death. The house had been empty more or less ever since. Bancom had rented it cheaply from the owner and presumably did not know of its reputation or, perhaps, they did. Anyway Plern and I decided that we could live with our unwanted guest and we put up with him. Doors continued to open and close mysteriously but there were no more spectres.

Bancom employed several thousand people in Manila based in adjacent buildings named Bancom 1, Bancom 2, and so on up to Bancom 7. I spent some time in each department or subsidiary learning the workings of the organisation. I was their only non-Filipino employee and I was generally viewed with curiosity. In spite of their extrovert natures, the Filipinos were not as friendly as the Thais who would go out of their way to be hospitable. The Filipinos very rarely invited us to their homes and made little effort to include us in their activities. A couple of times we were invited on weekend trips to Vigan or nearby Batangas but we were generally left to our own devices. It was difficult for Plern, who knew nobody in Manila and found it hard to make friends amongst the Filipinos who, in spite of their English skills and outward-going personalities, were not particularly welcoming to strangers.

The Philippines seemed to be going nowhere: other countries in the region were all in a state of accelerating development. Their governments were watching the war in Vietnam with mounting anxiety and there was a general realisation that the best method to stop encroaching communism was to raise the standard of living of their rural inhabitants. Thus with the help of overseas economic assistance, especially from the United States, enormous efforts were made to build roads, schools, hospitals and open up the remoter parts of the hinterland. Thailand benefited from being in the front line as hosts to the American airbases and their attendant infrastructure, which needed modern ports and highways.

The Philippines, with its vast U.S. naval base at Subic Bay and the equally extensive air force base at Clarke Field, was also a close client state of the U.S. but did not seem to take the threat too seriously. Like all the neighbouring countries, the Philippines had its own insurgency problems with the Moro National Liberation Front who were creating trouble from time to time but little effort was made either to put an end to the insurgency or to raise the people's living standards.

It was not long before we moved to Hong Kong, somewhat to our relief. I rented a spacious apartment in Midlevels, halfway up Victoria Peak, in Bowen Road. The 17th floor of Fairlane Towers had a commanding view over Hong Kong's fabled harbour, Kowloon and the Lion Rock beyond. I used to sit on the balcony transfixed by the beauty of the view and the busy city stretching in front of me with its clanging trams, miniature Star ferries wending their way across the harbour far below and distant airplanes seemingly threading their way between apartment blocks before landing at Kai Tak airport.

I started work with Bancom International in their smart offices in the Connaught Centre, Hong Kong's newest building. It was a fifty-two storey monolithic block with six-foot round windows looking out in every direction. Called the 'house of a thousand rear orifices' by the earthy Cantonese, and owned by Hong Kong Land – a Jardine Matheson satellite – it was nevertheless the place to be. Bancom International had its offices on the 29th floor where it employed about thirty staff under the loose, benevolent management of Noel Escaler.

It was not completely clear to me exactly how Bancom International earned its daily bread and there was very little management information circulated amongst the executive team. Noel played his cards very close to his chest and did not believe in sharing information with anyone, certainly not his new non-Filipino deputy. It gradually dawned on me that Bancom was engaged in some quasi-legal activities, mainly the provision of foreign exchange to wealthy Filipinos who were unable to buy foreign exchange with their blocked Filipino Pesos. Bancom had money-market and foreign exchange trading departments but the main activity appeared to be lending money to Filipinos who might, or more likely might not, decide to repay the loans. If they did not, nobody seemed too concerned, as they were presumably well known to the head office back in Manila.

I told Noel of my concerns and he patiently explained that the Filipinos would surely repay their loans one day together with the accrued interest and he could not possibly reclassify these loans as bad debts as the borrowers had sufficient resources in the Philippines. Some of these loans, without proper documentation or collateral, had been rolled over for years without a cent returned as principal repayments or interest.

"Come on, Evelyn," purred Noel. "This is the Philippines after all!" That may have been the case but we were operating in Hong Kong where the government took a dim view of such activities. This state of affairs continued for some years after I left the company when the edifice crumbled and Bancom went the way of so many companies.

Days and months passed and I found that I had few responsibilities and very little work. My job, I realised, was to lend Bancom International a little respectability. It was not easy for the Filipinos in Hong Kong: not readily accepted by the Chinese, who looked down their noses at all non-Chinese, but especially at members of the 'brown race', and not particularly welcomed by the British who peered over their long noses at everyone. I was to provide an entrée for Bancom through doors previously closed to them.

I was reasonably successful and enabled them to initiate a banking relationship with Li Ka Shing, a small property developer at the time but soon to become one of the richest people in the world. Others too: the Swire Group, the owners of Cathay Pacific Airways; local Chinese developers and contractors who were still finding their feet in the early 1970s but were soon to become magnates controlling assets around the world. It was hard graft but merchant banks were still an innovation at that time and it was not difficult for an Englishman to open the right doors.

The British community found me to be, as usual, an oddball. Most young Englishmen working in Hong Kong had either been through the Jardines mill or brought out fresh from university to join Butterfield & Swire, Wheelock Marden or the Hong Kong & Shanghai Bank (which did not insist on a university degree). The Jardines executives had generally worked in other Asian countries but had absorbed little in their training tending to create their own little world wherever they were posted. The Hong Kong & Shanghai Bank expatriates were even more extreme: desperately clinging on to their Britishness for fear of 'going native'. Only the Inchcape executives, amongst the great British Far Eastern trading houses, seemed different but then one rarely met an Inchcape man within business circles.

Robert Friend, the first *farang* I had met in Bangkok, came back into my life. He was now a senior executive in Jardine Matheson responsible for their extensive consumer goods operations in Hong Kong. My cousin Emma Chetwode had married Simon Keswick, one of the two brothers who controlled Jardines then as now, and lived in the expatriate enclave of Shek-O, on the eastern tip of Hong Kong Island. I met several people I used to know from my motor-racing days in Bangkok, especially from the Macau Grand Prix in 1970 as some people still remembered my Elva-BMW. Many friends I had known in Singapore had moved to Hong Kong. Compared to Manila, Hong Kong proved to be a much more hospitable place and Plern and I began to put down roots.

Bancom must have been pleased with my contributions as I was soon given another title and a salary rise. But life was proving rather hollow compared to the stimulating excitement of my years in Bangkok and Vietnam and the challenge of managing the tile factory in Singapore. I began to think of the future: I was twenty-nine years old, had been married for four years and I was wondering what should be the next step. Bancom was not a long term career; I was a tool for the Filipinos to use but I realised that as the sole foreigner in a Filipino company, there were no prospects outside the small Hong Kong operation. The future looked, if not bleak, then unexciting.

Events took a turn for the worse with the arrival of Manuel Pangilinan on the Bancom scene. Manny, a scion of a rich Filipino-Chinese family, had been sent to Hong Kong with an equal position to mine: we were both Noel's deputies. Manny was an austere humourless individual with no apparent interests other than work. He shut himself in his room and pored over the Bancom accounts, which had been generally locked away from my sight. Undoubtedly brilliant in many ways, people did not warm to Manny easily. Although he did not involve himself within my area of responsibilities, he was nevertheless an added irritant and I decided to look for another job.

When Bancom closed its doors Manny Pangilinan applied himself to forming a new Indonesian-backed Asian-based conglomerate and nearly all the Filipinos working at Bancom International transferred en bloc to work for Manny and his new organisation, First Pacific. Manny became a reluctant celebrity as First Pacific started to make headline-grabbing deals. His solemn, expressionless face began to appear on the front covers of business magazines lauding him as a new Asian tycoon. I cannot imagine that he was at peace with all this attention; he remained then as he does today, a very private man addicted to his work. He was later to take over the largest telecommunications company in the Philippines, the Philippine Long Distance Telephone Company, and concentrated his efforts on his native country but by then First Pacific had become one of the largest conglomerates in Hong Kong.

Luis Villafuerte became a minister for a short time in one of the post-Marcos administrations and then faded from view. Rolly Gapud was revealed as the man behind Imelda Marcos's billions and was forced to leave the Philippines for fear of being called to testify at the many investigations into where Marcos had hidden his money. He was occasionally to be seen in Hong Kong, disguised in casual clothes and behind a moustache. He never spoke out and the Marcos secrets remained safe with him. 'Ting' Roxas also left the Philippines, gave up banking and grew a ponytail.

One of the more colourful personalities I had met in Singapore was Louise Foo, an attractive feisty Hainanese who spoke perfect English with a cut-glass accent and was entirely confident of her own many abilities. She had moved to Hong Kong where she was working as an executive for the American bank, Morgan Guaranty. I lunched with Louise one day at the Hong Kong Club's Red Room and Louise explained that she had a new challenge in her life: she had decided to find a husband. Most women tend to drift into marriage but not Louise. She intended to set about the identification of her future mate in a thorough and scientific manner. First she needed to determine the type of man and she patiently described the necessary qualifications:

He had to be an Englishman, certainly no oriental male would do and other nationalities had been considered but rejected. He must be tall (she was petite herself), good breeding material, well educated, passably good-looking, a sportsman, and, most important of all, gainfully employed with good prospects. She did not mention money, I asked her why.

"Oh, that's not important," she replied with a shake of her pretty head. "If he has the other qualifications, I will make sure that the money flows."

I was sceptical for, as remarked before, many expatriates, and especially those 'gainfully employed' by the great Asian trading houses like Jardine Matheson, Inchcape and Swires, were often wont to enter into short-term liaisons with oriental girls but were difficult to tie down to a marriage contract. Louise brushed my concerns aside and went further.

"Not only will I find my man but I will march him up the aisle within twelve months from today!" she retorted.

"Twelve months? Not a chance," said I. "You haven't even got a short list yet!"

"Just watch me!"

"A thousand dollars, if you can make it."

"You're on. We will meet here, at the Hong Kong Club, ten months from today so that you can meet the target. That will leave me two months to complete the arrangements and book the church."

She was going to approach this project with the same single-minded purposefulness which so impressed her various employers. Our wager faded from my mind and I did not hear from Louise for a long time, but some nine months later I received a call from her in my office.

"Do you remember our bet?" I assured her that I did. "Well, please book a table for three at the Hong Kong Club next Monday for lunch."

When I arrived at the club I found Louise already sitting at the table; a broad grin on her face, and beside her was a tall, athletic-looking, fair-haired young Englishman.

"I would like you to meet Chris Buttery," she said with a smile.

Chris was working in the ship management division of Jardine Matheson. No newcomer to Asia, he had spent several years in Japan before being relocated back to headquarters in Hong Kong. Chris seemed an earnest young man of undoubted intelligence who, most importantly, seemed besotted with Louise. He could hardly take his eyes off her and I was far from sure what was going on underneath the table. When Chris left the table for a few minutes, Louise turned to me and asked what I thought of her find.

"Incredible, Louise," I told her. "Exactly according to your specifications. How did you do it?" She smiled enigmatically.

"He doesn't know it yet but I still have two months left before he will be walking up the aisle in St. John's Cathedral."

"Let's see about that, there's many a slip 'twixt cup and lip."

Then another month went by and once again Louise called me.

"Right, Evelyn. It's all planned. The wedding will be at St. John's Cathedral a week from today. Neither of my parents will be there so I would like to ask you to give me away."

So it was on the 18th February, 1976 that I walked down the central aisle at St. John's Cathedral in Hong Kong, with Louise, resplendent in white, gently holding my arm. As we reached the altar, where groom and best man awaited, she turned to me and winked.

Louise had chosen well; it was to be a successful marriage, still going strong at the time of writing after thirty-one years. Chris and Louise had three children (I was invited to be God-father to the first born), and Chris eventually was to found a shipping company and to join the heady ranks of a select group of Shanghai émigrés, who had replaced the Greeks as the world's largest ship owners. Chris and I became firm friends and, many years later, I was invited to join the board of directors of his company.

In October 1975 Hong Kong was hit by a late-season typhoon. The winds started to intensify from midnight onwards and I was awakened at 3 a.m. by a slight feeling of queasiness. Fairlane Towers seemed to be moving under my feet. I walked unsteadily to the window and peered out into the tempest, which roared outside like an express train. I gradually became aware that the whole building was swaying. At one moment the building seemed to bend over Bowen

Road, twenty stories below, and then it swung away so that I could see down the hillside far below. An apartment building had collapsed during a typhoon a short while before with great loss of life. I knew that buildings were designed to flex in typhoons and earthquakes but, as I stood at the window swaying with the building, I wondered just how much they were meant to flex; presumably a few centimetres too far and the walls would start to crack. I looked around the room; there were no cracks in the concrete, just the roar of the typhoon outside and a deep groaning from the bowels of the building. The windows, on the other hand, presented a fearsome site: they were bent inwards by the force of the wind and looked as if they could shatter at any moment.

By lunchtime the winds had abated and Chris and Louise were able to drive through the fallen branches, telephone poles and other debris deposited by the storm, from their flat on Victoria Peak to Bowen Road in Midlevels. Typhoon parties were a tradition in Hong Kong as once the number eight signal had been hoisted, Hong Kong closed down: public transport ceased, offices closed, people hurried home to safeguard their own properties. Cross-harbour ferries stopped and in those years before the tunnels under the harbour it was possible to become trapped on the wrong side of the harbour for the duration of the storm. Many a husband had been known to telephone their wives claiming that they had been stranded for the night on the Kowloon mainland and were unable to make it back across the harbour to Hong Kong Island leaving them free for a night of mayhem!

Over a long lunch, during which we had to shout to make ourselves heard above the hundred knot wind gusts, I told Chris that I felt I was marking time at Bancom and was considering looking around for other employment. When Chris was working in Tokyo he had been friendly with a young man of his own age called Ronnie Colson. Ronnie's father Walter, a South African, had founded a trading company which he called the Waco Corporation and based its headquarters in Japan. Waco expanded over the years and had several branches in other Asian cities and appeared to be prospering.

Ronnie was looking for an independent-minded young executive to take over the Hong Kong office and work with him on expanding the business. He offered Chris the job and he had been tempted by the substantial share of the profits that Ronnie was prepared to offer the right man, but Chris had decided that he was not yet ready to leave Jardine Matheson. Would I be interested?

Thus a new, and unhappy, chapter was to start in my life.

4

Tan Mair

I slipped off my carved wooden red and gold four-poster Chinese marriage bed, bought out of rare winnings in a Jakarta casino, at my usual time of 7 a.m. on the 17th February, 1977. I knotted a sarong around my waist and walked into the sitting room. Tropical sunshine was already flooding the room, high on the seventeenth floor of Fairlane Towers. I walked out onto the balcony. The sky was azure, not a puff of cloud in sight. The visibility was unusually clear and the massive profile of the lion's head stood out sharply on the Lion Rock hillside on the other side of the harbour. The distant miniature apartment blocks in Kowloon spread out at its feet like so many match boxes. Immediately below me the foothills of Victoria Peak fell away sharply to Hong Kong Island's Central District with its few prominent tall buildings: Hutchison House, the Furama Hotel, the Bank of America building and the Connaught Centre with its round windows. I was surrounded by Hong Kong's lush vegetation cascading down the hillside in front of my flat. White cockatoos swooped between the apartment blocks. Directly in front, but seven hundred feet below me, new barracks were being constructed on the harbour's edge for the British army. The weather looked promising. It was going to be another fine day.

Plern had gone out to play tennis half an hour earlier. Our Thai maid, Duangjan, had left some freshly made ginger tea for me beside the morning's newspapers: the *South China Morning Post, Hong Kong Standard* and the *Bangkok Post*. Chula, the shih tzu dog which had accompanied us from Singapore, fussed around my feet. I picked up the *Bangkok Post* and glanced at the headlines

COMMUNIST GUNS KILL AIDE TO QUEEN

At that instant a fist grabbed my stomach. The newspaper seemed to float away from me. Denial flashed through my mind but I knew it could only be one person. I did not need to read any further. I knew what the newspapers would say. I looked back at the view of Hong Kong spread out before me as it rushed towards me blurring into a haze of colours.

The Private Secretary to Her Majesty the Queen, M.C. Vibhavadi Rangsit, was fatally wounded while on a helicopter flight over the communist-infested district of Viengsa yesterday while on her way to distribute Royal gifts to Border Patrol policemen.

The Princess died on her way to the provincial hospital after a machinegun bullet pierced her lung. The first pilot, two police officers and a doctor were also slightly injured.

Police said yesterday that before the incident, a unit of twelve Border Patrol policemen guarding a building construction site at Ban Nua Klong had been rushed to a spot near the construction site, where communist terrorists were reported to have blocked a stream to prevent water from flowing down to the Ban Nua Klong village. While on their way to the spot, a land-mine planted by the terrorists wounded two soldiers one of whom had his left leg blown off by the explosion. At the same time Princess Vibhavadi was distributing necessary supplies to policemen and villagers in Ban Dorn on behalf of Their Majesties the King and Queen. The Princess and her team had just flown to the village from Thung Song where she had set up a headquarters for the distribution activities.

When she heard of the land-mine explosion, Princess Vibhavadi ordered her police helicopter to pick up the two wounded policemen despite warnings of danger from the policemen.

While approaching the site the helicopter with nine persons on board came under heavy ground-fire from the terrorists hiding on a small hill in a rubber plantation. The Princess, who sat on the extreme left side of the front row was hit by a shot which pierced her lung while the helicopter was raked with machinegun fire.

Reports said the Princess exclaimed "I am hit" to Dr. Suparb Burapat and then fell unconscious. The helicopter returned fire briefly and then quickly pulled away and landed at Wat Ban Song.

A new helicopter was called in while doctors applied first aid to try to save the life of the Princess but she died......

Reports of the death of Princess Vibhavadi were flashed to the Royal Household which dispatched a special airplane to bring the body of the Princess back to Bangkok for funeral ceremonies.

The special police airplane arrived at Don Muang Military Airport at about 5 p.m. yesterday. On hand to express condolences were Prime Minister Tanin Kraivixien, Lord Chamberlain of the Royal Household Dr. Kalaya Isarasena, Police Director General Montchai Pankongchuen and other high ranking officials.[1]

---

[1] Reproduced from the Bangkok Post of the 17th February 1977 by kind permission of The Post Publishing Public Company Limited.

Grief overwhelmed me. I was devastated. I owed Tan Mair so much and yet had allowed our relationship to falter in recent years. She had been a greater influence on my life than I ever appreciated: without her I would not have stayed in the Far East.

I quickly made arrangements to attend her funeral in Bangkok. I stood alone under the *boddhi* tree outside *Wat Benjamabopit*, the Marble Temple, the same temple where Tan Mair had taken me so many years before to show me its extensive collection of Buddha images. Nobody noticed me, I was just another *farang*. Black-clad Thai ladies chattered merrily as they entered the temple. Life goes on. I reminded myself that Tan Mair had told me so many times that Buddhists believe funerals are for celebrating the birth of a new life but somehow I could not find consolation in this. I visited the *Wang* but it was deserted. The shutters closed, dry leaves crackled as they eddied around the house.

Only Maria, the blind Vietnamese girl who answered the *Wang*'s telephone, was still there. She recognised my footsteps long before she heard my voice although I had not visited the *Wang* for many years. She held my hand as her sightless eyes gushed silent tears. Sobs wracked her slight body.

"Oh, Tan Lord," she gasped between sobs, "whatever will happen to me now?"

H.M. King Bhumibol and the Thai people were shocked and deeply wounded by H.S.H. Princess Vibhavadi Rangsit's death. The communists had made a major error which they quickly acknowledged. This was not the way to win the support of the people. Tan Mair would have taken wry amusement from knowing that the main highway from Bangkok to the international airport at Don Muang was renamed the Vibhavadi Rangsit Highway and thus her name will remain in our memories.

5

Japanese Jews

I flew to Tokyo to meet the Colsons. My first meeting with Ronnie was inauspicious. I found him shallow, boastful and arrogant. Of medium height, with dark oily hair and a deep voice that defied his slender frame, and some years younger than myself, he talked of the mega-deals that he was planning. This raised my suspicions. A Chinese saying sprung to mind 'empty vessels make the most noise'. But the offer was attractive. Waco was prepared to honour Bancom's terms of employment, it would pay the rent on the Fairlane Towers flat, and I was to receive a twenty-five percent share of the profits from Waco's Hong Kong business.

Ronnie's father, Walter, clinched the deal. Walter had made his fortune from importing Japanese steel into South Africa. He then moved to Japan and started his own company, a general exporter of manufactured merchandise which he sold to importers and department store chains in the West. Waco was what was known as an 'independent trader', not linked to any of the major trading houses and was thus able to handle business that the larger companies either considered too small or too risky. Walter was diminutive, mean-faced, gentle-voiced until aggravated, and spoke with a pronounced Israeli accent with South African overtones.

Walter set out to seduce me. "It will be like joining a family, not a company," purred Walter. "All my employees are like my children. I look after them when they are in need, I nurture them through their difficulties. That is why they give their best to me. They love me, you see."

Certainly in the large office in Tokyo, Walter was clearly respected by the office staff. I spoke privately with his senior Japanese manager, Sakai-san, who told me that he and all the staff were lucky to work there and they were all indebted to their father-figure, Walter. I had had little contact with the Japanese during my years in Asia so far and did not know their ways but the story was compelling. Ronnie's attitude was not quite so business-like. He flitted in and out of meetings unable to concentrate on one thing for more than a few seconds at a time. He was constantly on the telephone and as far as I could make out from his mixture of Japanese and English, he seemed to be more interested in lining up girls for the evening's entertainment than discussing business.

That night Ronnie gave a party in his apartment to welcome me to Tokyo. He and I were the only males. The other twelve guests were all international models working in Tokyo. I last saw Ronnie disappearing into a bedroom with Beatrice, his Argentinian girl-friend on one arm, and a long-legged American blonde on the other.

This was looking like an enormous jump into the unknown. The business seemed secure, Walter's silky assurances were beguiling but what about his wild-card son? He had the capability of inflicting much damage. I agonised over the decision, instinct telling me not to trust the Colsons, but Walter was persuasive and sensed my reservations over Ronnie. He brushed his son aside with a wave of his gold-ringed hand, "Ah, don't worry about the boy, he is young and will learn. You will answer to me only."

The decision made, I resigned from Bancom. I was sorry to leave the Filipinos. It had been an interesting experience and I had learned how Asians manage their own organisations. They were not surprised to see me go and I remained on good terms with my former colleagues in the Philippines and continued to see them from time to time.

On Walter's instructions the small Waco office in Hong Kong was renovated in my honour. Housed in a run-down old building in Duddell Street, a concealed cul-de-sac in Hong Kong's Central business district, it had just a single room for its dozen employees. Now it boasted a reception area and small private offices for me and Parvez Kerawala, the Pakistani general manager. Not so long after, when the honeymoon was over, Walter criticised me for disturbing the equilibrium in the office by allowing these private offices, saying it had been more efficient when everyone could see and hear each other in one large room.

The business consisted of courting other importers from many parts of the world and convincing them to buy commercial quantities of garments, textiles and consumer electronics. The importers only had one interest: price. It was up to Waco to put the squeeze on manufacturers in Hong Kong to drive down their prices to the generally unrealistic expectations of our clients. The importers, self-made men with one-man operations in their home country, would then resell the products to chain stores. They were jealously guarded clients and had to be followed from the moment their airplane touched down in Hong Kong until the second they departed. Leave them alone for a moment would have risked the possibility that they would fall into the hands of our competitors who would offer the same products at even lower prices than we could obtain. Loss leaders no doubt, but difficult to explain to the clients.

One of our more interesting clients was Alan Sugar, the bearded founder of an electronics company which was to become a household name in the United

Kingdom. The budding entrepreneur asked us to make a prototype clock-radio with some special features and in due course he visited Hong Kong to inspect the product. He weighed it in his right hand.

"It's too light, it doesn't feel heavy enough for someone to pay £49 in a shop in England," he mumbled to himself.

"Well, that's all those new integrated circuits we use these days. They don't weigh anything," I said.

"Can't you make it heavier? The heavier it is the more people will pay."

"Um, well, what do you want to put inside it?"

"Can you fit a brick in there?" asked Alan, smiling.

There then followed a long conversation as to what would happen if someone discovered there was a brick inside their clock-radio. Eventually it was decided to place a solid lump of steel in the bottom of the cabinet. Alan weighed it again.

"Ah, now that's more like it!" He looked delighted. "Perhaps I can even sell it for £99 now!"

Parvez Kerawala had long-standing relationships with most of these importers and undertook the chores of airport pick-ups and drop-offs. We both shared in the factory visits and negotiating marathons with the Cantonese[1] manufacturers. I learned to find my way around the concrete jungles of industrial Kowloon intimately, in contrast to many expatriates who very rarely ever left Hong Kong Island except to visit the Peninsula Hotel in Kowloon and trips to the airport. Kowloon, the New Territories and the areas where most of the Cantonese lived and worked was a foreign land to them. Before the first tunnel was built under the harbour (there are now five) pedestrians took the Star Ferry from Hong Kong Island to Kowloon and car-owners used the vehicular ferry, a time consuming process.

I was surprised at first that Hong Kong's factories were located in vast high-rise purpose-built buildings. These 'flatted factories' could cover ten or twenty thousand square feet on the fifteenth floor of an industrial building and employ hundreds of workers. Many of the factories worked on three shifts and the buildings would hum with industry twenty-four hours a day. The Chinese 'towkay' or boss seemed to be the only one who did not exert himself to the maximum: rarely in the factory before 11 a.m. in the morning, long lunches and then on their way home by 4 p.m. What they were up to when they were not working was a mystery, but I suspected gambling or could it perhaps be their minor wives demanding attention? These

---

[1] Throughout this book I have differentiated between the people of Hong Kong and the people of China. I refer to the people of Hong Kong as Cantonese, for that is their dialectic grouping, and to the people of China as Chinese. Likewise, Mandarin or putonghua, the standard Chinese language spoken in China is referred to here as 'Chinese' and the dialect spoken by the people of Hong Kong and in Guangdong Province as 'Cantonese'.

were the days when Hong Kong was still a manufacturing power house. Within ten years most of these industries had migrated into China.

Waco acted for buyers from European department store chains, large enough to do their own importing without using the services of an import agent. These were sharp company men with their eyes fixed firmly on a discreet villa in Spain and spoke openly of payoffs to be deposited in offshore bank accounts. We retained an escort agency to provide 'superior' call-girl services. I soon learned that the first telephone call these buyers expected when they checked into their hotel was from our escort service, never mind the business which was the purpose of their visit. The quality of the escort agency's services was very important to Waco as a client satisfied between the sheets would not quibble over the price of ten thousand pairs of jeans. Several buyers, generally those from the larger British department store chains, never left their hotel rooms during their stay in Hong Kong, completing their business with us over the telephone between snacks in bed.

It was a cut-throat business, the nett margins of less than one percent leaving little profit at the end of the day to cover the office overheads and the new costs that I had brought to the company. Competition was very tough, not only from the other small exporters but from the huge corporate exporters. Inchcape's Dodwell Buying Services was the largest of these, employing over a thousand people with their own show-rooms and collections. John Swire and the other *Hongs* had similar but smaller operations. The manufacturers were also not well disposed towards the exporters, tending to believe that our five percent gross mark-up should have ended up in their pockets rather than ours.

Waco's was a sunset business: exporters had justified their existence at a time when the Cantonese manufacturers spoke no English and did not have telex machines so could not easily deal directly with their 'foreign-devil' buyers. The exporters then did provide a real service to the Cantonese manufacturer: to earn their modest commission they insulated the manufacturers from negotiating in a foreign language and pandering to all the difficult habits of the foreigners. But by the 1970s the business was already changing. The Cantonese were sending their children to the U.S.A. to be educated and they were now returning from their American colleges fluent in English, with MBA's in their pockets and bursting with new management ideas. They began to install their own telex machines, form marketing and sales departments, and slowly the overseas importer or department store chain found that it paid to do business directly with the manufacturer and cut out the middleman.

Waco began to lose clients. Then I saw the other side of the Colson family. Paternal enough when the money was flowing in, the concept of one big happy family swiftly fell by the wayside when conditions changed. "What are you doing about it?" Walter would wail down the telephone from Tokyo. "Get off your arse and find me some more business!" Easier said than done but there was one little ray of light on the horizon: enter once again the Prince from Laos.

Panya Souvanna Phouma had been through some interesting times. Seized by the Pathet Lao and their Vietnamese allies, he had been committed to a 're-education' camp in Laos. If there was one person who was going to prove a tough case to be 're-educated' into a good communist, that had to be Panya. Unfortunately such hardened capitalist cases had a very short life expectancy in the hands of the Pathet Lao and so Panya decided that it would be best to take his chances while still in good health. He escaped from the camp and walked across Laos until he reached the mighty Mekong River, the border between Laos and Thailand, fast-flowing and half a mile wide. Showing immense courage, he swam across the river and gave himself up to the Thai border guards.

He was now living in comfort in the Souvanna Phouma family apartment in the Place de Barcelone in Paris. He was also trying to start a business in the consumer electronics field and there was a chance that I might be able to do some business with him and the French buyers with whom he had been developing relationships. I stayed with him for a week and he had not lost his ability to entertain in a most generous manner. Panya believed in spending his last penny on his friends, a most endearing characteristic to us, though possibly not to his family – Sali was losing patience with his philandering ways and the couple were soon to divorce.

It was not long before I once again met the girl whom I had seen briefly with Panya at the Vientiane airport so many years previously. Banyen had not changed. She was as beautiful and full of life as I remembered from our first brief meeting. Her thick black hair still cascaded to her waist and she had a long-legged, full-breasted figure more often found on a European than an oriental girl.

I asked her to dinner. She accepted. I asked her to come to Rome with me that weekend. She accepted. I had been married to Plern for exactly seven years and so, according to the saying, I was ripe for an adventure. Banyen and I fell in love and I moved into her apartment whenever I was in Paris which was very frequently that spring and summer. She showed me a Paris I did not know, made even more alluring through the eyes of lovers. In the way lovers do, we picnicked in Neuilly, tramped the streets of Montmartre, lay on the banks of the Seine gazing at the white puffy clouds dashing across the sky and then returned to her flat for long nights together.

Of course such diversions in life are not destined to last. I pondered over leaving Plern but I was not ready for such a step. Plern had been a good wife over the occasionally difficult times that we had gone through together. But

Banyen was beautiful, considerate and in many ways the opposite to my wife. Plern was becoming increasingly testy, reluctantly accustoming herself to rarely seeing her husband, and instinct warned her that her spouse had a new interest in life. Walter was making ever more irascible telephone calls from Tokyo and wondered aloud whether the French electronics business was ever going to yield fruit. Towards the end of that torrid summer I reluctantly parted from Banyen, never to see her again, and returned to my routine life in Hong Kong. The French electronics business never worked out and it was soon time to find other means to appease Walter. This came from a surprising direction: the People's Republic of China.

It was 1976 and China's ten-year experiment with anarchy, known as the Cultural Revolution, was winding down. China was a closed book to those living in Hong Kong. As few people could visit the Middle Kingdom and knowledge was limited, there was much speculation but few hard facts ever penetrated through the Bamboo Curtain. Hong Kong-based China-watchers, and the legions of 'experts' listening to Chinese radio transmissions, could only speculate at what they thought was happening over the border. Visitors were not welcome and the only access point to China was the heavily-guarded pedestrian bridge over the Shenzhen River at Lowu. The railway line also crossed the bridge but no train had travelled between Hong Kong and China since 1946. There was no other means of access to China: the only foreign airlines flying into Beijing were a weekly Pakistan International Airways flight from Karachi and irregular Aeroflot flights from Moscow. Visas were difficult to obtain. China was closed to all.

The only regular occasion that most foreigners could enter China was to be invited to attend the semi-annual China Export Commodities Fair, normally known as the 'Guangzhou Trade Fair[2]'. For this carefully selected merchants were invited by the Chinese Government to visit Guangzhou for one month every spring and autumn in a time-honoured custom that dated back to the earliest days when foreigners had been permitted to trade with China. Throughout the 18th and much of the 19th century, foreign traders were forced to spend ten months of the year in Macau, and then sail up the Pearl River to Guangzhou where they were allowed to trade with the Chinese from their thirteen 'factories' or warehouses located on a narrow patch of reclaimed land outside the city walls. China was forcibly opened to the world progressively from 1839 onwards, but the communists turned the clock back in 1949 when they closed all foreign enclaves except for Macau and Hong Kong and this remained

---

2 'Canton' is an Anglicisation of the Chinese city Guangzhou.

the status quo for the next thirty years with foreigners generally banned from China, albeit with rare exceptions.

China's official presence in Hong Kong was the New China News Agency, not so much a news agency, more an information gatherer. There was also the Bank of China's looming 1920's edifice next to the Hong Kong & Shanghai Banking Corporation's similarly dated building in Queen's Road. The Bank of China building was the nerve-centre of China's boisterous activities during the Cultural Revolution and loudspeakers were mounted on its roof blaring communist slogans. This was until loudspeakers were also installed on the roof of the Hong Kong and Shanghai Bank next door proclaiming capitalist slogans at a greater volume until the resultant cacophony became a meaningless noise, at which time both propagandists fell silent.

China uses trade as a diplomatic tool. It traded (and still does) with countries where it wished to make an impression or develop goodwill. At some point in the 1970s China decided that it wished to befriend South Africa, struggling under a trade embargo and the world's disdain for its apartheid policies. Always going against the grain, always supporting the lame dog where it could achieve the maximum impact for the smallest investment, China's friends included the otherwise pariah nations of Albania, North Korea, Cuba, Tanzania, Iraq, Pakistan, Yemen, Libya, et al. In later years China used its resources to favour such countries with large purchase contracts and subsidised arms sales, but in the mid-1970s China's foreign exchange reserves were modest and its imports were carefully controlled.

With everything in short supply in China, there was little to spare for export. But the Chinese were used to starving their own domestic market in order to export and earn what little foreign exchange they could. With the South Africans in dire need of many imported products, China stepped into the breach by offering cut-price commodities which slipped through the embargo, and there was little the rest of the world could do to stop them. Enter the humble yellow cotton duster.

This was a typical Chinese export: right at the bottom of the technology pile alongside pig bristle and aluminium saucepans. Yellow dusters were a product that was needed in every South African household and they were made cheaply in China. The Chinese sniffed around for a trader that could handle exports to South Africa, find buyers, and negotiate South African letters of credit. Walter Colson was their man (although he did not know it): a South African national, low profile, well-known to the closely-knit world of jewish traders, not linked to any major power and trusted to keep his mouth shut. No doubt the commercial department of the Embassy of the People's Republic of China's in Tokyo had examined Waco from top to toe.

One day, with no prior warning, a letter dropped on my desk from the Hong Kong office of China Resources, located on the twelfth floor of the Bank of China building in Hong Kong, inviting Waco Corporation to send a representative to Guangzhou to discuss the export of yellow dusters to South Africa.

So I duly applied for a visa to enter the People's Republic and one day in April I boarded the old train which left from Kowloon's railway station next to the Star Ferry[3]. An hour and a half later I crossed the pedestrian bridge over the Shenzhen River and was confronted for the first time by the sloppy olive green uniforms of the Chinese border guards. The first impression of Chinese officialdom is always a disappointment: all Chinese official uniforms were provided without boots or shoes, the result being that whatever the uniform, the wearer always sported plastic sandals. Many times in the future I would smile to see a column of People's Liberation Army soldiers shambling along each at their own pace, for it is impossible to march in time wearing flip-flops.

The Chinese train shuddered through the countryside to Guangzhou, a two hour trip. All the passengers, merchants from all over the world, peered with fascination at the Chinese farmers looking more or less the same as farmers anywhere else in Asia: tending their melon plots, knee-deep in flooded padi fields, or driving a laden donkey along a dusty track. Because this was a forbidden land, even the most banal event caused a ripple of excitement amongst the passengers. I heard some murmurs that what we were seeing was an elaborate façade, a hundred mile long Potemkin village; only what we could see was cultivated, just the other side of that hill or beyond the horizon lurked a wasteland littered with concentration camps and people living in unspeakable squalor. But, for me anyway, the sight of so many farmers working away in their fields with the occasional hand-tractor or water buffalo was just reassuringly familiar. It could have been Thailand or Indonesia.

The Dong Feng Hotel, on the other hand, was deeply depressing and, I was to discover, uniquely Chinese. A cavernous series of interconnected timeless buildings housing over two thousand rooms, it lay across the road from the spreading permanent exhibition site.

I had been warned before-hand that one inevitably shared rooms with strangers at the Dong Feng Hotel, and I had been advised, when I paid for my hotel room in Hong Kong before leaving, to invent a 'friend' and pay double in the hope that one could have a private room. I joined an endless queue in the dirt-encrusted lobby of the Dong Feng. The black floor was grimy with years of

[3] Only the clock tower now remains. The main station has been inconveniently moved a mile away to Hung Hom. Until 1930 it was possible to travel by rail from Victoria Station in London to the Kowloon Star Ferry terminal without leaving the train.

caked filth[4]. At the front was a plywood desk where a sour-faced woman with a pudding-basin haircut was allocating rooms. When I reached the front of the queue, I showed my receipt and asked for a room for my 'friend' and I.

"Where the other one?" grunted the woman.

"He'll be along in a minute," I said, eyes scanning the crowds looking for an imaginary face.

"Back of the queue!" ordered the woman.

I begged and pleaded but she was having none of it; she had seen this particular scam many times before. She looked up from her table and surveyed the waiting queue. Half way down the line was a robed and bearded man of vast bulk from a Francophone African nation. She crooked her finger at him and, when he waddled forward, she wagged it at both of us saying, "You two, room 1003."

"But, but," I stuttered. "What about my friend?"

The woman peered at me through cracked, wire-rimmed spectacles and admonished me.

"You very poor socialist attitude. You capitalists think you can pay money and get different service. Here everyone same-same. Next time you try this trick, hotel will be full. Understand?"

My enforced room-mate revealed many undesirable habits: although it was extremely hot in the room (air-conditioning was not to come to China for many a long summer), I never saw him have a shower and his animal odour was almost more than I could stand. When he slept, he snored, but he did not sleep often. Prayers to Allah were offered frequently, emphatically and, depending on how his day had gone, sometimes in anger and sometimes in a wheedling, chiding manner. Ignoring me completely, he would burst into the room long after I had gone to sleep, turn on all the lights, invite a couple of his similarly garbed and evil-smelling compatriots around and would drink whisky (a good Moslem, this one) until the early hours.

On my first morning I registered with the authorities, who occupied a room in the hotel, and strolled across the road into the cavernous exhibition building. On the ground floor there were displays of every type of manufactured merchandise, textiles, machine tools, agricultural produce, chemicals and minerals known to man. Although the exhibits were new, they somehow looked as if they had been loaned from a museum - dusty, antiquated and obsolete. Nevertheless, the sheer range and variety of products on display was a surprise. It took me a

---

[4] Some years later an industrial scraper was used to clean the floor. A most beautiful and rare red marble surface was revealed.

little while to understand that the products on display were not actually for sale; they were just proof that at one time a Chinese factory had been capable of making such and such a machine tool; it did not mean that they were manufacturing them on a production line for sale.

The first floor of the exhibition centre was given over to long, gloomy corridors with negotiation rooms on each side, each room handling a different type of merchandise. The traders perched on a line of wooden benches until summoned inside. This was a long process, depending on the popularity of the product, and might entail a two or three day wait until the summons came. And yellow dusters were hot, very hot that year. There was a line of dozens of merchants queuing outside room number 2010 from all over the world.

There was little to do in Guangzhou. There were no taxis, no other hotels, nothing to see but wander around the exhibition site or the park next door. The nights were stifling, the mornings started at dawn with political exhortations blaring from unseen loudspeakers throughout the city proclaiming, for all I knew, the masses' achievements in yet another record rice harvest. There was little traffic in the streets, just an endless flow of bicycles and pedestrians, a sea of black hair, white cotton shirts, ill-fitting blue trousers and plastic sandals. This human river also flowed down Xi Cun road outside the Dong Feng Hotel. But at lunchtime the flow suddenly ceased and a human wall built up as those at the front dismounted and those behind backed up. It was somewhat akin to the parting of the Red Sea: a narrow channel formed, maybe twenty feet wide and a couple of hundred feet long through which the foreigners walked on their way from the Exhibition Centre back to the Dong Feng for their lunch. The crowds on either side of the channel, as thick as the front row at a football match, stared unselfconsciously with mouths wide and eyes rounded as the 'foreign devils' of all different shapes and sizes crossed the road.

This was a world totally alien to anything I had so far encountered. I had been to other communist countries, Yugoslavia, Bulgaria, Czechoslovakia and the Soviet Union amongst them, and was well aware of the poverty and diminished standards of living that the system had brought to countries which once had been richer, but China was in a class of its own. So far, my knowledge of contemporary China was limited to its expansionary ambitions in Korea in the 1950s, Malaysia in the 1960s and now its backing of the North Vietnamese in the 1970s which had so alarmed the peoples of the region as well as the western powers. But here was a concentration of humanity that made Calcutta look under-populated. Years later a Chinese was to ask me, as we walked together down the crowded streets of Chicago, "Where have all the people gone?'

The morning of the third day brought me to the front of the queue. I was called into a bare room with a wooden table covered with a cotton table cloth upon which were six Chinese tea cups, a can of green tea leaves, an over-flowing ashtray and the omnipresent giant-size 'Peony Brand' thermos flask of hot water. Three men and one woman sat opposite. All wore identical *zhongshan zuan* blue suits, which the world incorrectly attributes to Chairman Mao. They were probably in their fifties, as much as it is possible to guess the age of any Chinese. The woman wore no make-up and had a weather-beaten but educated face as if she might have been a university professor who had found herself working in the fields by mistake.

The oldest man spoke first in Chinese which was interpreted by the woman.

"Welcome to China, Lord Errington. This is your first visit. I must apologise for keeping you waiting."

I was taken aback; how did they know whether I had been to China before, and, as good communists, how did they know I had a title? The name on my business card did describe me as *Zijue*, the precise translation of a Viscount into Chinese, but not a single Cantonese I had met in Hong Kong had understood the meaning of the word. All English titles have an equivalent in Chinese and all educated Chinese should be familiar with the system of hereditary ranks found in China before 1949, but if this had not been the case in Hong Kong then surely it would be even less so in China. The Chinese aristocracy was eliminated during the anti-landlord and subsequent campaigns in the early 1950s during which an entire class of over five million people were murdered by their tenants, employees, debtors or anybody with a grudge. However in the seventeen years that I was to spend in the 'China trade', I found nothing but interest and fascination in the British system of titles. Again and again I had to explain the workings of the British Parliament and the House of Lords to fascinated Chinese audiences.

There then followed a fifteen minute lecture on the benefits of communism, the long term destiny of capitalism, the impressive achievements and giant steps that the Chinese people had taken between 1949 and 1977 and a general critique of the decadence and failures of the west. "It is destined that our system will prevail and yours will fail," I was reminded. Only the man speaking was looking at me, the interpreter was playing with her fingers, the other two men were scribbling furiously in their note books. I took all this in excellent humour. I nodded my head in agreement and enthusiastically endorsed all that had been said. After all, I was there to buy yellow dusters not to enter into a philosophical discussion on the benefits of Marxism. All three men peered at me with suspicion: they had been expecting me to give the usual answer along the lines of what might suit China does not necessarily suit everyone else. I may have been mistaken but I thought the interpreter struggled for a second to conceal a smile.

The older man cleared his throat to bring the meeting to order and introduce himself.

"My name is Wang and my two colleagues are also called Wang." This certainly made life easier, I was not going to make any mistakes with their names. Later I discovered that there were one hundred and twenty million 'Wangs' in China: double the population of the United Kingdom, or as if every other person in the United States was called Wang, and Wang is far from being the only family name. China is not like Korea which has only a handful of family names. There are the 'old two hundred' of the most common family names and many more apart. But no business cards were produced so I really had no idea with whom I was dealing. Mr. Wang the Elder, looking satisfied at my confusion, decided to turn the subject to yellow dusters and offered me a large quantity at a price very much higher than what Walter had in mind. We bargained. There were appeals to my conscience; it was morally wrong to squeeze prices when China was so short of foreign exchange and the people could benefit from the proceeds.

By the next day we had reached a compromise and the deal was done. It was followed by several more over the coming months handled through the office in the Bank of China Building in Hong Kong. Walter seemed mollified and Waco's profits that year increased substantially on the back of the duster business. But not many more months passed before Walter started his wheedling calls once again, moaning about the lack of business and why could I not magically produce business out of a hat? On one occasion he told me "the trouble with you, my son, is that you have never been hungry."

Then Ronnie stepped in with predictably disastrous results. He had stumbled across Peter Ortmann, a fast-talking German salesman, who had been living in Japan working in the hi-fi business. He claimed to have a large order in his hands for a type of hi-fi music centre popular in the American market but his Japanese supplier had gone bankrupt and he needed a million dollars in working capital to arrange manufacture elsewhere. Peter owned the patents and the design rights to the hi-fi and he managed to convince Ronnie that this was a workable deal. Ronnie decided to divide the management of Waco's business in Hong Kong between Peter and myself.

Peter arrived in Hong Kong, took one look at Waco's modest offices, whose extravagance had attracted so much derision from Walter, and announced that his clients expected better. Without consulting Walter, but on a vague nod from Ronnie who rather liked the idea of luxurious prestige offices, Peter moved the offices into much larger premises in the Wing On Tower, a brand new building on the fringes of the Central business district with panoramic views over the harbour. He fired some of the old staff and hired many new people including a personnel manager, office administrator and associated bureaucrats. The overheads shot through the roof. Not to worry, smarmed Peter, the profits on the hi-fi business will easily cover the extra costs.

I could sense trouble but by that time I was deeply involved in a new project. My visits to the Guangzhou Fairs continued fruitlessly, the yellow duster business having faded as quickly as it had bloomed. The Chinese had either lost interest in South Africa or had moved on to different commodities. I tried other products without success: whatever area I looked at, from piano wire to rolled steel, there were experts who specialised in such a commodity and the Chinese preferred to deal with their long term 'friends'. They showed a rigid loyalty to their old 'friends' that I found intriguing. But encouraged by Chris Buttery, I persevered. "China knowledge will pay off in the long run," he wisely said.

Then I noticed that amongst China's very limited imports was coal mining machinery. The Chinese, I learned, had the world's largest coal mining industry and coal was the main source of power in China. The Chinese practised a mechanised coal-mining technique known as 'long wall' extraction which required imports of specialised equipment. This machinery was bought from Germany. The British also made the same type of machinery but they tended to be dilatory in developing new markets in Asia and probably had little idea how to enter the Chinese market. This seemed to be an opportunity.

I set about building an agency portfolio of British companies which made the same type of machinery. The British, none of whom had realised that there might be a huge export potential for their products in China, were delighted to award me their sales rights and very soon I had a list of some twenty companies with signed agency agreements. This was not the sort of business that Walter could understand. "Stick to the knitting, my boy. There's money in dusters but not in machinery."

Peter Ortmann, in the meanwhile, was freely spending Waco's hard-earned cash resources. I warned him that separating Walter from his money was not a wise step. "Nonsense," he said, "the Colsons are going to reap great riches from my hi-fi's." But where were these hi-fi's? It seemed that a new manufacturer had been found but was having difficulty with Peter's designs. More months of delay were forecast. Ronnie came to Hong Kong to investigate. He was delighted with the new prestigious offices, the enlarged staff was evidence that Peter was seeing 'the big picture'. He readily swallowed Peter's ambitious stories, imaginative forecasts, and the hi-fi fairy-tale, and flew back to Tokyo a happy man.

By now my fascination with China was growing and it occurred to me that there might be other companies who could be interested in backing my coal mining machinery concept. My father, at that time, was a non-executive director of P&O, the shipping company in which the Inchcape family had a substantial interest and of which the Earl of Inchcape was the chairman. I asked my father whether he could arrange an introduction to Lord Inchcape himself. After I had explained the whole project to my sceptical father, he agreed to drop a word 'when the time is right'. I heard nothing for months but then one day I received a note saying that Lord Inchcape would like to receive a proposal from me.

One month later I received a letter from Inchcape's head office asking me to drop in to see Lord Inchcape when next in London. And so before long I walked through the impressive portals of 40, St. Mary Axe just behind the old Barings offices in the City of London. I was shown into the chairman's office where I met the Earl, a stocky, bespectacled man, and the group chief executive, Peter Foxon, known as 'the Fuhrer' in the company due to his short, bristly moustache and authoritarian manner. I explained my plan to sell British coal-mining machinery in China. Kenneth Inchcape, a man of very few words, turned to Peter Foxon, and asked whether it would work. Peter Foxon barked, "Possibly." This was a monosyllabic office. I waited, but neither moved or said anything. Peter Foxon stared out of the window at the Wren churches outside, the Earl seemed mesmerised by his gold pen on the table. Things were not going well. Eventually Kenneth Inchcape stood up and thanked me for coming. I shook both their hands and headed, crest-fallen, for the door. Just as I was about to leave, the Earl said, "So that's agreed then. Please call Peter Williams at the Inchcape office in Hong Kong," and then turned away to exchange another word with the Fuhrer.

Later, much later, I was to discover that this was how Inchcape functioned. Decisions were made either in London or in the field, often by one man and often on a hunch. It was the quality of the individual who counted. Planners, accountants, spread sheets and forecasts were all secondary to the skills of the man behind the business plan. If he was the right man then the business would prosper. If he was the wrong man then it would fail and his Inchcape career would come to an end. It was a system that depended on the shrewd judgement of the key executives. Inchcape at that time was prospering and there were many entrepreneurs labouring within the world-wide conglomerate who were allowed very long leashes. The Earl had led Inchcape to acquire some substantial businesses in Asia in recent years including the 1973 purchase of the House of Dodwell for £13 million (the manager's house in Tokyo alone was sold some years later for £47 million) as well as the trading houses of Gibb Livingston, Gilman, the Borneo Company and the Anglo-Thai Corporation – all household names in the Far East.

Inchcape did, however, insist on some due diligence. They wanted me to spend ten days with one of their men travelling around the north of England visiting each one of the mining machinery companies to ascertain whether they had indeed signed agency agreements with Waco and whether they would be prepared to move the franchises to Inchcape were I to leave Waco. Without exception the mining machinery companies were delighted to think that their companies would be represented by such a prestigious organisation, with a substantial engineering background, rather than an unknown trader in Japan.

Having passed this hurdle, I was then called in to see Peter Williams, the chairman of Inchcape (Hong Kong) and also the chairman of the Hong Kong Jockey Club (some said the most influential organisation in the colony at that time), the power generator Hong Kong Electric, and many other local companies. He was a much respected and powerful man in Hong Kong. As I walked along the elevated walkway between the Wing On Building and the Connaught Centre, where Inchcape had its Hong Kong head office at the time, passed the outlying islands ferry terminus, the Macau ferry concourse, and gazed at the swarms of junks and sampans busily going about their business in the harbour, I wondered what lay in store for me.

When entering the Inchcape regional head office I was surprised to meet Dickie Arblaster coming the other way. He winked at me and whispered, "I put in a good word." What was he doing here? He should have been in Singapore managing his automotive company! Then I was face-to-face with the chairman himself. He was a huge man, tall and stout, with a fleshy face but sly, clever eyes. He had a cigarette dangling from the corner of his mouth and the ash had fallen down his jacket lapels and onto his generous stomach where it mingled with what looked like the remains of his lunch. Peter Williams was his own man who did not take orders lightly from London. He ran his empire as a benevolent fiefdom making major investment decisions without interference from the group head office. My proposal was open on his desk. He did not like receiving instructions from London and had the power to over-rule any suggestion that came down from above.

His opening words were not encouraging. "Why did you not come to me with this project in the first place? Why did you go straight to Lord Inchcape? These sort of decisions are made here, not there."

I mumbled some explanation but Peter Williams had lapsed into silence. He looked out of the large round window at the harbour far beneath. His brain had moved on. "Have you ever been to China?" he rumbled. I was transfixed by his cigarette, the ash was now nearly an inch long and, sure enough, it suddenly broke away and dropped in a cascade down his necktie. He did not notice. "Inchcape used to own coal mines in China, you know. We operated the mines in northern Shandong Province. Some of the largest in the world. Hundreds of thousands of coolies worked there. The Japanese seized them during the war. We flooded the shafts before we left. The Japanese never got them to work." More silence. If I was to work for this company I was going to have to learn to be more taciturn.

He picked up my proposal and the report prepared by the man who had accompanied me around northern England. "Very interesting idea, this," he waved the papers at me. "It might just work, you know. And very kind of you to do all this work. Now we have all the names of the companies you represent, and indications that they are prepared to work with Inchcape. So with all this information, why do we need you?"

I was flabbergasted! I had assumed that I was dealing with a reputable company and now I was being threatened. Would they really steal the idea, the whole plan, the agencies, and set about it themselves? I looked at him askance, and wondered whether I should walk out.

"We couldn't pay you much." He mentioned a figure far below what I was being paid by Waco. No other benefits, perhaps the possibility of a pension in the far off future. I had had enough.

"Thank you for your time, Mr. Williams, but if that is the best you can do, then I am not interested." I stood up to leave. Peter Williams shook my hand and turned away. I let myself out of his office and, seething, made my way back to the Wing On Centre.

Three days later I received a call from Peter Williams' secretary. Mr. Williams would like to see me again. He greeted me courteously, put his hand behind my shoulder and propelled me into an armchair. He had drawn up a list of employment details: salary (much increased but still fairly modest), housing allowance, company car, medical benefits, children's education allowances, free utilities, six weeks leave with paid airfares and a raft of other expatriate benefits not even considered by the parsimonious Walter. Peter Williams had been testing me in his own way; he knew I wanted to bring the business to Inchcape, but was I prepared to tell him to 'stuff it' and walk out? It was probably the best move I had ever made.

Walter Colson descended on Hong Kong the next week. Maybe Ronnie's exuberance had rung a warning bell, or perhaps he had noticed that the Hong Kong bank accounts were running dry. Whatever the reason, he stalked solemnly through the spanking new offices with a grim, set expression on his crinkley, yellow face. He stormed into my new office, "What the hell have you been doing? What is the meaning of all this extravagance?" I gestured in the direction of Peter Ortmann's vast spread of private offices, and he stomped off to confront Peter. Ronnie flew in the next day. Accountants and lawyers arrived on the scene. There was no hi-fi business. Ronnie had been duped. Walter flew into an apoplectic rage. Peter was in tears. Ronnie sat in the corner telephoning a new escort service to arrange his date that night. Walter looked as if he might become violent at any moment, jumping up and down underneath the tall German's nose, brandishing his fist, while Peter looked as if he was patting the old man's head in an effort to calm him down.

I chose this moment to submit my resignation.

PART THREE

The People's Republic of China

1979–1995

1

Hong Kong 1979

It was January, 1979 and I had been living in Hong Kong for five years. I was thirty-two. After Bangkok, Singapore and Manila I found Hong Kong too western for my taste. I was used to living in Asian cities run by Asians in their own eclectic ways. Bangkok had taught me that telephones do not generally work, that electricity is an inconsistent luxury, that traffic does stop for elephants, that a well-placed bribe can be an expedient and that the white man does not belong to a superior race. In all Asian countries one can choose to mix with the nationals or the expatriate community or both. Most caucasians delight in mixing with other nationalities, while others weave their lives around their indigenous clubs trying forlornly to create a little England, a miniature United States or a France away from home. I always preferred the company of the Thais, Singaporeans or the nationals of whichever country I was in at the time to that of the overseas 'Brit'.

The last British colony in the Far East, Hong Kong appeared to be a highly efficient city-state governed in a light-handed way by a handful of Britons who had gained their administrative experience in ex-colonies or protectorates all over the world, and were now concentrated into this last colonial outpost. They had either joined Her Majesty's Overseas Colonial Service as a career or were on three-year contracts. In the 1970s they were nearly all British but as time went by they were replaced by Australians, South Africans and New Zealanders. "They expect fewer perks than the Brits and do what they are told," confided one senior civil servant to me over a drink in the Hong Kong Club.

I had visited Hong Kong on countless occasions while I was living in Bangkok and although I did not know the city well, I had never really warmed to the place. Although the Cantonese comprised 98% of the population of three and a half million (shortly to grow to five million over the next few years), it seemed to possess a rather contrived British identity with Union Jacks flying from every building. For many British, Hong Kong was an escape hole, they could forget their past, and strut their stuff in a way they could never do back in the 'old country'. It was an Asian city in appearance, but in reality it was not only a British city, but also a much better managed one than any in Britain.

The contrast between the colony and its colonial master became ever more evident as Hong Kong continued to modernise and the United Kingdom continued to stagnate. The British expatriate found Hong Kong to be an acceptable half-way house between the chaotic free-wheeling Far East I had known in Bangkok and the familiarities of old England. There were English clubs, bars, and supermarkets selling all the household products that the British were used to buying in Sainsbury's. The cricket ground was in the middle of the city; there was much to make the English feel at home.

Not everything however: one morning as I drove to work I stopped at traffic lights beside the Hilton Hotel in Garden Road. A spry old man walked along the pavement beside my car. He stopped, looked around and carefully spread a piece of newspaper on the ground. He then took down his trousers, squatted over the neat square of newspaper and defecated. His task completed he folded up the newspaper, dropped it in a nearby rubbish bin and walked on.

The slopes of Victoria Peak above the city were sprinkled with high-rise apartment blocks where the expatriates and some better-off Cantonese lived. The top of the Peak itself was home to an almost exclusively caucasian community where bank managers and successful merchants lived in grand mansions or low rise apartments set in spacious gardens with swimming pools and tennis courts. Very few of these houses belonged to the inhabitants; they were nearly all rented by, or belonged to, the *hongs* and multinationals for the use of their executives and families.

The British community appeared to be omnipresent but in fact only numbered some twenty thousand, and was shortly to be outnumbered by both the Japanese and the Americans as well as the Filipinos who provided all the domestic staff. This came as a surprise: where were the Cantonese domestic servants? In Thailand I had a Thai maid, in Singapore my staff had been Malay, in Manila I had a Filipina maid, but why did the Cantonese not provide such services? The curious answer, I was told by one expatriate wife, was that the Cantonese in Hong Kong were mainly refugees from the mainland, had only recently discovered flushing lavatories and had only vague ideas of personal hygiene.

At the eastern end of Hong Kong Island lay the expatriate ghetto of Shek-O where some ordinary, suburban houses dwelt on the lower slopes of a high ridge known as the Dragon's Back with views over a dusty brown golf course overlooking the South China Sea. Here the social elite lived; the *taipans* of the *hongs*, the Keswicks, the Mardens and the bosses of Swires, Gilmans and the other large companies that had dominated Hong Kong since the 1850s. It was a cosy life of long lunches, tennis, swimming, or walks along the spine of the Dragon's Back with its commanding view over the islands to the east and south of Hong Kong.

Kowloon, just across the harbour from Hong Kong Island was where over seventy-five percent of Hong Kong's population lived, packed together in tiny apartments, several to a room, many in cages for security. Others lived in squatters' huts which covered the hillsides of Kowloon and parts of the Island in a chaotic jumble of corrugated iron, plywood, cardboard and electric cables. The squatter huts were the first port of call for new refugees from China and it was from this lowly point that they would begin their scramble up the ladder of capitalism. But there were slums in every city in Asia, some far worse than the squatter areas of Hong Kong.

I was surprised by the lack of contact between the Cantonese and the expatriates. There was always a sprinkling of western-educated Cantonese who could be found at expatriate parties, trying a little too hard to demonstrate how British or American they had become (known as 'bananas': yellow on the outside, white on the inside), but by and large the two communities rarely met. At a party in Bangkok one would find a majority of Thais with a smattering of *farang*, but in Hong Kong it would be the other way around. It seemed a mutually agreeable arrangement: the Cantonese did not wish to mix with the Caucasians and vice versa. I was puzzled by this attitude until I started to travel to China where I was to find an organised form of racial separation.

My situation seemed to be complicated by having a Thai wife. This had never been a problem in Bangkok, the Thais being a cosmopolitan people, and neither had it been in Singapore, a melting pot of many races. But in Hong Kong I was faced with the indomitable ranks of expatriate wives who gathered in sufficient numbers to make life uneasy for the oriental wife.

Particularly so for Plern. She found it difficult to mix with either the Cantonese or the expatriate wives. Plern suffered all sorts of minor slights and insults from the white wives of Hong Kong and I would occasionally return home after work to find her in tears after she had yet again been excluded from a group of parochial expat wives.

The British seemed by far the worst offenders. Drawing comfort from the Union Jacks, the Scottish Governor resplendent in his white uniform, two superb English-language newspapers, two equally good English-language television stations, and daily cocktail parties where they were relieved to find themselves in a large majority, the English wives could almost pretend that they were still in Surrey. Plern was invited to play tennis, a game at which she excelled, and then found herself ostracised at the end of the game when the British women would lapse into parochialism and chat about school days in England, friends they had left behind, English schools for their children, and the many inconveniences, real or imagined, that they encountered living in Hong Kong.

Some Hong Kong-based expatriates had previously been posted to other

Far Eastern countries, where, as we saw in Bangkok, they tended to live their lives surrounded by others of their own nationality. Once in Hong Kong the British thought they had landed in paradise: here was a little piece of Britain with an oriental veneer which could be overlooked if one wished. Others had only known life in Hong Kong and their experience of other Far Eastern countries was limited to the occasional business trip to Singapore and a weekend in Phuket.

I, on the other hand, had been living amongst Asians in their own environment for many years by now, and did not wish to find myself mixing with the British once again. My work was also very different from that of other expatriates. I had arrived in Hong Kong employed by a Filipino company, which was considered very exotic, I joined an unknown Japanese-based company as an independent trader; that was also not quite the 'done thing'. I was earning myself a reputation of being something of an outsider, but there was nothing new about that.

I did enjoy my early years in Hong Kong. It was a strikingly beautiful place and in those days it was possible to spend a day walking over the scrub-covered hills in the New Territories without meeting a single person. The beaches were sandy and clean, the sea warm and clear, the local food delicious. But in only a few years the population was to be boosted by millions as a new rash of refugees descended from the Mainland and the government introduced a softer line on immigration. This had an adverse impact on the quality of life as much of the countryside was taken over for the creation of new towns to house the refugees. I bought a small power boat, the *Parika*, which Plern and I took to secluded coves in the New Territories for quiet weekends swimming in the crystal clear waters and sun-bathing on the pristine sands of Tai Long Wan.

Although I was to be based in Hong Kong for twenty-three years, I really only spent the first few years living there. Once I had the China bit between my teeth, I spent more and more time in China only returning to Hong Kong to catch my breath, report to the Inchcape monthly board meeting and attend to routine office matters, before setting off once more. I did not therefore consider myself as a 'Hong Kong belonger', more a peripatetic traveller struggling to understand the People's Republic of China, a subject of little interest to the average Hong Kong expatriate for many years to come.

I was constantly surprised by how well the British administered Hong Kong compared to the mess they made of their own country. There was, of course, no politics in Hong Kong. The Governor-in-Council had the first and last word. The Executive Council met in secret, the Legislative Council boasted a handful of elected representatives and was a useful place for venting steam. By and large the government ran a highly efficient administration confronting and solving problems as they arose, in marked contrast to the motherland, labouring under the yoke of unions, creeping socialism and a paralysed decision-making process. If ever there was an argument against democracy, Hong Kong was it. Dedicated to a pure form of capitalism, the people wanted only to be left in peace to make money, improve their lot and eventually to move on to the United States or Canada. Hong Kong was a huge transit camp for many Chinese.

A fine example of how the Hong Kong Government speedily addressed problems was the sudden arrival of thousands of refugees from Vietnam in the late 1970s. The 'boat people' were not welcomed by other Southeast Asian countries who either isolated them in island camps, slaughtered them or gave them provisions and shoved their flimsy boats out to sea. The Thais specialised in raiding the refugee boats, murdering the men and any women over thirty, while keeping the younger women and children for their own devices before they too were consigned to the sharks. The humanitarian Hong Kong Government decided that they had to accept these people, much against the wishes of the Cantonese who pointed to their own kith and kin who were unceremoniously rounded up and returned to an uncertain fate in China when caught trying to cross the border between China and Hong Kong.

The 'boat people' were incarcerated in purpose-built camps, complete with fifteen-foot barbed-wire fences guarded by the Prison Service, while the lucky ones were processed by the United Nations High Commissioner for Refugees for acceptance by the United States and other countries. They were fed and received medical attention but, with the exception of a few experimental camps where the inmates were allowed to work outside during the daytime, could not leave the camps.

To the outside world the camps looked suspiciously like concentration camps and the inmates did riot from time to time to protest against their incarceration. The usual cast of NGOs, wearing their compassion on their sleeves, stridently protested at the treatment that the Vietnamese received but the Hong Kong Government took a firm line and refused to allow these refugees to be released into the community. One particularly shrill female American activist was deported back to the United States. After many years some refugees were forcibly repatriated by aircraft to Vietnam. The sight of a screaming Vietnamese child being dragged on to an aeroplane brought howls of dismay from the do-gooders but the Hong Kong Government remained resolute.

British governors came and went. Sir Murray (later Lord) Maclehose was the redoubtable Scottish Governor when I arrived. He frequently asked Plern and I to dinner or lunch at Government House where we met a fascinating array of important visitors passing through Hong Kong. Murray knew his China; he had walked from Amoy (now Xiamen) to Hong Kong, a very substantial distance, ahead of the invading Japanese. He was succeeded by Sir Edward Youde, an insipid career diplomat who took up the position not long after major heart surgery and died only a few years later when a guest at the British embassy in Beijing. His body was returned to Hong Kong with appropriate fanfare, a Union Jack covering the oak and brass coffin born by a ceremonial guard of honour provided by the British garrison in Hong Kong. In marked contrast, the South China Morning Post published a photograph of Youde's Chinese-supplied standard-issue unadorned metal coffin lying on the tarmac at Beijing Airport waiting for its flight to Hong Kong with a scruffy coolie sitting on one corner smoking a cigarette.

Youde was followed by an excellent governor, Sir David (later Lord) Wilson. Like Murray Maclehose, David was a China specialist who had been political advisor in Hong Kong earlier, spoke Chinese and had a lucid understanding of the Chinese in China, as opposed to the Cantonese in Hong Kong. He was the right man for the difficult times that Hong Kong was facing in the late 1980s and was widely considered the best man to lead Hong Kong through the uncertain period leading up to Britain's cession of sovereignty to the People's Republic in 1997. To Hong Kong's lasting loss, a campaign was mounted by a clique of businessmen with Hong Kong interests, led by one of the Keswick clan, who decided that Hong Kong needed a more dynamic politically-attuned governor prepared to confront the Chinese directly. David was supplanted by Chris Patten, a one-time politician who knew nothing about China or the Chinese and was not prepared to listen or learn. On his way to Hong Kong, Patten stopped off in Singapore to consult Lee Kuan Yew, one of Asia's greatest political intellects and an authority on matters Chinese. Lee was later to round on Patten criticising him for not listening to a single word he had said. But that was all in the future. In 1979, when I started with Inchcape, the world was beginning to turn its face towards China.

The Middle Kingdom had been closed to all but its ragbag of pariah friends since Liberation in 1949. For thirty years one of the world's oldest extant cultures, and one third of its inhabitants, had been enduring the most extreme form of social engineering since the Spanish Inquisition. Tens of millions of people had died as one wave of revolution succeeded another. The land-owning class had been annihilated, personal belongings seized, self-esteem torn away, families destroyed, a proud people reduced to amongst the lowest standards of living on earth, too scared to utter a word against their government for fear of ostracism or worse.

The cost was not only in broken families, deaths and stolen property but also in cultural terms. Chinese traditional culture, in decline for a couple of centuries, was finally dispatched by the Chinese communists who taught that China was reborn in 1949 and that anything that had passed before was perverse and evil. Thus a generation of Chinese was brought up in the knowledge that the Chinese Communist Party had rescued them from a capitalist scourge. It is a disappointment to most visitors to China, especially those that know India and other Asian countries so full of life with their vibrant cultures, to find there are few remaining signs of culture in China, and that today's Chinese have scant interest in their great history and the culture that made the Chinese people the fountain of art and literature that it was for so many centuries.

Culture was dropped altogether from the educational curriculum. Music was no longer taught in Chinese universities and neither were fine arts, psychology or economics. All of these were considered politically sensitive. By 1979 the people were beginning to demand more. All the improvements in China had been in the 1950s; the 1960s were wasted in fruitless campaigns, and then the Cultural Revolution erupted into the 'ten years of chaos' which ended in 1976, to be followed by the uncertainties of the 'Gang of Four' episode. By 1979 China's six hundred million people under the age of thirty knew little of pre-Liberation hardships or even the 'improvements' that had taken place in the 1950s. They could only recall the extremes of the Cultural Revolution.

The China I was entering in 1979 was a China ripe for change. But change was going to be managed in a slow and careful way. Changes got underway in fits and starts in the 1980s and seemed glacial in pace but looking back from the vantage point of two decades later, those changes were much more revolutionary than anything I could have expected at that time.

1979 was to be a pivotal year for China and a major turning point in the history of modern China. One man in the government, Deng Xiao-Ping, started to push the line that China must modernise and must open itself to the outside world.

Seizing my new responsibilities with enthusiasm, I read all I could about modern China. There was not a lot to study: after 1949 there were few visitors to China, other than trusted left-leaning sympathisers who could only extol the virtues of China's experiments with Marxism. Nevertheless, there was a cadre of 'China watchers' in Hong Kong who wrote learned articles on what they thought was happening in China gleaned from travellers' stories, diplomats (often the last to know anything in China) and, most importantly, tales from those Chinese who had been able to escape China and flee to Hong Kong, many risking their lives by swimming across the shark-infested Mirs Bay clutching rubber inner-tubes, bales of hay or inflated pig bellies.

I devoured these articles hungrily and began to appreciate the difficulties that lay ahead of me. China, quite simply, was closed to all. How was I going to penetrate this formidable barrier? The first problem was how to obtain regular Chinese visas. It was not just a question of submitting one's passport, paying a fee, handing over a photograph and waiting three days. The only visas granted were those to the Guangzhou Trade Fair and they were only valid for one week and only for the city of Guangzhou. They were also not issued upon application: one needed an invitation first.

How was I going to sell my coal mining machinery if I could not visit a coal mine?

It was time for another talk with Peter Williams.

2

Elizabeth House

I joined the House of Inchcape on the 1st January, 1979. I did not realise it at the time but Inchcape was another *Ben Nevis*, a mighty ocean-going ship in its day but stained with rust, and patched where the corrosion had been exorcised leaving a weakness through which seawater would occasionally burst. It steamed on, occasionally wavering from its course, under a number of bewildered captains for many years. From time to time it was re-engined to give a little extra speed but the old hulk could not bear it for long and another leak would develop. But none of this was apparent in 1979: Inchcape was at the pinnacle of its power.

Inchcape's operations in Hong Kong were vast, employing nearly 6,000 people in a multitude of different businesses. But Hong Kong was just a dot on Inchcape's world map. Inchcape plc had been assembled by Kenneth Inchcape from the many hundreds of trading companies and partnerships that his family had owned or founded from the end of the 18th century onwards. Early merchants in India, the family owned river boats before the advent of the railway and had expanded into whatever opportunity caught their sharp Scottish eyes. Inchcape companies were to be found everywhere in the world from Easter Island to Vladivostok, from the American Great Lakes to New Guinea, from Assam to Aberdeen. Inchcape's 49,000 employees were spread all over the world with a common allegiance to the company's head office in St. Mary Axe in the City of London.

Inchcape's history in China was similar to that of the other great *Hongs*. Gibb Livingston, an Inchcape company, was one of the first China tea traders and was founded in Guangzhou in 1836. Gilman, another large Inchcape subsidiary, had a similar history and was one of the founders of the Hong Kong & Shanghai Bank in 1864 while the House of Dodwell, the famous Japanese traders and Chinese silk merchants, was founded in Shanghai in 1858. By 1949 the Inchcape companies owned extensive operations in China from mineral water bottling to textile factories.

Between 1949 and 1951 the Chinese government 'nationalised' all foreign corporate assets in China. The last Dodwell manager in Shanghai was forced to stand on his desk for three days before signing over the business. All the *Hongs* suffered. Some refused to look at China again for forty years, others such as John Swire invested their money in mobile assets like ships and aircraft that could be moved quickly should the communists decide to take back Hong Kong. Inchcape suffered the least, not because it had fewer assets in China than the other *Hongs*, but because its investments were spread more globally than its competitors.

In 1979 Inchcape had just moved into new purpose-built headquarters for its Hong Kong operations. Elizabeth House, just opposite the Cross-Harbour Tunnel on the Hong Kong side, was like a skyscraper that had been laid on its side. Seven floors high, it was a full city block in length and width. Their Rolls-Royce and Toyota motor car showrooms took up the ground floor and the executive offices, dining rooms and guest flats occupied the seventh floor. Between them were packed the offices of Inchcape's many businesses in Hong Kong. Above the offices towered three twenty-storey blocks of apartments which mainly housed prostitutes working in the bars and nightclubs of neighbouring Wanchai. Into Elizabeth House were moved all the corporate head offices of the Hong Kong divisions, most of which maintained their own identity and private offices. Inchcape China, my one-man company, was allocated a vacant space at the back of the building overlooking the New World Night Club and a live snake shop where I would select a snake for lunch every day during the winter months. The snakes were kept in wooden boxes piled on the floor, pulled out with a steel hook and skinned and cooked on the spot. While most of my colleagues tucked into their shepherd's pie in the executive dining room, I preferred to slurp my snake soup in the alley behind Elizabeth House.

The best time to catch Peter Williams, known to all by his initials 'PG', was at the end of the day before he was driven home in the company's Rolls-Royce to one of Inchcape's many colonial mansions on Victoria Peak. I entered his new office to find him staring out of the window at a fleet of sailing junks slowly threading their way through the harbour, their brown sails and red Chinese ensigns catching the setting sun. His waistcoat was liberally covered with cigarette ash. A souvenir from lunch had left a tear-shaped stain on his necktie. His cigarette was lodged in the corner of his mouth, the ash drooping, about to fall.

He gestured for me to sit. I waited a long while, but he did not move or say anything. I thought of Lao Tzu's words, 'Those who know don't talk, and those who talk don't know'. PG's eyes were following the fleet of glinting junks on their majestic passage between the anchored American guided-missile cruisers and the outlying-island ferries which churned passed the old wooden vessels leaving them wallowing in their wake. Without looking at me PG mumbled rhetorically, "They are poor now, but for how much longer?" Turning quickly, the ash fell onto his trousers, and he looked at me for an uncomfortably long period of time. "The Chinese made Hong Kong what it is. Not us. The British just provide the framework. It is the Chinese who created Hong Kong." Another long silence. "One day China will awake, one day………," and he lapsed once again into silence.

I brought up a subject that had bothered me.

"Uh, Mr. Williams, you know I don't speak Mandarin. That will put me at a disadvantage. Could Inchcape send me to Taiwan for six months to learn Chinese?"

He thought about this for several minutes, his eyes sliding to a small antique cannon beside the window, the barrel pointing directly down the entrance to the Cross-Harbour Tunnel. He noticed me staring at the gun.

"*Feng shui*, you know. The *feng shui* doctor told me that the moving water in the harbour will bring us great fortune but our luck could disappear down that hole in the ground where a dragon lurks. That cannon is to deter the dragon from poking its nose in this direction." Oh no, I thought, not another dragon, I had quite enough of dragons and *feng shui* in Singapore! Then without hesitating he answered my question. "Learning a language is a form of training. We don't train people at Inchcape. Either they know how to do the job or they don't. If they do, they get on with it. If they don't they leave. I don't believe in wasting the company's money on training. If you want to learn Chinese, get yourself a Chinese girl friend."

He leaned towards me and added with a piercing look, "Were you aware that under the Qing dynasty the Chinese were forbidden on penalty of death to teach their language to foreigners?"

He returned to watching the junks. The interview was over. This was fairly typical of meetings with the chairman; one never knew quite what to expect. Two weeks after I joined Inchcape I was again called into his office one evening.

"How long will it take you to sell your mining machinery to the Chinese?" PG enquired. As I was still scratching my head wondering how to enter the country in the first place, this was a question that I was beginning to ask myself. I hesitated.

"I give you two years. If you are not making a profit at the end of two years then I will close you down. You have no long term tenure here, you know."

When I returned to my office I found a letter had already been placed on my desk confirming his ultimatum. I had manoeuvred myself into a corner: somehow I had to squeeze myself through the bamboo curtain in fairly short order. My first task was to find myself a 'number two': he had to be a Chinese who knew something about China. Certainly not a Hong Kong Chinese as they usually only spoke the Cantonese dialect and were generally refugees from China with their eyes set on the U.S. or Canada – the one future they would not consider was a return to China, for many had risked their lives and lost all in leaving the country.

Inchcape would have preferred me to recruit a Mandarin-speaking expatriate but this I resisted. PG was more blunt; he suggested that I should hire one of his sons who was fluent in Mandarin. Even with my limited experience in China trade, I had noticed that foreigners who spoke Chinese generally dedicated themselves to absorbing the language during a three year course at university in Taiwan. They tended to be rather more academic than commercial. Later they were to be labelled the 'China Lovers', apologists for any Chinese action that might not please the outside world and generally taking the Chinese side in any negotiation. Consequently they made poor negotiators. A certain strength of will was needed in dealing with the Chinese who enjoyed gaining 'face' by driving a hard bargain.

The recruitment consultants I employed were doubtful whether they could find anyone to match the unusual parameters of the job but they finally produced three candidates amongst whom one stood out: Dick Chan Yuen Chung. Not only had Dick lived in China most of his life, he had at one time been a leader of the Communist Youth League so understood the political system. He had also worked directly for one of China's key ministries so was intimate with the labyrinthine structures of the Chinese government. Dick spoke no Cantonese and little English. The first interview was tortuous for both of us but instinct told me that no matter what, our paths were destined to coincide.

Only the refugees, mainly farmers from the towns within walking range of the Hong Kong border, managed to get out of China. Those that wanted to leave legally were stuck: the Chinese government did not grant exit visas to its people at that time. Chinese were only allowed to leave their country under very strict conditions and in groups. Dick was amongst the first to be allowed to leave China after the Cultural Revolution as he was born in Indonesia and so classified as an 'Overseas Chinese'. He arrived in Hong Kong from China in June 1977 and was still struggling to find his way in this alien new environment. He was fortunate in finding a position as a technical librarian for Cathay Pacific Airways, a job not requiring Cantonese. Within a year Dick was heading a team of twelve staff. He was happy in the safe confines of the technical library but responded to the recruitment consultant's advertisement out of curiosity. The pay was attractive and the job specification suited his own credentials with one important detraction: the job at Inchcape needed him to spend much of his time in China, away from his family. Having just escaped China's clutches, he had no intention of returning there. Like so many others, the further away he was from China the happier he would be. He was haunted by memories of hardship and misery that came to him every night in his sleep.

He was surprised when the consultant called him to say he had got the job. The salary was tempting but he asked himself whether he could face the risks of continuing his relationship with China. Now the government seemed to be edging down the right track, but what if they changed policy? Supposing there was another irrational campaign? Could he get out again?

His mind made up, Dick visited me in my new office in Elizabeth House and explained why he could not take the position. I was bitterly disappointed. The consultants had taken three months to find Dick and I would now have to face a further three months delay while the position was re-advertised. I had little confidence that the right man could be found for few educated Chinese had found their way out of China over the previous twenty years. Then there was Dick himself: I had formed an immediate liking to this stocky, curly-haired, plain-speaking Chinese so different to the slick Hong Kong Cantonese.

I tried to convince Dick that returning to China under the Inchcape umbrella would provide some security, that China was changing and that he would be at the forefront of a new breed of China traders but his mind was determined. He politely but firmly turned me down: China may be a safe place today but the country's record of political upheavals was too great a risk. I shook Dick by the hand and bade him farewell whilst wishing him luck at Cathay Pacific. I collapsed into my chair, dejected.

PG was examining a Ming scroll spread over his desk. It was a very fine scroll, probably stolen from a Chinese museum and smuggled into Hong Kong concealed in a sack of rice. We discussed its merits for a while. PG had not risen to the chairmanship of all of Inchcape's hundreds of businesses throughout Northeast Asia through seniority alone. Behind his lugubrious manner there was a business mind as sharp as the épée he had wielded as an Olympic fencer many years before. He was also an excellent judge of character and had a great appreciation of literature and oriental art. He was the only one of the four chairmen of what became Inchcape Pacific in my time who would visit my office in the evening and spend an hour casually reminiscing about China as it used to be, and listening to my perceptions of modern China.

He stared avidly and with great concentration at the Chinese signature characters running vertically down the scroll. Suddenly with chameleon-like speed, a podgy hand shot out and caught in mid-air an inch of ash that had dropped from his cigar. With the same movement, surprising for such a large and overweight man, he turned and looked at me over his spectacles. He asked why I was looking saddened.

I told him Dick's story, of the campaigns and revolutions he had lived through, how he was one of the few people in Hong Kong to have escaped China but was still allowed to return due to his 'Overseas Chinese' status, how I had liked the man but he had slipped through my fingers. I doubted whether we would meet such a well-qualified person in the future. It was a long story. PG sank into an armchair and faded into the gloom, occasionally erupting with a cloud of smoke, sparks and ashes from his cigar. Nobody turned on the lights; we saw each other as in an old film – illuminated by the passing headlights of cars roaring out of the Cross-Harbour Tunnel.

When I finished we sat in silence for a long time. We had heard a story from new China. An age we had both lived through and yet had been ignorant of.

"I'll see what I can do," PG said quietly through the gloom.

"You will find that his mind is quite made up," I told him.

"We'll see."

Meanwhile, in Dick's own words, fate was to intervene.

'As I left Inchcape China's new offices, I noticed there was another private office adjacent to the boss's office, smaller but very attractive with new cream-coloured wooden furniture and apparently unoccupied. I do not know what caused me to ask the secretary, "By the way, who sits in that cozy little room, Patty?" She answered, "Why, it is intended for you, Dick." Instantly I regretted my decision. For the rest of the day I was so pre-occupied that I was unable to attend to any of my routine librarian work. Had I made a mistake? At 4.00 p.m., the next afternoon, the telephone awoke me from my ruminations. It was the Inchcape chairman himself. A surge of relief came over me. He asked whether I would reconsider my decision. I immediately responded that I will report to work as scheduled. He sounded most surprised.'

PG suggested that I should find out what other Inchcape subsidiaries traded with China. There were many small units within the Group all over the world which had been buying and selling all sorts of merchandise from pig bristles to camphor from China for decades uninterrupted by civil wars and revolutions. Individually the business was small but consolidated to Group statistics it appeared that Inchcape was already a significant trading partner with China.

After I had been working for Inchcape for about a month I wrote a letter to the China Council for the Promotion of International Trade (CCPIT) in Beijing which was one of the many governmental organisations in China with a watching brief over foreign businesses, requesting a meeting in Beijing. Six weeks later I was contacted in Hong Kong by the China Resources office in the Bank of China advising me that a Chinese visa had been approved and would I make arrangements to travel to Beijing the next week.

I did not recognise it at the time but I was falling victim to the China magnet effect. I was about to be drawn into the allure of China, to take a step from which there would be no retreat for the next seventeen years.

3

The Beijing Office

In 1979 China was not a modern country and this concerned the clique of 'elders', the so-called 'Long Marchers'[1] who succeeded Mao Zedong when he died in 1976. The Soviet model had proved effective at keeping power in the hands of the communist party but it was failing the people. It was no longer enough to tell the masses how much they had benefited since the communists had 'liberated' the country in 1949. China had not participated in the financial or technological boom that overtook the western post-war world. It remained comatose to the outside world, bypassed by the rapid development of its neighbours in East Asia, traumatised by events of its own making. There was a younger generation asking for more. Every family had a story similar to Dick Chan's experiences: some much more troubling.

The people wanted stability. The nation needed time to recover from the campaigns of the 1950s and the ordeal of the recently-ended Cultural Revolution, take stock, reorganise, plan and adopt a new strategy. That process was to take some twelve years beginning with the quashing of the 'Gang of Four' in 1978. Those years saw the gradual reappraisal of the Party's deepest tenets and the adoption of opposing views and the introduction of a market economy without too much political reform.

The 1980s were the decade of Deng Xiaoping: it was 'an era of genuine, deep-rooted and under-reported change in China'[2]. Deng finally emerged as the ultimate leader in 1978 and was not to fade from the scene until 1994. The massive changes underfoot in China were little noticed in the outside world as China was marginalized, almost an irrelevance. Cut off from the world, almost impossible to visit, the only analyses of events in China were made by specialist 'China watchers' living in Hong Kong but unable to enter the country itself. Except for occasional cataclysms, China was an exotic sideshow from 1949 when

---

[1] Survivors of the Long March when the communists retreated from their Red Bases in Jiangxi to their new centre in Yenan in 1933-1934.
[2] 'The China Dream' by Joe Studwell.

the communists took power until Deng's experiments started to attract the world's attention in the late 1980s.

The Chinese economy was also minute in size, smaller than Singapore's – an island of only 2.4 million people. And, much to the chagrin of the communists, considerably smaller than the 'renegade province' of Taiwan. China's foreign exchange reserves, now in the hundreds of billions of U.S. dollars, were less than 10 billion dollars in 1979, scarcely ten dollars for every Chinese citizen.

One of the reasons that China did not receive its fair share of attention was that it was a very difficult country to access. Travel between Hong Kong and Beijing was inconvenient until direct flights started in 1981. For me, in April 1979, on my first trip to Beijing, the only route was to take the train from Kowloon to Lowu on the British side of the border. It was a slow, hot ride taking an hour and a half to cover the nineteen miles to the frontier. Then it was a short walk across the bridge over the Shenzhen River, pass through Chinese border guard formalities and catch the Shenzhen-Guangzhou 'express' train. One then had to find a taxi for the short trip to Guangzhou's White Cloud airport. Taxis, much too expensive for local people, were few and far between.

The airport seethed with people. There was no concept of queueing. The Chinese have no distaste of physical proximity and happily push and shove. Where there was a queue, people stood so close together you could feel breath on your neck. Above the check-in counter was a board giving the destination of the flight in Chinese – I quickly learned the Chinese characters for Beijing. Behind the check-in desk two harassed women faced a sea of passengers waiving their tickets in the air and clamouring for attention. Every once in a while, one of the women reached into the forest of waving tickets and grabbed one for processing.

The departure lounge was a vast cavernous hangar furnished with cane chairs, all occupied. It looked and smelled like the waiting room to Hades with every type of fruit in bamboo carriers, bundles of struggling crabs, carry-on baggage of immense size, screaming children and unhappy looking farmers in stained singlets and rolled-up trousers. Mounds of sleeping bodies were heaped on every chair, propped against the wall or draped over the baggage. It was all I could do to find a square foot of floor space to place my bag.

Announcements blared constantly in Chinese. There was no flight information board, no shops, no food or drink available save for a large canteen of hot water guarded by an ill-tempered old lady. Flights were never on time. They sometimes departed many hours or even days late with never an explanation given. High on the wall in Chairman Mao's giant golden script was the exhortation 'Serve the People'.

The daily flight to Beijing left every evening at 8 p.m. If there were many passengers another flight would leave ten minutes later. Sometimes flights would be cancelled for days on end. I assumed that the number of passengers equalled the number of seats on the plane but it was difficult to tell. CAAC's fleet of aircraft included ten Boeing 707s, 36 British Tridents mostly bought new in gratitude for Britain being the first major Western nation to recognise the new People's Republic and the rest third hand from Pakistan International, and an extensive fleet of Russian-built planes.

I was met in Beijing by a 'minder' from the CCPIT. Single foreigners were not meant to wander alone in China and the CCPIT, by issuing a visa authorisation, was guaranteeing to the State that they would be responsible for me while in China. A responsibility all organisations took very seriously. The representative, an enthusiastic young man, was accompanied by a female shadow who said nothing but watched carefully. I was to become accustomed to this constant surveillance which was generally relaxed in Beijing but not in other cities. Like much in China, very little had changed down the centuries: a visitor to China had written in 1795 'they treat you politely, but are so incredibly suspicious that they will not let you take a single unescorted step in any city'[3].

We sedately made our way into Beijing in the formal comfort of a Shanghai motorcar, a boxy 1960s style saloon with net curtains over the rear windows. The only traffic were buses, trucks, hand tractors and horses – masses of horses, pulling heavily laden trailers, three horses per trailer. And bicycles by the million. We drove along the straight but narrow, two lane road into the city, peaceful this spring, with the pale green willow shoots meeting overhead and cascading over the road. Almost exactly ten years later I was to drive along the same road lined with jeering hostile crowds, many of the same willow trees chopped down and pulled across the road, with no certainty that I would be allowed through alive.

Beijing, as all Chinese cities in the 1970s and 80s, was drab in the extreme. Nothing had been cleaned or painted for decades. There were no fluorescent lights, no advertising, no posters, not a hint of colour to break the uniform greyness of the city. Grey had anyway always been Beijing's preferred colour, and houses, walls and roofs once painted with a grey wash had become even greyer after decades of industrial smog and ashes. Some years later when it was decreed that all buildings should be painted, the municipal government decided to paint Beijing pink and the grey walls were all repainted but the pink did not last and grey once again took over. When China unsuccessfully bid for the 2000 Olympic Games, Sydney portrayed itself as a blue city, other countries picked suitably

---

[3] A. Anderson. 'A Narrative of the British Embassy to China in the Years 1792, 1793 and 1794'.

bright colours but the Chinese government announced that Beijing's colour was grey. True but unappealing.

Our car took us west along Chang 'an Avenue past the Peking Hotel, the Forbidden City, Tienanmen Square, the Politburo's compound in Zhong Nan Hai, the Central Post Office and finally through the entrance to the Minzu Hotel about a mile from Tiananmen Square. The Minzu was a large dull brick building constructed to accommodate Russian technicians in the 1950s and had not been visited by maintenance men in twenty-five years. The CCPIT staff were stopped at the gate by a security guard who checked their identity documents and issued them with a pass. No attention was paid to the foreigner in the back of the car; foreigners were expected to stay in hotels but Chinese were not allowed to enter unless they could prove they had a reason.

Once inside the cavernous lobby of the hotel we went to the 'service desk' where more papers changed hands and a room number was issued, but no key. Although the lift had automatic controls, an old lady perched on a stool in a corner and punched the buttons while examining me closely. On the 8th Floor was a service desk manned by a detail of all-male attendants. They were lounging on some chairs, fooling around and pushing each other playfully. The room keys were kept on a board behind the counter. I handed over my room allocation ticket and was given the key to room 852.

I walked down the corridor to find the room while the attendants argued noisily with each other. The room was spartan but did have a small balcony where I could stand and watch the endless stream of bicycles pouring along Chang'an Avenue. This small room was to become the seed of our existence in China: by the end of the decade Inchcape's activities spread over much of the 8th floor of the Minzu Hotel and offices were to be opened in six other major cities in China. It was however to be more than ten years before modern office facilities became available and we were able to move out of the hotel, a far from ideal home for a modern business.

Although there was little traffic every vehicle drove with its horn blaring: the noise was overwhelming, even for someone who had lived in Bangkok for so long. Some years later the mayor of Beijing declared the blowing of horns illegal from six o'clock one Monday morning. I remember waking that morning to an unusual silence in the city. Many people had speculated that horn-blowing was such a deeply-engrained custom that drivers would not be able to desist but they underestimated the obedience all Chinese show to the State.

The CCPIT representative told me firmly "You must rest. You must be very tired after your long trip." I was soon to learn that this was a standard expression always used when speaking to travellers: it did not matter if one had travelled around the world or had taken a train from the next station, whoever met you at your destination would announce "You have to rest, you are very tired after your trip." Anyway, there was some truth in the suggestion on this occasion. The trip from Hong Kong had taken all day with more than its usual share of hassles.

The Minzu's restaurant was open for dinner between 5:30 and 8:00pm only. The menu was in Chinese and Russian. I ordered from a surly waitress by pointing at other people's food. A large bottle of warm Wu Xing 'Five Star' beer was placed on my table and I ate an excellent meal of hot and oily northern Chinese cuisine. Sure enough, at 8:00pm the waitress handed me the bill and stood by my table, foot tapping, until I paid. Within a few minutes the tables were cleared, the lights turned off and the staff on their way home.

I walked out into Chang 'an Avenue and was immediately surrounded by a small crowd of people, craning their necks to get a better look at the *waiguoren*, the 'outside person'. Wherever I walked the crowd followed me like a swarm of mosquitoes. They were not threatening, just curious, but nevertheless it certainly curtailed the pleasure of an after-dinner stroll. The populations of Beijing and Shanghai were in time to grow accustomed to the sight of *waiguoren* in their midst but even today a foreigner draws a crowd in more remote areas. In Shanghai today a mother will still lift up her baby in her arms and point out a long-nosed *waiguoren* as if distant contact with a foreigner at a young age forms a critical part of their education.

After the Russians had been ejected from China in the 1950s, the few 'long-nose' foreigners that were invited into China disappeared amongst the Chinese masses and there had been no exposure to western culture, views or current affairs over the prior twenty years except to exaggerate the evils of the West. A couple of years later the Chinese started to show carefully selected American television shows and one they favoured was called 'The Incredible Hulk'. This featured an actor who turned green when angered, burst his shirt buttons and turned into a monster. More than once some children would ask me if I also turned green and changed into a long-toothed monster when annoyed.

Back in my room I came to grips with life in a Chinese hotel. It was April so the harshness of the northern Chinese winter had passed and spring was in the air. Central heating, which is turned off on the 15th April (regardless of the weather at the time), made the room unpleasantly hot. I opened the window and enjoyed the cool breeze blowing down the Avenue outside. I looked at my watch. It was just eight o'clock. There was no television, no radio, no newspapers. There was only a single upright wooden chair in my room so I lay on the bed and read a book, but reading was not easy. The room was lit by only two 25-watt light bulbs. It looked as if I was going to read a lot of books in China in the future.

The city was asleep by nine o'clock. Only an occasional bicycle would speed passed on its way home. Later the water trucks would sprinkle the roads to keep down the dust and sand that blew in from the desert beyond the Great Wall. Later still the roads would be owned by the camel caravans, prohibited from entering the city during the day. One of my most enduring memories of Beijing was these trains of shaggy-haired twin-humped Bactrian camels, linked nose to tail by rough rope harnesses pulling loaded carts of fresh vegetables into the city from the fields of Hebei Province. The camels' soft feet and the carts' rubber tyres moved soundlessly through the empty streets with only the occasional call from the camel drivers breaking the silence.

The next morning I received a message that Mr Li Zhao-Li, one of the directors of the CCPIT had invited me for dinner at the Nationalities Palace at 6 p.m. that evening. Mr. Li was dark-skinned and hirsute for a Chinese indicating his origins from *Dong Bei*, the northeast provinces of China. He spoke Russian but no English. My first meal with a member of the Communist Party proceeded, although I did not know it at the time, precisely along the template used for welcoming foreigners to China.

The strained and difficult conversation between the six CCPIT officials present at the dinner and their single foreign guest brought home to me the gulf that the Chinese placed between themselves and any non-Chinese. I had long suspected that the Chinese are committed racists. I had always assumed this was due to their chosen isolation and to their conviction that China forms the centre of the world: the 'Middle Kingdom', the place between heaven and earth. For millennia the Chinese have dwelled in the comfortable assurance that their society was the most advanced in the world. There was much that was unique about China: the sophistication of its literature, the refined food, its ancient philosophies, commanding art and so much more that made China different. This certainty, found in every Chinese, is more than pride in their nation or race; it is a firm belief that China's strength has been sapped over the past two hundred years (largely, but not exclusively, at the hands of foreigners) but will rise to assume its correct position in the world when the time is ripe.

Traditionally, foreigners were to be pitied for not being Chinese. Coming from outside the Great Wall, they were barbarians by definition and could only be received by the Chinese as inferiors. In times gone by, neighbouring kingdoms such as Thailand, Korea, Burma and Vietnam, sent regular embassies to China bearing gifts, as well-mannered guests, but such gifts were seen by the Chinese as homage paid to the Celestial Kingdom by vassal states. Much has been written about the unhappy relationship between China and the Great Powers between 1840 and 1949 and although this may seem history to us today, it is not to the Chinese who frequently mention the 'unfair' treatment meted out by the western powers to China over the past one hundred and fifty years. The western powers did much to drag China into a modern world and save it from vegetating further as their system fell into one of its not-infrequent periods of lethargy. Compared to some other countries, China trod lightly through the era of colonialism.

The Chinese have always preferred to keep foreigners apart from their own people. One traveller had noted in 1617 that 'Chinese who treat or converse with foreigners, without permission of the Sovereign, are punished severely'[4]. The policy served them well in the 19th century but once the foreigners had forced their way into China, only problems ensued. The Japanese invaded the country and treated the Chinese with unspeakable cruelty, the Russians appropriated vast areas of Chinese territory, the British seized Hong Kong, opened many parts of a reluctant China to 'free trade', assumed certain sovereign rights and helped themselves to customs revenue, introduced 'extra-territoriality' and even set up their own city, Shanghai, in the centre of the richest part of the Chinese seaboard.

The Chinese seemed torn between superiority and inferiority. Everything in their being told them that they were fortunate to be born Chinese, the superior race. But when confronted by a caucasian *waiguoren* they felt uncomfortable, inadequate in front of a race which had produced empires greater than their own, invented most modern technologies and, most importantly, had created wealth for its people. China, on the other hand, while making some improvements after Liberation in 1949 had nevertheless slipped behind much of the world in so many ways and this proved deeply embarrassing to the Chinese.

Li Hongzhi, the leader of the U.S.-based dissident *Falun Gong* movement, but first and foremost a Han Chinese, was asked at a public rally of his supporters in San Francisco in 1999 whether foreigners were to be encountered in heaven, in which the movement believes, and if so then how should they be treated.

Li surveyed the audience and noted to his approval that it was nearly all Chinese, and decreed "There are no *waiguoren* in heaven. Only Chinese are to be found in heaven."

Then warming to his theme, he continued "If there were *waiguoren* in heaven, then it wouldn't be heaven would it?"

"But where do the *waiguoren* go when they die?" persisted the follower.

"Oh, they have their own heaven somewhere else. A *waiguoren*-only heaven, but Chinese don't go there."

Although innately superior, the hard evidence brought home by the Chinese as they started to travel, was that China had become a backward nation. The

---

[4] Nicolas Trigault. 'Histoire de l'expedition chretienne au royaume de la Chine 1582-1610. Paris 1617, reprinted 1978.

Chinese did not have washing machines, disposable nappies, televisions or vacuum cleaners. They were surprised to travel to neighbouring Asian countries, which they had been told were labouring under capitalist systems and were far worse off than they were, to find much higher standards of living and more advanced economies. It worried the *People's Daily*, China's official newspaper, as well:

'A few young people are deluded by the temporary prosperity of the capitalist countries. They see the prosperity and the technological advances of the capitalist nations and the backwardness of the socialist states and conclude that capitalism is better than socialism. That leads them astray. But this is completely wrong. Only socialism can save China.'

There are many causes that have led to an awkwardness in dealing with foreigners, something the Chinese are well aware of themselves. The problem was best summarised by the famous Chinese writer Lu Xun, 'throughout the ages, the Chinese had only two ways of looking at foreigners: up to them as superior beings or down at them as wild animals. They have never been able to treat them as friends, to consider them as people like themselves.'

I began to see that the lack of contact between the Cantonese and non-Chinese in Hong Kong which I had at first superficially blamed on British colonial superiority actually ran much deeper. Whilst I am sure British attitudes did not help, the reason seemed to lurk deep in the Chinese psyche. The further I investigated this strange society the more illogical it appeared to be. The violence of Mao's revolution and the seismic after-shocks that ravaged the world's oldest civilisation were still felt thirty years later. So many years of constant revolution, campaigns for this or that, and constant changes in political line had left the people tired and confused.

The Cultural Revolution ended in 1976, the same year that both Mao Ze-Dong and Zhou En-Lai died. Mao's widow Jiang Qing and the other members of her 'Gang of Four', the much feared architects of the Cultural Revolution, were arrested the same year on the grounds that they were planning to overthrow the government. They were detained in the harsh Qin Cheng Number One detention centre outside Beijing, a deliberate choice as over five hundred of China's top leaders had been detained at Qin Cheng during the Cultural Revolution, many at Jiang Qing's behest, of whom 'thirty-four were tortured to death, twenty permanently maimed and sixty went insane.'[5]

The Gang of Four were not put on trial until November 1980 and in the meanwhile they were paraded in the press to remind people of the privations, murders and suicides that had gone before. The years after the Cultural

---

[5] New China News Agency report.

Revolution were for 'settling accounts'; now the persecutors had become the persecuted according to the political wheel of life devised by the communists.

Such were the horrors that the Chinese had suffered during the decade before I arrived in China. When nearly a million people died from the excesses of the Red Guards and millions more had their lives traumatised, it was little surprise that the people were scared to talk, least of all to a foreigner. The most expedient reaction was to disengage, become smooth as a pebble washed in the stream, seek no confrontation. Foreigners, for the Chinese, were not only barbarians they were also dangerous and even a casual contact could be perilous: they were better avoided.

Back in the Nationalities Palace, I was presenting Inchcape's international strengths to Mr. Li but I could see he was hardly listening, he knew it all already. He had been well briefed: his staff probably knew more about my employers than I did. But I persevered and Mr. Li politely listened as the interpreter struggled and his five colleagues scribbled in their five notebooks. Towards the end of dinner, when the soup was served, Mr. Li made a surprising announcement.

"*Yalingdun Zizue,*" he said using my formal Chinese name, "the Chinese Government is mindful to allow certain foreign companies to open representative offices in Beijing."

Although there had been rumours circulating in Hong Kong for some months to this effect, this was the first time that a Chinese official had made such a statement. It could mean that Inchcape might be allowed to establish a base in Beijing and gain a permanent presence in China for the first time in thirty years. The world of course had been here before: China's boundless market infinitely large in numbers yet minute in financial terms, had caused bouts of euphoria down the centuries. The last China boom had been between the world wars when foreigners queued to open representative offices in Shanghai. Carl Crow, an astute observer, wrote in 1937, 'it is either vanity or the romantic idea that business is like an adventure story that, in many cases, provides the urge to make them open expensive branch offices [in Shanghai]'[6]. History was well on the way to repeating itself again.

"What excellent news!" I said. "But where would these foreign representative offices find office space?" There was not a single commercial office building in the city. The ministries and government commissions were housed in their own immense complexes but there were no other buildings that could possibly be used as offices.

"You are staying at the Minzu Hotel – that might become your office," suggested Mr. Li.

---

[6] '400 Million Chinese' by Carl Crow (Harpers, 1937)

"But foreigners cannot reserve hotel rooms," I was referring to the exotic Chinese practice of allocating hotel rooms. All hotels in Beijing were under the control of Beijing Service Bureau Number One. The form was that the same day a foreigner arrived in China, the Chinese unit who had invited the foreigner into the country had to visit Bureau No. 1 and he would be allocated a room in one of the city's hotels. Thus hotels had no control over their occupancy. They simply reported their room availability to the Bureau every day and received allocated guests. One never knew where one was going to stay until one arrived at the airport. Some ministries had more clout than others and could always find a room in the sought-after Peking Hotel; others, lower on the list, scrounged to find a room in a more basic guest house.

"*Yalingdun zijue*, I may be able to arrange for room 852 at the Minzu Hotel to remain yours." Mr. Li then stood, remarked that I must be very tired after such a long day and that I must rest. This is the template for 'dinner's over' and was followed by another old standard, "You must visit China again soon. My hospitality was insufficient on this occasion," a comment often mistaken by foreigners as an invitation to return but in fact is a politely meaningless statement.

Mr. Li's hint was enough however. When I left Beijing the next day I paid for thirty days' rent somewhat to the service staff's surprise. Inchcape now had an office in Beijing. This was a singular honour. None of the other major '*hongs*' in Hong Kong had received such an invitation mainly, it became apparent, due to their history in China: most of them had played inglorious roles as opium peddlers in the 19th century but Inchcape alone had not been tainted by this trade. Inchcape's vast portfolio of agency representation was of considerable interest to the Chinese: it enabled them to make indirect contact with international exporters of high-tech products and, most interesting of all, they could use Inchcape to make contact with Americans – there was an official embargo on U.S. trade with China at that time introduced in 1949 and never withdrawn.

Upon my return to Hong Kong I applied, as instructed, to the CCPIT for formal permission to open an office. I received a positive response some eighteen months later but by that time our office was up and running.

Dick and I began to take it in turns to live in our room in the Minzu, ten days or so at a time. Of the many problems we encountered in China, one of the more difficult was communications. International telephone calls were awkward: a call to Hong Kong had to be booked forty-eight hours in advance and there were so many people on the line it was almost impossible to hear. Calling home to speak to our families was an exercise in frustration. Telexes formed the only credible international link but private telexes were not allowed. The only telex machines were in a room at the back of the Central Post Office some half a mile from the Minzu. There we had to cut the telex tape and operate the machines ourselves. As no individual inbound messages could be received, we arranged for the Hong Kong office to have a prepared tape ready with their messages and as soon as we completed our transmission from Beijing then the Hong Kong office would start their tape and we would receive their news.

Transport was the next problem. Beijing taxis were rare and generally only found at hotels; local people never used them. They were also expensive and had to be hired by the hour as there was no way to find a taxi once released. To give us some mobility I purchased a 'Flying Pigeon' bicycle at the Friendship Store, had it licensed, and started to explore Beijing. I spent many hours cycling around Beijing's maze of *hutongs* exploring the inner depths of this city which in the 1980s had changed little over the centuries. The land clearance and modernisation campaigns were still well in the future and the modern skyscrapers now seen in the city were not even a distant gleam in some architect's eye.

After a couple of months my bike was stolen. I was incensed, China was proud of its overseas image of a crime-free society (something of a surprise to the local residents of Beijing who saw plenty of crime, barred their windows and triple locked their bikes). I went to the local Public Security Bureau and told a surprised officer that I wished to report a theft.

"That will not be possible," I was told.

"And why not?"

"As there is no theft in China there is no mechanism to report a theft. You must have misplaced your bicycle."

"But I didn't. I know precisely where I left it: in its usual place in the bicycle shelter at the Minzu Hotel."

"You must be mistaken," persisted the officer reassuringly.

So it was my fault. I pondered on this surprising turn of events for a while. I was beginning to understand that China is a place where black is never black and white may be something quite different from what you expect. Over the years to come I often noted that if there is another way of doing anything to the accepted norm, then one could almost guarantee that the Chinese had found it.

It was not long before Dick and I decided to take on a local staff member. We were pointed in the direction of the Foreign Enterprises Service Corporation or Fesco which provided carefully vetted staff to the diplomatic corps but had now been charged with supplying staff to the new influx of representative offices and news agencies. The Chinese government's system of allocating staff to foreign representatives became the single largest impediment to foreign business in the 1980s and '90s.

The foreign company signed a contract with Fesco to provide staff at a salary some ten times what the individual received. The difference was explained away as the cost of state pensions, medical care, education and subsidies that the individual received from the State but for which the foreign company should pay anyway. Only then was a controlled 'interview' arranged in the presence of a Fesco official. It was possible to politely refuse the first interviewee but this was met with a hint of displeasure from the Fesco official and the next candidate would always be less-suited than the first, but by then there was no going back and a request for a third choice would be huffily rejected by Fesco.

Many staff members were eventually allocated to Inchcape and we would view them as our own company employees, but their allegiance remained to Fesco as it remained their *danwei* or work unit. Foreign companies could not become a *danwei* and thus were unable to do many things in China. For years I tried to convert our Fesco staff into 'Inchcape men' and introduce a sense of corporate loyalty and belonging but it was generally a wasted effort. Even after many years of employment, if I was to ask a staff member whether they worked for Inchcape or Fesco, they would respond without hesitation that they worked for Fesco.

Every Saturday afternoon our local staff reported to Fesco to receive the latest political line, to be checked for 'spiritual contamination' from close contact with foreigners and to provide a written report on their precise work over the previous week. I, as the chief representative, was always under close scrutiny to see whether I harboured any anti-Chinese thoughts or was conducting some activity which might not be approved by the State. In effect we were inviting spies into our camp but I took the view that it was best for the authorities to know what we were doing.

The two staff members first provided by Fesco stayed with us the longest. Sun Chaogen was a stolid thick-set man from Anhui province, one of the poorest in China. He was of impeccable 'worker/peasant' lineage, the type that formed the backbone of the Party. Sun was an affable bear, speaking atrocious English with a strong Beijing accent, rolling his r's and talking from the back of his throat. We called him 'Lao' Sun, an honorific reserved for older people as he acted much older than his real age – in his early 30s. Lao Sun's mind worked in its own ponderous way and he had a knack of misunderstanding almost everything that anyone told him, be it in English or Mandarin. Lao Sun drove me to the far limits of desperation but however impatient and testy I became with him, he always remained cordial, self-deprecating and keen to please.

Liu Guoxin was the opposite. He was also in his 30s, tall with a square face and an attention deficiency. He paced the room, his hands restlessly picking things up and putting them down somewhere else without looking at them, talking continuously. He had an alert brain and was quick to grasp whatever new ideas he could glean from Dick and myself. A Red Guard only a few years before, 'GX' would recall with delight the horrors he had witnessed during the Cultural Revolution. During 'struggle' sessions GX was always at the forefront, burning books and private property and humiliating the intellectuals. GX slightly regretted that the Cultural Revolution was over. They had been happy times for him. In the West men like GX would have ended up in trouble but the Chinese system had found a way to rein in his wilder side.

Now it was time to identify some business opportunities that I could realise quicker than selling coal mining machinery. Enter Michael Beutler. Michael was a German from Bremen, living in New York and working for Stinnes AG, the large German logistics and trading company. Michael was enthused by the world's passion for China, in full flood in 1979, and was looking for somebody with whom to share his fervour. Over a lunch of fresh snake soup in Hong Kong I listened carefully to Michael's ideas. He had correctly calculated that the Americans would jump into China as soon as the U.S. embargo on trade with China was lifted. Michael thought that he could introduce some American companies for Inchcape to represent in China. The American embargo was placing their own companies at a disadvantage and Michael thought that the Americans might see advantages in appointing a British company to represent them.

Before I met Michael I had been searching Inchcape's extensive list of the companies it represented in different markets around the world for those which might be interested in the China potential. I was not surprised to find that most of Inchape's 'principals', of which there were many thousands, were British-oriented, a legacy from colonial times. There were many world-class British companies but apart from a small handful who already had ongoing trading relationships, the rest of the corporate sector seemed completely disinterested in China. Twenty-five years later, nothing has changed. The British remain laggards in China with British exports to China comprising only 8% of European Union exports, much less than German, French or Italian. Although I gave endless presentations to British companies to exhort them to look at the potential, I was successful with very few. In 2006 a director of a company that had been previously owned by Inchcape was quoted in the *Daily Telegraph* as saying that he 'really didn't see any [British companies in the market]'.

So with the British showing their customary dilatory attitude, the possibility of working with the Americans, in spite of the embargo, seemed a refreshing concept.

My relationship with Michael Beutler was to last for nearly fifteen years during which he was instrumental in introducing a great deal of business to Inchcape from the United States. Michael had a keen eye for detail, was fastidious in the extreme, and not easy to work with. He expected immediate results and found it difficult to work in the Chinese business environment where everything was opaque, there were no easy answers or short cuts and there was no urgency. His impatience grated on most of my staff, Dick in particular. But the business model was excellent: if it was difficult to earn money from selling to the Chinese, then why not make the Americans pay Inchcape a fee to represent them in China? Throughout my career with Inchcape in China this formula provided us with the profits to pacify PG and subsequent chairmen of Inchcape in Hong Kong. It was to be nearly ten years before Inchcape started to earn significant commissions from actual sales of equipment to China.

One year later, with Inchcape's China activities showing a substantial profit, PG was taking the credit for recruiting me in the first place. One evening he called me into his office. The sun was setting over the harbour, the cannon in its usual place taking aim at the traffic pouring out of the tunnel. He ignored my presence for five minutes and then turned to me with the question,

"Can the Chinese build high chimneys?"

I had become the China guru. I was expected to wax knowledgably on every subject from rice yields in Sichuan to the inside fulminations of the Politburo to the cost of cooking oil in Harbin. But chimneys? This was a new one to me.

"You do see high chimneys in China," I responded guardedly.

"Well of course you do," he brushed me aside impatiently. "But how many workers are killed building the bloody things? Do they know anything about safety?"

This I doubted. All Chinese factories I had visited had almost no safety measures. I had just visited a plywood factory and seen the workers risking severed hands and arms, not to mention losing their eyesight, at every turn. At another factory I had seen workers pulling pressed steel sheets from a huge automatic press with no hint of safety precautions. I relayed my reservations to my chairman. He was disappointed. As chairman of Hong Kong Electric he was inviting tenders for the construction of a tall chimney for a new power station. The image of Chinese workers falling off the new chimney would not please the Hong Kong Government.

He changed tack. "I see your business is doing well in China. Congratulations," he thought for a moment. "But you still have not sold any coal mining machinery. It is strange how many times I am presented with well designed business plans and then either the concept does not work and we all lose our investment or something quite unforeseen comes along and we make money from an entirely unexpected source."

The letter on my personal file was forgotten. I had proved that I could make money on my own for Inchcape (a rarity as most managers were in charge of long established businesses with no need to start anything new). I had become Inchcape's China expert at an important time: Deng's reforms and the open-door policy were just igniting a China craze which was set to run and run.

As for the chimney? PG awarded the contract to the Chinese anyway. In the ultimate analyses the low bid overcame any qualms over industrial safety. No Chinese died during its construction.

4

Dick's Story: Part 1

After the overthrow of the Gang of Four in September 1976, a few people were allowed to leave China and I was one of the lucky ones. I was forty years old.

I was born into a wealthy Indonesian Chinese family and brought up in Jakarta, then known as Batavia. After the Dutch withdrew from Indonesia in 1948 anti-Chinese sentiment was rife and the ethnic Chinese began to turn their eyes to their motherland where the new People's Republic was finding its feet. Mao Ze-Dong had won the long civil war, the Japanese had been defeated, the country was alive with new ideas and for the first time in decades a new unified China seemed to hold exciting prospects.

I left Indonesia at the age of sixteen on a ship bound for Hong Kong together with many other young enthusiasts. When I left my parents on the quay at Tanjong Priok port I had little idea that I would not see them for nearly twenty-one years. I was accepted by the prestigious Qinghua University in Beijing which specialised in engineering. The university had been restructured along Russian lines in 1952 and it was still considered the best learning institution in the country. But during the political campaigns between 1957 and 1959, the main concentration at the university shifted from engineering, the subject of my choice, to political education. I had to attend daily lectures on Marxism-Leninism fostered by the Communist Youth League whose members penetrated every aspect of life on the campus.

I decided to join the League not because I was convinced by the ideology but because it seemed to be the road to advancement in China. After I applied to join the League I was instructed that a rite of passage was to betray my 'bourgeois' family by denouncing them as exploiters of the working class. I was greatly pained at having to censure my parents, especially my father who had never exploited anybody in his life. Nevertheless I was forced to write page after page on how my parents had brutally exploited the working masses and how the 'excessive labour' of the workers was transformed into my family's own wealth. My painful efforts were rewarded by membership of the League and eventual promotion to become the deputy Secretary of the League's branch in the university.

Survival in China depended to a large extent on political savvy and on showing the right restrained enthusiasm for the prevailing campaign, for campaigns spread over China with the regularity of the seasons. The summer of 1957 heralded the 'Party Rectification Campaign' in which many students fervently put forward ideas as to how the Party could be improved only to find themselves castigated in the 'Struggle Against the Rightists' which was launched two months later. Those unfortunate students who had supported Party Rectification as a means to show their loyalty to the Party (and with the distant ambition of joining the Communist Party of China itself after graduation) found themselves labelled as Rightists and suffered political discrimination, harassment and humiliation for the next twenty years. I had learned to be wary of such movements and while my friends were avid supporters of Party Rectification, I kept my distance.

Political activism became the *raison d'etre* of university life. Qinghua was transformed into an ideological cleansing institution. Career professors were branded 'white specialists' while young inexperienced teachers with the right proletarian origin took over the classes and management of the university – and this was nine years before the launch of the Cultural Revolution.

The consequences for my education were disastrous. Final examinations were suspended, 'social practice' superseded classroom theory, graduation dissertations were no longer required and students were judged according to their 'socialistic ideological consciousness' rather than their academic achievements. Against this background I graduated in 1958 with a degree in mechanical engineering. I achieved a *san-hao*, or triple credit, with distinctions in ideology, study and sports.

Individual career choice was not introduced in China until the 1990s. Before then the State Personnel Bureau allocated fresh graduates according to demand from the ministries and provincial institutions. I was instructed to report for work at the Forestry Research Institute in the north-eastern city of Harbin, which had been largely populated by 'white' Russians and Cossacks from 1918 until 1949 when the Chinese ejected them. The city still retained a strong Russian character in its architecture and daily life (people from Harbin are the only Chinese who eat cheese). Harbin is the capital of Heilongjiang Province – which translates as 'black dragon river'.

Heilongjiang lies along the Amur River, bordering Russian Siberia. It is bitterly cold in the winter, hot and dry in the summer. Coming from tropical Indonesia I had found the winters in Beijing icily raw but nothing could have prepared me for Harbin where the temperature can drop to minus fifty degrees Celsius. There was little heating; coal was rationed to a few lumps a week despite China's coal reserves being amongst the largest in the world. Essential foodstuffs such as rice, flour and cooking oil were severely rationed. There were shortages of every daily necessity. The temperature inside the houses hovered at freezing level; I did not take off my thick clothes for weeks on end. I lay on my bed at night, fully clothed, unable to sleep for cold and hunger. I wondered what had gone wrong; why had China been reduced to such a low subsistence level? The new China was not meant to be like this. We were told that these years of hardship were due to 'natural calamities' but few believed the official line.

The 1960s were troubling years for the Chinese government. Apart from the constant campaigns wreaking havoc on the home front, we were alarmed at the activities of the Americans in Vietnam. We saw ourselves as becoming isolated on every side: to the north the Soviets had turned against us, relations with the Indians to the south had been poor after border conflicts. It looked as if the Americans might defeat our political allies in North Vietnam and there had been an escalation of enmity with the 'renegade province' of Taiwan.

Mao Ze-Dong decided to construct a 'third front' in the remote mountainous areas of Yunnan and Sichuan Provinces that could be protected from a Russian invasion. Tens of thousands of workers, engineers and administrators were relocated into this forbidding land of mountains and rivers to build steel plants, power stations, machinery factories, military installations and hospitals in spite of a total lack of infrastructure or communications or awareness that the raw materials for the new factories needed to be transported hundreds or thousands of miles.

I was one of eight people from the Forestry Research Institute told to report to the Third Front. I was only recently married, was not allowed to bring my wife with me and was told that my transfer to Yunnan, some three thousand miles from Harbin, would be 'indefinite'.

With heavy heart I began my long trek to the Third Front. My seven colleagues and I were driven in an ancient Russian lorry for hundreds of miles through dense forests, across wild rivers on tottering bridges, zigzagging up and down mountains until the truck finally came to the end of the road facing a river flowing swiftly through a gorge. Dripping black cliffs rose above the river into a dank mist. We climbed slowly out of the back of the truck, stretching our limbs after the long drive. I looked around. I was standing on a rotting wooden platform over the riverbank. There was no sign of human habitation, just dripping sodden trees fading into that mist. The lorry turned and rattled away into the mist. The sheer desolation of the place was profoundly depressing. I wondered if I had been delivered to the veritable end of the earth.

After some hours of waiting in the wind and the rain, a small wooden rowing boat loomed out of the mist and we climbed aboard. I felt like I was crossing the River Styx into the underworld. Eventually I reached what was known as the 'Headquarters': a grim collection of single story concrete buildings in a forest clearing surrounded by military canvas tents pitched in a field of mud. After an uneasy night I was told that another lorry would take us as far as it could into the forest. Several hours later the road petered out and we had to walk a further ten miles until we reached our destination, a small settlement in the forest.

Our task was to erect aerial cableways to extract timber in the mountainous terrain. It was tough, dangerous work. Living conditions were primitive and harsh. Food was scarce; often all we had to eat were forest berries and wild mushrooms mixed with a little rice. If we were lucky we trapped rabbits, pheasants and the occasional wild boar. Some times we managed to buy some meat from the local farmers but it was generally putrid and inedible. I became emaciated and ill but there was no medical attention. I began to wonder whether I would survive.

Then in August 1966, after I had been working in the forest for four months, news filtered through that a new campaign had been launched: 'The Great Proletarian Revolution'. The 'Cultural Revolution' spread over China like wild fire. Suddenly Red Guards were everywhere, taking over the reins of power, destroying anything they thought 'feudalistic', reminiscent of pre-1949 China, or even slightly foreign. China fell under the 'Reign of Red Terror'. High-ranking officials were forcibly removed from their offices, humiliated, tortured and frequently murdered. Chaos spread to every corner of the nation. But I spied an opportunity amidst the pandemonium: during the first surge of anarchy the traditional authority of the *danwei* or work unit had been challenged and many had become dysfunctional. The expression on everyone's lips was 'we have the right to *zhao-fan*' or to rebel. I applied for permission to return to Harbin so that I could better participate in the revolution. Due to my impeccable political background at Qinghua my request was granted and before long I was back with my wife and son once more.

As the Revolution spread over the following months, the world was turned on its head. Rebellious factions fought with other rebellious factions, each outdoing the other in revolutionary fervour. The winning faction established revolutionary committees with their own chairmen until they in turn were superseded by another faction. The Party secretaries, normally the seat of power in every organisation and unit, found themselves sidelined or even incarcerated. The Communist Party itself was completely eclipsed from the autumn of 1966 until the middle of 1970.

During those years my colleagues in the Forestry Research Institute and I were released from our routine work. Our every waking hour was spent on attending meetings to repudiate the 'class enemies' (whoever they were, I was never quite sure and there did not seem to be any class enemies in Harbin), writing 'big character' posters proclaiming the glory of the revolution which were stuck on every available wall space, or singing revolutionary songs. I had to learn Mao's 'little red book' by heart and recite quotations from it in a suitably ardent manner. Every morning I summoned my wife and son and we would stand in front of Mao's portrait (for every house must have at least one large picture of the Chairman on a wall) and bow three times, recite a few paragraphs from the red book and devoutly pray that the 'never setting sun' would live for a million years. I hated this absurd ritual but 'pictures have ears' and any hint of scepticism would have branded me as a counter-revolutionary.

Nevertheless there were always some people who became so fed up with this nonsense that they would write anonymous letters to the media or official institutions querying the wisdom of the Revolution and the anarchy that it had brought. Such letters threw the provincial revolutionary headquarters in Harbin into an orgy of activity and a city-wide hunt would be launched for this most dangerous of all counter-revolutionaries living in our midst. Samples of handwriting were taken at political meetings to be compared with that of the complainer. The Party secretary instructed attendees at political meetings to watch each other in case the culprit might betray himself by appearing nervous. This 'psychological warfare' technique was used to flush out the enemies of the people by using the 'penetrating eyes of the masses'. On each occasion I stared at my feet, holding my breath in anxiety for fear of a sudden and unintentional blush or cough, which might be interpreted as the wrongdoer inadvertently revealing himself.

As an Overseas Chinese I was in a vulnerable position. Many of the Indonesian Chinese who arrived in China with me to participate in the birth of the new China were labelled as spies or counter-revolutionaries and sent to work camps for 'reform through labour'. Many never returned. But my behaviour was above reproach and my status in the Communist Youth League served me well. I was spared any particular punishment but still was told that I was to be given the 'opportunity' to be 're-educated by the working masses'. My family was to be resettled in a remote rural area. This process was called *cha dei luo hu* meaning to settle down to be a new member of the farming brigade. In May 1970 my wife, five year old son, one month old baby and I were settled in a small village set in the midst of a dense forest of fir trees in the most northern part of China just a hundred miles from the border with Russian Siberia.

The narrow-gauge logging train deposited us on a bright sunny day in a clearing in the forest. We were attacked by swarms of gnats, which landed on any exposed skin and inflicted painful bites. My oldest son stood patiently beside his father seeming to realise the seriousness of the situation. Honey, my wife, held the baby. Nobody said a word or made a noise. I shivered in a cold sweat and wished that I was dreaming and would soon wake to find myself back in Harbin. We spent our first night in a woodcutter's timber shed lit by a tiny oil lamp that cast ominous shadows on the rough mud walls. Once again I was overwhelmed with despair at what had happened to me and my family. I remembered my happy carefree youth in Indonesia where the sun was always hot, where there was always plenty of food and fruit of every description, the familiar noises and spicy smells of Java. I thought of my parents and wondered what had happened to them over the years. My father could never have contemplated the ravages that the Chinese people had inflicted upon themselves since the heady days of 1950 when China was reborn as a new nation amidst so much hope. Tears sprung to my eyes, it all seemed such a waste.

I and one other man were assigned to work in a farming brigade consisting of the wives and female relatives of the loggers who in turn had been sent to work in other areas. I worked in the fields from dawn to dusk, day after day, tilling the soil and planting whatever scant crops could be grown during the short summer season. The first snow fell in September and soon after the ground froze so instead of working in the fields I was assigned as a labourer to build a dormitory out of wood and mud. I wondered for how long this could go on – were my Qinghua University qualifications going to be wasted like this? I was told that my relocation was to be permanent but surely one day sanity would prevail and I would be sent back to my Institute.

Before long the little settlement was bolstered by the arrival of teenagers from the city, fresh graduates from middle school who had responded to a new campaign: 'going up to the mountains and down to the villages'. These youngsters enthusiastically set off for the country believing that they could labour side-by-side with the farmers bathing in the rosy glow of revolutionary dedication. But when they disembarked from the logging train and saw my mud dormitory, their faces fell. Their spirits dropped further when they faced their first meal. Soon they just sat around, hugging each other and stamping their feet for warmth.

The winters were even colder than in Harbin. The temperature was minus twenty degrees Celsius at midday, colder still at night. By now I was working in the forest for ten hours a day cutting down young trees with a hatchet, dragging the felled trees to a small clearing and loading them onto a rail cart. There was no machinery, everything was done by hand. My lunch consisted of a small chunk of corn bread that froze solid in the cold air. At lunchtime I was permitted to light a small fire to melt some snow and thaw my bread, frozen hands and feet.

Then, just when I thought things could not get any worse, a new nightmare arose. Relations between China and the Soviet Union had been deteriorating for some time and now skirmishes broke out along the Amur River over some disputed islands in mid-stream. One day a People's Liberation Army cadre visited my camp and called everyone to attend a meeting. He told us that the situation was serious: hundreds of Russian spies had crossed the river and penetrated China to gather intelligence and sabotage infrastructure. The settlement was placed on full alert.

I, as a trusted member of the Communist Youth League, was instructed to keep all-night vigils in a particularly lonely and deserted place for several nights each week. I did not think that this invasion of Russian spies would be very successful. They did not look like Chinese and would face a walk of hundreds of miles to reach the nearest civilisation. There was also not much in the way of infrastructure to sabotage, possibly the mud dormitory or even the narrow gauge logging railway but it would hardly be worth the effort. Nevertheless, armed with a stout stick, I was prepared for the enemy. Night after night I stood behind a large tree watching and listening carefully for any suspicious sound or movement. Every creaking branch made me jump. I often wondered what use my stick would have been against a burly Russian armed with an AK-47 assault rifle.[1]

The winters were dry in Heilongjiang and the very low humidity desiccated the trees, which burned like tinder in spontaneous forest fires, destroying vast areas of woodland and burning the small logging settlements. One night an alarm sounded and everyone in the settlement was summoned to the schoolyard and told that a forest fire was threatening the settlement. I was told to arm myself with mops, spades, anything I could lay my hands on and be prepared to fight the fire 'to the bitter end'. All the elderly people, wives and children were instructed to abandon their houses and hide themselves in ditches, dykes or gullies until the all clear sounded. All the able-bodied men were trucked to the face of the fire. The wind was roaring, the sky turned red, sparks and burning twigs fell onto the amateur fire fighters. I saw the fire around me on every side, in front there was a wall of fire sixty feet high rushing towards me. It seemed that all might be lost but at the last moment the wind miraculously changed course. As I stood in my charred clothes staring at the retreating flames I felt the first drops of rain on my head.

By 1972 other winds were changing too. The fervour of the Cultural Revolution was beginning to ebb. The government had decided that little was to be gained from turning university graduates and intellectuals into a breed of

---

[1] In April 1969 Mao instigated a border clash with the Soviet Union over the uninhabited Zhenbao island in the Amur River. This small skirmish which left 32 dead Russians provoked the Soviet Union to launch a much larger retaliation in which over 800 Chinese died. Mao became genuinely concerned that the Russians might indeed invade China: a constant concern to the Chinese leadership.

farmers. New policies were introduced stipulating that some intellectuals-cum-farmers considered to have worked well in the countryside could return to their hometowns and their previous jobs. In April of that year I was told that I had 'successfully' accomplished my re-education programme and had been selected to be included in the first batch of returnees. I did not know it at the time but my parents in Indonesia had been applying pressure on the Chinese Ministry of Foreign Affairs to find out the location of their third son and his family who were apparently 'missing' somewhere in Northeast China.

Two days later my family and I boarded the narrow-gauge logging train for the last time. One month later I reported to the Ministry of Forestry in Beijing where I was told that I was to be trained to deal with foreigners. I was to be posted to the Foreign Affairs Bureau. The ministry had decided that I would be well suited to work with *waiguoren*: my political status was unimpeachable and my knowledge of English was considered to be 'tolerably proficient'. That I was an Overseas Chinese was no longer something to hide, it suddenly became an advantage.

5

China in 1980

Dick's story was very far from unusual. Everyone in China had been traumatised by the events in China after the founding of the People's Republic on the 1st October 1949. It has been estimated that as many as 27 million people could have died in prison and in labour camps under the rule of Chairman Mao.[1]

There were few countries as forbidding as China in the late 1970s. After a few days in Beijing my eyes gradually became accustomed to the universal drabness, the lack of colour and vibrancy, the unpainted concrete buildings, the pervading sense of living in an under-world. Mao had left China a wretchedly poor country: clothing, food and all daily necessities were still rationed and families were squeezed into one or two small rooms. Very little housing had been built since the 1940s while the urban population alone had increased by over 100 million. In the countryside people were still living in semi-starvation conditions and in many places were poorer than they had been in 1949. In Yenan, Mao's base after the Long March, adult women walked the streets naked for lack of clothes and the streets teemed with beggars.

On my trips back to Hong Kong, I crossed the border and caught the familiar train to Kowloon. I stared out of the window absorbing the various colours of the cars and vans, fashionable clothes, flashing neon signs, bright red lipstick, different hair styles and Hong Kong's busy frantic pulsating life. It was as if life clicked into fast forward the moment I crossed the border from China.

China was a world apart, covered with a thick coating of dust. People rarely smiled, the masses circled slowly and aimlessly on black bicycles; there was an atmosphere of unease, distrust, anxiety. People pressed in on me from every quarter but as in a surrealistic film, I could see them but not talk to them, touch them but not feel them.

Passers-by stopped to stare at the *waiguoren*, eyes and mouths wide open, occasionally calling to a friend to come and view this obscure apparition. In 1979

---

[1] 'Mao the Unknown Story' by Jung Chang and Jon Halliday, Jonathan Cape, 2005.

and for many years after it could be dangerous for a Chinese to talk to a *waiguoren*. The contact had to be reported to a senior cadre and was an unnecessary risk. The office bicycle brought more fleeting contacts as mystery figures glided alongside in the dark and practised a few hesitant words of English before silently disappearing.

Two Chinese phrases rung constantly in the ears of foreigners in China. One was '*mei-you*' roughly translating as 'no' in a hundred different ways. There were always *mei-you* train tickets, *mei-you* food, *mei-you* anything you wanted. A *mei-you* was tossed over the shoulder at every instance to remind you that you were in a land of want.

'*Neibu*' was almost as universal, meaning 'internal information' usually in the form of a State secret. Almost everything was *neibu*: street maps of Beijing were *neibu* (but not bus maps where some streets had been intentionally relocated), as was the weather forecast, train time tables and the whereabouts of official buildings. Most day to day information was *neibu* in China unless it had officially been declassified as not *neibu*. Telephone numbers were *neibu* so an operator could never confirm that you had called the right number. Many an undesirable or critical foreigner was evicted from China after being discovered with some perfectly anodyne data, probably given to him at a technical exchange, but *neibu* nevertheless.

The authorities went to great lengths to keep foreigners apart from Chinese. To enter the Minzu Hotel, a Chinese was stopped by security guards at the gates, ordered to surrender his ID card and handed a form to be signed by the person he saw in the hotel. It angered many Chinese that they were not allowed to enter the hotels where foreigners stayed without being humiliated in this manner.

For the foreigners in China, contact with the Chinese was as limited as it was to be for Dick to meet Italians when he was based at the Chinese delegation to the United Nations Food and Agriculture Organisation in Rome. The same rules applied: foreigners could only make contact with Chinese ministries or organisations through their Foreign Affairs Offices when at least two, preferably more, officials were present. Notes had to be taken at all times so that a record was kept of the conversation.

State Secrets apart, the enforced segregation of *waiguoren* from Chinese puzzled me. It was most evident when travelling together with Chinese cadres. Each railway station had a comfortable waiting room with cane armchairs marked 'Foreign Friends Only'[2]. Foreign businessmen had to travel 'Soft Class' in individual compartments where supervision was easier, but not 'hard class' as this entailed mixing with the Chinese. Foreigners were only allowed into the dining

---

[2] Later changed to "Foreign Friends & Returning Compatriots from Hong Kong" and finally to "Taiwanese Only" when Taiwanese investment was especially sought.

car when the Chinese had finished eating and returned to their seats.

When we checked into an hotel in a provincial city, I stayed in the 'foreigners section' replete with individual rooms, basic bathrooms, threadbare curtains, a wooden chair or two, heating in the winter, a mosquito net, hot water thermos and, if extremely fortunate, a creaky air-conditioner. Our Chinese colleagues were shepherded into a separate wing where they stayed in scruffy unheated dormitories with communal washing facilities.

Every restaurant was divided into foreign and Chinese sections. Foreigners' tables were decorated with a plastic flower and a soiled table cloth while the Chinese ate off bare wooden tables. I suspected the food was better on the Chinese side. The service in the State-owned hotels (foreign managed hotels were not to appear for some years) was deplorable, generally a fact in communist countries. Service on the Chinese side was non-existent: self-service from aluminium tubs, as an occasional figure with a white hat waddled around brushing used plates, crab claws, chicken toe-nails and other detritus from which no more nourishment could be squeezed, into a farmer's bucket.

Another difference was price. Little irritated foreigners more in China than the double pricing standards. There was one price for the foreigners and another for the Chinese for any sort of travel: a foreigner generally paid three times as much for an air or train ticket or in a restaurant.

A kind of apartheid was practised to keep foreigners and Chinese separate. Those who enquired into this arrangement were told that it reflected the different standards of living to be found inside China. This was a sensitive subject and embarrassed the Chinese. Why was there such a large difference in the standards of living? Why should they have to sleep in a dormitory while the rich foreigners lived in such 'luxury'? Why were they so poor? I invited my travelling companions to eat in the foreigners' section with me but this was refused; social eating in an unstructured setting with *waiguoren* could be dangerous.

This apartheid was the latest revelation of China's historic instinct to repel outside influences. China's experiences over many centuries had taught that foreigners, especially caucasians, nearly always brought trouble. They needed to be watched, avoided if possible. Our telephones were tapped, doubtless our rooms bugged also, the room boys examined whatever we threw away and spent a long time tidying our desks but there was no need to follow us too closely. The authorities could rely implicitly upon the reports from our Fesco staff every Saturday afternoon. Although on friendly terms with my staff it was never possible to associate with them after hours. They were specially selected and trained how to handle themselves with foreigners. In particular they had been told to 'draw a clear line' on this subject which was a firm communist instruction never to mix personal curiosity with business. This policy was known as *wai-song nei-jin* or 'outwardly relaxed, inwardly tight'.

Life in Beijing was a dull, lonely affair. There was no entertainment, cinemas, television, casual restaurants or social life. The diplomats laid low in their guarded compounds and incestuously entertained each other. Most other resident foreigners were lecturers or students from the large universities in the city. The small number of foreign businessmen resident in Beijing gathered around the bar in the Peking Hotel – and complained. I went there a couple of times but saw little point in whingeing about China's many shortcomings.

In the winter of 1980 we were allowed to import a car into China. I ordered a Land-Rover from an Inchcape company managed by Dickie Arblaster now metamorphosed in Hong Kong. Dick Chan was in favour of hiring a driver but I thought we would learn more about Beijing if we drove ourselves. This was a wise decision.

One wintry day Dick and I took the train to Tianjin and a taxi across the windy salt pans to Xingang, Beijing's nearest port on the Gulf of Bohai. We walked around the container yard with a blue uniformed customs inspector until we found our shipping container, unlocked it and revealed our gleaming white estate car proudly displaying Inchcape China symbols on its front doors. It had snowed hard during the night and the surrounding fields were covered with thick fresh snow. The road had not been cleared but the Land-Rover roared down the icy road to Beijing, slipping and sliding the whole way back to the city. It was a beautiful sunny, crisp morning and the land was so flat it was difficult to see where the road ended and the fields began.

Now I needed to acquire a driving licence. The only Chinese who drove were professional drivers: chauffeurs, truck and bus drivers. As there were no privately-owned vehicles in China it was unnecessary for others to learn. So the authority that issues driving licences was used to examining a different kind of driver to an amateur like myself. I duly arrived at the appointed place to be handed a long questionnaire in Chinese. I looked puzzled, the examiner roared with laughter. We both knew there was only one way to bridge this particular culture gap: two hundred Marlboro cigarettes. I became the holder of non-diplomatic foreign driving licence number one.

The car transformed my life in China. It gave me a sense of freedom even if it was only a mirage. I could stretch my arms although I knew I was still inside a box. Drive out of Beijing in any direction on any road and after ten miles I faced a sign in Russian, French and English warning 'Foreigners not allowed beyond this point'. I spent hours exploring lanes hoping that I might find a secret way through this cordon but whichever track I chose, however remote, I always found the same sign, sometimes rusty and bent but the message clear. There was no guard enforcing this restriction and at times I would probe their defences by continuing but within a few miles some soldiers or security bureau officers always waved me down and politely pointed me back into the city. Even when these restrictions were finally lifted I was only allowed to buy petrol at a single petrol station in Beijing so expeditions were limited to the car's range on a tank of petrol.

Maps were *neibu* so it was quite difficult to find my way around Beijing although the general layout is not complicated. The bus map was inaccurate and the only tourist map had been doctored. A friend in the American embassy solved my problem by procuring several large and accurate wall maps of Beijing and Shanghai produced by the CIA based on satellite photographs. The maps perplexed my staff: they could not understand how foreigners' maps showed ministries in their actual positions, whilst on maps available to them important buildings were intentionally placed a few hundred yards away on a different road.

Beijing lies on the edge of the desert which rolls for thousands of miles westwards beyond the Great Wall; mountains rise to the north. Frequently I drove the twenty odd miles to the necropolis of the Valley of Eternal Peace for picnic lunches amidst the unexcavated remains of the Ming dynasty imperial tombs. I lay on the warm cracked stones and sipped cool Chablis, as the expatriate population in Beijing had done for a hundred years and more, Tourists could be spied in the far distance through the peach trees but they always went to the same restored tomb with its guides and tacky souvenir stalls. The other tombs lay faded and crumbling, undisturbed down the centuries.

Dick and I were very conspicuous as we drove Beijing's only Land-Rover around the city. There were few foreigners behind steering wheels. Many government cadres used to seeing cars with their drivers found the owner-driver concept to be startlingly original. Cadres, crisp in their *zhongshan zhuang* suits would look around and ask after a meeting at their ministry, "And where is your driver?" But it delighted them to see me start the car and drive off, just the same as a *si-ji*, a Chinese professional driver. "These *waiguoren*! So resourceful!"

On crisp winter Sundays we would drive into the dusty Fragrant Hills rimming one side of Beijing or to one of the many deserted temples in the surrounding hills, still damaged from the Cultural Revolution. There were no tourists. One winter's morning I crunched fresh snow underfoot through courtyard after muffled courtyard from one end of the Forbidden City to the other. Nightly I drove from the Minzu to where I was staying at the time, maybe the Peking Hotel, perhaps another, slowly weaving between camel trains, green tanker trucks silently hosing the streets, lightless bicycles and dare-devil child-carrying pedestrians used to crossing the empty streets without looking.

Driving brought me in contact with the Public Security Bureau and their traffic police. I had long noticed that the Chinese showed little respect for their police. Shouting matches with them over a dispute seemed to be the normal form. I was frequently flagged down for some perceived infraction of the rules, to be castigated by a policeman in Chinese for some unknown infringement. I would respond in English in similar fashion until there was an impasse and I would be waved on with a dismissive gesture. The right response seemed to be to vociferously deny any wrong doing and fight for the moral high ground while accusing the policeman of interfering with one's legal business.

One night I was driving to Tianjin when a horse and cart laden with crates of tomatoes suddenly crossed the road without warning. I swerved but clipped the back of the cart spilling two crates onto the ground. I stopped the car, helped the farmer pick up the damaged fruit, offered a little compensation far in excess of the value of the tomatoes, apologised and drove on. Many weeks later I was summoned to appear at the headquarters of the Public Security Bureau's traffic division. Driving the only Land-Rover in Beijing had not made it too difficult for them to find me. I noticed that there was a file detailing the accident with the farmer.

"Why did you hit the cart?" I was asked by a uniformed PSB officer as if it had been my intention to do so. "Were you smoking?" I admitted this might have been a possibility, I did occasionally smoke twisted Burmese cheroots. Most drivers in China seem to have a cigarette permanently lodged in the corner of their mouths.

"You are not allowed to smoke when driving in China." There was much scribbling in note books. "Were you talking at the time?" I concurred that I might have been talking as well. "Talking and smoking at the same time as driving? You are not allowed to talk and drive. They are both serious offences." This was an even greater surprise, most chauffeurs in China never draw breath.

Three more PSB officers entered the room and I was ordered to make a detailed self-criticism in front of a row of uniformed officers to the effect that I must not in future abuse rural farmers or their carts and would never smoke or talk while driving again. I was then fined ten Renminbi, slightly less than one U.S. dollar and sent on my way.

Beijing was a wounded city. Evidence of the Red Guards' zeal was clear to the eye. Historic buildings, palaces and temples were boarded up. Dusty, broken furniture lay heaped in corners of courtyards. Grass grew in the courts of the Forbidden City. Young bushes sprouted between the yellow tiled dragons on the eaves. The emperor's astronomy instruments which had perched on a platform on the edge of the city wall tumbled down in an earthquake while I was staying nearby one Sunday and lay there unrepaired. The city was in decay. China's ancient capital was crumbling through earthquakes and neglect. The Red Guards had given it a shove on its inexorable way. The Maoists had not cared. Beijing was not a symbol they needed. The Long Marchers' hearts lay in the country.

Not much had changed in Beijing since Liberation thirty years before. A few slums had been cleared, some factories built in the centre of the city, occasional roads widened and the old Foreign Legation quarter reborn into ministries. The most significant change was the almost total destruction of Beijing's fabled wall: only hidden fragments and the great gates remained.

Travel was a problem: every visit to China required a Chinese visa and these were only issued on the instructions of certain Chinese organisations holding the right to bring in foreigners. A visa was only valid for the cities one intended to travel to. Sometimes I was in Beijing and wanted to travel to Shanghai but found I could not because Shanghai was not on my visa. This required a visit to the department of the Public Security Bureau responsible for foreigners. It was housed in a beautiful old Chinese building around a courtyard where pomegranate trees grew in large tubs. The PSB were well-practised in dealing with foreigners and skilful at the art of making everything an impossibility.

"May I obtain permission to visit Shanghai?" would be the opening line in a typical visit to the PSB.

"Why do you want to go there?"

"To visit the Shanghai government."

"Where is your invitation from the Shanghai government?"

"They will not issue one until I have obtained your permission to travel to Shanghai."

"You know that we cannot issue our permission until we have evidence that you have an official invitation to visit Shanghai." And so on.

The authorities were still nervous about allowing foreigners to wander freely. After some years the government announced that there would be three 'open' cities, Beijing, Shanghai and Guangzhou which foreigners could visit without permission. Over many years more and more cities were added to this list until eventually it became possible to travel almost anywhere in China but this was a very gradual process.

Another problem was the impossibility of buying a return ticket. As soon as I arrived in a city the first task was to visit the CAAC office to buy an onward airticket. This was especially difficult with railway travel, the normal means of travel for the Chinese. Trains were always full and a visit to the booking office generally involved a long wait to have an uncooperative and offhand clerk sing out 'mei-you' whenever one wanted a ticket. It was possible to be stranded for several days in a distant Chinese city waiting for a berth on an express train.

I found my lack of Chinese, and the difficulties I was encountering in learning the language, proved frustrating in a country where no English was spoken. Later, one cadre told me that my lack of Chinese was actually to my advantage. "All cadres would like to come into contact with foreigners if they dare," he told me quietly one night as we shared a swaying sleeping compartment on the long train trip between Loyang and the central desert city of Lanzhou, "but we have been told to be especially wary of foreigners who speak Chinese. Who do you think trained all these foreigners? The Taiwanese of course, those American running dogs," he lapsed into Cultural Revolution-talk. I was fascinated but he had not finished, "And why do they want to learn our language? They have some dark reason. Things may not be what they seem. We have to be careful of such people."

This may have been the case but I did notice that Chinese became uncomfortable in the presence of a Mandarin-speaking foreigner. Normally they merrily talked amongst themselves quite ignoring my presence but if there was a Mandarin-speaker present they would speak formally and huddle whispering in little groups. Over the years I developed a working knowledge of the language and was often not in the dark as much as the cadres thought. I often interviewed foreigners for selection in China-based work, generally short-term machinery installations, and found that it was the successful Chinese-speaking candidates that were resisted the most by their Chinese hosts and sometimes had to be replaced.

I had been in Beijing for some months and was becoming bored with the food in the Minzu Hotel although its two restaurants, one Chinese and one Russian, were amongst the best in the capital. Sometimes we ventured to one of the few other restaurants which accepted foreigners. These restaurants were divided into two parts. The larger section had bare tables, bamboo chopsticks, wooden stools and a mass of local people jostling and pushing while unkempt waitresses shouted at the customers and passed around steaming bowls of soup. The other section, sometimes just behind a green cloth divider but more often on a different floor, was the foreigners-only area. There were starched tablecloths, paper napkins, upholstered chairs and red velvet curtains with neat waitresses in aprons. I beseeched Dick to take me to a local restaurant as I wanted to see what choice the local people really had. I had seen one not far from the Minzu on Chang'an Avenue. He was reluctant and viewed the venture with distaste but eventually conceded.

As we walked into the hot and noisy restaurant all talk ceased. Waitresses balancing trays of food froze where they stood. A hundred pairs of eyes watched. I spied two empty stools around a table where eight other men in blue *zhongshan zuan* were sitting. We sat down. The eight men were also imitating statues, chopsticks poised in mid air, mouths frozen in mid chew. Then as suddenly as it stopped, life resumed. The old man next to me waved a pile of gnawed bones away with his sleeve, pushed a plate overflowing with debris over to the other side of the table and cleared enough space for a couple of bowls. Producing a jug of beer he filled a glass that had been used by the previous guest and offered it to me. Food choices were written on a blackboard. The kitchen was partitioned from the restaurant by a glass wall. Food was cooked in vats and ladled into buckets which were carried to a serving station in the restaurant. The broken grey rice was unlike the fragrant long grain rice that foreigners were served. When we left all the customers stood up and craned their necks to see us. Somehow eating in the Minzu seemed a better prospect after all.

Our office expanded over the years to take up nearly half a floor of the Minzu Hotel as more and more staff from Fesco joined Inchcape China. Our staff were considerably more stress-free than their colleagues in the Hong Kong office. Any morning tension was eased by the right to *xiuxi* or mid-day rest as enshrined in the Chinese constitution. The custom dates to the days when the new communist leaders were fresh from the country and used to rising with the sun to work in the fields and sleep during the hottest part of the day. Urban dwellers had enthusiastically adopted the system.

Government offices closed at mid-day and reopened at 3 p.m. Most Chinese staff kept a bedroll in their offices which they rolled out on the top of their desks and promptly fell asleep for two hours. I forbade my staff from sleeping on their desks in the Inchcape offices. So they found other places and went to sleep anyway.

Our offices were ordinary hotel rooms with the hotel furniture removed and our own desks and filing cabinets moved in[3]. Each room had its own en-suite bathroom. I was however taken aback to see my staff in dressing gowns towelling their recently shampooed hair in the middle of the day or GX dressing in front of a mirror after taking a shower.

"Why," I asked Dick, "can't they do this at home? Why are they bathing during working hours?" As I talked, Jane, our exquisitely svelte secretary, strolled past in a woolly bath-robe smiling at us sweetly.

Dick and I went to the Russian restaurant where we picked at a greyish substance in a pink watery broth.

"Our staff," he grasped my arm, "you know how they live? In a dismal appartment with the rest of their family. Bare concrete floor. One light bulb. A squat toilet and a hose. Only a dribble of water, sometimes none. They had probably been promised central heating but it never worked. Like the lift. Do you know what it is to live when the temperature inside your home never rises above minus ten degrees for months?" He let go of my arm and prodded a lump of fat in his soup bowl. He knew, he had been there.

Dick paused for a while, blowing at the broth in his spoon, undecided

---

[3] A source of perennial dissent with the Minzu Hotel management committee which insisted on charging Inchcape rent to store the hotel furniture we did not use as well as extra rent for the furniture we brought in.

whether to swallow. He let it slowly drip back into the bowl and lowered his voice, "They get a hot shower twice a week in the winter if they are fortunate at the public bath house. They are lucky if they get a couple of minutes each. So is it so bad if they help themselves to those piping hot showers and baths so conveniently located next to their workplace?"

Shelley, my future wife, was eleven years old at the time. She was attending the Peijin Junior High School in Shanghai, one of the best. She tells of broken window panes still unrepaired from the Cultural Revolution through which snow would drift in the winter. All the children suffered severely from chillblains, some even frost-bite,

The early 1980s were the years of the 'four must-haves' when for the first time that the Chinese could remember, some useful consumer goods appeared on the shelves and rapidly became status symbols. The first four consumer goods to which all aspired were a wrist-watch, bicycle, radio and sewing machine. Once these demands had been satisfied, consumers moved on to the 'big four': a washing machine, refigerator, electric fan and television. Gone were the days when villages had a single television set mounted on a pole in the village centre for everyone to crowd around.

Hotels in China were a particular delight. Mostly built in the 1950s to house visiting Russian technicians and little improved since, the Dong Feng hotel in Guangzhou was one of the worst. On one stay I was troubled by creatures living in a threadbare sofa in my room which sprang to life when I turned out the single light-bulb at night. I complained to the room attendants that I was not alone in my room but they showed little interest. On the third night I became increasingly irritated at the scuffling and thumping coming from the sofa and turned on the light to catch a surprised-looking rat peering at me from the end of my bed. The next morning I remonstrated again with the attendants who continued to lounge around their work station. So I pushed the sofa out into the corridor and with a huge heave turned it upside down. This upset the family of rats who jumped out of the sofa and scampered down the corridor towards the room attendants who leapt onto the counter to escape the rampaging rodents.

Shanghai, which today houses a plethora of five-star hotels, had only six government-owned hotels, all built in the early 1900s. By the mid-1980s it was well-nigh impossible to obtain an hotel room, bearing in mind that one could not make reservations but depended upon the influence of the 'host organisation' with the government bureau in charge of issuing hotel rooms. There were however, a few very grand houses in the old French concession that had been abandoned by their owners in 1949 and which the municipality decided to rent out on a per-room basis to visiting businessmen. Many of them still had some of the belongings of their previous owners which was surprising given the amount of looting that had taken place during the intervening thirty odd years. On one occasion I came across a set of sterling silver tea-spoons that the previous owners had forgotten to stuff into their suitcase before they left. I persuaded the attendant to let me have them in exchange for a litre of cooking oil.

There was one vast house with extensive gardens near the airport surrounded with a high brick wall. I was told that after 1949 the masses, who had looted all privately-owned properties, did not dare to enter this particular estate for fear that it might be occupied by Party leaders. In fact it had been the residence of one of the Sassoons, a wealthy family in Shanghai, and the owner had told his staff in 1949 that he would be going to Hong Kong for a few days but then never returned. For the next thirty years his staff, and presumably their successors, maintained the house and manicured the gardens waiting for the owner to return. It was not until 1982 that the municipal government finally plucked up enough courage to force open the grand gates and discover the empty palace that lay within.

Shanghai had a total of eight restaurants in 1979 of which one, the Red House, was China's only remaining western restaurant. The menu offered such delights as cocktail de crevettes, tournedos, crepes suzettes and Grand Marnier soufflé. The only snag was that the ingredients had to be brought from Hong Kong and given to the French-speaking chef the day before.

Cockroaches in hotels were a constant hazard. The venerable Peking Hotel had three wings that were built during different eras of recent Chinese history. The old section was built under the imperial Ch'ing dynasty, another wing was added by the nationalists and a huge 'new' wing was built under the communists. It was the hotel of choice for all visitors but difficult to get into. It was the new wing which seemed to house the largest population of cockroaches. If one was unwise enough to visit the bathroom at night one turned on the light to find a virtual carpet of cockroaches on the floor, in the bath, the shower, the basin and perched on the fittings.

On one occasion I was accompanying an American delegation to China and one of their members woke me in the middle of the night to complain of a searing pain in his head. He was scarcely lucid with agony and asked to be taken to the nearest hospital. Fortunately the Peking Hospital, normally reserved for high-ranking Party members only, was just across the street next to a famous duck restaurant which residents used to call the 'Sick Duck'. There were few staff on duty at the hospital and the American sat and waited for an hour cradling his head in his hands and moaning as I searched for a doctor. Finally I ran one down and he checked the American over: he examined his eyes, looked down his throat and eventually peered into his ears when he suddenly jumped back with an explanation. "Good lord," he shouted in excitement. "You have a cockroach in your ear!"

He called for other Chinese nurses and doctors who suddenly materialised as one after the other they lined up to examine the strange sight of the American with a cockroach in his ear. It was scratching on his eardrum and apparently seemed intent to work its way through his head. "Get it out!" pleaded the American but it took some time before all the Chinese had sated their curiosity and with a long pair of tweezers the doctor reached in and pulled it out.

For ever after I wore ear-plugs when I stayed in the Peking Hotel.

The Chinese Communist Party kept control of the country with a firm fist, there was no question of a velvet glove. There are over five thousand executions yearly, most in public – every city has an execution ground. In Beijing it was generally the gravel riverbed beside the Marco Polo bridge but other places sufficed. Any number of crimes merit execution from the most serious to mere hooliganism. The State sees no reason why it should foot the bill for the bullets expended and it is customary for a security officer to call on the family the day before an execution to demand payment of a small pittance for the cost of the single bullet to be fired into the back of the kneeling victim's neck.

In 1984 I took a boat from Wuhan to Chongqing, a four day trip chugging slowly up the muddy Yangzi River. More than ten miles wide in some places, it was more like a sea than a river. At other times, especially as it roared through the now vanished gorges, the torrent narrowed to a few hundred yards. It was on the second day, when I was standing at the rail idly watching the cormorants diving for fish, that a headless human corpse floated by. I paid little attention until a few minutes later I saw a second and then a third. After I had counted at least six I pointed out one of the swollen corpses to a ship's officer and asked him where these bodies were coming from. He studiously avoided looking at the body bobbing in the water and said, "Corpse, what corpse? I see no bodies." Over the next couple of days I must have seen a couple of dozen, all headless, and was wondering whether we were about to view some terrible massacre around the next corner.

I was met in Chongqing by GX who had flown from Beijing to meet me. I told him what I had seen and asked him the reason. He looked uncomfortable, this was not something that a foreigner was meant to see. He took me to a tea-house where we shared a warm bottle of beer. Over two hundred executions had taken place in Chongqing over the previous week. The normal procedure, he told me, was that the family was meant to collect the body of the executed criminal and arrange a cremation but often the family thought it unwise to be associated with the criminal and so left the body on the execution ground. Who knows whether the authorities might come looking for the family to see if they might be in some way responsible for the miscreant's behaviour.

If the body was not collected fairly sharply then eager suppliers to the Chinese medical profession would fall upon the bodies to see what could be salvaged. There were all sorts of body parts which could be usefully recycled; especially the head where the brain could be extracted, dried, treated, ground-up and used in various potions. The quickest procedure was to cut off the heads and collect them in jute sacks, slice out the choicest organs and chuck the body in the river.

Outside most security bureau offices in China there is a notice board displaying photographs of criminals due for execution and a short synopsis of their crime. Once the criminal has been executed a large red tick is printed on the photograph. As I walked past one of these notice boards in Chongqing I saw that all the photographs had recently been ticked.

6

Delegations

Foreign business people were invited to China in delegations, never singly. An incoming delegation was generally headed by a senior officer in the company, frequently very senior as even in the 1980s the elusive China market raised inordinate interest and the prospect of a billion consumers was always at the forefront of every businessman's mind. I reckoned that it took a minimum of four years for a foreign company to achieve a direct sale in China and four years of concentrated dedication at that. This meant a sizeable budget had to be allocated to the China market: people needed to be taken away from their normal jobs and instructed to travel to China at regular intervals. Chinese delegations to the U.S. had to be planned and accompanied, there were marketing expenses and, not the least, the Inchcape China fee had to be paid.

For these reasons I insisted that the chairman, president or CEO should lead the team. He would inevitably be swayed during his first visit, bowled over by Chinese hospitality and convinced by the promise of the potential that such a huge market held for the future. A convert was made who then ensured that the China budget was sustained throughout the long barren years that always followed. The more senior the leader, the more serious the Chinese took the delegation and protocol dictated that their team had to be led by a cadre of equivalent rank.

The Chinese host organisation handled incoming foreign businessmen according to a carefully planned template. They knew that foreigners visiting China for the first time were apprehensive of entering this intimidating communist world and often held deep-seated prejudices. Horror stories, mostly grossly exaggerated, abounded, and first-time visitors anticipated a cold and possibly hostile reception. The Chinese understood these concerns and made huge efforts to ensure that their most skilled, but trustworthy, staff were allocated to the Foreign Affairs Bureaux of the various ministries and were accustomed to accommodate, within reason, the curious tastes and customs of the foreigners.

It took Dick and I anything up to nine months to arrange for a Chinese ministry to receive a delegation consisting of half a dozen Americans: the leader, frequently the president of the corporation (whom the Chinese would always address as 'Mr. President' much the delight of the businessman), a senior vice president in the international department. a couple of technical people and miscellaneous aides. Much needed to be done during those nine months: brochures were translated into simplified Chinese (as used only in China and thus not known to Hong Kong-Chinese, Taiwanese or American-born Chinese), slide presentations to be translated with a Mandarin sound-track, there were business cards and data sheets of technical presentations to be printed, large and small gifts to be prepared and every effort made so that the Chinese appreciated and remembered this particular delegation.

When the delegation arrived in Beijing, having entered via the difficult route from Hong Kong and endured the vicissitudes of the White Cloud Airport and CAAC's eccentric inflight service, they were surprised to be met as they stepped off the aircraft by a ministerial representative who guided them away from the other passengers into a VIP reception area. Here they were plied with mugs of green tea which they found difficult to drink through the thick mat of leaves floating on top, while being urged to rest after their long flight. Passports were taken away, much troubling the Americans who had been coached by the State Department never to let their passports out of their sight, but were soon returned after processing by invisible border guards.

A fleet of cars would then arrive, often led by a formidable 'Red Flag' limousine and the entourage set off for their hotel sometimes accompanied by police outriders with sirens blaring. Such a reception boosted the egos of the visiting Americans way out of proportion to their own importance. All of this required intensive preparation by the Inchcape China team in Beijing and all had to be paid for: even the police out-riders were available for a fee paid to the Ministry of Public Security. But the Americans, never short on self-importance, thought that it was only right that they should be treated in such a way!

During their first two days in Beijing we arranged for the senior Americans to meet vice ministers or appropriate senior Chinese politicians in the formal surroundings of the Ministry or occasionally even State leaders and members of the Politburo in the hallowed Great Hall of the People amidst television and other media coverage. Simultaneously the American technical people embarked on what was the first of many 'technical exchanges': a one-way flow of information during which a room full of Chinese from factories, research institutes, universities and anybody with an official interest in the subject listened to the Americans explain why their technology was the best in the world. Sometimes these 'exchanges' were the sole rationale for the Chinese invitation, a gap in their technical knowledge needing to be filled.

On the second or third evening the Chinese hosted a banquet at one of the restaurants specialising in such events. Such banquets included as many as twelve or more courses of food exotic to western tastes and involving a free flow of Mao Tai, a sorghum-based harsh liquor that foreigners were told to knock back in a single gulp to increasingly raucous toasts and much shouting of the word 'gan-bei' or bottoms up. After a few gan-bei's the Americans were delighted to find that their hosts, previously considered remote and austere, were human after all and enjoyed a drink or two too many. The visitors were encouraged to drink too much thus releasing the tension accumulated during the high-pressure technical exchanges and the awkward discussions with the ministerial officials.

They did not notice that their hosts and the senior officials at the banquet only proposed a single toast and left it to their juniors to challenge the foreigners with more and more toasts. While the Americans drank more and often became unguarded and tactless in their comments, the senior Chinese quietly observed. When a foreigner realised that he was becoming the worse for wear while his host remained surprisingly sober, he would ply his host with more gan-bei's not detecting the Chinese technique, perfected by Dick, of apparently swallowing the slug of Mao Tai but actually holding it in his mouth and then discreetly spitting it into a half full glass of orange juice. I often watched Dick's glass of juice getting steadily fuller as the banquet progressed.

With a few exceptions the Chinese are not great drinkers of alcohol. They absorb the alcohol too quickly and become red-faced and over-heated not enjoying the process or the knowledge that they might be losing control and possibly saying something better left unsaid. Penalties could be huge for an indiscreet word muttered in a tipsy moment at a banquet.

Once outside Beijing, or especially after a major contract had been signed when a banquet was held for celebratory reasons, then the atmosphere could become very charged and the foreigners, and some Chinese, became very drunk indeed. The further one travelled from Beijing the more serious the drinking and the more the Chinese relaxed with their foreign guests.

My most memorable banquet was at the guest-house of the Wuhan Steel Plant after a contract signing. That evening I was to be the victim and one after the other a procession of the steel plant's executives proposed a gan-bei to me personally. At some time during the dinner I felt the need to relieve myself and staggered to the door in search of the W.C. But outside the banquet hall there were no electric lights and so I wandered down a dark corridor before hearing the sound of running water through a pitch dark doorway. I stumbled through the gloom into even deeper darkness and walked in the direction of the tinkling water until I guessed it was in front of me. Thinking this must be the urinal I let out a pressurised stream of processed Mao-Tai. Imagine my surprise when there was a sudden yell of annoyance from directly in front of me and a figure moved out of the gloom hastily bumping into me and swearing in Chinese. Once back in the banquet hall I was deeply embarrassed to find my host brushing himself down after I had clearly achieved a direct hit all over his smart uniform!

Banquets could take place at any time of the day. I remember one twelve course banquet held in a remote town in the Pearl River Delta that started at 7 a.m. complete with Mao-Tai toasts – not a good start to the day. The Chinese often eat their lunch at 1130 a.m. and dinner would start at 5.30 p.m. Every city, town, village or factory insisted on holding a banquet for their visitors. Whereas in Beijing it was a formal way to greet the foreigners and demonstrate a friendly face, in the countryside it was an opportunity for the factory managers to gorge themselves in a grand manner and charge the expenses to the work unit. Many factories ran very high class cuisines for their management; the Guangzhou Glass Works employed the chef from the Chinese Embassy in Germany who produced delectable Chinese meals.

Food was always by far the greatest priority to the Chinese when they travelled away from home. Not for nothing did Confucius write 'Eat, drink, man, woman: herein are man's great desires'. As soon as I arrived at a new destination after an overnight train journey my priority was to find an hotel for the night but my Chinese travelling companions would first ask the local officials where they could find the best meal. Whatever the time of day immediate preparations were laid for a succession of grand meals. One did not have to look far into recent Chinese history to understand the reason. Scarcity of food, even famines, have been an everyday risk in China for centuries. As recently as 1960, very fresh in their memories for most of the Chinese I met, many millions died of starvation; 38 million people died from government-created hunger between 1958 and 1961 during the Great Leap Forward.

The return banquet held by the foreign delegation was often a protocol minefield. It was not always obvious who was the most senior Chinese present. In the early days many Chinese did not have business cards and sometimes the most important person deliberately kept himself, or frequently herself, in the background. Many foreigners made the mistake of treating the one or two English-speakers as the guests of honour and had to be guided by Dick or myself.

Soon it became apparent to the Chinese that their choice of Inchcape as one of the first foreign companies invited to open a representative office in Beijing was a wise one. Most companies were single industry businesses whereas Inchcape was a multinational with extensive interests in a multitude of different businesses. We therefore began to cultivate contacts in a wide variety of ministries from Agriculture to Public Health, Communications to Ship Building, Defence to Light Industry. This was a unique advantage: all our principals and other companies endeavouring to break into China dealt exclusively with the ministry responsible for their particular activity.

The Chinese themselves, once allocated to a particular industry upon leaving university, never ventured far from their work unit. The *danwei* provided their housing, their welfare, the workplace, their friendships and their social life. They would rarely meet people from other walks of life. So it came as a considerable surprise to them when they were invited to an Inchcape China banquet which we would give from time to time when a main board director visited from London.

On such occasions Dick and I spent many months arranging a large banquet for as many as a hundred and fifty senior representatives from fifty or so different State commissions, ministries, research institutes and federal bodies. Each guest entered the banqueting room flabbergasted to meet so many senior Chinese from different organisations. We often entertained a dozen or so officials of ministerial rank and all had to be seated according to the correct level of seniority – a protocol nightmare. Who ranked higher, the Minister of Coal Industry or the Minister of Public Health? This was resolved by seating the most senior people around a huge round table.

During such visits we invited the British ambassador and, as we needed a host for each of the dozen or so tables at the banquet, we asked other high-ranking diplomats from the British embassy to host tables. One might have thought that embassy people, who lived in Beijing full time, might have previously met some of the officials that we entertained but this was rarely the case. They knew officials from the Ministry of Foreign Affairs, as one might expect, but few others. Indeed they valued an Inchcape banquet as a source of contacts. I thought this strange: for many businessmen the embassy was their first port of call when arriving in China. They were looking for contacts, market information and general assistance in this alien and difficult country. But the reality was that the embassy seemed to know little of what was happening in China and knew few people outside their own orbit. I thought this reflected poorly on Britain's diplomats, who had a much more comfortable life than Dick and I, but showed also the success of the Chinese system in deliberately keeping the diplomats, whom they were convinced were only interested in subversion, in the dark.

I had hoped that the diplomats might be able to solve some of our protocol problems, for was that not one of their specialities? But on more than one occasion they created problems of their own. I remember one instance when we invited the British ambassador and four or five of his colleagues to a banquet at the Peking Hotel. The ambassador was rightly sitting on the top table together with an Inchcape director and a collection of ministers. As the senior Inchcape officer in China I hosted the second table and I invited the commercial counsellor from the embassy to host the third table. As soon as he saw his *placement* he took me on one side and remonstrated that he should be on the top table together with his ambassador. I politely explained that there was no spare seat for him and that his position did not merit such an honour and that there were many officials on table number three whom he should find interesting to meet. He rejected my explanation and threatened to withdraw from the dinner taking his staff with him. Only a word in the ambassador's ear prevented a diplomatic walk-out.

Difficulties with the British embassy in Beijing were not restricted to petty protocol matters. I visited the embassy not long after we opened the Beijing office to investigate what services it might provide, but the news that a British company had been one of the very first to open a permanent representative office in China, was met with boredom and raised eye-brows. "What on earth for?" asked the diplomat I met at the time.

When Lord Inchcape made his first visit to China I advised the embassy of the dates that the chairman would be visiting and suggested a couple of days that would be suitable for lunch with the ambassador. "Oh I don't think that would be possible!" came the fruity voice of the blue-rinse Foreign Office secretary down the telephone line. "His Excellency only meets businessmen on very rare occasions." I reported this comment to an amazed Inchcape officer in London who must have made the right call for within a few days I was told that the ambassador would be delighted to invite Lord Inchcape for lunch. I made a point of calling on the commercial counsellor from time to time to brief him generally on Inchcape's rapidly expanding interests in China. I then found that whatever I told him was circulated not only widely within the Foreign Office, which one might expect, but he also used the information as part of his briefing to any visiting British businessman. In the highly competitive and very secretive world that China was, such indiscretion was quite out of order.

A year or two later I hosted a visit to China by Rear Admiral Sir Rae McKaig, recently retired from responsibility for command of NATO's North Atlantic fleet and now a director of Inchcape plc. Sir Rae was only in Beijing for three days and had a series of meetings with the Minister of Communications but he did want to see the new commercial counsellor at the Embassy. By this time I was increasingly wary of the embassy and suggested that Sir Rae might give them a miss but he was adamant. He was of the school that believed that wherever he was in the world, it was proper to call in at the embassy.

I was told that the counsellor would be available at 4 p.m. one afternoon but only for fifteen minutes. This was inconvenient for Sir Rae as it entailed

Bukit Chermin, my house in Singapore

Charles Letts and Plern

Prince and Princess Panya Souvanna Phouma at their wedding (me behind)

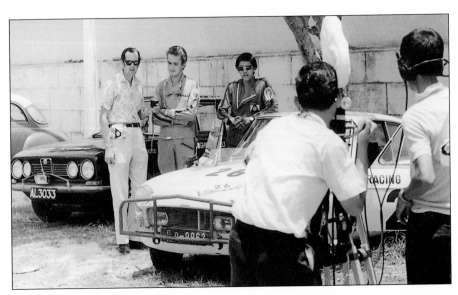

Dickie Arblaster interviewing me for Radio Television Singapore

Dick Chan in one of the
Okanagan/Inchcape helicopters

The Inchcape Land-Rover in front
of the Monument to the Heroes of
the People's Rebublic, Tiananmen
Square, Beijing

P.G. Williams, chairman of Inchcape
Hong Kong

P.G. and the Governor of
Guangdong at the launch of
the bus service

The main highway between Beijing and Tianjin

In northern Manchuria

Travel by camel in the Gobi Desert, west China

Most travel in China was by train

Chinese life in 1980

My daughter Venetia and Shelley

Shelley, me and my son Alexander

cutting short a meeting with the Minister. We arrived at the embassy five minutes late to be met by a very impatient counsellor wearing white shorts, socks and tennis shoes. The admiral was resplendent in his very best civilian dark suit. The counsellor gave Sir Rae's hand a quick shake and garbled "Sorry about this but we'll have to keep this to five minutes as I have a tennis game waiting." He pushed Sir Rae into a chair and spoke for three minutes on China's economy.

Sir Rae tried to explain what he was doing in China which could have led to an investment of many millions of pounds in Chinese port construction, an important 'first' for a British company. "Look," said the counsellor jumping to his feet. "I really don't have time for this. I'm sorry," and dashed out of the room grabbing his tennis racket on the way.

Sir Rae was so incensed he wrote a letter to Margaret Thatcher, the prime minister. This counsellor left Beijing fairly soon afterwards. I never heard of him again. My last contact with the British embassy in Beijing was after the Tiananmen Square riots of 1989 and was equally unsatisfactory but that was in the future.

It was not long before we were arranging Chinese delegations to travel overseas. Few Chinese were allowed to travel and in the early 80s it became hugely prestigious to be invited to a foreign country and there was only one country that they wanted to visit: the U.S.A. America, the mountain of gold, was every Chinese' eldorado. It was the land of eternal opportunity, the fountain of technology, nirvana on earth. Europe was a poor substitute, full of old buildings and secondary technology. The developing world held no interest. Towards the end of an American delegation's visit to China there was a palpable crescendo as the Chinese hosts awaited those magic words "We would like to invite you to visit our operations in the United States."

This was the trigger for immediate and hasty negotiations. How many people can we send? When can we come? Who was to pay the airfares? The travel expenses in America? So many important matters needed to be clarified. Many months, sometimes up to a year, would go by while visas were arranged amidst frantic jockeying to see who would be on the select list of those allowed to travel. Frequently the American hosts had firm ideas as to who should be on the delegation – factory managers, senior engineers, foreign trade officials and people who could influence their future business prospects in China. All too often quite the wrong people made the trip: Party members, often completely unrelated to the particular industry, local government officials, even Long Marchers wangled themselves onto the list much to the frustration of the hosts. Translators rarely made it and so it often fell to Dick or one of the Inchcape China team to travel with the Chinese to act as interpreters.

To make the most of their chance-in-a-lifetime, they wanted to travel to the most places, do as much sightseeing as possible and stay as long as they could in the States. A typical delegation might consist of as many as ten Chinese and they needed to be ferried around in a fleet of cars and sometimes private aircraft. Their inexperience in the outside world often led to a considerable degree of awkwardness.

The first problem was food: a new custom became apparent to us which stated that when foreigners visited China they were expected to eat Chinese food only and when the Chinese went overseas then they would also only expect to eat Chinese food. They would of course be introduced to local delicacies such as hamburgers and T-bone steaks but these would be poked at and tasted but where were the noodles? As reports reached home that Chinese food was not always available in Ohio and Nebraska, delegations started to bring their own sacks of dried noodles and rice with them when they travelled. Home cooking facilities needed to be provided in hotels often with disastrous results necessitating redecoration of the rooms after they had been used by the Chinese.

In the early 1980s the behaviour of the Chinese as they travelled was always under close scrutiny by a Party member but this was relaxed as time went by and more and more Chinese travelled overseas for longer periods. Sometimes they needed to spend months overseas to be trained in a technology or learn how to operate complex machinery. It was about this time that they discovered the earthy delights of American night-clubs, pole-dancing, prostitutes and other temptations not available back home in China. I recall one delegation that spent some weeks in Finland and who were meant to visit the Finnish plant daily for training but never left their hotel rooms insisting instead that a fresh selection of pornographic videos should be delivered to their rooms every day.

Delegations, both inward and outward, led to the same results. American executives would arrive home after visits to China to boast of their trip, give public speeches at chambers of commerce and private dinner parties and to receive accolades for their far-sighted vision and commercial imagination in taking the first steps to pick the forbidden fruit of China. The Chinese came home with greatly enhanced prestige as one of the few Chinese to have visited the United States. They also underwent intensive debriefing and doubtless bored their colleagues at great length with the wonders they had beheld.

7

Dick's Story Continued

I worked for five years, from June 1972 until April 1977 as a Chinese Foreign Affairs official. During these years my experiences were the mirror image of those encountered by foreigners in their dealings with the Chinese, many of which made little sense to the western mind.

When a foreigner came to China, generally as part of an official delegation, those of us who were likely to be in contact with the foreigners were encouraged to spruce up our appearance. For this purpose each ministry kept a large warehouse outside Beijing where there was a vast array of different clothes: well-tailored Mao-style *zhongshan zuan* in fine woollen fabric, normally reserved for the most senior cadres, and sets of old-fashioned western suits, shirts and ties to be issued to Chinese when they travelled overseas. All such clothes belonged to the respective ministry and had to be returned after use.

I was told that a delegation was to visit China from the University of Helsinki led by Professor Putkisto, a noted scholar on forestry. I was appointed the chief coordinator for the visit and this brought me into regular contact with the commercial attaché at the Finnish embassy, a young diplomat by the name of Kokonen. During the visit of the delegation I sat next to Kokonen at the welcome banquet and again when the Finnish embassy hosted a reciprocal banquet. Every time I met Kokonen I was meticulously turned out in a clean wool tunic with neatly pressed trousers and polished shoes.

Once the delegation had departed I was allowed a few days' leave to return to Harbin to see my family. I returned the smart clothes to the ministry and changed into my usual travelling clothes, aware that I had to face many long hours squeezed on to a wooden 'hard class' railway seat for the long two-day trip to Heilongjiang. I put on my ordinary faded blue padded cotton coat, padded trousers and green canvas boots. Underneath I had several layers of thick woollen sweaters, vests and long johns. I strapped countless canvas bags of all shapes and sizes to my back. I needed to bring many foodstuffs and nearly twenty kilogrammes of frozen meat with me as many products were still in short supply or rationed in Harbin. As I entered the Beijing Central railway station I had become one of the masses, indistinguishable amongst the churning sea of similarly clad Chinese jostling each other in their rush to catch their trains.

Suddenly a large figure bumped into me and I looked up into the surprised face of Kokonen from the Finnish embassy. The Finn took a step backwards, shocked to see my transformation, and asked hesitantly, "Mr. Chan?" unsure whether this could be the same person as the elegantly dressed official whom he had met so many times previously. "Is that you Mr Chan?" he asked again.

I was so overwhelmed with embarrassment and confusion that for a moment I was at a loss how to react. I gambled that most foreigners think Chinese look alike with their pale skin, black hair and dark hooded eyes, and with a polite nod of my head and a mumbled "*tuibu qi*," or "excuse me," I strode ahead briskly and disappeared into the crowd without turning. The Finn, sensitive as all foreigners become to every gesture or sign in a controlled alien world, could only stand and stare at my vanishing back, wondering why this smart, sophisticated cadre from the Ministry of Forestry had suddenly reverted to one of the masses and would not acknowledge a foreigner whom he knew well.

In March 1974 Charles Priestley, the section chief of the United Nations Food and Agriculture Organization made a visit to China. His objective was to write a detailed report on forestry development in China to be delivered as a research document upon his return to the FAO's headquarters in Rome. Priestley was renowned for persevering with difficult questions. As tension mounted he began to sweat. It was March and very cold and foreigners and Chinese alike were clad in thick coats and sweaters. One never knew whether a meeting room would be heated or not. If it was then layers of clothes had to be peeled off. But Priestley never seemed to get this balancing act right and was frequently found in a heated room wearing far too many woollies and perspiring profusely.

During his stay in Beijing the Forestry Ministry officials gave Priestley a generic introduction to China's forestry industry ensuring that all the information provided had previously been released into the public domain and that no State Secrets were revealed. Priestley was far from satisfied at the answers he received but was pacified when assured that more details would be provided as he toured the forestry areas in the provinces. I and my team, who were to accompany Priestley upon his travels, were given strict instructions that under no circumstances were we to mention any statistics to foreigners that had not previously been made known to the public. This was a risky proposition as nobody was quite sure what was a State Secret and what had been released into the public domain. Caution was required!

At that time provincial officials had only rare opportunities to meet foreigners and a heightened perception of risk accompanied such visits. The local officials were intimidated by the guidelines directed by the Ministry and were very much aware that a simple and inadvertent blunder in any foreign affairs-related activity could land the unfortunate in deep water that could affect the perpetrator and his family for the rest of their lives.

Priestley and my team from the Ministry flew to Harbin and were greeted by a group of local officials. As is the custom, a twelve-course dinner was hosted that night, attended by the same group of officials who met Priestley at the airport; they were specially selected members of the local provincial reception team. As usual, the hosts and the only guest toasted each other with fiery Mao Tai while continually expressing everlasting friendship between both parties. Priestley was heard, before the Mao Tai reduced him to mumbles, to repeat again and again that he hoped that he would receive straight answers to his many questions at the next morning's meeting with the local foresters.

The following morning I was surprised to see that as many as thirty of my colleagues arrived for the meeting. We sat quietly in rows, notebooks poised on our laps. We had been told in advance that only the director of the Provincial Forestry Bureau would be allowed to speak, the rest of us must remain a silent audience. As soon as the introductions and welcomes were over, Priestley launched himself into his research. His first question was, "Director Wang, could you please give me the number and size of the local forestry bureaux under the supervision of the Heilongjiang Provincial Forestry Bureau?"

Such an anodyne question was almost certainly a State Secret and Director Wang was not to be caught out. He launched into a thirty-minute monologue describing the structure of the forestry administration within the province, the functioning of each level of organisation and how they filled the State's production plans. Priestley's attention started to waver mid-way through the dissertation and by the conclusion he realised that his question was not going to be answered. Little beads of sweat began to form on his forehead.

Priestley tried a different approach, "Director Wang, could you please let me know the annual volume of timber harvested in your province?"

Most certainly another State Secret! But Director Wang was quite unfazed and began another thirty minute speech, deftly side-stepping any statistics and patiently explaining that it was almost impossible to provide any accurate figures as the ownership of China's forests was a complicated structure consisting of State-owned, commune-owned and privately-owned land, and only the State sector maintained statistics which were not comprehensive as they did not include the other two sectors.

By now Priestley, sweat dripping down his face, had begun to lose patience with all this prevarication and was becoming slightly annoyed that his notebook remained blank. I noticed that my colleagues were enthralled by the skill of their boss at speaking for such a long time without revealing anything of relevance. Priestley tried again "Director Wang, could you please let me have the precise annual volume of cut timber in the State sector?"

The director found it more difficult to circumvent this very straight question but successfully beat around the bush a few more times, despite some goading from Priestley who by now was in obvious discomfort with sweat dripping onto his thick cardigan. The director finally answered the question with a vague "several million cubic metres a year" and immediately proposed a tea break.

That evening I was called to a meeting where I found Director Wang quite distraught. He confessed that he had found the morning's session with Priestley an ordeal. "How can I, a full director of the Forestry Bureau, pretend not to know how many bureaux are under my jurisdiction? As chief of the provincial administration I have to know exactly how many cubic meters of wood we harvest in this province!" he thundered. "Mr. Priestley must think that I am incompetent, good-for-nothing or crack-brained!" I felt for him, but how else could he have answered such questions under the circumstances? Almost any visitor to China over the following two decades experienced something similar: questions that were never answered or answered evasively, often put down to poor interpretation but the usual reality was that the answers were *neibu*.

In late October 1974, I was transferred to the Chinese embassy in Rome and attached to the United Nations Food & Agricultural Organisation. I welcomed the opportunity to retreat from the ravages of the Cultural Revolution but worried constantly over my family who were still in Harbin. I and the other Chinese assigned to the FAO lived in a residential compound within the high walls of the embassy. In contrast to China where food was very scarce, the embassy served three excellent meals a day, an almost unheard of luxury. But there were house rules which had to be followed.

No one was allowed to leave the compound without permission. Whenever it was necessary to attend an official function or carry out any duties outside the embassy then a minimum of two people were allowed to leave the embassy. There was to be no mixing with Italians or other nationalities. Although there was television inside the embassy, it was strictly forbidden to watch any programmes except for sport. Only the *People's Daily* newspaper could be read, no foreign reading materials were allowed.

Saturdays were mainly committed to tedious political studies but Sundays were free – alas, there was nothing to do: I was not allowed to leave the embassy building, could not watch television and the *People's Daily* was not exactly recreational reading. So I and my colleagues, well fed from the embassy's excellent kitchens, could only digest their lunches by strolling around the embassy compound. I estimated that I could make seventy complete trips around the compound over a three-hour period. I did not walk alone, the entire embassy staff, numbering over a hundred, were similarly walking in groups around the courtyard.

During the working week the restrictions were lifted slightly: although an embassy bus drove us to the FAO every morning and collected us in the evening, we were quite free to walk anywhere inside the FAO compound or even explore the streets of Rome. The embassy's political section was terrified that one of our number might be seduced by the bright lights and seek political asylum but this was a rash step to take unless one had outside contacts (and much screening had taken place to make sure this was not the case). During my three years in Rome no Chinese 'disappeared' or was 'reported missing'.

Soon after the conclusion of the FAO World Congress in November 1975 I received my first invitation to visit the United States' embassy as the interpreter to Mr. Li, the senior Chinese Representative to the FAO. Three years had passed since the 'Shanghai Communiqué' which laid out the road map for improved U.S./China relations but the relationship between the two countries had remained tense and cold. I approached the American embassy with trepidation, which was not allayed when one of the hulky marines at the gate immediately started talking into his walkie-talkie when he espied two Chinese. I felt like I was stepping into enemy territory. But Mr. Li, a veteran diplomat, was calm and unperturbed, and assured me that this was normal American behaviour.

Mr. Li knew many of the other representatives attending the reception, particularly those from developing countries. He moved easily from one group to another, smoothly acknowledging this person and chatting briefly with others, all the time demonstrating his diplomatic skills. Then he was approached by an attractive young Asian journalist, who asked him in fluent Mandarin whether it was now possible to obtain a visa to the 'Mainland'. Mr. Li's urbane smile disappeared, a frown furrowed his head and to my surprise he admonished the poor woman, "I really hate to hear this word 'Mainland'. Do you think that there is more than one China? You must be more respectful when you refer to the People's Republic of China!" and he moved away leaving her gaping. He was referring to the American custom of differentiating between the 'Republic of China' on Taiwan and the 'People's Republic' on the Asian continent – a sore point in Beijing. I of course knew, as everyone learns in time, that she had transgressed a sacred taboo, but the young lady was innocently unaware of the political subtlety.

In September 1976 I was accompanying a forestry delegation to visit a logging centre two hundred kilometres north of Oslo when one of the Norwegians accompanying the delegation whispered that he had just heard on his portable radio that Chairman Mao had died. The Norwegian Foreign Office confirmed the news half an hour later and the delegation was officially informed. We stared at our feet in sorrow, overwhelmed with emotion. One of our party suddenly burst into a long wail and many of the others followed suit. I was curiously numbed by this news. I had grown impervious to such emotions over the years. Even the death of my father, whom I had loved and respected, earlier the same year had little emotional impact upon me. Nevertheless, I bowed my head like the others and stared at the ground in shock.

The leader of our delegation suggested that we should immediately return to China but it was decided that the mission should continue and that we would return to Oslo where the Chinese embassy was certain to have prepared a hall for people to mourn and grieve. From that day on, no one in the delegation laughed, made jokes, or wore any bright colours. There was no drinking alcohol, banquets were cancelled, and we could only stand in little groups looking sad and devastated. The next day we continued to Stockholm where the Swedish government hosted a banquet in our honour. I remember the dinner as an ordeal for the hosts had to endure the long dinner with their silent, solemn and mourning guests. There were no alcoholic drinks served that evening, no 'gan-bei' and the ever-present background music ceased playing.

Many of the members of our delegation were openly weeping over their food. My well-honed political instincts told me that at such times every move was watched and could be used against one in the future, so I squeezed a raw onion with my fingers and rubbed my eyes so that it looked as if I too had been deeply upset at the passing of the 'most beloved Great Helmsman'. But in my heart I dared to hope that with Mao dead life in China might start to improve.

8

Inchcape in the 1980s

Each of Inchcape's geographical regions held monthly board meetings presided over by the regional chairmen and attended by the heads of the largest business units in the area. The ten directors of Inchcape's North East Asian region, which included Japan, Korea, Taiwan, Hong Kong and China, were all British except for a single Chinese, Samson Sun, who acted as the comprador handling any sensitivities to do with the local Cantonese. None of the directors ever visited China or had any intention of doing so, although most had been living in the region for decades. Their responsibilities were to manage Inchcape's huge and growing presence in the area, to report ever increasing profits and to reinvest these profits wisely in local projects.

China was a closed book to my directors as it was to most expatriates in Hong Kong. Most of my colleagues had lived in Hong Kong through the vicissitudes of the Cultural Revolution which frequently threatened to boil over into the colony, as indeed it did from time to time. These had been difficult times in Hong Kong and China had not endeared itself to the local residents. As there was little prospect of profitable business in China for years to come, the vast nation to the north did not deserve a second (or even a first) look. The Inchcape directors thought privately that PG was wasting his time in supporting my endeavours in China.

Once a month I was expected to present my activities in China to the directors in the windowless boardroom in Elizabeth House. I would discuss the political situation and the deals on which we were working with some of our American principals. To the Inchcape directors, used to selling motorcars or consumer goods, our efforts to sell military hardware, advanced technology or turnkey plants to China sounded very exotic. My presentations were received in silence, with never a question or comment from my directors. Only PG, irritated by the lack of interest shown by his colleagues, would occasionally rumble into life and remind them that they could not continue to pretend that China did not exist.

This lack of enthusiasm for the greatest untapped market in the world was in contrast to the reactions of businessmen in the U.S. and Europe who were once again becoming over-excited at the thought of selling their products to China's billions. But Inchcape's ennui pervaded nearly all of its many operating units in Hong Kong. Their business in China was insignificant compared to that of Hong Kong and was often left in the hands of a single 'specialist' who generally took the easy route and sold products to a middleman in Hong Kong. It was understood that the 'specialist' received benefits directly from the middleman but the attitude of our Hong Kong management was to leave things alone and not ask too many questions.

At one meeting in April 1982 however, there was something new to discuss. The previous week I had received a summons to PG's office late one afternoon. PG was showing some untypical signs of animation: he paced the room, cigarette smoke billowing behind him. As I entered the room, he fixed me with a glare.

"Do you know a man called Algy Cluff?" he demanded, as if this was a capital crime. I had indeed met Algy, he was a friend of Charles Letts. Cluff Oil was a successful independent oil explorer in the North Sea. Algy was an ex-Guards officer, tall, ramrod straight, and with a penchant for wearing snappy chalk-stripe suits. It was rumoured that as a soldier based on the Malaysian/Indonesian border in Borneo, he had arranged for hampers of delicacies from Fortnum & Mason to be dropped into the jungle. He was a charmer and a clever businessman. I admitted that I did have the pleasure of knowing Algy.

"Ha! I thought you would!" said PG ambiguously. "It looks as if we are going to have to invest some money in his company. What do you think, you are the China expert?" he growled, thrusting a file of papers into my hand. It seemed that Algy had been invited by the Chinese Ministry of Oil to bid for some offshore oil exploration concessions, a new 'first' for China. Algy had come to Hong Kong to raise money for his exploration activities and had started with his friends at the Hong Kong & Shanghai Bank.

"Mike Sandberg, (the chairman of the Hong Kong & Shanghai Bank at that time), tells me that the Bank is going to put in five million. John Marden, (the chairman of Wheelock Marden, another major trading house) is to put in another five, Swires are going to invest as well as is Li Ka-Shing. I think we have to invest as well. What is your view?"

Inchcape had not, as far as I knew, ever invested in oil exploration and I bore in mind Kenneth Inchcape's words of wisdom about not investing in an unfamiliar business in a new country. Furthermore, the only offshore oil reserves in China were in the Gulf of Bohai. I counselled caution.

"You don't get it, do you?" said my chairman. "It is not a question of whether the business makes any sense or not. It is a club. We have been invited to invest along with all the other *Hongs*. If we turn it down then Inchcape will not be invited into such opportunities in the future. We have to do it."

I somewhat doubted whether PG would get permission from London for this particular speculation but I was wrong. As soon as the Fuhrer heard that the investment group was an elite club (and especially when he heard that our traditional rivals Jardine Matheson were not invited to join the club on the grounds that 'they are not team players') he immediately gave his approval over the telephone.

The deal was done. We invested five million dollars in Algy's Hong Kong company[1]. Inchcape's regional board meeting that day was told by the chairman that a decision had been made and approved by London. No director asked a question or said a word, continueing to study their papers. It was China business, it did not concern them.

Thus were major investment decisions made by Inchcape's management in those days. In later years, when Inchcape boasted of its 'professional management', such proposals became so obfuscated by corporate planners, management consultants, accountants and analysts that decision-making became constipated and uninspired. Inchcape, like all the Far Eastern trading houses, had achieved its success over the centuries by making buccaneering decisions by instinct; the moment that this entrepreneurialism was taken away, the company began to wane.

Throughout the 1980s I led an ideal life. I was running my own profitable business within Inchcape and was left completely to my own devices. There was no boss peering over my shoulder, no-one to give instructions, nobody to query how I spent my time or question my policies. It was as if I was running my own company without the problems of cash-flow or other niggling matters that can inhibit small traders. I appreciated Inchcape's massive prestige and reputation but most of all I enjoyed the total trust and independence that I was given. All this was to come to a grinding halt in the 1990s as Inchcape lost its way in its world but the 1980s were peak years for the company. Its empire straddled the globe and its 500 subsidiaries were active in a vast array of different businesses many of which eventually beat their way to China through doors opened by Dick and myself.

PG retired and was replaced by another Inchcape 'lifer' and he in turn by another. Whilst none of PG's successors showed the same eccentric approach to China, all continued to support my activities and none had any wish to interfere in what remained a poorly understood corner of the Inchcape world.

We began to look at investing in China and considered buying into tea estates in the Himalayan foothills, container ports on the Chinese seaboard,

---

[1] Cluff Oil (Hong Kong) drilled for oil for many years offshore China but only found hydrocarbon traces. There had been oil once but it had 'migrated'.

forestry concessions in Hainan, chocolate manufacturing in Guangdong, consumer goods distribution, assembly of copying machines and many other projects. But in most cases China was not ready for foreign investment and the cultural gap was too wide. The profit motive was still very suspect and there were many sensitivities on the Chinese side and distrust amongst foreign investors. The first foreign investment regulations were introduced in 1982 but they were vague and did not provide investors with much security.

Distant storm clouds began to gather over the Inchcape Group. Kenneth Inchcape, whose brilliance it had been to consolidate the company out of his family's disparate investments in India and whose inventive mind rapidly expanded the company by acquisition throughout the 1960s and 1970s was removed in a board room coup at the end of 1982. Leadership became less inspired as a new chairman arrived on the scene in London. Regional or sector fiefdoms began to materialise within the group and management errors caused huge losses. It was imperceptible at the time, certainly from my remote vantage point in China, but the Inchcape ship was beginning to take on water.

9

Close Encounters

My first impression of Chinese women was a disappointment: they were hard to tell from the men. Some of the loveliest and liveliest women in the world are the Chinese in Singapore, Kuala Lumpur, Hong Kong and, especially, Taipei. Not so in China: the Chinese Communist Party had purged physical beauty.

A Maoist policy had been to discourage sexual relations, not out of concern over the burgeoning birth-rate, but for fear of the love that binds families or the lust that the young or straying may seek as a distraction from an unfettered dedication to the Communist Party. That the authorities split up families so that they only saw each other for two weeks a year was one thing. That a strictly prudish high-minded regimen should be imposed on an oriental race with a healthy history of sexual interest predating human habitation of Europe was another. Prostitution, a popular pre-1949 pastime, was dealt with summarily: the 'john' was ejected from the brothel and shot in the street. Concubines and minor wives, all ancient Chinese traditions, were suddenly prohibited.

Overcrowding made even licit sex something of a rushed task. With one or more families squeezed into a single room, special arrangements had to be made to secure fifteen minutes of privacy. During his 're-education' Dick shared a single room for many years between his wife and children and another couple and their children. In the winter both families huddled around the five-foot-wide *kang* for warmth. Dick waited until he thought everyone was asleep before with undetectable movement, he stealthily made silent love to his wife.

The quality of sex understandably plummeted under the Maoists. Sex became a rushed and furtive physical imperative. Men could not marry before twenty-eight, women twenty-five. The Maoists liked us to believe that the Chinese had subjugated sexual desire to a mere decadent, bourgeois conceit. Most visitors to China listened to the high moral tone, observed the lack of vanity in the baggy clothes that both sexes wore and swallowed the Party line. The reality was that young Chinese were no different: most young people enjoyed their share of exploratory fumblings beneath the duvet. Indeed, I only had to walk through a public park in the summer evenings to see every bush, plant and hedge rustling and vibrating with covert activity not caused by the wind. It is no coincidence that there are one billion, two hundred million Chinese and expanding by fourteen million a year.

This was a highly frustrated society. I entered our Shanghai office one morning to find Katie Yu, our attractive Shanghainese secretary, in tears. We were the only people in the office and I did not expect anybody else to arrive for at least another half hour. I invited her into my office. I sat behind my desk. She perched primly opposite me, her legs tightly closed, knees turning white with the effort. Her light cotton dress had a couple of recent wet stains on her bottom. She cried a little and then, staring at her sandals, she sobbed, "Every day I squeeze into the number 16 bus from Xinja Road to Yanan Road West, and every day a different man rubs his penis against my back until he comes." She continued graphically in precise English with no embarrassment, "I try to move away but we are packed so tight that the men just smile and sway with the movement of the bus. And I am so close to these sordid strangers I can see the hairs in their nostrils. I am so angry but I cannot even raise my hand. Sometimes, if I am very lucky," she continued between sobs, " I get a seat but that doesn't help. They just unzip their trousers and reveal themselves just a few inches from my nose. Chinese men can be very disgusting!"

The Maoists had great success in persuading Chinese women that plain is good and beautiful is nasty. The Maoists eliminated the Chinese upper classes in the 1950s, where some of the most beautiful women might have been suspected to hide. Women were forced by the Maoists to wear the same loose-fitting clothes as men, make up was banned, body-shaving discouraged, sanitary towels no longer available. The "Three Hair Styles" policy was introduced: pudding basin with fringe, short bunches or two short pigtails. The "Breast Suppression' policy was a Chinese tradition to which the Party adhered in the belief that breasts should be flattened and concealed by a top garment between shirt and bra.

Chinese women's modesty in the 1980s seemed only to concern the top half of the body. During the summer it was quite usual to see smiling young women bicycling along Nanjing's shady lanes with cotton skirts blowing in their faces. During the hot weather in southern China I was quite used to Chinese officials fanning themselves with a piece of paper, collapsing into an armchair and rolling their baggy trousers high up their thighs to reveal nobbly knees and straggly leg hairs.

In spite of these handicaps, Chinese women did stand out: the paleness of the unblemished skin, the lustre of the pigtail, the line of the eyebrow, the gleam in the corner of a tilted eye could still prove irresistible to the foreigner. The Chinese authorities were well aware of the latent attractions of the female sex and went out of their way to make sure that only the plainest, sincerest, most reliable girls were allowed to make contact with foreigners. Any hint of flirtation was reported to the authorities and the girl, and maybe her family, could be banished to a distant factory.

Such was my sad experience with Li Yu-Tian, a 21 year-old interpreter allocated to the CCPIT. Every night I dreamed of her heart-shaped face and panther-like body. She tried unsuccessfully to keep her hair in bunches held by rubber bands behind her head. But the dusty Beijing wind blew loose strands across her mouth. Her hair was the colour of polished coal: the deepest black, glinting a reddish copper in the sun. She was a Ming-dynasty beauty transported into the twentieth century and somehow she had slipped through the Party's net.

She had recently arrived from Xian, a walled city on the edge of the desert and one of China's ancient capitals. A fresh graduate from Xian's Foreign Language Institute, she studied hard and must have attracted someone's eye to gain a much-sought position in the Beijing head office. She thought she had won the lottery; it was a break that might provide opportunities for all her family. As we drove around Beijing arranging meetings for Lord Inchcape's impending visit, she breathlessly told me of her excitement at living within the seat of civilisation, at bicycling daily past the Great Hall of the People, the Monument to the Heroes of the People's Republic, the Forbidden City and all the famed revolutionary sites. She was reassured by Beijing's proximity to the desert, like her own city some thousand miles away, with its sudden yellow sand storms and the chains of camels padding through the streets at night. She was a very happy girl, full of youth and enthusiasm.

Business called for me to see Li Yu-Tian daily for weeks during Beijing's ephemeral autumn. In the last week of October a sudden drop in the temperature causes the sycamore, maple and willow leaves to turn a vivid red and drop in a scarlet blizzard over a few days. The desert beyond the Great Wall is whipped by westerly winds and a sandy haze settles on the city through which the orange sun hangs in etched silhouette. A sudden chill falls across the old city, the bicyclists appear in fur hats and long coats, the hotel rooms begin to feel cold with no prospect of central heating for more than a fortnight to come.

One freezing dusk, with the sun sinking over the jagged outline of the Fragrant Hills, Li Yu-Tian and I waited for our driver in a Ming-dynasty lacquered gateway outside the Temple of Heaven. A bitter wind blew the red and yellow leaves into our faces. Her shiny hair, loosened from its bands, whipped across my mouth. We snuggled against each other for warmth, our shivering hands finding each others. She raised her head and looked at me, her dark eyes glinting gold with the last crimson rays of the dying sun. I raised one hand and gently brushed her cheek with my numb fingertips. She smiled. My lips touched her cheek, I smelled her fragrance. A car horn blew, the driver had returned. The moment was lost. Later we shared a bowl of noodles in a local tea-house and for a fleeting moment were happy together.

The next morning she was not at our daily meeting. She had been replaced by a grim grandmother-type in her sixties with dark grey hair cut very short in the Party approved manner. My enquiries as to the whereabouts of Li Yu-Tian were met with a slightly truculent stare.

Two days later I was called to see Li Yu-Tian's superior, Madam[1] Hao Su-Yun, on a routine matter. After she had completed her repetition of her previous day's statement which was identical to those that I had received daily for quite some time, there was a pause. Her shadow, in this case a junior clerk, ceased writing down her every word, a precise copy of which he had taken down the previous day, and closed his notebook. At a glance from Madam Hao, he slipped through the door leaving us alone, a highly unusual, if not to say uncomfortable, situation. Madam Hao was in her fifties, with very sharp eyes, a slightly softer version of the Party's approved pudding basin hair-style, and a knowing face. She smiled rarely but when she did her face burst suddenly into life, her eyes crinkling and many hidden smile lines revealing her true character, so carefully suppressed in front of a *waiguoren*. She was an anglophile, had been stationed at the Chinese embassy in London, and we got on well together.

"And, er, Lord Errington……"

"May I help, Madam Hao?"

"It's Miss Li." Her face lit up with a forced smile.

"Miss Li? What happened to her?"

"Such happy news! She has been promoted. She has been transferred to a training school in Guizhou." She beamed mentioning a particularly drab tropical provincial city some two thousand miles south of Beijing. "It is an honour for her. She will like it there."

I doubted that, she was a desert girl and liked the cold winters and dry heat of the Shaanxi summers. She had told me she hated the dampness of South China, with its little people and strange languages. "I see. Curious she never mentioned it to me. When will she go?"

"Oh, she went last night, as soon as she heard the good news. We should be happy for her."

Madam Hao stood up to shake my hand, taking care that our eyes did not meet. The scribe re-entered. The meeting was over.

Ever since I have feared that my gentle but innocent gesture of affection in that deserted gateway, and that to dare to share a smile over some steaming

---

[1] I was never able to find a satisfactory explanation as to why Chinese women of a certain age expect to be referred to as 'madam' rather than 'mrs'. It seemed an unnecessary pretension in an equal society.

dandan noodles with a forbidden foreigner had led to Li Yu-Tian's 'promotion'.

That was in 1980. There was no breaking down the wall between foreign men and Chinese women for many years to come but as more and more foreigners arrived in China for longer and longer periods, there were bound to be some indiscretions.

Our contract with Okanagan Helicopters brought about our first incident. To keep the four helicopters operational for the offshore oil industry, we based teams of Canadian pilots and engineers in a compound in Zhuhai, adjacent to the border with the Portuguese colony of Macau. This was no hardship posting: Macau was a taxi-drive away where any sort of entertainment was readily available. But in spite of these temptations one of the pilots seduced a girl working in the hotel (or v.v.). As soon as her work unit discovered the girl was pregnant she disappeared from view. But that was not enough for the authorities. I was called to see the Party Secretary within the Civil Aviation Authority's offices in Guangzhou, the provincial capital. The Party Secretary was incandescent with anger.

"You must accept responsibility for this incident and ensure that it is not repeated!" he ordered, quite forgetting to offer me the obligatory mug of green tea.

"And how can I do that? How can I stop Chinese girls if they choose to sleep with Canadian airmen?" I replied.

It was rare to see a Chinese man become really angry with a foreigner. It was outside the template. The manual instructed emotional control at all times. But this Party Secretary found the subject distasteful and embarrassing. It was an affront to the moral standards of the Party.

"He forced himself upon her! Chinese girls do not care to have intimate relations with foreigners!"

"He tells me the opposite. Apparently she used to come into his room at night entirely of her own free will."

"Lies, lies, lies! You must sign a statement confirming that this will never happen again. Has the pilot been punished?"

"In the outside world you cannot punish a single man who wishes to make love to a willing woman. It is one of our particularly cherished freedoms."

"But this is China!" thundered the Party Secretary. "We cannot permit such amoral behaviour."

Sure enough, the pilot's work permit was withdrawn within a week and he was sent back to Vancouver.

During the 1980s the Chinese started to travel abroad in delegations of 'experts' purportedly to study foreign technology but in truth glorified sight-seeing jaunts with a thin veneer of serious business. A typical group of ten

Chinese always included one or more eagle-eyed Party members to ensure high moral standards were maintained. On one occasion we arranged for a delegation from the Ministry of Railways to visit Germany. The delegation was led by a splendidly handsome, six foot tall Manchurian by the name of Qi Zi-Hong. He was the director of the Ministry's Foreign Affairs Bureau, a senior position. He spoke Russian and English fluently, had an easy and charming manner, a certain presence, and an un-Chinese penchant for bear hugs. He was held in awe by his colleagues and was clearly slated for higher responsibilities.

The trip to Germany passed off smoothly and Dick and I were pleased at our improved *guanxi* within the Ministry. Then one week after the delegation returned from Germany Director Qi disappeared. Our enquiries were deflected and we wondered what had gone amiss. It was not until a month or two later that we learned that while in Hamburg the delegation had been taken to a nightclub. A tall, cool blonde had noticed Director Qi's striking appearance and had been seen to chat with him. Later that night one of the Chinese women in the delegation claimed that she had seen the same blonde entering Director Qi's room. The Chinese always share rooms when travelling but we had given Director Qi his own room in recognition of his seniority which might have caused some jealousy amongst the egalitarian group. Once such an allegation had been made it was likely to be supported by others content to see the leader's downfall, and was virtually impossible to refute.

It was months later before I was able to discreetly enquire from another contact within the Ministry as to Director Qi's fate. Apparently he, as well as his wife, who was also a senior official within the Ministry and his two children had been dispatched to Lanzhou, a remote polluted city in the Taklamakan Desert, where he was working as a porter at the railway station. I found it hard to understand how the punishment fitted the crime.

By 1988 things had changed greatly. The Okanagan helicopters flew with a crew of three: a Canadian captain, a Chinese first officer and a Chinese interpreter who relayed air traffic control instructions to the captain. Chan Ku-Ku had been the senior interpreter for a couple of years. No beauty, Ku-Ku was short, with spectacles, protruding teeth and a single long pig-tail. When she spoke she tended to spit. I thought that she was very safe with any of the Canadian flight crews but evidently she developed a crush upon Captain Donahue, a tall gangly Canadian with a relaxed and easy-going attitude.

One day they completed their run out to the offshore rigs and upon returning to Zhuhai Ku-Ku asked Captain Donahue if he could fly her to Guangzhou, about one hundred miles away as she had some business there. The two of them flew to the White Cloud Airport in Guangzhou. Once there Ku-Ku hired a cab and they drove to her home. Captain Donahue waited inside the cab. After a while a number of Chinese came out of the house shouting and laughing and reached through the cab's window to shake a somewhat perplexed Captain Donahue by the hand. The cab then drove on to a government building where once again Ku-Ku disappeared inside while Captain Donahue waited in the cab.

After an hour, Ku-Ku ran excitedly down the stairs outside the building waving a piece of paper, and jumped into the cab.

"All finished," she beamed. "We're married now!"

"Married? MARRIED? But how? I haven't even signed anything!"

"Oh, that's not necessary. I told them that you are a dumb foreigner and can't read Chinese so no need to trouble you."

And that apparently was that. She should have got the Party Secretary's permission but somehow, using some *guanxi* inside the government offices, she had managed to cut through the red tape. This time the Party Secretary controlled his temper — he knew he had been outmanoeuvred and could only mutter expletives to me when we met but by that time Party Secretaries were beginning to lose their power all over China.

The couple could not stay in China so they moved to Vancouver where they started a Chinese take-away. The unfortunate pilot always maintained that he had had no intimate relations with Ku-Ku prior to the 'wedding' and it had never occurred to him to marry the girl, indeed he had a long-standing girl-friend back home in Canada. Nevertheless he stuck with his new commitment and, as far as I know, the couple are still married.

By the late 1980s there were many changes afoot. The Open Door policy was, as Deng Xiao-Ping had so pertinently noted, allowing in a lot of flies. Hair styles were liberated and some of the younger women started to put on lipstick which, to the matrons of the Party, was scandalous behaviour. The *zhongshan zuan* faded away and Chinese women began to wear their rendition of western clothes. As international fashion magazines had yet to enter the country and there were no dress-makers who had any idea what women wore outside China, Chinese women could only attempt to copy what they saw western women wearing in the few movies allowed into China such as classics like 'Gone with the Wind' or 'Brief Encounter'.

Textiles were also in short supply, the only available fabric being upholstery material. So Chinese women made their dresses out of the green or burgundy velvet normally used for curtain hangings in official buildings. Rubber sandals remained in vogue as did knee-length white socks which together with the velvet dress presented an eye-catching ensemble. Once dress-makers started to use their imagination, they specialised in night-club hostess gowns with plunging necklines and bows and chiffon which looked conspicuous on the back of a bicycle in the middle of the day. The Chinese invented a fashion sense entirely of their own: something between an armchair in sandals and a coiffeured mosquito net.

Prostitution began to raise its head once more after its elimination in 1949. By 1990 it was becoming more and more common to be accosted in an hotel lobby or telephoned in a room seconds after arrival. The authorities were not happy about this development and in a softer version of the 'Shoot the John' policy, clients were arrested and had a Chinese stamp placed in their passports stating 'Consorts with Prostitutes' which might have induced some amused looks from immigration officers, but would certainly take some explaining to a wife! The girls were (and still are) rounded up in occasional swoops and sent off to a morality school from where they were eventually released back onto the market.

Throughout history the Chinese have always excelled themselves at inventing appropriate punishments and I recall walking down Wang Fujing, Beijing's crowded main shopping street, one summer's day to be confronted by a forlorn Frenchman standing on a small round platform, of the type the police use to direct traffic. His head was bowed and there was a placard hanging around his neck proclaiming in large Chinese characters 'Polluter of Chinese girls'. I fought my way through the crowd taunting and shouting at him and enquired what had brought him to this sorry state. He told me his hotel room was raided at 3 a.m. that morning and he had been found in bed with a local girl. The Public Security officers ordered him to stand in this conspicuous position all day. He was an engineer with Renault, had been in China for only three days and was in no hurry to return.

Towards the end of the 1980s Inchcape sent James Yang, a flash young Cantonese, to manage one of our joint-ventures in Shanghai. James was a typical Hong Kong salesman: smooth, urbane, good-looking if one overlooked his small stature and a bachelor with a keen eye for the girls. By that time the Chinese had graduated from velvet and chiffon to clothes that would be deemed elegant anywhere in the world. The Shanghainese in particular rapidly regained their reputation as the Parisiennes of the orient. James salivated at the thought of moving to Shanghai and threw himself into nocturnal life with great vigour.

I was working in my office in Shanghai one morning when my secretary told me that James had vanished. His hotel room had not been slept in and his belongings were intact, but of James there was not a sign. We searched for him for three days but in vain. Eventually on the fourth morning, an untidy, unwashed and unshaved James tottered into my office. He had been a guest of the Public Security Bureau for three days.

He told me that he had been asleep, alone, in his hotel room when there was a loud banging on his door at 4 a.m. and six Public Security Bureau officers barged into his room and peered into every corner and cupboard.

"So where is she?" they demanded.

"Who are you looking for?" asked James.

"We know that you have a prostitute here."

"As you can see, I am alone in my bed."

"Did you have a prostitute earlier?"

"No."

"Ha! Are you planning to have a prostitute later?"

"Certainly not. I was trying to get some sleep before you......."

He was interrupted by a shout of excitement from one of the guards who had been rifling through James' papers and was now waiving a business card in the air. The card was closely examined.

"This card," announced the senior officer with glee, "probably belongs to a prostitute! Has she been here?"

"No," insisted James.

"But you must have been planning to invite her to your room or you would not have her business card," said the officer with confident logic.

"Nonsense." retorted James.

"In this case we have no option but to detain you on the grounds that you may have been intending to invite a prostitute to your room."

The hapless James was bundled into a van and deposited at the Public Security Bureau's Shanghai detention centre where he was kept for three days and denied any outside contact. Eventually he was released with a stern warning never again to think of what he might have been thinking the night he was arrested. James requested to be posted back to Hong Kong.

By the end of the 1980s free-spending Taiwanese were moving to China and taking over all available and eligible Chinese girls in cities such as Shanghai and elsewhere. They spoke Mandarin (few pretty girls bothered to learn any foreign languages), were much less conspicuous than *waiguoren* and, above all, threw their money around. Unlike the transient foreigners, the Taiwanese had come to stay. They quickly acquired apartments and cars and filled their offices with the best looking girls, setting up households with their favourites. They were on a hiding to nothing: the Chinese government did not allow their Chinese girlfriends to visit Taiwan and the Taiwanese government would not permit their wives to visit China. Most important of all, the Taiwanese had money. Much more money than the salaried *waiguoren*. They used their money to buy small presents for their girlfriends (a small present went a long way when there was little money available in China) and on endless *karaoke* evenings and banquets featuring the rarest of CITES protected species.

The Taiwanese did, however, lack one commodity precious to all Chinese:

a useful passport. Any ambitious young Chinese, of either sex, concentrated on a single target: how to get out of China. In this the Taiwanese were most ineffective. The Chinese did not consider Taiwan a desirable overseas destination even if they had been allowed to travel there. Their sights were set on the U.S., Canada, England or some other European country. A *waiguoren* could provide a passport but catching a *waiguoren* was not an easy task. Chinese girls also earned a poor reputation in a very short time. They called the target *waiguoren* a '*feijipiao*' or 'aeroplane ticket' and were not averse to ditching their new husband as soon as the vital service had been supplied.

When inter-racial marriages became possible in the late 1980s many Chinese women found it difficult to assimilate into their foreign husband's culture. At one party I hosted in Shanghai I was introduced to a German working for Volkswagen who was one of the first foreigners to marry a local Chinese girl. She was a tall Shanghainese beauty. He was a fairly typical Bavarian – wide of girth and noisy in manner. He was delighted with his new wife. She was radiant at attaining her wildest ambition. To her great excitement the couple were transferred to Wolfsburg, Volkswagen's head office in Germany. She spoke no German, hated the weather, missed Chinese food, had no friends, resented being stared at by the Germans and begged her husband to return to China. He eventually settled for a more junior position at lower pay at Volkswagen's other Chinese factory in Manchuria. It was not Shanghai but at least it was in China. But she hated the provincialism of Manchuria and eventually left her husband and returned to Shanghai with their children.

Not all stories ended so unsatisfactorily; many other Chinese women fell genuinely in love with foreign men and happily moved overseas as did two girls in my Beijing office.

Certainly China had moved a long way from 1980 when the Beijing Government announced a decree totally prohibiting marriage between foreigners and Chinese belonging to a number of categories including 'diplomats, China Travel Service Guides and interpreters'.

Today, twenty-five years after I arrived in China, most of these shibboleths have long gone. It is possible to meet, court and marry girls from China as in any other country. It is as if the Maoists and their extreme ideas on women, sex and morality had never existed.

10

China Investments

In January 1979 the Chinese government made the surprise announcement that limited foreign investment would be allowed in China for the first time since the communists took power. A new law and operating regulations would be announced within a year or two which were to form the legal framework for foreign investment. This proclamation was greeted with considerable scepticism by international business. Many multinational corporations still nursed their wounds from the way the Chinese had seized their investments after Liberation: no compensation was ever paid and there had been torture and loss of life amongst the expatriate staff left at their stations in China. Could the Chinese ever be trusted to allow foreigners to invest in China again?

Whilst most foreigners took a wait and see attitude, the Overseas Chinese community pricked up its ears. Was this the sign they had been waiting for? It was the Overseas Chinese, especially the Hong Kong Chinese, who were going to provide the money and the impetus that would get China back on its feet. The Chinese diaspora consists of thirty million ethnic Chinese spread in almost every country: the largest expatriate community in the world. The Chinese have been fleeing their country from floods, poverty, famine and persecution for centuries. Unlike most foreign communities, who put down roots and absorb their adopted nationality, the Chinese retain their Chinese-ness wherever they are and for however long they have been in their new country. Once a Chinese, always a Chinese.

Inspite of the massacres and privations inflicted on the Chinese by their own people, all overseas Chinese feel that a debt is owed to their motherland and something, no matter what, has to be given back. Another Chinese characteristic about to rise to the surface was the deeply ingrained notion of honouring past favours. Whenever the Chinese perceive that a favour had been granted, then this represents an obligation which has to be returned.

The 1970s saw the surprising appearance of Hong Kong Chinese benefiting from 'favours' they had extended to the People's Republic during the early years after its birth. Turmoil was a consistent theme in China from the 1930s and particularly since Liberation. The anti-rightist campaigns of the 1950s which saw the annihilation of over five million landlords and businessmen, the Korean War, the Great Leap Forward, the Cultural Revolution and the countless other campaigns over the years had all led to massive loss of life and deepening poverty. Throughout all these phases there were some Overseas Chinese who never turned their backs on China. Now it was pay-back time.

Some benefited hugely. The building contractor who helped the Chinese government buy arms during the Korean War was given the monopoly to import Chinese river sand for the construction industry into Hong Kong so becoming one of the world's richest men. Others were the recipients of important-looking documents from government departments giving them the exclusive right to import or export some valuable commodity or develop a strategic piece of land. People began to appear in my office waving these documents and asking whether we would like to exploit such opportunities with them.

Amongst its many businesses, Inchcape owned oil-field bases and workshops around the world and a fleet of offshore supply boats to service drilling rigs. We were interested in supplying such services to the oil industry then considering exploration in Chinese offshore waters. But how were we to introduce our capabilities? One morning a men's shirt manufacturer from one of the poorer areas of Kowloon came into my office. He was an old man, owned a small tailor's shop and had scratched a poor living all his life. He placed in front of me an important-looking document apparently issued by the Ministry of Oil appointing the tailor as the sole channel through which the Ministry intended to charter oilfield supply vessels. He would not tell me how he had got hold of this document but I guessed that for years the tailor had been supplying information to communist agents in Hong Kong as a 'sleeper'. Or perhaps he too had been a gun-runner.

Some of these claims were spurious, others genuine: it was difficult to sort the grain from the chaff. In each case the promoter had little idea of what was involved but they believed they were holding a valuable piece of paper. Certainly the tailor had no idea what a supply boat was, but he thought the Chinese government was granting him a favour so the document must have some value.

In early March 1979 Dickie Arblaster and I lunched in Inchcape's executive dining suite, the Tower Rooms, in Elizabeth House. Dickie told me a surprising story. His automotive company used a sub-contractor to beat out bent truck panels in Kowloon and the sub-contractor's father had just returned from Guangzhou with a document asking him to start a company to operate bus services between Guangzhou and Hong Kong. We never found out what service he had provided to the Chinese government to be rewarded in such a way. It hardly mattered.

Dickie asked what I thought of such a scheme. At that time, as we have seen, the only access to China was to take the train on the Hong Kong-side to Lowu, walk across the bridge at Shenzhen, just a halt on the railway with a few houses, and then take the Chinese train to Guangzhou. There was no road access and no vehicular bridge across the narrow Shenzhen River. And was there even a road from Shenzhen to Guangzhou? Nobody knew. The road had been closed to foreigners since 1949 and the Chinese always took the train.

Dickie's interest was awakened as he wanted to sell buses in China and this might be an original way into the market. I agreed to investigate. Dick Chan and I met some officials from the Guangdong Provincial Bureau of Transport in Guangzhou. It seemed they were serious. I asked whether I could survey the road between Guangzhou and Shenzhen, a distance of one hundred and thirty miles, and this was arranged for the following week.

I left Guangzhou at 7 a.m. one freezing winter's day in a Soviet-style Beijing jeep with a driver, an official and a security guard. We drove all day along an unsurfaced track winding through lychee orchards and villages, across rice paddies and over tottering wooden bridges, stopping for at least three ferries. We eventually reached Shenzhen at 5 p.m. to find the immigration office had closed an hour earlier for the night. I slept in a dormitory on a camp bed covered by an ancient yellow mosquito net with thirty other Chinese travellers. The following morning I walked alone across the bridge into Hong Kong surprising the Hong Kong border guards who did not often see solitary travellers walking across the Shenzhen Bridge coming out of China.

I reported to Dickie that the venture looked difficult to say the least. The road needed to be rebuilt, new bridges would have to replace the ferries and it was going to take much longer to reach Guangzhou by bus than by train. But Dickie was not to be deterred: it was not so much the route to Guangzhou that he was after but other routes that could be opened up elsewhere in Guangdong Province which could deliver Hong Kong people direct to their families in the remote parts of the province where there was little local transport.

All through that hot summer of 1979 Dick Chan and I worked on this project and eventually succeeded in drawing up a joint-venture agreement, the first of its kind in China and months before the draft law on foreign investment was promulgated. Our final document was no more than three pages long and left a great deal on trust. It was time for a talk with PG.

The chairman was unconvinced. "Let me get this right, Evelyn," he said. "You want me to invest a million Hong Kong dollars in a bus company in China but there are no roads, no bridges, no customs and immigration on either side and neither of the partners have ever run a bus company before. Also there is no law to protect our investment. Is that right?"

This was not going to work out. "That is correct, but, if it succeeds, we will be the first. Now that would be quite something!"

"Remember Lord Inchcape's dictum?" PG was no longer looking at me. His eyes had drifted to the window as he watched a Chinese-flagged cargo ship slowly feeling its way into Hong Kong harbour. He lit a cigarette. I had caught his imagination. "Kenneth Inchcape said that we should never consider a new activity in a new country. And here we are talking about running a bus company, a first for Inchcape, in China, where we have never invested before. The Earl would not approve." He lapsed into one of his prolonged silences with which I was quite familiar by now.

"A million Hong Kong dollars? Hmmm." I could see that PG was considering the kudos. This would be a first for any company, perhaps in the world. Friends would be buying him drinks in the Jockey Club. "Take me to Guangzhou," he said. "Introduce me to the officials there. Let me see if this is for real."

So in March 1980 a small delegation from Inchcape led by PG, and including Peter Carrodus, the finance director, Dickie Arblaster, Dick Chan and myself assembled in the forbidding lobby of the Dong Feng Hotel. We had flown from Hong Kong in one of the first CAAC Trident flights from Hong Kong to Guangzhou. PG had taken one look at the dilapidated unpainted aircraft and sent Dickie to the bar. "Two double vodkas for me," he ordered.

Even PG found the entertainment laid on by the Guangdong authorities somewhat excessive as one twelve-course banquet followed another, exotic specialities forbidden in Hong Kong being served with eager anticipation by our Chinese hosts. The rarest of wild animals were procured, endangered species from all over China were salted, braised, triple-boiled or baked in mud shells. Glasses of vintage Mao Tai were drunk, toasted, refilled, spilt, refilled and toasted again. Amidst all this bonhomie, the Governor of Guangdong Province, an area larger than France, stood wavering on his feet and in loud, clear tones gave formal instructions to his officials to proceed with the bus company without further ado. PG was delighted, another feather in his cap.

Not many months later Lord Inchcape made a visit to Hong Kong. Before his routine press conference he was groomed by Inchcape's press relations specialist in how to answer the jounalists' questions. "In the unlikely event that you should be asked about our bus company, say nothing," he was told.

"What bus company?" asked the Earl. In the event embarrassment was compounded as all the journalists wanted to know about was the bus company.

"When is it going to start?"

"How much money have you invested?"

"But are there any roads?"

"What sort of agreement do you have?" The questions burst from the journalists scenting a new story. Lord Inchcape looked uncomfortable and confused. PG stood impassive, a slight smile on his lips, a fresh stain on his shirt front.

Over the coming months intensive negotiations with the Hong Kong government concluded with their decision to build a new bridge across the Shenzhen River, construct a building for the immigration and customs on the British side and to allocate a terminal from where our fleet of buses could operate in Kowloon. In marked comparison to the British government in England where things move glacially and generally not in a positive direction, the Hong Kong government realised that immense changes were in the wind and that their giant Chinese neighbour was stirring, and enthusiastically supported our venture. The Chinese side also started civil construction work on their side of the border but at a more measured pace.

By the end of 1980 it was clear that the bus service was going to start some six months behind schedule but our million dollars had all been spent. The buses had been ordered but there had been many other costs we had not anticipated and the delays had eaten into our reserves. I had to face PG to explain that the first million dollars had gone and that we needed another million. In later years, when Inchcape's management was sanitised somebody's head might have rolled over such a miscalculation but this was a mere detail to PG.

"Another million? Are you sure that is the last?" enquired the chairman. He stared at me for what seemed an eternity. "Right. Done! But no more do you hear?" He went back to studying the racing form in the Hong Kong Standard for that evening's races at Happy Valley. He never asked what I had done with the first million and he never enquired why I needed a second.

By June 1981 the civil construction had been completed and the first thirty British Leyland buses with Singapore-made bodies arrived in Hong Kong. Dickie Arblaster set off for Guangzhou in one of the buses on a proving run together with a British Leyland engineer to show the future Chinese bus drivers how a modern bus operated. The bus drivers could not have been less interested, they thought that there was nothing new under the sun for them to learn.

Not all buses are created equal however. The BL buses had servo-assisted air brakes which needed the engine on at all times to provide pressurised air. In the event that the air pressure fell then a buzzer sounded in the driver's cabin. Now the Chinese have invented certain driving techniques over the years to which they adhere with compulsion. One of these techniques is driving at night with the head-lights off in the belief that they are saving fuel. If you see something coming the other way, you flash your headlights at full beam into the eyes of the other driver and then revert to your sidelights. Another fuel-saving measure is to put the engine into neutral and coast when going down hill.

When the BL bus faced its first steep descent, the engineer advised the driver to put the bus in third gear to keep the engine revolutions up and the air pressure high. The driver immediately put the engine into neutral and the bus rolled down the hill with increasing speed. Within seconds the emergency buzzer sounded as the brakes lost pressure. There was nothing that the BL engineer could do to modify the driver's technique and so both Dickie and the engineer completed the trip sitting anxiously in the back seat of the bus. The Chinese requested the buzzers to be removed. Quite unnecessary, they thought.

Once the service started in June 1981 it proved immediately popular with the public and was to become a beacon of success amongst foreign investments in China at a time when others were failing. But as the years went by and success grew, Inchcape found that its original fifty per cent shareholding was whittled down as other Chinese shareholders in the form of state-owned travel agents and regional governments jumped on the band-wagon. I was appointed deputy chairman of the company and remained in that position for fifteen years. When I left, the company had grown to own over 200 buses and 150 trucks.

Inchcape management input was limited to Cyril Lau, a retired Inchcape motors executive, who worked in the company trying to understand the thought processes of the Chinese who were sent to Hong Kong to run the company. Cyril reported to me regularly on the communist cadres struggle to make sense out of life in free-wheeling Hong Kong.

Inchcape also set up an accounting system for the joint-venture as there were no formal accounting systems in Chinese organisations. This was well-received by the board of directors as they found for the first time that they could see where the money went and how much profit they made. Our first board meeting started in a very hostile atmosphere. I was, as usual, the only non-Chinese present and I felt that there were some unpleasant undertones throughout the meeting. At the end of the meeting the chairman made a formal speech.

"We are much obliged to Inchcape for their assistance in setting up the financial system, especially so as we have now noticed that a substantial sum of money has been removed from the company. We haven't got it, so who has?" He looked accusingly at me.

"Well, we certainly haven't taken anything!" I protested.

"So what is this?" demanded the chairman stubbing the accounts with his finger. "There is a large amount of money missing here. It's called 'depreciation'. Where's it gone and who's got it?"

Not being an accountant myself, I struggled to explain that depreciation is a notional figure put on one side with which one can buy new buses in the future.

"Put on one side? Where is it then? Can you show me?" persisted the chairman.

I did my best to clarify the concept of depreciation but I realised that the more I explained the more suspicious were the other directors at my laboured account.

There were countless similar incidents when the communist and capitalist world collided and the two had to find some compatible ground but it was these surprises that provided the challenge.

Shortly afterwards Inchcape made a small investment in another project in China. As one of the largest distributors of wines and spirits in the Far East, Inchcape was induced to invest in a winery together with Pernod-Ricard, a French company well-known for its wines. China has long produced some low quality wine and Pernod-Ricard were confident that they could make a better quality wine in China which would sell well throughout the Far East. A modern, state-of-the-art winery was built near Yantai and the first batch of white wine was produced. I was offered a glass at the winery: it tasted alright but was the colour of water. The French wine-maker was non-plussed. He recommended adding caramel, "to make it more yellow," he said.

The first vintage of 'Great Wall White Wine' was not a success. The bottles developed a habit of exploding, fortunately more often in our warehouse than at the table.

When the winery re-opened the following year we were horrified to find that our Chinese partners had been busy during the winter months faithfully copying the process system, machinery and even the building of our winery. Now, just one hundred yards away, we found a new winery had been created owned by our partners. Worse news came when the grapes started arriving from the vineyards. Pressure was exerted on the farmers to channel the best grapes to the new factory while ours received the left-overs.

This became a common and unendearing Chinese characteristic: use foreign capital and expertise and then copy it.

Some years later we considered investing in the Chinese tea industry, where one might surmise they would have little to learn. Although there are countless high-grade tea gardens all over China, we were taken to see a plantation in one of the most remote corners of the country. From Kunming, a large city in the south of China, we took a ricketty airplane to Simao. After spending the night in a small guesthouse (where the only food consisted of frogs cooked in eight different ways), we drove through dense forest for five hours until we reached a large patch of cleared jungle, several thousand acres, where the Chinese were trying to grow tea. It was very cold and snowed as we examined the meagre-looking tea plants. The workers were not happy: tigers roamed the forest at will and frequently raided the tea estate. Our small team was dejected; we could not see any Inchcape tea planters living in such a remote place.

With other tea gardens so much more accessible, why had this particular estate been selected for Inchcape's investment? "Because," the cadre answered with commendable honesty, "of all the tea estates in China, this is the only one where we are unable to grow even passable tea. We thought with your money and technology, you could put it right."

After our delegation had spent a few days on the tea plantation we drove south through dense jungle to Shixiangbanna the traditional source of the ethnic Thai people. Here I was to see first hand what had only been whispered to me before: the arrogant way in which the Han Chinese treat the more than one hundred 'minority' nationalities who dwell inside the People's Republic. There are some 60 million people in China who are not Han Chinese but belong to many different tribal groupings. Although the Han created so-called 'autonomous regions' for these people so that their traditions are apparently respected, in truth the Han view these people with disdain.

During my years in Thailand I had learned many Thai customs such as removing shoes before entering a house, not pointing with one's feet, not touching the top of someone's head and many others. The 'Dai' people in Shixiangbanna had preserved their Thai culture down the centuries and showed the hospitality typical of the Thais. As I walked around the town, the first *farang* for a long time, I was invited into their wooden stilted houses. I carefully removed my shoes, avoided stepping on the threshold, sat on the polished wooden floors and spoke softly to my host while some tea was prepared. In the meanwhile my Han Chinese companions from the Ministry of Agriculture's provincial headquarters in Kunming, clumped around the house in their shoes, kicked the furniture, ridiculed the Buddhist icons and made derogatory comments loudly in Mandarin. My Dai hosts looked pained and reserved, biting their tongues in anger.

Inchcape's next investment in China was in the shipping container industry. A joint-venture company was set up, Land-Ocean Inchcape, to operate a hazardous cargo container terminus in Shanghai with a fleet of container trucks and trailers which delivered containers all over China. This time Inchcape was in control of the management of the venture and was exposed for the first time to the curious ways in which Chinese companies operated.

Typical of our many experiences was a discussion regarding taxation. We considered that we had been over-charged by the taxation authorities. After a three hour meeting to discuss theproblem, Shi Fubao, the general manager, said, "Well, I guess it doesn't matter anyway. The money's gone, we won't get it back." Eight pairs of eyes swivelled in his direction, "Gone? Gone where?"

Mr Shi explained that whenever the government wants money from a company, for tax or any other reason, then they simply remove the money from the company's bank account. "Just like that!" said Mr. Shi. "They don't tell you that they are going to do it. One day the money is there, the next day it is gone! You can't argue with the State as there is nobody to argue with. I suggest we might as well forget the whole thing."

Compared to other foreign-Chinese joint-ventures in the 1980s, Land-Ocean Inchcape was considered a success. Many ventures failed due to management disagreements or the difference between the communist system and the thought processes this entailed and the mindset of the capitalist businessman.

I was also exposed to the exotic ways that the French deploy to pursue business in China. As joint chairman of Land-Ocean Inchcape I had some influence over purchase of equipment. At one time we were negotiating the purchase of a dozen container tractors, a deal worth some millions of dollars. One of the possibilities was to buy Renault tractors from France which were the cheapest but not the best. One day a French Renault representative insisted on visiting me in my office in Hong Kong. Scarcely had he introduced himself when he brazenly announced that 'of course' should Renault tractors be chosen then a 2% commission would be paid into a secret bank account in my name. It was therefore no surprise at all when at a meeting the following week in Shanghai all my Chinese fellow-directors suddenly announced that they could find no fault at all with Renault tractors, having totally rejected them only the week before, and that we should proceed to award the contract to Renault without further consideration. They were very disappointed when I vetoed their proposal.

By 1992 Inchcape had invested in only a handful of other ventures in China. The momentum created by Inchcape's arrival in China in 1979 and the speed with which its Chinese name became known through ministerial corridors had been largely dissipated by the 1990s, when China's foreign investment boom really got under way. By that time Inchcape's ship was steering a confused course. The bridge had become over-crowded with its officers pointing in different directions.

Charles Mackay, the new chairman of Inchcape Pacific and an outsider to the company, had vision and could see China's long term attractions but was diverted by opportunities elsewhere. Many large American companies sensed the future and made China their international priority allocating resources to develop their business in China. Inchcape, better positioned in every way with its huge Chinese-speaking staff base in Hong Kong, centuries of experience in operating in developing countries and an unrivalled portfolio of international principals, allowed these advantages to go to waste. The new 'professional' management in London turned introspective and failed to meet the challenge.

Head office management had become embroiled in petty politics and parochial priorities and ignored its team of specialists within Inchcape China with its unparalleled network of Chinese offices and its hard-won access to top officials in the Chinese government, the envy of other multinationals. This was a commercial tragedy of some magnitude. The Inchcape directors in London failed to see the jewel within their own company. While Inchcape China was setting the China strategy for many Fortune 500 companies in America, most much larger than Inchcape, the new planners and strategists within Inchcape could only theorise and commission yet another management consultancy report. After so many years courting the powers in Beijing and so successfully establishing the name of Inchcape ascross China, we found ourselves sidelined. The shattering changes that swept China in the 1990s creating business opportunities on a massive scale, managed to bypass Inchcape unheeded.

11

The Business

Since the beginning of time China has been an agricultural country – perennially overpopulated, its hoards struggling to make a living off frequently poor, arid land blighted by floods and droughts. Although containing a third of the world's population it only has 17% of the world's agricultural land. The Chinese nevertheless consider themselves to be true sons of the soil. This was certainly true until the advent of the communist dynasty in 1949, but then superhuman efforts were made to turn China into an industrial powerhouse. In the thirty years between 1949 and 1979 the Chinese built 355,000 factories causing the greatest famine in the history of the human race in the process as millions left the land to work in the factories.

In our initial search for business opportunities in China, Dick and I quickly realised that with China's meagre foreign exchange reserves and with negligible consumer spending power we could only sell industrial products and technology in China. We considered the industrial export market; exports of consumer goods from China were already being handled on a rapidly growing scale by Inchcape's buying offices. Most traditional exports were channelled through well established unshakeable trading relationships – the famed 'old friends'. But China was beginning to become interested in manufacturing low-technology component parts, forgings, castings, and the suchlike. American industry made these components themselves or used a lower cost source such as Japan, Mexico or Korea. As China's cost of labour seemed so low and other costs also should be lower than in the industrialised west, then iron and steel forgings and castings should be competitive. We were a long way ahead of ourselves, it was to be another twenty years before China became a major exporter of industrial manufactured products.

It was 1981 and we were working with an American ship-builder in Seattle. This was the type of company the Chinese should have welcomed with open arms: high-tech, state-of-the art plasma machinery, a builder of warships for the

U.S. Navy, a company from which the Chinese could learn much to improve their own capabilities. We struggled to find common ground for cooperation. Eventually we picked on anchor chain. Forged anchor chain is a commodity, sold by the ton. The Dalien Shipyard, one of the largest in China, had built a new anchor chain factory with the latest machinery and we were invited to have a look.

It was a large factory building with two production lines. One was an old Soviet line dating back many decades, the other brand new and recently imported from Germany. Both lines were idle. On one side of the factory there was a pile of recently completed chain. The workers, and there were many, were sitting around playing cards or watching a game of netball in the factory yard.

"Is it the morning break?" I asked the plant manager. "Oh no, we have finished our production plan for the year," he told me.

"But it is only February."

"Yes, I know. With the old equipment we used to finish our annual production quota in November which left us a month to maintain the machinery. But with this marvellous new German machinery we can finish our entire year's quota in six weeks and there it is!" He pointed proudly at a mound of chain alongside one wall.

"What are you going to do with the workers for the next ten months?"

He shrugged his shoulders.

In the meeting room, over a mug of green tea, I asked the plant manager, who had a marked resemblance to Mao Zedong, at what price could he sell us the chain. "Price, price?" he looked confused. "We do not have prices. The chain belongs to the China State Shipbuilding Corporation and we hand it over to them. They do not pay us. How much do you think we could sell it for?"

There lay a problem which the Chinese would not overcome for many years. When they did finally unlock that door, they were able to turn themselves into the world's greatest supplier of low-cost manufactures. But in 1981 the Americans could only suggest taking their lowest cost of manufacture, deduct the shipping costs from China and import duties, take away a margin for the extra risk in ordering from such a long distance and tell the Chinese what they thought it should cost. The Chinese would then have a stab at what they guessed it cost them to manufacture a length of chain and always came up with a much higher figure.

Paradoxically the costs were indeed much higher in China. Although workers' salaries were a few yuan a month, there were many of them. And they had wives who also needed jobs, probably in the same concern. Hospitals had to be provided, accommodation for the workers, schools, crèches, the entire cradle-to-grave cocoon in which the Chinese lived all had a cost. It seemed that Chinese chain might be the most expensive in the world!

The Americans looked around at the poverty surrounding them and the drabness of Dalien in the winter, took in the skinny workers squatting on piles of chain shuffling rice into their hungry mouths from battered enamel bowls and decided they were being cheated by the Chinese. They were asking for too much money. In the meantime, the Chinese, not trusting the Americans, asked their embassy to find out the price of chain in the U.S. The only price available to them was the retail price which was considerably more than the ex-factory wholesale price quoted by the Americans. The Chinese, not understanding the American system, thought they also were being cheated.

The Americans suggested that the plant run both lines at full capacity to bring down the production cost. The plant manager was horrified, "We couldn't possibly do that! We would never receive the steel to make the chain from our head office. And what would we do with all the chain? And the workers? They would never put up with having to work so hard!"

Over the years Dick and I escorted numerous teams of foreign businessmen to China all desperately searching for a grain of hope which might grow into that most elusive of all objectives: a profitable China business. One of the first delegations we took to China came from Precision National Corporation, one of Michael Beutler's introductions from the United States. PNC was a rebuilder of American diesel locomotives for the railways. It mattered not that American railways were in decline while China ran one of the most sophisticated railway networks in the world. The equipment may have been old-fashioned, there were plenty of coal-fired steam engines still at work, but the railway system was the only form of transport which worked efficiently in China. It was a vast industry coordinated under the Ministry of Railways which ran the track and trains and an extensive industrial infrastructure which built the rolling stock and the locomotives. The ministry employed over a million people.

PNC's delegation to China was headed by its president, Hansjoerg Schudel. Hansjoerg brought his Iranian mistress, an emotional harridan with green eyes, and skin and hair of conflicting orange hues. She wore a turquoise floor-length down-filled coat. Her name was Irena and she terrified the Chinese. They did not look at her for fear of the evil eye. They were deeply shocked that she shared the same bed as 'President' Schudel, as they called him much to his smug delight. On one occasion she objected to the Chinese-style plumbing in her bathroom. Whatever she flushed down the loo reappeared up the bath drain every time she turned the shower on. She ordered the young interpreter to scrub the damage in the bathroom. He was not amused. The 'interpreter' was actually the son of the PLA chief of general staff undergoing a six-month exposure to western life before taking up a senior post in the Ministry of Defence.

Irena was shortly to receive her comeuppance. Chinese postage stamps and envelopes are not adhesive and there was a small pot of glue in each hotel room for the use of the guests in the shape of a plastic bird. Irena found the 'bird' in her bathroom and thinking it must be a small container of shampoo, she washed her hair with it.

The Ministry of Railways was determined to do business. There was no question of investment, it was much too early for that. The ministerial cadres wanted to prove that they were able to generate foreign exchange on their own, a new privilege for the ministry, which they could then spend on imports circumventing the Ministry of Foreign Trade. They were determined that we should leave China deeply impressed with their capabilities. Over three long weeks we travelled the breadth and depth of China. We visited a factory making locomotive wheels on the coast in Qingdao, a bogey plant by the lake in Kunming, and a signals factory in Shanghai. We traversed the mountains to see a diesel engine factory in Chengdu and lived for days in the Politburo's own railcar attached to the back of a local train as it chugged across the frozen Taklamakan Desert to Xinjiang in the far west of China.

We stayed, as usual, in a government guest-house in Urumqi, the capital of Xinjiang. Our Chinese hosts were visibly uncomfortable here. Mandarin was spoken poorly and they became frustrated at not being able to make themselves understood in their own country. The Uighurs who live there are a Turkic people with fair, caucasian complexions, green eyes and light brown hair. Here it was the Han Chinese who were conspicuous and the Americans were no longer the attraction. A snow-fall closed the airport in Urumqi and we found ourselves marooned there for three days waiting for our flight to Beijing.

The Chinese were at a loss as to how to entertain us when Bill, the obese American engineer, sprung to life.

"Say, what I'd really like to do is see a Chinese home. Just a typical house, an ordinary family. I'd like to see how they live here."

The ministry officials were horrified. It was absolutely forbidden to invite a foreigner into your home without extensive explanations to the security apparatus, the Party Secretary, the street committee and countless officials. But Bill was not to be put off and he badgered the Chinese all morning. Eventually at lunch time, with no sign of the snow easing, the Chinese announced that we were to visit an ordinary family home that afternoon.

We were taken to an attractive modern brick house standing in its own garden. It seemed that the Uighurs in Urumqi lived very well. The Americans were impressed. The furniture was comfortable and looked new. There was a television set, a rug on the floor, a polished table with a vase of plastic flowers. The kitchen was well-equipped with a modern refigerator. The smiling owner obligingly opened the door to show it was well stocked with a chicken, a hunk of lamb, milk and vegetables. Fresh apples, rare in January, lay on the table. Then I saw something so surprising that I realised we were being treated to a Chinese charade. A banana. Just a banana. But bananas in China were reserved only for top cadres and only available in the shops reserved for senior officials. There was no way our lovely Uighur hostess, undoubtably chosen to entertain us for her looks, could have access to bananas.

I whispered to Dick to find out what was going on. He reported to me later that the Uighur family had been told two hours before we arrived that they were to be visited by some Americans: a great honour. One hour later a truck delivered the furniture, the kitchen equipment and the food. They were told that on no account were they to touch anything, especially the food, and the truck would return to collect everything as soon as the Americans had left.

Throughout our tour of China with the Ministry of Railways we found vast gloomy factories with ancient equipment surrounded by crowds of workers nonchalantly watching the machinery as they chatted and slurped tea from jam jars. Every factory was its own self-sustaining community with hospitals, crèches, schools and workers' housing. This was the iron rice bowl, the famed Chinese communist system of total control, the surrender of choice in favour of three meals a day.

In many places we were a sensation. Factories stopped production as their workers flooded outside to line the streets to see the foreigners. We felt, and indeed looked, like aliens marching through crowds which opened up as we walked. It was always the same look: mouth gaping slightly open, eyes unblinking, a look of slight amusement on their faces, rather as one might look at a performing Panda walking down the street. One of the American engineers, a huge round man with a pumpkin-like bald head, played to the crowd and roared and beat his chest producing near panic amongst those who ventured the closest.

Our Chinese hosts were unerringly courteous and hospitable. We provided the excuse for every factory manager to push the boat out. Twelve course banquets, complete with *baijiu*. At every city, every plant, we were toasted at banquets, overfed and made to believe that the ministry had chosen PNC as its long-lost and most-favoured industrial partner. The Chinese team was led by the affable Director Qi whose fall from grace we have already followed. The Chinese always showed a particular skill at relaxing visitors while keeping their distance.

For Americans to visit China was to enter the devil's lair: they had been indoctrinated for years on the evils of the communist Chinese, had fought them in Korea, feared them in Vietnam and read about the atrocities of the Cultural Revolution. China's heinous reputation had been stoked for years by the émigrés on Taiwan. The Chinese reacted to this suspicion and occasional hostility with a charm offensive. Soon I found the Americans praising the most banal everyday event as if it was a matter of national importance to discover that the Chinese were only a little different from everybody else.

Throughout our long trip we were not asked to pay for our hotels, food or transport. We discussed this amongst ourselves and decided that it was most unlikely that we were the 'guests' of the ministry and that sooner or later we would be faced with a large bill. So it was on the last night of the trip that Director Qi asked for a private audience with President Schudel. He had a suggestion to make. The ministry offered to pay all the Americans' expenses in China but in return the Americans would invite a team from the ministry to visit the United States. This was scarcely a fair deal as travel in America is much more expensive than it is in China. But the deal was done and it set the precedent that we were to follow until travel costs in China caught up with international levels.

Back in Beijing, President Schudel and Director Qi exchanged bear hugs and promises of eternal friendship but who was bringing the bacon home? Where was the business? Once again the Americans prepared a long list of widgets that they would like the ministry to forge and cast and once again we could not agree on a price. Whichever way we looked at it, the production costs in one of the poorest countries in the world were several times higher than in the United States.

There is a reason why both export efforts failed. China maintained an unrealistically high exchange rate – the opposite to conditions today. There was no incentive to export as foreign exchange earnings were surrendered to the State and the exporter was paid in the local currency at the same price as if he had sold the products on the domestic market. The over-valued currency meant that the international market price would usually be lower than the domestic cost of production. The result was that the State had to subsidise exports through the use of state trading corporations. Both the China State Shipbuilding Corporation and the Ministry of Railways were trying to circumvent the system but found this impossible. By the end of the decade the State rectified its system allowing a true export boom to commence.

So my efforts to find new export businesses from China seemed doomed to failure. I would not have guessed that within a decade China would become the manufacturing shop of the world. I turned again to the import market. But China had scant foreign exchange reserves, received few funds from international agencies and did not have access to the international capital markets. Realising China's penchant for big-ticket capital process equipment, recently undergoing a revival during the 1980s, I concentrated on representing companies at the leading edge of technology: process equipment, aerospace, computerised machine tools, cryogenics and oil exploration equipment. Nearly all these companies were American.

Dick and I had to hide a fundamental secret from the Fortune 500 companies we represented in China: it took an average of *five years* to win a contract to sell capital equipment in China. It needed the same amount of time to sell a machine that cost ten thousand dollars or an integrated production line that could cost twenty million. Americans were always looking for sales around the corner; if they had known that they would still be beating their heads against the Great Wall of China so many years down the road, they would have switched their sales efforts to an easier country.

The road map to a deal in China started with a visit by the American company's top executives to China. This always, without fail, resulted in an insane and unreasonable 'China euphoria' emanating from the Chairman's office instructing all company departments to shift China into a top priority. The well-honed Chinese technique at seducing possibly critical foreigners was always fascinating to observe. They were courted with lavish meals, expressions of sincerity, an apparent openness, a firm desire to succeed, charm and friendliness. Dick and I often laughed at the comments expressed behind the foreigners' backs but he was a rare man who left China for the first time not bursting with enthusiasm to spread the word that China was ready for business.

Of course it was not to be, not for many years. The Chinese government had earned itself a good business reputation under the Maoist days when, with much of the world against it, it was known for honesty and prompt payment of bills. But as time went by, China was revealed as a country where there was only one winner and where foreigners should tread with caution.

With the senior management all fired up with enthusiasm, it became the turn of the engineers and salesmen to invade China. Armed with Chinese-language brochures and Mandarin slide presentations they found themselves locked into an overcrowded, smoke-filled room with twenty or thirty Chinese as their technology was picked to pieces day after day. Tolerances, temperatures and metal content were analysed and argued over. Some of the audience came from the end-user plant, many more from different Chinese research institutes, universities and commercial companies. Questioning was relentless, often confused, frequently at cross-purposes, often mis-interpreted and sometimes bad-tempered. The foreigners could not understand why it was necessary to go into such minute technical detail with the Chinese writing every word into their note-books. The foreigners were no fools, they could see that most of the information was to be used by the Chinese so that they could replicate the process themselves.

Although called a 'technical exchange', it was in fact a one-way flow of information. Should a foreigner ask about Chinese machinery or operating conditions, there was a hush: he had ventured into *neibu* territory. Might this be a State Secret? The Chinese intention was then, as it is today, to seek self-sufficiency. They reasoned that given their historical isolation it was unwise to become dependant on foreign equipment or technology and that there was no reason why their own people could not do whatever the westerners could do. It was just a question of extracting the technology from the foreigners. All they needed was the know-how and then the Chinese could also send a man to the moon or build a Boeing 747. So for our American clients it became a high risk game – to sell the maximum amount of high-tech equipment while giving away the minimum amount of technology. The Chinese aim was the precise opposite.

The tactic the Chinese used was to lure the foreigners with hints of huge equipment imports. Our experiences with American Steriliser Corporation from Erie, Pennsylvania was one of the more extreme examples. Amsco was the world's leading manufacturer of sterilisers for the hospital industry. Chinese hospitals were not equipped with disposable supplies and all syringes and medical equipment had to be sterilised in their own far from adequate sterilisers. But the Ministry of Public Health reasoned that a steriliser was not such an advanced technology and there was no reason why they could not make a modern steriliser with a little help from the outside world. So the Ministry set about courting Amsco with hints of an order so large that the factory in Erie would be busy for years to come making equipment for the Chinese market.

We set off down the by then familiar long march of Chinese delegations to Erie and American team visits to the Chinese steriliser factory in Zibo, a particularly unappealing town in Shandong Province, an overnight train journey from Beijing. The Chinese made visits to Zibo more alluring by rolling out the red carpet on a massive scale. On one occasion the mayor of Erie was invited to visit Zibo accompanied by Amsco's President Fish. When the couple's train arrived in Zibo they were astounded to find the railway station full of children lining the platform waving Chinese and American flags and chanting 'Welcome Erie Mayor to Zibo!' The whole town was festooned with American flags and banners proclaiming 'Hail to Amsco' and 'Long Live US/China Friendship'. We sped through the city in a cavalcade of Red Flag limousines amidst rows of cheering Chinese all recorded by Chinese television cameras and, not to be outdone, by Amsco's own NBC cameraman specially flown in for the occasion.

The banquets over the next few days and the speeches from the top provincial leaders exceeded all the hyperbole that we had seen before. It appeared that a deal of earth-shattering importance was in the making. The Chinese talked of several hundred of the latest generation of sterilisers which kept President Fish in a lather and the mayor of Erie salivating at the thought of the speeches he would give at Chambers of Commerce across the United States on how the small town of Erie had been able to crack open the Chinese market.

The cold light of reality dawned when the Chinese broke the news to

Amsco on the last day of their visit that there was no money available and that they would buy only three sterilisers (but at the heavily discounted price Amsco had offered for several hundred) and they would pay only a nominal fee to buy the technology to make sterilisers in China. The Amsco team left China in a huff, scarcely shaking the hands of their Chinese hosts. A 100 million dollar dream had been reduced to less than a single million.

The relationship did however continue. Amsco sold a few sterilisers and there was a half-hearted effort to teach the Chinese to manufacturer them. Over time the Chinese became tired of the very tight manufacturing tolerances that the Americans insisted were needed to achieve the correct medical standards and they started to use their own looser tolerances. Quite good enough for Chinese hospitals, they said.

We came across many such cases: Hughes Aircraft approached us with a problem. They thought they had landed a major contract to sell wire-guided anti-tank missile systems to the Ministry of Defence but in the end they mistakenly sold only a single missile which the Chinese tried unsuccessfully to reverse manufacture.

For many years the Chinese tried to copy a Boeing 707 and produce a similar aircraft which they called the Y-10. Originally CAAC purchased ten Boeing 707s, the last ever made for an airline, but one was secretly ear-marked for reverse manufacture and was disassembled at a factory in Shanghai. The 707 first flew in the 1950s and by that time it was twenty-year old technology but still represented a huge leap forward for the Chinese. It had cost Boeing US$16 million to develop and build the Boeing 367-80 in the 1950s which later became the 707.[1] The Chinese built two Y-10's over a period of eight years and at a cost of US$300 million. They got little for their pains – the project was dropped and the world never saw the Y-10.

The final hurdle in our protracted efforts to sell high-tech equipment and manufacturing processes was the negotiating stage. The foreign supplier was invited to China and then found, much to his surprise, that he was not the single chosen supplier that he had been encouraged to believe. He found himself in a room in the Ministry of Foreign Trade's Negotiations Building in the tree-lined avenue of Erligou in Beijing with his competition from all over the world in other rooms in the building. The Chinese buyers dashed from room to room to announce that the Germans had cut their price or the French had offered some more free benefits or the Italians claimed that their machine could run faster, to unnerve the wretched American negotiators.

[1] 'China Takes Off' by E.E. Bauer published by University of Washington Press, 1986.

Each team spent days, maybe weeks, negotiating the minute terms of a commercial contract supported by pages of technical specifications. Chinese had once preferred to sign one-page contracts but by the end of the 1980s a typical machinery contract could run to a hundred pages or more. The introduction of a lawyer was considered bad faith: the Chinese did not have lawyers and neither should the foreigners. On one occasion I saw the Chinese walk away from negotiations because the Americans insisted in having an attorney present. So China traders became very skilful in the arcane art of negotiating Chinese contracts based on imprecise Chinese laws. In early 1979 there were no commercial laws, much went on trust, but that commodity was beginning to wear thin by the end of the 1980s as the Chinese started to bend the rules of engagement.

The final decision, and no decision was ever truly final, was often reached at dawn after an all-night negotiating session. Sometimes the lowest price won the contract. Frequently the winner was the one who had struck the greatest rapport with the Chinese or who had looked after them the most generously during overseas visits. There was an arbitrary unfairness to the process. The Americans, arms tied behind their backs by the U.S. Foreign Corrupt Practices Act, had a strong sense of fair play and felt themselves disadvantaged.

The negotiations were often timed to start in early December, the Chinese being well aware that foreigners liked to be home by Christmas. Two weeks would go by as little progress was made, the same technical points being investigated by the Chinese technicians again and again. The same clauses in the contract argued over endlessly. By the 20th December the foreigners became desperate but the Chinese showed no sign of urgency. Come the 23rd December and the foreigners were prepared to work all night and started to surrender key negotiating points and by the 24th prices had reached rock bottom and suitcases were packed.

Sometimes the Chinese, skilled at cliff-edge timing brought the contract to the airport for signing as the foreigners disappeared behind the immigration counters. On other occasions the Americans refused to play the game and would walk out of the negotiations in disgust. This caused great consternation in the Chinese camp. They had a tendency to overplay their hand perhaps over-confident in their analyses that the foreigners had spent so much time and money to reach the negotiation stage that they would agree to almost anything to bring home a contract.

The Chinese were very cunning negotiators. Indeed the head negotiator, nearly always from one of the State trading organisations within the Ministry of Foreign Trade had studied negotiating tactics at the Foreign Trade Institute and they would deploy every psychological tactic they could summon during the negotiations. One time we negotiated the sale of an edible oil plant and the

American in charge of the negotiating team admitted in an unguarded moment to the Chinese that he had a weak heart and needed plenty of regular sleep. Almost immediately the Chinese called meetings starting in the evening and continuing until 3 a.m.

Although it was always preferable to have the negotiations at Erligou in Beijing as the hotels, restaurants and entertainment were better than elsewhere, they could be arranged anywhere. One cold winter Owens-Illinois was invited to attend negotiations in Wuhan, a city in the middle of China, for the sale of eight glass bottle forming machines. This multi-million dollar deal was to be a major break-through for them. The negotiations took place in a dingy hotel without central heating. One side of the hotel warmed up during the daytime as the sunshine streamed through the windows but the other side of the hotel remained glacial.

Then it snowed. It does not often snow in Wuhan and the city was not prepared. It snowed for two days and nights until there was two feet of snow on the ground. The staff could not come to work in the hotel. Worse, food supplies stopped reaching the city. We inspected the empty kitchens to see if we could find anything to eat but the shelves were bare. We were forced to trek through the snow to the ubiquitous Friendship Store where we found two cases of Chinese canned ham and a box of miniature Kahlua chocolate-liqueur bottles which we dragged back to the hotel. We lived off the canned ham and warmed ourselves with the Kahlua for the next three days until the snow melted and horse-drawn carts started to re-supply the city with fresh food.

Throughout the 1980s and early 1990s, Dick and I accompanied countless delegations to China. We had very few accidents, never lost anyone and, fortunately, few of our clients became sick. There was one incident in 1983 when an Owens-Illinois executive complained that he was urinating blood. I arranged for him to see an American embassy doctor who advised he should return to the U.S. forthwith. At that time Pan American and CAAC offered two flights a week to the U.S. Both airlines were fully booked for the foreseeable future. I reasoned with the Pan Am manager.

"I have a sick American national on my hands who should be repatriated immediately. Can you not find him a seat?"

"How sick is he?" came the answer. I explained the symptoms and said that the doctor did not think it infectious.

"We would need to get the Pan Am doctor to look at him."

" How are you going to do that in Beijing?"

"We could get some samples taken and send them over to our office in San Francisco."

"How long will all that take?"

"Maybe a week or two."

"But he could be dead by then!"

"I'm sorry, we must follow procedures."

Living in China made one think that everything was impossible. It was reassuring to find that even outside China nothing was as straightforward as it should be. I called CAAC, secured a seat by paying a small premium, never told the airline the man was sick and he arrived safely in Ohio the next day.

Dick and I frequently gave talks on China to fact-finding teams and chief executives of multi-national companies who in the 1980s were again becoming intoxicated with the "if only every Chinese would take a single aspirin once a month ......" mirage. One day we had lunch at Elizabeth House with the Inchcape chairman of the day and a high-powered team from Unilever, the world's largest soap and detergent company. Dick dutifully mentioned what he calculated was the total annual consumption of detergent products in China. The Unilever executives shook their heads "That is just not possible," the leader spoke up. "We make or sell detergents in every country in the world and we have consumption habits down to a fine art. A small European country would consume that much detergents in car-washes, shampoo, washing-up liquid, and household cleansers let alone bath soap. But China has over a billion people! Your statistics have to be wrong!"

Dick slowly and patiently explained that the Chinese do not own cars or washing machines. They wash their single bowl and two chop-sticks under a cold water tap. Most of the Chinese living in the colder northern part of the country only remove their outer clothes at night and take off their underwear very occasionally between the end of October and mid-April. "Soap is used sparingly in China." As the Unilever executives sat in silence absorbing this surprising statement, Dick added, "And the Chinese have no body-smell, you know."

They would have been even more surprised if they had learned that Chairman Mao never had a bath or shower, or washed his hair, or brushed his teeth once during his twenty-seven year reign.

There was a gap of understanding between the west and China that had yawned down the centuries and in the years of China's reopening after 1978 that difference was greater than it had ever been before. For me it was a period of rapid learning as I came to grips with the mysteries of the Middle Kingdom – a process without end.

'The more you know, the less you understand.'

12

Born in the Clouds

Captain 'Born in the Clouds' Chen, as we were all to know him, was a Chinese war hero. He was reputed to have shot down more American airplanes during the Korean War than any other flier in the Chinese Air Force. He certainly looked the part. In the winter he strode around Guangzhou's 'White Cloud' airport in a worn leather flying jacket looking like a Chinese version of John Wayne. With a thorough disdain for all foreigners, but especially Americans, it was ironic that Chen should have found himself in charge of the Chinese Southern Region Helicopter Service Company responsible for supplying helicopters to an array of foreign oil companies operating offshore drilling rigs in the South China Sea. Chen was in his late 40s and was retired from the PLA-AF[1] but, as is their custom, his valiant efforts on the field of battle had to be rewarded and hence he had been allocated this position.

It was, however, a civilian posting. Not that that was unusual, most of the Civil Aviation Administration of China's flight crews came from the Air Force. But Chen had little time for civilians and even less for foreigners. He was also not pleased with his company: it had a ragbag of staff, its offices were based in a disused radar shack at one corner of the airfield, and it had no helicopters. The oil companies were putting pressure on Chen to find some helicopters, the rigs were moving into position and the workers needed to be flown out to their rigs.

I had teamed up with a large Canadian helicopter company called Okanagan, based in Vancouver. Okanagan had several hundred helicopters based all over the world and specialised in servicing the oil industry. Okanagan also used state-of-the art twin-engine Sikorsky S-76 helicopters, after which Chen lusted. I arranged to meet Chen in his lair in the radar shack. I waited all morning and then all afternoon, but no sign of Chen. He slouched into his office on the third day, threw his worn flying jacket into a corner, sat at the battered wooden table, glared at me and spat. He looked like he had not slept, brushed his hair or teeth, or

---

[1] The People's Liberation Army [PLA] embraces all services of the Chinese military

shaved for a week. His clothes were dirty and crumpled and he reeked of alcohol.

He listened, ill-attentively, to my proposal to lease him two S-76 helicopters. He wanted them to be based at White Cloud Airport in Guangzhou, a hundred and twenty miles from the mouth of the Pearl River, so poorly located to service the rigs further out in the South China Sea. In addition I needed to base six Canadian flight crew and three ground engineers in China. I mentioned the sort of money that we would intend to charge for the helicopters (which anyway Chen was to triple and then recover from the oil companies). I was treated to an outburst as to how foreigners were determined to seize China's wealth (which was not very apparent in the 1970s) and exploit the country as the British had been doing for centuries. This was to be a long drawn-out battle.

As the oil companies became increasingly anxious, Chen sat on his hands. I had meetings with the oil companies who were concerned that their expensive rigs were about to start drilling and still there were no helicopters. They complained to the ministries in Beijing, they complained to the head office of CAAC, they complained to their embassies, they did everything they could to bring Chen to the negotiating table but still Chen did nothing. I had a few meals with him: his terrified staff ate silently while he boasted at length of the bravery of the Chinese airforce and the weakness of the Americans in combat. His version of the Korean war was very different from what I recalled but I was there to do business not fight his wars over again.

Chen's line was that urgency was a western concept and he was not going to be pushed along or around by a bunch of foreign oil men, predominantly American. It became clear that Chen was a law unto himself. Such was his reputation as a fearless anti-imperialist on the battle-field, no one dared to reprimand him. He was a rare specimen in China; he had no time for anyone in authority and did not give a hoot about the many strictures under which the Chinese lived. I had a private session with his Party Secretary, generally a very powerful position, but the secretary just shrugged, powerless to intervene in the life of this maverick.

After many weeks a deal was done and our helicopters and crew arrived in China. Okanagan provided the captains but Chen insisted that the first officer should be one of his men and that an interpreter should sit behind them on the flight deck. Much later the Chinese built a helicopter base at Zhuhai on the border with Macau and much closer to the oil rigs. The base suffered from having a fifteen-story building right at the end of the runway which led to a rather complicated landing and take-off routine. Chen promised that he would arrange for the building to be demolished but, like so much else, it was a promise too far.

Some months later I found myself faced with an example of China's rampant racism. A new crew, led by Captain Williams, had arrived on rotation from Vancouver. I was called in to see Chen as a matter of great urgency. For once Chen was on time and had not been drinking.

"Have you met Captain Williams?" he demanded.

"Not yet," I said, "but I understand he is one of Okanagan's most senior captains."

"He must go. Send him back," barked Chen. "Today."

Wondering what particular Chinese sensitivity Captain Williams had ruffled, I enquired as to what was his offence.

"He's black!" shouted Chen. "A black man. You cannot have Chinese being flown by a black man!"

"Uh, why ever not?" I enquired.

"You foreigners invented the helicopter. We Chinese learn how to fly them. But the black men, where do they come into this? They do not know how to fly."

Chen would not have him. Furthermore the Chinese crew at the base refused to go anywhere near him. In his own interests more than anything else, Captain Williams returned to Canada. He came back to China a few years later when Chen had moved on, and became one of our most successful training pilots in China.

The helicopters were occasionally required to evacuate injured people from the rigs to the shore. The most modern medical facilities were in Hong Kong but our helicopters with their strange crewing arrangements were not allowed into Hong Kong except for serious emergencies. One evening I was in my office in Hong Kong when I got a call from China alerting me that one of our helicopters was bringing a badly injured American to Hong Kong. I advised the Civil Aviation Department as to the unscheduled arrival of our helicopter, arranged an ambulance and booked a room at a nearby hotel for the four Chinese crew on the helicopter. Chinese nationals were not allowed into Hong Kong at that time except on very special business, and I had to make arrangements with the immigration department to allow the crew to enter Hong Kong for twelve hours.

The crew were delighted with their accommodation in the Regal Hotel, never having stayed in a western hotel before. After a while they became hungry and found a room service menu – a new concept to the Chinese. When ordering Chinese food one orders many individual courses and so the Chinese thought this was the best thing to do with the alien food on the menu.

They ordered almost every single western dish assuming they would all arrive together as a Chinese meal. They were therefore amazed to find a traffic jam of room service trolleys backing up in the corridor outside their rooms as meal after meal of western food began to arrive. The helicopter and its crew departed on schedule the next morning back to China leaving me with a small bill for crew accommodation, but a room service bill running into many thousand of dollars!

Very slowly I built up a rapport with Chen. We met in other Chinese cities, sometimes in the old French settlement of Zhanjiang, sometimes in Beijing, and gradually he began to accept me. Once we shared some apples and a bottle of imported wine as we lay on the grass under a tree watching the old CAAC propeller airplanes slowly climbing into the sky from White Cloud airport. He ruled his staff with complete authority but generally had a softer touch with the girls. On several occasions I was introduced to a new and comely female staff member, who would simper and flirt with a freshly-shaved Captain Chen. But they never lasted. Within a week or two they had been sent elsewhere and a new girl was in her place.

After a while I heard that the oil companies were also planning to drill offshore from Shanghai, some thousand miles to the north. With considerable difficulty I located a man within CAAC's Shanghai office who had been given the responsibility of setting up helicopter services for this central region. The exact opposite of Chen, Captain Wang was a quietly-spoken bureaucrat. I visited Captain Wang on many occasions but he was always very vague as to when he needed the helicopter services to start. By now many of the world's helicopter operators had watched Okanagan's success in Guangzhou with some envy and with the possibility of new business in the Shanghai area, Captain Wang was deluged with offers of cooperation from every corner of the globe.

One day I received a message that Captain Wang would like to see me. He greeted me cordially over lunch and, as my heart sank, he told me of the many offers that he had received. Some companies were prepared to send in a helicopter free of charge, others offered free training in the United States (almost irresistible to the Chinese), or a range of other benefits which we could not offer without upsetting our arrangements with Chen.

Then just as I could see that Captain Wang was preparing to let me down softly, he said: "But, I have decided to give this business to you. You are not the cheapest and I have better offers but I would like to work with Okanagan and Inchcape."

"But why?" I blurted out. The Chinese would always negotiate with all and sundry and generally, but not always, give the business to the lowest bidder.

"Because, *Yalingdun*, you were the first to find me. You have always shown the utmost respect and sincerity and I trust you."

'Respect' and 'sincerity' were magic words to the Chinese. The other competitors never got a look in. They must have been wondering for months what had passed between Captain Wang and Inchcape to lock out the competition but in reality it had been a very Chinese decision. With all business owned by the State at that time, it was not uncommon for the Chinese to make commercial decisions that favoured the people they liked or, in their parlance, their *lao pengyou* or 'old friends'. Over the years there were many similar experiences of the Chinese favouring Inchcape, or sometimes Dick and myself personally, due to small or large favours that we had been able to provide, personal gestures, or just by being there over a long period of time. The Chinese instinctively distrust all foreigners but once one has been accepted, and this might take many years, then favours would be granted in an entirely surprising way.

At about this time we had a new recruit in Inchcape China by the name of Georgiana Pang. Georgiana was a feisty, attractive girl who spoke good English and passable Mandarin. It was difficult finding staff in Hong Kong who could speak credible English as well as Mandarin: generally they either spoke English and Cantonese or Mandarin and Cantonese but not all three. Georgiana, it soon turned out, was brilliant at her work but was theatrical and unstable, quite how unstable we would only find out as time went by.

The interpreter was always the key person in negotiations. Do the job badly and the two sides would never understand each other's point of view. Dick and Georgiana excelled at translation, passionately throwing themselves into the discussion and often speaking at great length in Mandarin in an effort to explain a few subtle English words. Georgiana however, had her moods and was prone to stage one-girl strikes at the most inopportune moment.

Georgiana handled the Okanagan account with aplomb, bullying Canadian crew and Chinese bureaucrats around with total confidence. Girls who entered the China trade were a brave race. Although there is complete sexual equality in China on the surface, beneath that veneer there are some old-fashioned Asian beliefs. Chinese men tended to view Hong Kong girls, with their long hair, make-up and short skirts, as promiscuous strumpets and showed them little respect. On the many times that Georgiana accompanied Chinese delegations abroad, there were occasions when normally respectable cadres tried to force their way into her bedroom. But Georgiana was not to be fazed by a few randy Chinese. There was little that Georgiana could not handle.

Sadly she was gradually overwhelmed by her own monsters and I was awoken early one morning in Hong Kong by a telephone call from Georgiana. "I called to say goodbye," she said. I asked her where she was going, aware that no trip to China was planned for that week. "A long way away," she replied and hung up. Later that morning I was called out of a China conference in the Mandarin Hotel to be told that Georgiana had thrown herself off the balcony of her 23rd floor flat.

Air travel in China was an ongoing nightmare throughout the early 1980s. The aircraft were old and, one assumed, poorly maintained. Seat covers were worn and stained, seat belts frequently missing. The Chinese had tried to stretch some fuselages by cutting them and inserting new sections. These experiments had not been entirely successful and reinforcing hoops were inserted inside the fuselage where the surgery had taken place. Tyres were worn down to the canvas. Beside the emergency exit hung a length of rope with a sign 'Only to be used in Emergency' – quite how was left to one's imagination. One could have sought confidence from CAAC's safety record but the unfortunate truth lay in CAAC's acronym - 'Chinese Aircraft Always Crashing'.

I could not guess at the amount of time I spent sitting in Chinese airports waiting for flights to leave. The airports themselves were largely built in the Russian era in the 1950s and were huge granite monoliths furnished with grimy cane chairs of which there were never enough. Passengers lay on the spittle-covered floor accepting the long waits, as one waited for everything in China. There were no announcements, no food, no refreshments except for the jam-jars of room-temperature tea with which no Chinese would be seen without.

Inflight service was no better. Elderly ladies waddled down the aisle holding large blackened aluminium kettles from which warm brownish tea would be sloshed into paper cups. There were no restrictions on hand baggage so one was squeezed into a narrow seat hemmed in on all sides by miscellaneous bags, baskets and bundles. On one occasion a basket full of long-legged hairy Shanghai crabs got loose and resulted in hundreds of crabs scuttling all over the floor of the aircraft much to the delight of the passengers.

Maurice Donnelly, who was later to work for me in Vietnam, experienced the ultimate in inflight service while on a flight from Wuhan to Nanjing. After over-indulging with Mao Tai the previous evening, he climbed on to a small turboprop Antonov early one morning and made a dive for the back row where he thought he could nurse his hangover in peace. A matronly 'stewardess' ordered him to sit near the front to balance the weight of the aircraft. Maurice refused. The harridan publicly berated him for his poor attitude and again stridently ordered Maurice to move forward, but he remained in his seat. There were only a few passengers and he was comfortable where he was. With no further ado, the stewardess walked up to Maurice and slapped him hard across the face. "Now, will you move?" she demanded. Maurice, his face hot and stinging, slunk to the front row.

One of CAAC's stranger procedures was the need to stop for lunch. An hour or two out of Nanjing *en route* for Chengdu, my aircraft started descending at around eleven o'clock. The aircraft then made an unscheduled landing at some out-of-the-way spot and the passengers were taken to what passed for a terminal building for lunch. Steel buckets of food arrived and the passengers retrieved a bowl and chopsticks from their luggage and tucked in. After an hour the passengers finished eating and were ready to fly on, but no, the crew needed their *xiu-xi* or siesta which in the heat of the summer could be a two or three hour affair. By mid-afternoon the airplane was ready to continue its flight.

The *xiu-xi* is hallowed ground: occasionally I suggested to our office staff that when we had an urgent job on hand we might work through the *xiu-xi* period. I could have been asking for a major personal sacrifice for all the cooperation I received. Article 49 of the Chinese Constitution solemnly declares 'The working people have the right to *xui-xi*'.

CAAC's Boeing 707's, and the new aircraft they were to buy later, were configured with first class seating. Social classes had been successfully and painfully eliminated by the Chinese over the years and the idea of separate accommodation designated as 'classes' on aeroplanes made the Chinese decidedly uneasy. The first class section was therefore reserved as a rest area for the crew or as a convenient storage place for the crew's extensive luggage. After a while first class tickets were sold to foreigners only, which caused great consternation amongst the crew. I took many flights where I was the only first class passenger but all the available seats were taken up by the crew who had little to do and so took off their uniforms and generally lounged around in the first class cabin talking, smoking and clipping their toe nails, maybe with the matched pair of nail-clippers offered as somewhat esoteric give-aways by CAAC.

Flying on CAAC aeroplanes was often an adventure. There was the celebrated case of an Antonov flying between Harbin and Dalien when the captain had a call of nature. When he returned to the cockpit he found the door between the cockpit and the passenger compartment was jammed. He called out for the first officer to push while he pulled and suddenly the door sprung open to disgorge the first officer and then slammed once again. Now both the captain and the first officer were on the wrong side of the door while the automatic pilot took sole charge of the 'plane. However hard the two officers pulled at the door, it remained immobile. By this time the passengers were transfixed by the performance of the crew. Finally the captain found a fire axe and chopped a hole in the door large enough for a stewardess to squeeze through and with her pushing and the other two pulling the door eventually opened.

Inchcape China had taken on the agency for Short Brothers, the British builder of twin-engine turboprop passenger airplanes, just before Margaret Thatcher, the prime minister, made a visit to China. The Chinese government often likes to flatter a visiting statesman by announcing trade deals at the same time as the visit and aircraft purchases are the sort of relatively straightforward big-ticket capital equipment that the Chinese favour. We were told that CAAC could be interested in buying up to thirty Short Brothers' aircraft. With such a large contract in the offing, Shorts mobilised a negotiating team which was destined to spend some months in Beijing in the middle of winter.

There are many colder places in the world than Beijing in the winter but none more exotic. While the thermometer falls far below freezing and stays there for weeks on end, the city sinks into a man–made soup of pollution exacerbated by the charcoal briquette stoves that the Beijing-*ren* use for cooking and keeping themselves warm. Although some apartments receive a sort of central heating in the capital, most flats have concrete walls and floors and there is little warmth. The Chinese roll themselves in layer upon layer of woollen clothes. Through the smog can be seen mountains of Chinese cabbages adorning every balcony. The winter freezes the cabbages and keeps them fresh, but grimy, until the spring.

The Short's negotiating team stayed in the newly opened Sheraton Great Wall Hotel, the first hotel in Beijing to be operated by an international management group. The clash of cultures was proving too great for the confused foreign management team. In a country where there is no concept of service, it was too much to expect that the cadres would be prepared to improve their attitude to others, let alone learn personal hygiene, manners and courtesy. It was all the managers could do to stop the local staff from spitting on the magnificent new Chinese carpets.

Our day fell into a routine: we left the hotel at 8 a.m, meetings until 11, return to the hotel for lunch and *xiu-xi*, reconvene at 3 p.m. and then finish for the day at 4:30 p.m. – a typical working day for most Chinese officials. One day I returned to the Great Wall in the middle of the morning to find my room in darkness with the curtains drawn. As I fumbled for the light switch I heard some anxious male mumblings coming from the direction of the bed. Imagine my surprise when I turned on the light to find the two male room attendants on my floor snuggling up to each other under the bedclothes. I telephoned the house-keeper to complain. "Oh, no! Not again!" she said. "Whatever can I do? Whenever they feel cold they jump into the nearest bed!"

On another occasion I walked into my bathroom to find the room attendant brushing his teeth with my toothbrush and toothpaste. He paused in mid-brush stroke to tell me that foreign toothpaste tasted much better than Chinese toothpaste and then continued brushing.

The negotiations however, were going well. For thirty aircraft a very special price was negotiated. Mr. Xu Zheng-Le, the avuncular director of the China Aviation Supplies Corporation who headed the Chinese team was an old-school Chinese scholar who had learned English at the renowned St. John's College in Shanghai before Liberation. But even he was not past a little local chicanery: once the price had been agreed the order was suddenly reduced to twelve aircraft. Short Brothers were not happy but Mr. Xu played another card which always pacifies the foreign businessman. "Remember the size of our market: a few airplanes today could mean many hundreds tomorrow." For both Airbus and Boeing that was indeed to prove to be the case but for Short Brothers this was the first and last sale in China.

Under the contract Short Brothers agreed to convert forty Chinese pilots to fly the Shorts 360 aircraft. Shorts insisted that the Chinese pilots should be qualified to fly turboprop aircraft and so the conversion course should have been relatively quick. But the Chinese pilots' log-books were considered to be 'State Secrets' and could not be released to foreigners. It also became readily apparent to Short Brothers that the Chinese pilots had no experience on turboprops and most of their experience was gained from flying single petrol-engine crop-dusting aircraft. They were duly sent to a British flying school to learn some flying rudimentaries before tackling the more sophisticated Shorts 360.

The CAAC crews arrived in Belfast, the Shorts' head office, with US$50,000 in cash to cover their living expenses. Shorts offered to keep the cash safe for them but they viewed the westerners with suspicion and instead handed the money to the Hong Kong-Chinese manager of the small hotel where they were staying who promised that the money would earn them a little interest. Within a couple of weeks the hotel manager absconded with their cash. A shame-faced CAAC crew leader admitted to the Shorts liaison officer that they might have made a mistake. The Hong Kong-Chinese was arrested at Heathrow airport with a suitcase full of cash but the event left the Chinese pilots in trouble with their bosses in Beijing.

Soon the first aircraft were delivered to Wuhan in China. Within days there had been an incident. One of the Chinese pilots was making his final approach when the control tower advised him to make another circle as he was coming in too high and too fast. The pilot landed anyway, half way down the runway, failed to brake in time, came off the end of the runway, went through a brick wall and demolished a school (fortunately empty at the time). It is considered loss of face for a pilot to abort a landing and make a second attempt and Chinese pilots prefer to keep their fingers crossed and have a go regardless of advice from the control tower. In the years I spent in China there were many such instances of Chinese (and Taiwanese) pilots crashing their aircraft when a more prudent course could have been taken.

Over the years the Chinese bought more and more aircraft from Airbus and Boeing and their safety record improved. But even at the time of writing, in 2007, I have just returned from a visit to China and noticed that as I sat in my first class no-smoking seat, every time the door opened into the flight deck a cloud of cigarette smoke surged outward and crew could be seen sitting on the floor, lounging around with mugs of tea with the first officers' legs resting on the instrument panel.

Much has changed in China but under the surface a great deal has remained the same.

13

Turmoil in Beijing

If only this man would remove his boot from my face. I was lying on the floor in the back seat well of my Toyota station wagon with this boot pushing hard into my left cheek, the other cheek rammed into the rubber mat. It was dark but my right eye could make out my smashed spectacles on the floor beside me in the flashes of the street lights. My left eye had filled with blood which ran over my face and down my neck. Upon the back seat, designed for three, five people sat or squatted, another three were sitting on top of me. There had to be at least another four people squeezed into the front of the car. Everyone was shouting, at each other or at John, my driver, who was still valiantly driving the car. I could not see his face from where I was but could make out that one of the men sitting on my legs kept hitting the back of his head with a piece of wood.

Suddenly the car swerved to one side of the road and skidded to a stop. The engine shut off and I heard a door open and slam shut. The hubbub in the car silenced for a second and then resumed at a higher volume. Nobody paid any attention to me, lying prone on the floor. Then the doors opened and the hijackers jumped out and ran away. I lay there without moving. Perhaps they would be back. The car was suddenly silent, dark and cold. After a while I raised my head and peered out of the side window.

I knew precisely where I was; it was not easy for me to lose my way in Beijing. I was near Chegongzhuang on the Second Ring Road, a mile from the junction with Fuxingmenwai, the main boulevard which leads into Tiananmen Square. The six-lane highway, normally packed with traffic, was deserted. Most of the street lamps were smashed, shards of glass littered the road. A few lamps leaned at absurd angles where vehicles had crashed into their bases. On the other side of the road a traffic sign had fallen across an electric bus, breaking its back. The road was strewn with rocks, bottles and bricks and near me a four wheel cart had upset spilling its load of water melons onto the concrete. The cart's traces and one shaft had snapped, the horse long gone.

I waited a few minutes longer. There was an eery silence. Nobody moved or walked on the streets. John had vanished. Smoke drifted across the road from the dying remains of a burned-out Nissan Patrol. I looked at my watch, it was smeered with blood but still working. The time was nearly mid-night.

It was the 30th May, 1989.

Beijing does not have a spring. One moment it is freezing cold and then suddenly a warm wind blasts across the city announcing the advent of summer. For a week or two the early mornings and late evenings hold a little cool air but soon the stifling heat of north China descends on the city. The spring of 1989 had lasted longer than most people could remember. Long brilliant days of warm sunshine and cool breezes; the Western Hills, normally hidden in the smog, clearly stood out against the brilliant sky.

In April 1989 I was in Beijing negotiating a contract to supply an American sunflower oil factory to a work unit in Jilin, Manchuria. The negotiations were progressing even slower than usual, nine Chinese engineers arguing daily with two Americans over very fine performance parametres. The Americans insisted their technology was the best, the Chinese were unconvinced. This type of impasse was common with the Chinese: it was all part of their well-trodden technique to draw out the negotiating process indefinitely. The Chinese had time on their side, the Americans paying for their food, hotel bills and Inchcape's expenses. They missed their families and their golf courses and wanted to go home as quickly as they could.

The political situation in China appeared normal and, in fact, was entering a more liberal phase. Zhao Ziyang, the reform minded Party secretary was opening China's doors to the western world and conditions were improving. Hu Yaobang had been removed as Party general secretary in 1987 but was still a member of the Politburo. He was considered by the establishment to be something of a wild card, not always following the Party line, but was revered as a reformist by the people. His death of a heart attack on the 8th April provided the surprising catalyst for Chinese students to take to the streets.

On 17th April several hundred students began a sit-in in the hundred-acre Tiananmen Square, the largest public square in the world, to insist on investigations into corruption, freedom of the press and a few other demands, modest in nature, but anathema to the authorities. Within a week the demonstrations moved on from praising Hu Yaobang to a coordinated attack on the Chinese government. Student leaders appeared from nowhere and the crowd in the vast Square expanded to several thousand. The tone was becoming more strident.

By the end of April the situation had deteriorated. Students were now permanently encamped in the Square. There had been several city-wide student demonstrations which had closed the city, protests were beginning in other cities and the Politburo agonised as to what action should be taken. Most of the demonstrators were from Beijing's prestigious universities, many the children of top officials. The leaders realised they had to tread softly and were showing commendable tolerance in spite of increasingly shrill and unreasonable demands from the students.

Some of the student claims however, were right on the mark. Corruption had become endemic in China with many ministers' children holding high positions. Chen Xitong, the mayor of Beijing, presented a fine example. He told a meeting of students, "My salary is three hundred yuan a month. The combined salaries of my wife and two children total less than five hundred yuan a month. Some people say my son embezzles and takes bribes, but that's false. Rumours like that remind me of the Cultural Revolution." Chen was charged with corruption in 1996 and was sentenced to sixteen years in prison. Evidence showed that his corruption began the day he assumed office and grew to massive proportions.

By 12th May the 'turmoil' had deepened. The Politburo was split as to what action should be taken and Russian President Mikhail Gorbachev was scheduled to arrive on the 15th May for an historic visit to normalise diplomatic relations with China, tense for many decades.

Trouble was breaking out all over the country. The students in Beijing decided that Mr. Gorbachev would support them as he had led Russian reforms much further than the Chinese Politburo would consider. A hunger strike was planned. Deng Xiaoping wondered whether the situation was already beyond control. He told Zhao Ziyang, "The opposition is not just some students but a bunch of rebels and a lot of riffraff.........these people want to overthrow our Party and our State." Battle lines were hardening. The Gorbachev visit was a disaster. The Square was taken over by the hunger strikers, over three thousand of them, and demands were surfacing from every dissident or aggrieved group in the country. Gorbachev's meetings had to be rescheduled and moved from place to place around the city. The temptation to send in the troops must have been hard to resist but still the Politburo argued amongst themselves not so much as to what to do, but as to the deep reasons behind the dissent.

I arrived in Beijing on the 14th May to find a carnival atmosphere in the city. From the Inchcape office's balcony directly overlooking Chang 'an Avenue, less than a mile from the Square, I watched the endless stream of protesters marching down the avenue towards the Square. Almost every institution in the city had its own contingent of fifty or a hundred people marching with placards and posters demanding government change. I saw units from most ministries, hospitals, the New China News Agency, research institutes, academies and state-owned industries. As they marched they shouted in unison, *"Dar Dao Li Peng!"* "Down with Li Peng," China's prime minister.

I saw onlookers darting amongst the marchers hailing old friends. Others handed out bottles of water and gave away home-made dumplings to the hungry. A lot of people were hanging back, there were many more onlookers than participants. A large number of official-looking men seemed to be photographing the demonstrators. Later I was told that even the traffic cameras were retrained to record the demonstrators on the streets. I wondered whether they were doing the right thing. The Chinese say the tallest bamboo catches the wind.

The attitude in my office was not supportive. Nobody left their desks except for a brief glimpse out of the window. Nobody talked, everybody trying to pretend that conditions were normal. My enquiry as to whether Fesco had sent a delegation of marchers demanding overthrow of the prime minister, was met with a gasp of horror. I walked into the meeting room where discussions on the sunflower oil plant continued with difficulty against the roar of protesters marching outside the window. I asked the plant's negotiator what he thought of the protests. "Protests? What protests?" he said as another huge roar burst through the open windows. My staff were embarrassed; this was not the China they wanted foreigners to see.

That afternoon I walked along Chang 'an Avenue to Tiananmen Square. I knew almost every inch of this vast space having driven, bicycled or walked around it a thousand times. I knew all the surrounding buildings intimately from inside and out: the Great Hall of the People on the west side, the Museum of Chinese History facing from the east, the vibrant Monument to the People's Heroes in the centre of the Square. In front of Chairman Mao's Memorial Hall are two large statues of workers and soldiers looking as if they are poised to march across the Jinshui Bridges into the Imperial Palace itself. At the north end of the square rises the enormous stone Zhengyangmen, the great south gate through the city wall.

Yet that day the Square had become a tented camp surrounded by ranks of Public Security Bureau officers. As I walked through the ranks, no-one tried to stop me. I strolled amongst the students most of them, like students everywhere, sitting or lying around on the ground, reading magazines, chatting, flirting or just hanging out. A few were making much noise with loud-hailers but nobody was listening. Most students smiled or waved at me, a few wanted to talk and one offered me a toffee apple.

I stayed in Beijing for four days and then flew back to Hong Kong. The situation deteriorated markedly during those four days: the number of students in the Square swelled to ten thousand and it was said that over a million people had taken to the streets in Beijing, while demonstrations were spreading like wildfire in the provinces. The Politburo imposed martial law on 18th May and Zhao Ziyang resigned. That night 180,000 Chinese troops from the Beijing, Shengyang and Jinan Military Regions moved into the city.

The imposition of martial law, under which it was illegal to hold demonstrations, inflamed some passions but also caused some of the students in the Square to reappraise their position. Maybe they could read the runes, perhaps they were warned by their parents or instinct took over. Many hundreds of students from the main universities of Beijing, Qinghua and others in Beijing quietly left the Square and went home. They were immediately replaced by organised masses of provincial students coming in from the country, many never having been to Beijing before. The Ministry of Railways reported that over 56,000 students entered Beijing overnight on the 19th May.

The city rapidly fell into chaos as students and citizens set up road-blocks and check points around the city to delay the arrival of the troops. Whilst most soldiers reached their planned positions, other military columns were held up by road-blocks. The 38th Group Army, a Beijing garrison, initially refused to enter the city but was eventually to be the unit selected to clear the Square on the 4th June.

By the 30th May Beijing had been under martial law for eleven days. Not much had been accomplished. The situation looked as if it could turn worse at any moment. Foreigners had been evacuating the city for weeks and our office had recently received a call from the British Embassy reminding all British nationals to leave. Ian Nethercoat, a Lipton tea buyer based in our office and an ex-tank officer, paid no attention. "Diplomats are always the first out," he told me over the telephone. "But it is spring time in the tea gardens and I must stay." I could see that Ian was enjoying his sudden unanticipated break from the routine of Beijing life.

The sunflower oil plant negotiations were still stuck and the American negotiator, a highly-strung man in his sixties, was threatening to leave with the rest of the American population in China. I offered to take over allowing him to return home. I accordingly booked myself on a flight to Beijing on the evening of the 30th May. Not altogether to my surprise, I was the only passenger on the 'plane.

Beijing airport was closed. The escalators were not running, only a few lights were on. There was not a soul in the normally over-crowded arrivals hall. The immigration booths were unmanned. I walked straight through the airport but then realising that if I had no evidence of entry into the country then it might not be so easy to leave, I eventually found a rather bewildered immigration officer who stamped my passport while staring at me in confusion. He had spent all day dealing with frightened crowds of foreigners desperate to get on a flight, any flight, out of China.

John was waiting for me in the deserted car park outside the terminal. He looked at me anxiously. "We are going to have a difficult drive into the city tonight," he warned me with foreboding. For the first twenty kilometres the two-lane road runs in a straight line through an avenue of willow trees whose young branches hang pendulously over the road giving the impression of driving through a green tunnel. The road was quiet that night: no traffic, not even a solitary cyclist. Approaching the Lidu Hotel the car started to slow; peering ahead I could see at the furthest reach of the headlights that a tree had been cut down across the road and there was a heaving crowd of people blocking the road, some standing in front of the tree trunk and some on it. Realising that the grey Toyota station-wagon with its blacked-out windows could easily be mistaken for a senior cadres' official car, I rolled down the windows and turned on the interior light. True, this gave me little protection but I thought that if the crowd could see there was a foreigner inside then they might not bother me. The car slowed to walking pace and drove into the dense mass of people. They parted slightly to let the car through. On either side there was an impenetrable pack of men, all silently staring at me. Those with experience of crowd behaviour know that mood can change in an instant. I sat in the back seat, lit up like a statue with a fixed smile on my face knowing that any second a brick or stick could come through the window and the mob would erupt.

The car crept through and we emerged onto a clear road. In less than two weeks China's capital city had been reduced to a shambles. Piles of rubber tyres burned in the streets creating thick acrid smoke through which we drove. Shops had been smashed and looted. The detritus of street riots was everywhere. Burned out electric buses lay on their sides, pushed together with only just enough space for a single car to pass. Everywhere people milled aimlessly, some shouting, some throwing rocks. This did not seem a good place to be; certainly not in the back seat of the only private car on the roads.

At each intersection the car was stopped and I was appraised by the generally good-natured mob and allowed to pass. It was not until we reached the major intersection at Haidian that our luck ran out. The back door was suddenly pulled open and an unshaved thug punched me hard in the face. As I fell backwards, he thrust his body into the car and pushed me onto the floor. He shouted for his colleagues to join him and as they jumped into the car it dawned on me that I had been hijacked by 'peace-loving' students, the beneficiaries of so much encouragement and goodwill from people all over the world.

Once John had fled the car and the hijackers, realising they had lost their lift, had also disappeared into the night, I drove myself on to the Shangri-la Hotel using my spare car key. I must have looked a sight as I stumbled into the hotel's marble lobby dripping blood from a cut on my hairline but there was nobody to see me. The hotel was deserted, only a night-light shone feebly above the reception desk. A solitary clerk handed me a room key. He scarcely noticed my dishevelled appearance: perhaps he had seen much worse during the previous week.

The next morning I could see from my hotel window, high on the twelfth floor of the building, the total chaos that had overtaken Beijing. Right across the city palls of black smoke spiralled into the smog; beneath me, just by the main entrance to the hotel, some students had erected a road block out of several over-turned lorries. As I watched, a farmer's lorry drove in from the west, the driver was pulled out of his cab and pushed around. One of the 'students' got into the cab and reversed the lorry into a ditch. He then set fire to the truck while his colleagues stood around cheering.

I ventured to the car park and gingerly drove the Toyota through the empty streets, dodging the bricks and deserted cars on the roads. All the major government buildings, the head office of China Central Television, the blocks of flats where many ministers lived, were guarded by a few more soldiers than usual but nobody paid me much attention. In the office most of my staff had come to work. The delegation from Jilin looked unhappy: the American had left and they still had not bought their sunflower oil factory.

I took G.X. Liu, the senior member of our local staff, on one side.

"GX," I said. "How will all this end?"

"Oh, we will end this the traditional Chinese way of course."

"And what would that be?"

"About six inches of blood in the gutter. Want to hang around and see?"

The events of the 3rd and 4th June have been well chronicled although sometimes exaggerated. The truth, as much as it will ever be known, indicates that the protesters were armed with weapons seized previously from the military when the 38th Group Army moved in to clear Tiananmen Square at 9:30 p.m. on the night of the 3rd June. Certainly many two-sided fire-fights took place. Although the outcome was inevitable, it was not the total massacre as has sometimes been portrayed. The Chinese military was poorly equipped to handle civil unrest and the soldiers inadequately trained for such a mission. Hundreds of students, soldiers and innocent bystanders died and many more were wounded that warm, early summer's night in Beijing.

A few days later I was in the Inchcape office in the Minzu Hotel talking to GX.

He was sitting at his desk chain-smoking, his hair hanging over his left eye. He looked morose, as he often did. Opposite him, on the other side of the desk, sat the negotiator for the sunflower oil factory in Jilin. He was of my own age, forty-three at the time, and a Party man. His blue *zhongshan zhuang* was slightly soiled. He had only brought one set with him from Jilin and had not been able to get it washed. He had been in Beijing for seven weeks now, waiting for the Americans to arrive only to see them leave in a hurry on account of the students agitating in the Square. He was not a happy man either.

All three of us suddenly winced as a crane in Chang 'an Avenue dropped a concrete lane divider with a thud followed by shouts of anger. The dividers had been pushed across the avenue as tank traps and were slowly being moved back into place.

"All buggered up! Just shit! shit! shit!" observed GX in a cloud of smoke.

"Just when things were going right," added the negotiator.

"And I just got myself a washing machine."

"My wife was wanting a new watch."

"I even got to use this little motorbike that *Yalingdun* bought for the office." With a quick glance at me to make sure I was listening, GX went on, "and now this will put us all back five years or more."

"What about Gorbachev? Wah! We lost so much face over that!"

"Punished. They will get punished of course. The *lao-gai* will be overflowing again," contemplated the negotiator with a hint of pleasure referring to the government's labour camps.

"Why didn't they learn from history? Our government does this sort of thing whenever they think someone's out of line. We expect it, so why hadn't they learned?" GX was annoyed, thumping the side of his chair.

This was the general attitude I encountered. The Chinese, then and now, look for stability and security and the opportunity to prosper. These are the attributes the government gave its people from 1979 onwards. The majority was not looking for change in 1989 but stood as disinterested observers shaking their heads at the naivety of the protesters.

The fall-out from these tragic events worried me. The world had turned against China with horror and condemnation. President Bush Sr. considered recalling the U.S. Ambassador to China and gave sanctuary to Chinese students in America. Heads of all European governments considered what measures could be introduced to punish the Chinese government. The Italians called for economic sanctions and the British foreign office advised British nationals not to visit China. But all these sanctimonious outcries were not what concerned me. I was worried about the Chinese.

Long before the night of the 3rd June, the Chinese government had been pointing at the 'black hands' behind the rising tide of student unrest. The authorities did not think that the students had created all this mayhem by themselves. They did not have far to look. The State Security Ministry submitted a report to the Politburo on the 1st June entitled 'On ideological and political infiltration into our country from the United States and other international political forces'. This document traced the American government's well-defined policy to use their 'culture' to seduce China towards liberalisation. All the usual suspects were targeted: the Voice of America, the Fulbright programme, the U.S. Information Agency, the missionaries, businessmen, even George Soros, were all accused of playing their part to pull China down.

It seemed to me that foreigners would be quick to forget these events in China; one cannot punish a country with one third of the world's population for too long. But the Chinese government had received a nasty shock: it could have been brought down. If the foreigners could be proved to be the root of the problem then it was possible that the 'Open Door' policy might close as quickly as it had opened and China might once again isolate itself from the world.

So I asked Dick Chan to call in a few favours and arrange for me to see someone high in the government. The higher the better; I needed to say that I had talked to someone in a position of power. The risk, of course, was that I would allow myself to be used for government propaganda: the loud message being foreign politicians are keeping away from China but businessmen continue to do business. Normally requests to see China's secretive leaders are passed through convoluted channels, take a long time to process and interviews are only given to important foreign political figures or chairmen of large companies. The managing director of Inchcape China would not normally get his foot through the Politburo's door. But in this case Dick had a response within twenty-four hours: Vice Premier Tian Ziyuen would see me the following afternoon.

The Chinese Communist Party is the cream of the civil service and to rise to the very top requires a rare talent. Much more so than in a western democracy where one is favoured more by the luck of the ballot booth and friends in the right places than any innate political skill. Once at the top, Chinese leaders tend to stay there for the remainder of their lives as long as they support the right people and do not deviate from the Party line. A mandatory retirement age has only recently been introduced in China and even from the sidelines Chinese politicians continue to exercise political power until their deathbed, as the events of June 3rd and 4th 1989 amply proved. Vice Premier Tien was one of these men.

To my surprise the meeting was to be held in Zhongnanhai, the Politburo's 'Forbidden City' next to the Imperial Palace. It is a square-mile compound surrounded by a twelve-foot high red wall. On the rare occasions that I did meet State Councillors or Politburo members, it was always under carefully orchestrated surroundings in one of the grand rooms in the Great Hall of the People. Although I understand it is more common these days, at that time very few foreigners ever penetrated the walls of Zhongnanhai. The authorities would have known this: the location had been selected to underline the significance of the meeting.

It was therefore to my considerable satisfaction the following day to find myself standing on a flagstone terrace facing the tranquil beauty of Harmony Hall, a Ming-dynasty pavilion, beside the banks of the Zhonghai Lake, the 'Central Sea', inside Zhongnanhai, gazing out over the glistening waters at the yellow tiled curved roofs of the Imperial Palace. A row of ancient willow trees lined the banks of the lake. I felt a slight tug at my sleeve and turned to look directly into a pair of bright golden irises set in a Chinese face of incredible beauty framed by hair swept loosely into a chinon. I caught my breath for a second. She was wearing a formal bright blue silk *qipao*. Exactly my height, very tall for a Chinese, she was probably a Manchurian from the northern city of Harbin. Her amber eyes seemed equally fascinated with my blue eyes; she did not see too many foreigners in Zhongnanhai. "Please …………." She gestured me to follow her into the State Council's intimate audience hall.

As is customary, the Vice Premier and I sat in the centre of a semi-circle of armchairs, a spittoon separating us. My small team sat beside me on tall hard-back chairs: Dick Chan, GX, Karina Kwok, a new Inchcape China executive who had replaced Georgiana, and Ian Nethercoat. The State Councillor on the other hand sat on his own, an interpreter behind him. All the usual supporters had been dismissed. This was meant to be an intimate talk (although I had no illusions as far as hidden microphones and cameras were concerned). Such audiences are generally allotted fifteen minutes but the Vice Premier was in an expansive mood. I was treated to a two hour exchange on the difficulties and challenges of managing the Chinese Empire and its one and a quarter billion people – a quarter of the world's population.

Sometimes from behind the giant blue Ming vases or shady alcoves those deep ochre eyes flashed at me. Then suddenly she would be kneeling beside me, replenishing my cup of green tea, her *qipao* falling open to reveal an ivory leg. I could not tear my eyes away from hers. She was a cat and I was her morsel. Did the Deputy Premier notice my distraction? I glanced at him. No, he was expounding on the benefits of the United Front.

It was still not easy to drive around Beijing so I called the British ambassador to assess his feelings. The conversation went along these lines:

"Ambassador, I have just been to see a Chinese Deputy Premier in Zhongnanhai. I was told that I was the first westerner to see such a high official since the 4th June and I thought you might like to know what he said."

There was a brief silence and then the ambassador exploded "You've done what?"

I repeated myself.

"But, my military attaché had his flat destroyed by machine gun fire!"

"I do hope he kept his head down," I responded perhaps a little too flippantly, not quite seeing the relevance.

"You have no right.......! You are not allowed to speak to those murderers!"

"Oh? Who says?" I was beginning to think I was wasting my time.

"The Foreign Secretary, that's who! He has forbidden us from speaking to any senior official in the Chinese government."

"That hardly sounds like diplomacy to me. Isn't it the art of talking at difficult times? And anyway, I am a businessman − I don't need to follow the knee-jerk orders of your political bosses in London."

The ambassador spluttered so I asked him again whether he wanted to know what the deputy premier had said.

"Only if you come to the embassy and explain in person." I knew what that meant: a debriefing by embassy staff so that a cable could be sent to London to show that the embassy had its finger on the pulse. I was not to be used again as a source of intelligence by diplomats.

"Watch it on the television tonight then," I said and hung up.

I was not jesting. The half-hour main news on China Central Television, broadcasting to the world's largest television audience, was tiring of post-June 4th stories and there was no international news as all the foreign networks were still reeling from events in China. So the news that I had become the first international businessman to visit a high government official was given headline status, repeated at length and for ten days! Overnight I earned my fifteen minutes of fame in China. For a very short time I was accosted in the streets by strangers, even in Hong Kong, who had seen me on television. The overwhelming message was one of encouragement and admiration. As soon as the Chinese government had taken firm steps to stop the student demonstrations, all the Overseas Chinese fell over themselves in support.

Amongst the authorities, deep inside the Party, my fame did not fade. Articles were published in the extensive *neibu* internal publications network in

China bringing Party members' attention to my support of China in its time of trouble. On many occasions in the future I would meet a cadre who knew much more about me than he should have done. I was always aware throughout my years in China that dossiers were kept on any frequent visitors to the country and I can only assume that my dossier started to adopt a rosy hue as I became known as a 'Friend of China', an honour freely given but rarely meant.

Within days I was explaining to the board of directors of Inchcape Pacific that I had been assured by the highest authorities that the Chinese government's 'open door' policy to foreign companies remained unchanged, foreign investment was safe and business could continue as before. I went on to bring this message to the boards of companies represented by Inchcape China in Europe and the United States to the relief of all. Business in China was difficult enough without politicians intervening and by 1989 some companies were considering the first major wave of foreign investment into China. What they wanted was stability and that was what the political leaders in China, after so many decades of turmoil, were determined to provide.

14

Vietnam Revisited

In 1988 another communist country had noticed the changes in China and decided to follow suite. Vietnam closed itself to the outside world after the defeat of the Americans and the reunification of the North and South in 1975 and had embarked on a road of totalitarian misery and decline, centralised control from Hanoi and labour camps for the citizens of the old Republic of South Vietnam.

In 1989 I suggested to the Inchcape Pacific board that the company's very own specialist in communist regimes should investigate. So, once again, I approached a forbidding and reclusive country through their official representative in Hong Kong. This time it was a travel agency that posed as the Socialist Republic of Vietnam's agency in the territory. A letter was duly submitted to the Vietnamese Ministry of Foreign Trade and a few months later I received an invitation from the Vietnamese Chamber of Commerce, the equivalent of China's CCPIT, to visit them in Hanoi.

Just as it was difficult to visit Beijing in the 1970s, the same logistical problems faced a visitor to Hanoi in the 1980s. A visa could only be obtained at the embassy in Bangkok by invitation and there were infrequent flights from Bangkok to Hanoi on a particularly ancient Russian airplane belonging to Air Vietnam. Hanoi boasted only one hotel: it was a strange construction built on concrete piles in a mosquito-infested lake some kilometres outside the city. The building had been supplied in a prefabricated kit as Russian aid to Cuba. The Cubans had no need for it and gave it to the Vietnamese. Somewhere along the line either the assembly instructions were lost or parts of the kit never arrived in Hanoi. It was necessary to exercise great care when entering one's room as whereas some doors opened into rooms, others opened into mid-air and a long drop into the weed-filled lake.

The Vietnamese Chamber of Commerce's director was Mme Nguyen, a diminutive lady of very precise views. She had evidently done her homework, had most likely spoken to the CCPIT in Beijing, and was clearly anticipating my question when I asked whether Inchcape could open a representative office in Hanoi. Once again, Inchcape was the pioneer, setting the pace for others to follow. The hotel option for office space did not exist in Hanoi but houses could be made available and so we rented a small but attractive building not far from the defunct opera house. Staff for the office were provided by the Diplomatic Personnel Bureau of the Ministry of Labour but the office itself was rented to us by a private landlord, rather to my surprise.

I then recruited Philippe Rabaud to manage the office. Philippe, had a Mongolian wife and a small baby, was half French and half Vietnamese and spoke both languages. He had also worked in China for a while and so understood the communist system. On paper he seemed to be perfect. He could speak French to the Vietnamese, Chinese to our mandarin-speaking Hong Kong staff and English to me. He was born and brought up in Vietnam and so should have had a natural affinity for the country. I thought he was an excellent choice and dispatched him to Hanoi as quickly as I could.

I was therefore taken aback to receive a telex from him only ten days after he had arrived to tell me that the Ministry of Labour had unexpectedly withdrawn all their staff and that he was alone in the office. He provided no explanation but was asking for instructions.

So I flew to Bangkok, obtained a visa and one week later I arrived in Hanoi. I did not go to our office but instead went directly to the Ministry where I met Mr. Ngo Van Thoan, an austere official responsible for allocating staff to embassies and the very few foreign representative offices.

I asked him why he had withdrawn our staff.

"Why did you send us a Frenchman?" he asked angrily.

"I thought you got on well with the French. Certainly most of the Vietnamese I have met prefer to speak French to English," I responded truthfully. Admittedly it was more than 35 years since the French were forced to quit their Indochinese colonies but the French Embassy was by far the largest in Hanoi (other than the Chinese and the Russian) and the French government openly boasted of their excellent relations with the Vietnamese.

Mr. Thoan stood up and walked out of the room. "Come with me," he ordered over his shoulder.

I followed him out of his office and we got into a small (French) car and were driven in silence across the city. We drew up outside a museum. Without talking, he strode through the building until we reached a courtyard at the back of the building. In the middle stood a guillotine.

"See that?" he said. "I can remember the French operating that machine on my compatriots in the square every Saturday morning. Do you really think we like the French? We didn't give Inchcape permission to open an office here just to have you send us a Frenchman. You can have your staff back when he goes."

His point was well made. I asked him for some time for me to sort this out and after a while one or two of the staff returned to work, but refusing to accept instructions from Philippe they waited for orders by telex from Hong Kong. Within a few months a new opportunity presented itself in Cambodia and I dispatched Philippe to Phnom Penh. I replaced him with an Australian who was quite acceptable to the Vietnamese and our staff returned to work.

Over the next couple of years a company was formed, Inchcape Vietnam, offices were opened in Ho Chi Minh City, which most Vietnamese preferred to call by its old name of Saigon, and another in Danang. Investments were made in joint-ventures in the insurance broking and motor car distribution businesses and Inchcape became one of the most active foreign companies in the country. But business in Vietnam was no easier than it had been in China and required constant attention from the Hong Kong office. Unlike China, the country lacked critical mass and every contract was much smaller in size but involved the same range of problems requiring the same amount of attention as did much larger deals in China.

In December 1989 I was given permission to drive the 2,000 kilometres from Hanoi to Saigon, accompanied by our driver who was our official 'shadow', submitting weekly reports on our activities and movements to the Ministry of Internal Security. Our drive took us through landscape still heavily scarred from years of American bombing raids. In some places the road had only been patched, bridges still bore bomb damage, everywhere there were graveyards and memorials to the North Vietnamese killed during the war.

After a couple of days of driving, the Annamite Cordillera mountains drew near to the coast and we passed through what had been the DMZ, the de-militarised zone which marked the border between the old North and South Vietnams. Then we were in Dong Ha, dominated by a vintage Vietnamese tank marooned at a cross-roads where, nineteen years previously, I had waited for a helicopter to fly me to Phubai on that rainy day when I nearly met my demise at the hands of a bunch of drunken American GI's.

On a whim I asked the driver to take me up the highway to Khe Sanh. We drove past the old marine fire base at the Rockpile and the Special Forces base at Lang Vei. Soon I was walking over the base at Khe Sanh, now long since emptied of any trace of American presence. Or almost, as the local villagers had been busy collecting military residue and had assembled mounds of shell casings and strips of aluminium outside their houses. The metal-link airstrip had been ripped up and found a new use as fencing materials. The Co Soc mountains still loomed in the distance but were long since deserted by the North Vietnamese artillery. Now the base was the quiet home for pie dogs scratching themselves in the heat and ragged children darting in and out of the remains of the bunkers.

The tropical jungle, cleared by defoliation and shelling had strangely not grown back, the whole plain now a wilderness of scrub and elephant grass.

We opened our office in Saigon in a French colonial villa which the government was using as a school. On my frequent visits there I stayed either at the Rex Hotel, previously the U.S. officers club, or the old Caravelle where the North Vietnamese troops had been stationed after they conquered the South in 1974.

Our efforts to make profits in Vietnam were doomed to failure. At the end of every year we congratulated ourselves on achieving a small profit only to be invaded by an army of Vietnamese tax inspectors who announced that the amount of tax that we owed was always precisely the same as the profit we had achieved. We could never understand their method of calculation but the results were always the same.

In neighbouring Cambodia we had greater success. I had asked Karina Kwok, last seen in Beijing, to open the Inchcape office in Phnom Penh. She had been successful in winning a contract to set up a 'PX' for the United Nations army that moved into Cambodia for eighteen months to oversee Cambodia's first elections since the murderous Khmer Rouge had been defeated by the Vietnamese. There Philippe Rabaud would preside as a modern day French trader resembling a character out of a Joseph Conrad novel. He simmered, for he had not forgiven me for his precipitate removal from Hanoi.

It was late in 1989 when I was in Phnom Penh with Karina and we decided to visit the port of Kompong Som some 120 kilometres from Phnom Penh. Travel in Cambodia was dangerous with marauding bands of Khmer Rouge kidnapping foreigners and generally creating mayhem. I asked Philippe whether it was safe to make the trip. "*Mais oui,*" he assured me. "Completely safe, my friends make the trip all the time."

It was a pleasant two-hour drive in a hired elderly Toyota down to the coast. I was mildly disconcerted to find that every bridge along the way had been destroyed and we had to drive off the road down into dry culverts and then climb back up onto the road. This meant slowing to a crawl and on each occasion there were a number of suspicious looking Khmers with assault rifles lurking around looking at us with more than a glint of menace in their eyes.

We completed our business in Kompong Som, had lunch and at 2 p.m. asked the taxi driver to head back to Phnom Penh. The driver threw up his hands in horror. "That is impossible!" he exclaimed. "Everybody knows that the road is not safe after midday. We must spend the night here." But Karina and I were booked on a flight back to Hong Kong the next morning and there were only two flights a week. Philippe had assured us the road was safe; perhaps the driver had another motive to stay the night in Kompong Som.

More money changed hands and the driver agreed to take us back but he looked miserable at the prospect. Understandably so. After some thirty kilometres the road started to climb into a range of jungle-covered hills. As we rounded a corner, the Toyota struggling to climb in third gear, we were faced with a small group of bandits standing in the road waving guns at us and signalling at us to stop. I yelled at the driver to keep going and he charged at the men who dived out of the way at the last second. This was not very auspicious but it seemed that we had little choice but to continue.

Another few kilometres and round another corner we drove straight into an ambush. This time there were men lying on the ground with guns pointing at us and again we were signalled to stop. This time the car was going down hill and was able to pick up speed as we rushed them. There was a slight bump as we hit the man standing in the road and then we were passed and driving away fast as a crackle of gun-fire exploded behind us. It was beginning to look as if we were not going to make it back to Phnom Penh – and we still had the dried up river beds to cross.

Then we rounded a corner to find a United Nations road block made up of two white tanks with large U.N. signs painted on their sides and a platoon of French soldiers lounging around smoking. We stopped the car and I told the French officer what had happened to us. "Poof. What nonsense. There are no terrorists here. Drive on," he said with that arrogance that the French can adopt with such ease. A long discussion ensued, as the French insisted that there were no armed terrorists in the area and that we must have imagined the ambush. We were getting nowhere; the French soldiers could not have been less interested in our plight.

We were then joined by an armed U.N. patrol of two Canadian pick-up trucks with heavy machine guns mounted on their flat-beds. They drove along this road several times a day providing armed escorts to convoys of trucks plying their way between the port and Phnom Penh. I explained our situation to the Canadian officer who immediately offered to escort us to Phnom Penh and so we completed our trip safely with armed guards in front and behind us.

I went straight to the Inchcape office where I found Philippe relaxing on a sun lounger in the garden. He looked quite staggered to see me. "Surprised Philippe?" I asked him. He stuttered, "I.......I hadn't expected to see you back so soon." He had known all along that he had been sending us on a very dangerous mission.

I fired him on the spot. And enjoyed doing so.

15

Inchcape's Demise

Lord Inchcape made several visits to China in the early 1980s. In Beijing he stayed at Diaoyutai, the Emperor's erstwhile Fishing Lodge now reborn as the State Guest House, a collection of spacious villas in a peaceful lakeside park not far from the Negotiations Building in Erligou. During his visits we hosted banquets for Chinese ministers every evening or were the guests at banquets held in the earl's honour. The dinners ended by 7:30 p.m. and the earl then retired to his suite of rooms in the Fishing Lodge. I repaired to my room to work on the next day's round of meetings. It had been my custom since my Bangkok days to wear a long sarong in the privacy of my hotel room which gave the room attendants, who would walk into my room unannounced at any time of the day or night, considerable mirth.

One evening I was working in my room when I heard Lord Inchcape's door open along the corridor and my name was called loudly, "Errington! Errington! Come here!" Without changing from my sarong, I walked down the corridor to find the short, rotund figure of the earl similarly clad. He was also used to wearing a sarong from his days in Bengal. Evidently recognising me as a fellow man from Asia he invited me into his room to share his bottle of whisky. A shy and taciturn man, he then talked that evening, and for many others, of his experiences as he moulded the company that bore his name.

He believed in the light head office touch. He saw Inchcape as an investment holding company and believed that power should rest with the managers in the fifty countries around the world where the Inchcape companies were located. He had no need of corporate planners or strategists; he planned the strategy himself. There were also no requirements for corporate affairs, public relations or personnel departments. He knew all the managers and had selected most of them personally. Inchcape was the 28th largest company quoted on the London Stock Exchange and was universally admired. Lord Inchcape was an entrepreneurial legend, hailed as the 'man with the Midas touch.'

Once I asked him about the share price. "Irrelevant," he said, "if the company prospers then this will be reflected in the price. Otherwise it is a diversion." His family had millions of pounds invested in the company but the rise or fall of the share price was of little concern. All this was to change in subsequent years when share options were granted to senior management and the mood of the head office would change from day to day with the rise and fall of the share price. Then stock brokers' analysts, with scant interest or understanding of the business, were to be treated as royalty, as they tried with sparse success to make sense out of the convoluted network of businesses that the earl had forged. Lord Inchcape maintained a remote disdain for the stock market and its analysts.

Problems had begun to fester throughout the 1970s. Many of the most senior managers, like PG in Hong Kong, were happy to spend their entire working lives in a far-off country enjoying their autonomy and ability to make quick decisions. Their local knowledge and relationships with their principals became great assets. But their high level of loyalty was generally to Lord Inchcape the man, not to Inchcape the company. Those further down the tree were often disenchanted by the low pay, little opportunity for advancement, transfer to another country, or any effort to provide a career path. All too often the brightest people left, taking substantial chunks of the business with them, whilst those who stayed exploited their independence in nefarious ways. The culture was becoming stale. There was an air of lethargy in the company, that nobody could do it better than the 'Inchcape man' and that change was unnecessary. Most of the middle management was becoming rather second rate.

There had been some shocks to the empire in the late 1970s and early 1980s as the managers in the field made errors of judgement that cost the company dearly, and criticism mounted of Lord Inchcape's management style. This culminated in his eventual removal at the end of 1982, a shock to him and the family. He was succeeded by Sir David Orr, a former chairman of Unilever, a highly centralised world-wide business, who believed that power should be brought back to London.

He was succeeded in turn by Sir George Turnbull in 1986, a no-nonsense businessman from the motor industry who, depending upon your point of view, was either the creator of a modern company or the destroyer of all that Inchcape stood for. One of his earliest moves, which convinced Inchcape's many partners in Asia that the company was becoming out of touch, was to sell the company's huge property interests. The company owned its own regional head office buildings throughout the Far East as well as large tracts of land including much of the land bordering Orchard Road in Singapore, now the most desirable property in the country. Asians believe that real estate holdings are every company's crown jewels and to sell a head office building showed lack of faith in its own business.

Turnbull then set about changing Inchcape's corporate culture. The long leashes that the earl had given to his entrepreneurial managers had led to extraordinary profits but also greater risks. While some managers exceeded their profit forecasts, others produced sudden cataclysmic losses. He wondered whether the business was operating beyond the control of its head office in London. But he was an industrialist, a man from the assembly floor used to seeing motor cars rumbling out of the factory door. Turnbull was not interested in entrepreneurial deals and could not get his mind around the essence of what had made the company so successful. He thought that Inchcape's traditional business as a middleman was doomed to failure and yearned for 'simplicity'.

So he let the old managers go, people who had lived in the countries where they were based for most of their lives building up deep relationships with the businessmen and politicians in their adopted homes. Turnbull had no interest in this; he wanted what he called 'professional management'. He believed in a bloated head office and hired legions of planners and strategists and established a personnel department in London that soon became one of the most powerful departments in the company. Turnbull believed in 'focus, simplicity and synergy' but in reality he cut out the heart of the company. He, and his successors, allowed the company to be run by accountants, planners and personnel managers and become besotted with shareholder communications and placating the board of directors with consistent results. Turnbull did not want to have to explain to analysts why, apparently unforeseen, the tea business in India had done particularly well one year while the tractor business in Thailand had suddenly produced unexpected losses. He wanted predictability where no such thing could be offered.

Turnbull fell victim to two pernicious influences. One was the power of the management consultants. Many of his new recruits came from the consultancy world and were at home analysing other people's problems but less certain when they had to solve their own. The other was INSEAD, the French management school where all Inchcape senior managers were sent to attend courses run by academics who knew a great deal less about business in the developing world than the experienced Inchcape managers. Together with many of my contemporaries I was sent to INSEAD to undergo an 'advanced management programme' which gave my colleagues endless mirth. We were set infantile corporate case studies to analyse, having handled infinitely more complex problems ourselves on a regular basis.

For a couple of years after Turnbull took over, the company's prospects improved. Turnbull claimed that this was evidence that the new 'professional management culture that emphasised achievement through teamwork'[1] was

---

[1] 'Managers & Mantras' by Charlotte Butler and John Keary published by John Wiley & Sons, 2000.

starting to work, but others thought the sunny period was just inertia left over from the previous management regime. The earlier fiefdoms that Turnbull had eliminated were replaced by new fiefdoms of the bureaucrats, the faceless personnel and planning departments in London. The operating companies in the field now found that they were required to spend much of their time compiling endless and irrelevant reports to a distant head office. Decision making became paralysed and the company shuddered at the thought of taking a commercial risk. But without risk there is no opportunity.

Meanwhile the new corporate affairs department worked at a hysterical pitch to convince the City of London and the company's new managers that success was being achieved. Inchcape was hailed as 'coming back from the dead' and the *Financial Weekly* breathlessly reported in July 1987 that the new management team has 'completed one of the most dramatic and rapid corporate rehabilitations the City has seen for years'.

After the property fire-sale in 1986 Turnbull started to chip away at the pillars sustaining the business. Whereas Lord Inchcape had long term vision and invested for the future, Turnbull introduced a new short termism as if aware that he might not be there for long. His eye first fell on the tea business, Inchcape's last major activity in India, where the company was born centuries before. Inchcape's substantial tea business employed over 10,000 people and was one of the most outstanding plantation businesses in the world, consistently reporting profits of many millions of pounds. But Indian taxes were high and prospects for the immediate future were not encouraging. Turnbull sold it for a few million pounds. The new buyers were delighted and within a year Indian taxes came down and the government smiled once again on foreign investment.

Next Turnbull turned to Inchcape's extensive interests in the timber industry where the company held logging concessions, pulp mills and woodworking factories in Malaysia, Indonesia, Papua New Guinea, Chile and Australia. Turnbull worried that the shareholders did not care for such a business and was concerned that he might be criticised by ecologists. The whole business was sold on the cheap at a time when timber prices were rising strongly. And so the pattern continued. One by one businesses built up over the years were divested as the company's limbs were amputated while little new of value was added.

Back in Hong Kong a new regional chairman arrived on the scene in 1986. Charles Mackay, another ex-management consultant, was a breath of fresh air. He swiftly carried out a rationalisation of the Inchcape companies in his region and reinvigorated the local management. But he also believed in the big head office concept and the Inchcape Pacific head office swiftly expanded from 30 people to over 200. I took Charles Mackay to China several times and he was quick to see that the country was changing fast and with Hong Kong's days numbered, under a British administration due to surrender sovereignty in 1997, the future lay in China. He supported my endeavours to drag the reluctant Hong Kong-based Inchcape managers into China and challenged them to include China in their future plans.

Mackay had two failings. One was a tendency to micro-manage which stemmed from his high intellect. The other was a poor judgement of character. In particular he selected as his deputy in Hong Kong an American Chinese would-be politician named Paul Cheng. As 'minister without portfolio' Cheng interfered with most of the group's profitable businesses wherever he could, trying to craft a role for himself. His eye particularly fell on Inchcape China. Regardless of who had created this successful business he thought that an ethnic Chinese should be in charge and who better than himself? He convinced Mackay that he should be responsible for a 'Greater China' area embracing Hong Kong, the People's Republic and Taiwan (three completely unrelated territories) and was thus in a position to give me some grief.

Cheng was a corporate politician who had flitted from job to job, until he metamorphosed into a 'head hunter'. In this capacity he was hired by Mackay to identify a top grade Chinese executive to join the ranks of the Inchcape Pacific board of directors. Mackay thought poorly of the ethnic mix of the largely caucasian Inchcape Pacific board and allowed himself to be seduced by the smooth-talking Cheng into appointing him as his deputy chairman. Cheng did not take kindly to yet another Englishman running the China operation. As the only Chinese on the board, he decided that the China operation should report directly to him. There then began two forlorn years of corporate politics and back-stabbing as Cheng set about undermining my work of the previous seventeen years.

It was unfortunate that Cheng knew little about either China or the Chinese and only managed to spread fear and uncertainty throughout the China offices which by that time employed 150 people. These capable people so carefully recruited and trained by Dick and myself started to leave, the reputation of Inchcape in China began to wain and confusion followed as Cheng toured the China offices endeavouring to develop a fifth column. Cheng was certainly aware that he was viewed with suspicion throughout the company. He was later to state in an interview, playing the racial card, that, "we in the east feel that the total trust is not there with our western colleagues."

In 1991 Turnbull contracted cancer and retired appointing Mackay as chief executive in London. A new chairman was appointed. Sir David Plastow had been presiding over the stately realm of Rolls-Royce motor cars and Vickers, its parent company, and seemed unable to shake off his custom of mentally genuflecting to his financial and social superiors. He was more concerned with advancement in his local golf club. The complex world of Inchcape was not for him. Turnbull had cranked up the company to produce record profits and Mackay seemed to think that this could continue forever and dreamed of exponential growth. But the ship was shuddering and when hit by a couple of economic storms that normally would have passed smoothly under the hull with a few years of poor profits as had happened many times in previous years, on this occasion the 'professional management' was brought to panic stations. One third of the head office staff were retrenched.

Plastow was replaced by Sir Colin Marshall, an unsympathetic businessman with a varied reputation for managing companies. He had no time for history or culture, failed to see the immense prospects for growth in Asia and set about dismembering the old company. Traditionally half of Inchcape's profits had come from sales of motor cars, due to Lord Inchcape's visionary policies. The growth of that business was such that the earl had once said, "I hope they don't turn my business into a garage." But that is exactly what the management did and by 1996 all the traditional businesses had been sold, some at ridiculously low prices, and the company was reduced to selling motor cars in England and a few foreign outposts. The unique worldwide network of companies built up over centuries was sold for £650 million. The 'professional management' had no bright ideas as to how this money might be profitably invested and so gave it back to the shareholders.

All the many businesses that were sold went on to enjoy greater success and profitability as independent companies which showed that the problems were not within the individual businesses so much as created by the head office in London. Even today, with the 'garage' business prospering, it is the original motor businesses that were originally organised by Lord Inchcape, the Fuhrer, PG and others in the 1970s and earlier, that provide the main profit streams. The 'professional management' provided little but red–herrings and 'ego–nomics'. Lord Inchcape had remarked that evening long ago at the Fishing Lodge in Beijing that his success came down to 'vision, people and luck'.

It was unfortunate that at a time when a cool head was most needed the senior non-executive director of Inchcape plc was my distant cousin Peter Baring. Baring Brothers were Inchcape's long-standing investment bankers. Since my father's retirement, Barings had also pursued the route of 'professional management' and members of the Baring family who had overseen the prosperity of the bank for over 250 years were now few in number within the bank's ranks. The Barings management were shortly to prove their own incompetence when they allowed the bank to lose £850 million which brought about its bankruptcy in 1995. The same 'professionals' armed with their Phd's and MBA's and motivated with bloated salaries, disproportionate bonuses and share option schemes brought down both the House of Baring and the House of Inchcape. The epitaph on the tombstones of both the advisers and the advised had to be the same word: 'greed'.

With storm clouds gathering in London, I had been heartened in 1985 when it was announced that China was to be a key area of growth. I knew that as Inchcape was prohibited from distributing its principals' products in China the only way forward was to join them in manufacturing, using our expertise in this difficult market. But with one or two small exceptions the new management was lukewarm and diverted by prospects in Russia and elsewhere. My efforts in China, hailed by my Fortune 500 clients in America, seemed of little interest in my own company.

In 1994 I had grown tired of the meddlesome Cheng and lack of support from London and, after fifteen years with Inchcape, I began to look elsewhere. I was approached by Lord Hanson who had been formidably successful at building his own industrial group as a latter-day Lord Inchcape, and was planning to devote his considerable resources to start a 'Hanson Pacific'. Would I be interested in heading up this new initiative? I met Lord Hanson in the south of France and his partner Lord White in London and agreed on a much improved employment package and I resolved to leave Inchcape.

I flew to London to see Charles Mackay and tendered my resignation. Charles was horrified. Whilst he could fire people at will, he did not like to see his managers resign. Over many hours he convinced me to stay with Inchcape. I liked Charles, was flattered by his faith in me and allowed myself to be swayed. As I left his office, he said, "Evelyn, I do accept that in persuading you not to resign and take up the Hanson offer I am making a long term commitment of employment to you. Take my word." He looked me in the eye as we shook hands.

16

The House of Lords and the China Expert

It was 5 p.m. on the 21st September, 1981. Hong Kong was watching the relentless progress of Severe Tropical Storm Clara with gloomy foreboding as it passed over the Philippines and entered the South China Sea on its passage north-westwards towards the coast of China. Earlier that morning the storm had been reclassified to a full typhoon and by noon it was mid-way across the South China Sea heading directly towards Hong Kong. The typhoon warning signal number eight had been hoisted on the weatherman's mast to warn sailors of impending calamity but by then Hong Kong had already closed down, alerted by previous warnings. For most people it was a day to stay at home, play mah-jongg, watch and listen to news of the approaching storm, protecting themselves as well as they could from the advancing maelstrom.

As usual, I had driven early to my office in Elizabeth House on the waterfront in Wanchai. The last tram rattled passed swaying on its way to the terminal. The rain streamed off the sheer sides of the buildings in parallel sheets, the gaudy overhead neon signs in Wanchai swinging perilously as I drove underneath. The wind was already too strong for anybody to brave. Shop fronts shuttered, people were stringing masking tape across their windows to stop them shattering under the pressure of the winds.

I spent the afternoon at home in my flat gazing across the harbour far below. The last Star Ferry had crossed the harbour many hours before. Now nothing moved. A single American guided-missile cruiser pulled at its double anchors in mid-stream, engines at slow ahead to keep the ship into the wind. Hong Kong's fleet of junks and sampans had squeezed into the over-crowded typhoon shelters; the larger ships re-anchored in the off-lying storm anchorages. Mounting seas crashed into the ferry piers creating volcanos of spray and spume. The roads in

Central and Wanchai empty, only the occasional wailing ambulance splashed by. Some tree branches had fallen. I could see a wall of bamboo scaffolding had come adrift and was threatening to topple into Queen's Road below me. Sheets of corrugated iron were floating in the wind like pages of newspaper.

Suddenly the telephone rang. It was PG. There was silence down the line except for a laboured wheezing. It might have been the wind or was he taking a long puff on his cigar?

"Errington," he rasped. "I have just been reading this paper you sent me. You had better come and see me."

I suggested tomorrow might be a better time, when the typhoon would have blown inland.

"No," he replied. "Now."

I sat in my car staring out of the garage at the appalling conditions. Many people had died taking this sort of quite unnecessary risk. Then I plunged out into the tempest. Down Bowen Road and up the twisty Magazine Gap Road. There was no other traffic but it was all I could do to keep the heavy car on the road. I was pushed from side to side by the 120 mph gusts of wind, the car struggling to find a grip through the torrents of water gushing down from Victoria Peak. Leaves, twigs, branches and rubbish torn from garbage cans whipped the windscreen. I parked my car as close as I could get to PG's colonnaded colonial mansion in Middle Gap Road, one of many that Inchcape owned for the use of its directors in Hong Kong, and ran through the wall of water to the front door. Within a few seconds I was soaked, dripping, my shirt sticking to my skin.

PG's Chinese bare-footed 'house-boy', in truth a man in his late sixties, let me in and ushered me into PG's study. The room was dark save for a single lamp on his desk and a reading light over a large armchair where PG sat smoking a cigar, a cascade of ash pouring in a grey river over his un-buttoned waist coat. I stood in front of him dripping into a spreading puddle, suddenly frozen by the air-conditioning. The wind outside roared like an express train, with an occasional crash as a branch slammed into one of the large house's windows. The whole building seemed to be trembling like one of PG's many racehorses before a race.

He waved me into another armchair. "Boy," he called. "Bring Lord Errington a brandy and soda. And another for me."

He was holding my 27-page thesis in one hand, his cigar in the other. He waved it at me. "This will cause a stir, you know," he grumbled. "Where did you get this information from? It's not what they are saying at the Jockey Club or in the boardroom of the Hong Kong and Shanghai Bank. Or at Government House come to that," he said covering all the centres of power in the colony.

The paper I had written for PG in May 1982, 'Whither Hong Kong?' was one of the first attempts to address a subject that was to dominate people's lives in Hong Kong over the succeeding fifteen years: what would happen when the lease on the New Territories of Hong Kong ran out on the 30th June 1997? In 1982 this was not a subject of consideration. Hong Kong was a transient place to make a quick profit or a stepping-stone for the Chinese to pause before moving on to Canada, Australia or the United States. 'Whither Hong Kong?' had posed some intriguing questions that had not previously crossed the minds of the Inchcape directors.

"Lord Inchcape wants you to address the board in London next week," PG said. "I hope you've got your facts right."

We then discussed the document at some length. It set out to analyse the current status in Hong Kong, the British and Chinese opposing positions and the various scenarios that could develop between 1982 and 1997. At the time the popular view was that the Chinese realised they could not manage Hong Kong with its freewheeling capitalists and *laissez-faire* attitudes and would probably insist on a nominal recovery of sovereignty at some time and a continuance of British administration or possibly an extension of the lease. My colleagues could not see the situation changing very much in 1997 but I took a different point of view. Based on whispers I had been hearing in Beijing, I thought it more likely that China would insist on recovering Hong Kong fully in 1997 and the British administrators would be forced to leave. For Inchcape this was an important subject: many millions of pounds were invested in Hong Kong and the company employed over 350 British expatriates and 6,000 Chinese in the territory. Could life continue the same under the communists?

Five days later I walked into the dark, wood-panelled Inchcape boardroom in St. Mary Axe in the City of London to be confronted by a room-full of directors sitting around an oak table. Beside each director were their sector controllers, analysts and PAs. At the head of the table glowered the earl, the Fuhrer by his right hand. Every director had a copy of 'Whither Hong Kong?' in front of him. For the next three hours I was interrogated on the points I had raised. Finally Lord Inchcape took me on one side. "This has been one of the most interesting and well-analysed documents I have seen. I want you to take a keen interest in political developments in China. Keep the chairman in Hong Kong and myself informed at all times." I was taken aback; I had never heard him speak officially at such length before.

So it was that I became the in-house expert on Hong Kong/China politics and gradually assumed the aura of a sinologist. Down the years I briefed PG and all the subsequent Inchcape chairmen in Hong Kong on the changing political winds and the likely effects on Hong Kong. This ended only with the opening of China and the creation of the fast-track China-hand but by that time Hong

Kong's future was discussed on the front pages of every newspaper in the region on a daily basis and everyone had become an expert.

In the 1980s however, there were few sinologists outside the closed worlds of academics, diplomats, specialised traders and the league of 'China watchers' tapping into domestic broadcasts in China from their secret bases in Hong Kong. Although some tourists began to trickle into China at that time, all escaped with tales of physical hardship inflicted on intrepid foreign visitors. For the international businessman there were few reasons to enter the forbidding gates of the Middle Kingdom; foreign exchange was scarce and China's overseas trade was in the hands of a few specialist merchants.

Imperceptibly, almost glacially, conditions began to improve. By the mid-1980s it was possible to fly directly to Beijing from Hong Kong without walking across the bridge at the Lowu border. Modern hotels began to appear. There were more taxis available although it was to be many years before it was possible to hail one on the street. The advent of refrigerators meant no more tepid beer. Sketchy laws were promulgated. China was on the move.

Visitors to the huge Inchcape regional headquarters in Hong Kong began to ask what Inchcape could offer in China. Instead of being an exotic speciality I was suddenly in demand. Inchcape directors from all over the world started to seek me out to enquire about prospects for trade with the People's Republic. A stream, then a river of foreign businessmen, mainly American, passed through the doors of Inchcape China. Without intention and with little qualification, I had become that rarest of species: a 'China hand'.

The Chinese Government had also taken notice of Inchcape, and the business establishment in Hong Kong reacted with incredulity when the first Chinese Politburo member to ever visit Hong Kong arrived under the aegis of Inchcape China in 1980. PG was in a lather: Government House, Special Branch, the entire security establishment was calling him asking for information.

"What shall we do with him? What can we show the Minister?" demanded PG.

"There won't be just one. There will be a cohort of 'Mao'-suited Party members," I pointed out.

PG retreated into a cloud of cigar smoke as he dwelled on the pros and cons of being seen to entertain the first important delegation from China to Hong Kong since 1945. Then it struck him. Erupting in a spray of burning ash, he exclaimed: "I know, we'll take them horseracing. They won't have seen anything like that before. I can't wait to see the expressions on the faces in the Jardines and Swires boxes at Happy Valley when they see whom I'm entertaining!"

Horseracing had been banned in China along with prostitution as soon as the communists took power in 1949. The famed racecourse in Shanghai had been turned into a People's Park. All forms of gambling had been strictly outlawed. I duly submitted our proposed programme to the Politburo Secretariat in Beijing including 'an evening of horse-racing with the chairman of the Royal Hong Kong Jockey Club' and this passed without comment.

On the chosen day, PG revelled in the surprised stares of his fellow Jockey Club committee members as, Moses-like, he led the group of Chinese, all clad in identical black 'Mao' suits through throngs of punters who parted like the Red Sea.

"That'll show them who has friends in the right places!" grunted PG as he led the way. Our communist guests followed the racing with rapt attention and the Minister was overjoyed when PG managed to slip a winning ticket into the hands of one of the Chinese who had studiously avoided placing a bet themselves.

By 1990 everything was changing in China. People had more money and freedom both of choice and of thought. There was a wide variety of consumer goods available for the first time in decades. There was still the occasional political campaign but they were low-key and passed like ripples on China's often-turbulent ocean. The Chinese were travelling overseas more, foreigners were not such alien creatures, girls could choose any type of hair style, well-dressed women suddenly appeared on the streets, 'Mao' suits were consigned to the dustbin of history, traffic jams became a problem as bicycles became a rarity and the camels disappeared from the streets of Beijing. Everywhere there was construction: new roads, new shopping centres, and new apartment blocks. It was said that half the construction cranes in the world were now in China. Beijing and Shanghai were slowly beginning to emerge from their 1930s time warp. A new China was being born in front of my eyes.

Modern restaurants of every nationality were opening, as were *karaoke* bars, discos and nightclubs. Prostitutes were back on the streets. The days were gone when you might be detained on suspicion of frequenting hookers or forced to wear a dunce's cap in the middle of *wangfujing*. Now there was a new feeling of freshness pulsing through the streets of Shanghai. More people were leaving to study overseas; life was beginning to look up for most Chinese. Salaries increased by multiples. Stores sold out of consumer goods as soon as they received them, the streets were full of happy shoppers wheeling television sets home on their bikes. But older and wiser heads were suspicious. They had seen it all before: the Party was skilled at taking the pressure off to see how the ants behaved before slamming down hard on them again. Could it last?

The events of June 4th, 1989 were not discussed. Like the Cultural

Revolution and all the painful campaigns that had gone before, the events in Tiananmen Square had become a *neibu* subject, one of those unpleasant experiences about which it was safer not to talk. The dissident ringleaders had disappeared, some consigned to the *laogai* but many fleeing to America, thereby supporting the view that perhaps the Americans might have been the 'black hand' in the whole affair. Most of the demonstrators had not suffered too much: a little re-education, a few self-criticisms, all minor punishments. There was little talk of democracy these days, the Party had reacted quickly after the summer of 1989 to stifle dissent and the Chinese knew how to 'bend like the bamboo'. Deng Xiao-Ping had played his best card: allow the people to improve their standard of living. "To be rich is glorious!" this old communist found himself saying.

I had just moved the Inchcape office into its third, and last, address in Shanghai. I chose a smart new office building between the Equatorial and the Hilton Hotels. The Hilton was the best hotel in Shanghai in 1991 and much used by Inchcape's visiting principals. The Equatorial was a new Singapore-owned hotel, more modest in scope. Our office in Shanghai now had a staff of thirty people and was handling more and more business every year. We had just opened our fourth joint-venture in Shanghai, a factory to manufacture mattresses for the local market. For the first time, Chinese could afford to discard their old kapok mattresses, lumpy and hard as concrete, and buy a comfortable sprung mattress.

Now I was travelling to other emerging socialist countries in the region. We had opened offices in the Vietnamese cities of Hanoi and Ho Chi Minh City and in Cambodia and I was also making frequent visits to North Korea and the Russian Far East. I was spending less and less time in Hong Kong. With an eye on retiring in Asia I was building a house in Bangkok, designed in a startlingly original way by my old friend from Singapore, Remo Riva, now senior partner in Asia's largest firm of architects. With the house nearly finished Plern spent more of her time in Bangkok.

On the 16th March, 1991 my father died suddenly and unexpectedly and my life changed. My name also: I had grown attached to the name of Errington over the previous 38 years (it had already changed once before when my grandfather had died in 1953) and to be suddenly addressed by my father's title was not altogether welcome. With the name came the responsibility of a seat in the House of Lords, something I had never previously considered.

Few Earls of Cromer had showed much talent or interest in the House of Lords. My father attended rarely and only spoke on matters of finance from the

Cross Benches. His advice to me was that it was best left to those who can think on their feet. When I took my seat on the 7th May, 1991 I found the Palace of Westminster redolent of the very memories that I had willingly left behind when I embarked on the *Ben Nevis* that cold autumn day in 1967. Its long, gloomy corridors, gothic architecture and musty corners reminded me of the misery of dank weekends in English country houses. Worse, it was occupied by the same public school boys, now bald and cobwebby, with whom I had shared chilly classrooms 35 years previously. They strode, or occasionally tottered, down the panelled corridors with the same self-importance that they had affected in Eton as teenagers. When introduced they would peer at me in an off-hand way and then intentionally fail to recognise me when we next passed each other in the House with a certain type of English superciliousness perfected by those over-confident in their own position in the universe.

This attitude is very much a national trait. I had frequently noted when in the wilds of Afghanistan, the high Himalayas, the Indian Ghats or wherever I had wandered that one Englishman would always avoid another whereas other nationalities would greet a fellow national with enthusiasm. On many occasions a Filipino, Bhutanese or Lao would tell me with unconcealed delight that they had heard there was another Englishman in a nearby village or the next valley thinking this would bring me great joy whereas I viewed such news with dismay. If we were brought together an immediate guarded hostility would ensue as we sniffed each other out like two stray dogs.

I started to attend the House of Lords with dubious enthusiasm and would listen to debates with increasing wonder, not at the wisdom and knowledge expressed but by the exact opposite. One after another, Lords would unselfconsciously address the House on subjects about which they were completely ignorant. In any debate I found that at least three quarters of the speakers knew little of the subject and yet blithely spoke at great length irritating those who had something more substantial to contribute. There were always, on the other hand, one or two peers, often hereditary backwoodsmen, who were experts in some arcane subject but their insights seemed to become lost in the mass of verbiage spouted by those carried away by the enjoyment of their own voices.

I soon decided that it was only worth speaking on subjects upon which I was knowledgeable and for me that meant the Far East, Hong Kong and China in particular. Although many peers had visited Hong Kong, often as a result of a paid parliamentary trip and frequently staying at Government House, there were only two members of the House who had lived in Hong Kong at any time and only one with an in depth understanding of the People's Republic of China. Two ex-governors of Hong Kong, Lords Maclehose and Wilson, also spoke from time to time but were constrained in what they could say due to their previous positions.

I was encouraged by many to give my views, as the deteriorating relationship between Britain and China over the future of Hong Kong was beginning to catch people's attention. It seemed that I had something to offer and I began to pay more attention to the activities of Christopher Patten who had taken over as the governor of Hong Kong in July 1992.

At about the same time I was approached in Hong Kong by a group of influential Chinese businessmen who had become concerned that Patten's populist policies might rebound adversely on Hong Kong when it became part of China on the 1st July, 1997. They thought Patten, who had no previous experience of either Hong Kong or China, was leading the government in Westminster by the nose while the wise mandarins in the Foreign Office were being sidelined. Could I do anything about it?

On the 18th May, 1994 there was a debate in the House on Hong Kong and China and after listening to any number of peers pontificating on their experiences of shopping in Hong Kong, the delights of Chinese cuisine and the sumptuous entertainment they had received at Government House, I rose to address the House. A silence fell as I set out my qualifications for speaking and as I gathered steam I could see and feel an anxious shuffling on the Conservative front bench as I pointed out the failings in Governor Patten's policies and how the people of Hong Kong were being dangerously misled by this erstwhile Member of Parliament.

My speech received the press comment that it deserved and congratulations flowed in from many people who shared the same concerns but did not have a public platform from which to express them. Back in Hong Kong two days later the business community hailed me as a hero. At last someone had put into words the feelings of many in the community too cowed by Patten's publicity machine and too far from Westminster to have any effect themselves. Government House, of course, took a very different view.

Another sea-change also took place in my life in 1991.

From 1980 onwards my travels to China had taken me away from Hong Kong for longer and longer periods. In the early days I was in China for ten days a month but as the business started to take off and delegations of businessmen had to be accompanied in China this soon extended to half my time. Prolonged trips to the United States to meet new and existing clients took even more of my time away from Hong Kong and negotiations in China sometimes lasted for weeks at a time. Eventually I was in Hong Kong for only one week every month, sometimes less. Constant time away began to take its toll on my marriage: Plern made a life for herself in Hong Kong and formed her own circle of friends that did not include me. We saw each other less and when we did meet we had little in common. Our paths diverted and we realised that we were leading different lives without a mutual thread. Although she made several visits to China it was difficult for her to understand the vortex carrying me forward as China's development picked up pace.

Thus we decided to divorce. But Tan Mair had not been proved right: we were never an 'ill starred' couple. We had been married for twenty-two years, longer than many contemporary marriages and for most of that time we had been very happy together.

Some months after the divorce had been agreed, I had lunch with Joe Chan, one of my Hong Kong-based China managers, in the Equatorial Hotel in Shanghai. As I crossed the hotel lobby my eye was caught by a young woman sitting alone on a small sofa. She had long hair, which framed her face and cascaded down her back almost to the top of her tight and fashionable trousers. Her hair was sleeker than other Chinese, her skin paler, her lips pinker, and her legs longer. Her attitude was purely feminine, a quality only recently reappearing in China. Joe noticed my distraction and followed my line of sight.

We both looked at the girl in the admiring way that men do. She was joined by a middle-aged woman and both of them were sitting on the small sofa in animated conversation.

"Now she," I said to Joe, "is what I call a beautiful woman." My mind was in turmoil; I was unable to tear my eyes away from her.

"Would you like to meet her?" enquired Joe softly, always eager to please his boss. "I can find out where she works," he added slightly doubtfully.

"Yes, you must," I murmured. "She does not know it yet but she is going to change my life."

Joe interrupted my meeting later that afternoon and beckoned me into the corridor outside the meeting room. "Wang Wei knows her," he burst out excitedly, referring to the manager of the Shanghai office. "You won't believe this but she works in an office on the same floor as ours. Quick, let's go and investigate."

Like inquisitive schoolboys, Joe and I walked down the corridor where we found the offices of an American consultancy company. We peered through the glass door but all we could see was the receptionist and a few men ambling around with mugs of tea. No sign of the Shanghainese beauty. We pushed open the glass doors. The receptionist looked up from reading the *People's Daily* and asked if she could assist us.

I stalled for time, asking her about her business, the weather, anything, hoping that the girl in the Equatorial would walk passed. Just as I was about to give up, the door swung open and there she was. "Ah, here is Miss Hu. She will tell you all about our business," said the receptionist. Suddenly Joe and I found ourselves in a windowless room with this tall, cool Shanghainese woman in her early twenties, looking at us with some suspicion. I told her in English, which Joe translated into Mandarin, that we were her neighbours and had just come along to introduce ourselves.

"And I am Hu Cheng-Yu," she said, her face dimpling prettily as she smiled. "You can call me Shelley."

Shelley's family had been through the horrors that well-off Chinese families endured in the 1950s. Her grandfather's family had owned extensive estates on Chongming Island, Shanghai's breadbasket, and he and his brothers were murdered by the rampaging masses. The remaining family members converted their savings into gold bars, which they hid behind the masonry of the family home. In the 1970s the Red Guards found the bars and murdered the remaining members of the family. Only Shelley's grandmother, mother and aunt survived. Shelley, a graduate of Shanghai University, was an only child and almost the only survivor of her immediate family.

Shelley and I married in London in July 1993. One year later we had our first child, Alexander, followed four years later by a daughter, Venetia. Two years after our marriage I left Inchcape and we moved to England. After 29 years in the Far East my life had gone full circle and now with a new wife and a young family I wondered whether a more conventional life lay ahead of me.

For me however, the China story was not over. Just as the Chinese never forget those who have favoured the People's Republic, they did not forget the years that I had dedicated to China. When I moved to England I was sought out by various elements of the Chinese government who remembered my brushes with Patten and the stand that I had taken, had read the file that used to be opened on every regular visitor to China and showed their appreciation of what they considered to be a real 'old friend' of China. To my pleasurable surprise they rewarded me in ways that showed that China had indeed changed little over the years.

When the U.K. handed over sovereignty of Hong Kong on the 1st July 1997 there were extensive celebrations and a vast banquet was held at the new Convention Centre in Wanchai. The British submitted their list of proposed guests and the Chinese had their own list of special guests. Although the only resident member of the House of Lords in Hong Kong, Patten could not bring himself to invite me but instead I received a special invitation from the Chinese government and was placed on a high table amongst members of the Politburo many of whom I had known for decades.

This story has taken us on a passage spanning nearly three decades and through many countries in East Asia at a time when most were emerging either from colonialism or the rigours of dictatorial military or single-party regimes. They were the years that witnessed the birth and adolescence of the Asian 'tiger' economies. By the middle of the '90s many of the excitements and excesses I have described had already faded into history as the cities and countries where I lived adopted a uniformity brought by development, a growing affluence, the ease of intercontinental travel and a melding of cultures.

All around me everything had metamorphosed into something bland and grey in an astonishingly short period of time. Whole spanking new cities had arisen on the foundations of the quaint Far Eastern capitals that had greeted me in the 1960s. Bangkok had filled in its canals and was no longer the Venice of the East, Singapore bred sky-scrapers like ants, Hong Kong's fabled fragrant harbour shrank to a far-from-fragrant canal, Shanghai and Beijing tore out the hearts of their cities, new highways were struck through jungles and rubber estates, sparkling airports the envy of Europe awaited the avalanche of businessmen, tourists and travellers who descended on the Far East. Old customs were shed as more Asians were educated in the West. A boring uniformity spread across what had been a uniquely original patchwork of varying peoples, cultures and traditions.

But for most of the peoples of the Far East, life had improved beyond their wildest hopes. There were no more wars or genocide, communism had faded away, rampant diseases had largely been brought under control, education was now widespread, roads reached to the furthest Thai village and a new type of affluence spread across the region. As I look back over those three decades, I marvel at the extraordinary good fortune that brought me to those distant shores, at the kindness showed me by so many people, none less than my Tan Mair, and how the hand of fate guided me through so many vicissitudes.

The day I climbed the gangplank onto the rusty deck of the S.S. *Ben Nevis* in 1967 was the day I never looked back. Do I ever rue leaving my dusty desk at Baring Brothers? I would never have chosen a different path from the winding one I blindly followed.

Glossary

ao-dai – The Vietnamese 'national dress' consisting of a long silk tunic slit to the waist over silk trousers.

attap – The frond of the nipa palm, used for making roofs [Malay]

bomoh – Malay fortune teller

bukit – Hill [Malay]

charpoy – Bamboo bed frame, usually with a woven rope top in lieu of mattress [Hindi]

dandan – Hot and spicy noodle soup from Sichuan, China [Mandarin]

dhoti – Loin cloth [Hindi]

farang – A Caucasian [from the Portugese ferringhi]

FESCO – Foreign Enterprises Service Corporation. The organisation in China responsible for issuing local staff.

gai-yarng – Barbecued chicken served splayed on a bamboo frame

gamelan – Indonesian bamboo orchestra

ganja – Cannabis or marijuana [Thai]

guanxi – Connections [Mandarin]

hmong – One of the hill tribes found in Laos, Thailand, Vietnam and China

hong – The traditional mainly British-owned trading houses in Hong Kong, viz Jardine Matheson, John Swire, Inchcape and Wheelock Marden. The Hong Kong & Shanghai Banking Corporation (latterly HSBC) was not a 'hong', it was a commercial bank founded by the 'hongs'

howdah – Platform mounted on the back of an elephant, generally large enough for 2-4 people to sit [Hindi]

hutong – Small lane [Mandarin]

jek – Chinese [Thai derogatory slang]

jinjok – Gekko [Thai]

Kang – A flat brick bed often with a fire underneath

kampong – Native village [Malay]

khun – Mr or Mrs [Thai]

klong – Canal [Thai]

ko – Island [Thai]

lao gai – Re-education camp [Mandarin]

lord – Drinking straw [Thai]

LZ – Landing zone

MACV – Military Assistance Command Vietnam. The U.S. military headquarters in Saigon

mahout – An elephant trainer and handler [Hindi]

maidan – Large area of grass frequently found in the centre of towns in Malaysia, used for cricket, kite-flying, public ceremonies, etc.

mamasan – Woman in nightclub managing a group of girls [Japanese slang]

mea-noi – Minor wife [Thai]

mea-yai – Senior wife [Thai]

momchao – His Serene Highness, Prince ….. Often abbreviated to M.C. [Thai]

more doo – Fortune teller [Thai]

naga – Mythical serpent [Thai]. Stylised versions grace the gable ends of Thai, Burmese and Lao temples

NGO – Non-Governmental Organisation (i.e. charities)

NVA – North Vietnamese Army (regular)

neibu – Classified [Mandarin]

oleang – A coffee-like drink made from tamarind seeds generally served in a plastic bag with crushed ice, tied with a rubber band [Thai]

nai umphur – Village headman [Thai]

pakoma – Piece of chequered cotton cloth, 1.5m x 1m used by Thai peasants as a sarong [Thai]

paasaa – Language [Thai]

qipao – Floor length formal Chinese dress, generally split on both sides. Usually made from silk [Mandarin]

sanuk – The Thai sense of fun. Much behaviour can by justified in the pursuit of sanuk [Thai]

sawaddhi (-ka or -krap) – Form of greeting. *–ka* used by females, *-krap* used by men [Thai]

soi – Lane [Thai]

stupa – Cone shaped structure built of stone rising to a pinnacle, some a hundred feet high, built to house Buddhist holy relics. Frequently found in Thai temples

tuk-tuk – Motorised three-wheeler, low cost transport [Thai (colloq)]

towkay – Proprietor of a business [Hokkien]

umphur – A Thai regional administrative area

UNHCR – United Nations High Commission for Refugees

wai – To place one's hands together vertically and bow one's head in respect [Thai]

waiguoren – Foreigner [Mandarin]

Wang – A palace or any place of dwelling for a member of the Royal Family [Thai]

Wat – A Buddhist temple [Thai]

Xiu-xi – Siesta. As laid down in the Chinese constitution. [Mandarin]

Zhongshan zhuang – Chinese costume worn by most cadres, often incorrectly referred as the 'Mao suit', but more correctly the 'Sun Yatsen suit' after the founder of the Chinese Republic in 1912 [Mandarin]